Ernest Cruikshank

The documentary history of the campaign upon the Niagara frontier

In 1812-4. Vol. IX

Ernest Cruikshank

The documentary history of the campaign upon the Niagara frontier
In 1812-4. Vol. IX

ISBN/EAN: 9783337147761

Printed in Europe, USA, Canada, Australia, Japan

Cover: Foto ©ninafisch / pixelio.de

More available books at **www.hansebooks.com**

THE DOCUMENTARY
History of the Campaigns

—UPON THE—

Niagara Frontier

In 1812=4.

VOL. IX.

December, 1813, to May, 1814.

COLLECTED AND EDITED FOR THE LUNDY'S LANE HISTORICAL SOCIETY

BY LIEUT.-COL. E. CRUIKSHANK, F. R. S. C.

WELLAND:
TRIBUNE OFFICE
1908.

The Documentary History of the Campaign Upon the Niagara Frontier in 1812-4.

VOL. IX.

DECEMBER, 1813, TO MAY, 1814.

Lieut.-Colonel Harvey to Colonel Matthew Elliott.

HEADQUARTERS, ST. DAVID'S, 17th December, 1813.

SIR,—Lieutenant-General Drummond, having determined to avail himself of the services of his brethen and allies, the Western Indians, in an attack on the enemy's territory and fortress on the opposite shore, I have received His Honour's direction to request you will assemble the several chieftains of those nations and will impress upon them in the strongest manner the expediency of abstaining from plunder and all acts of violence or outrage on the persons of women and children and unarmed men, and, even in the case of prisoners taken in arms, the Lieutenant-General would willingly indulge the hope that, in conformity with the practice of their white brethren, the Western Indians will take a pride in shewing their clemency and forbearance. Indeed, I am commanded by the Lieutenant-General, that it is only upon their giving their promise and assurance of observing his wishes on this head that he can consent to employ them on the service above alluded to.

(Canadian Archives, C. 681, pp. 260-1.)

Lieut.-Colonel Harvey to Colonel John Murray.

ST. DAVID'S, December 17th, 1813,

SIR,—It appearing to Lieutenant-General Drummond that the present moment is highly favorable for an attack on Fort Niagara, I am directed to acquaint you that the Lieutenant-General has selected you to command the force to be employed on this service, and to add that it is his wish that the attack should be made this night if possible.

The 100th Regiment, the Grenadiers of the Royals, the flank companies 41st Regiment and a party of Royal Artillery are the troops placed at your disposal, and you will be pleased to make such a disposal of them for the attack as you may think proper. The remainder of the regular troops, with the whole body of the Indians, will be passed over to support you.

It is hoped that, with the batteaux just arrived from the head of the lake, you may be able to pass over the whole of the attacking troops in two embarkations, and by this means effect a surprise. It is further hoped that a sufficient number of militiamen will come forward as volunteers, not only to man the batteaux for the purpose of bringing them back to this shore, (as soon as the first embarkation shall have been effected,) but also to aid in the attack of the place by cutting down the pickets, for which purpose it should be recommended that every militia volunteer should come provided with a sharp axe.

The troops should carry scaling ladders (at least 18 or 20) and should be divided into at least two attacks, one to be made on the lake face and the other on the river. The troops must preserve the profoundest silence and the strictest discipline. They must on no account be suffered to load without the orders of their officers. It should be impressed on the mind of every man that the bayonet is the weapon on which the success of the attack must depend.

J. HARVEY, Lt.-Col., D. A. G.

N. B.

```
100th Regiment (say).....................350
Royals...................................100
41st.....................................100
Royal Artillery.......................... 12
                                         ---
                                         562
```

(Canadian Archives, C. 681, pp. 258-9.)

Commodore Chauncey to the Secretary of the Navy.

(No. 130.) U. S. SHIP GENERAL PIKE,

Sackett's Harbor, 17th Dec., 1813.

SIR,—I was last evening honored with your letter of the 1st instant, with the enclosures therein referred to.

I trust that in a day or two after the date of your letter you was relieved from your anxiety for the safety of the fleet by the receipt of my letters from this place.

I have had the honor in former communications of stating to you that the enemy had two vessels in a considerable state of forwardness, and that the keel of a third was laid, and recent advices state that materials are preparing for a fourth. Of this, however, there may be some doubts, but none whatever that he is building three vessels and that the length of keels as stated is pretty nearly correct; but of the breadth of beam, or the number of guns that they are to mount I can obtain no information that can be relied on. I have, however, employed a man who has promised to obtain that information for me from a friend in Kingston. The enemy has received, between the first of October and the last of November, a reinforcement of about five hundred seamen, with a proportionable number of officers. This additional force, I presume, is intended for the vessels building, but by the last accounts no stores, nor men to arm or equip these new vessels, had arrived at Kingston, but from the situation of our army no obstruction can be offered to the enemy's sending from Quebec or Montreal any quantity that he may require, and no doubt but that he will profit by the opportunity.

The enemy's physical force at this time is certainly equal, if not superior, to ours. Add to that force the three vessels which he is building, it will make him vastly superior. Therefore, to place ourselves upon an equality with him, we necessarily must build three vessels of a force corresponding with his. But I should recommend to add a fourth vessel, of the size of the *Sylph*, in lieu of all the heavy sailing schooners, for really they are of no manner of service except to carry troops or use as gunboats.

If it is determined to prosecute the war offensively and secure our conquests in Upper Canada, Kingston ought unquestionably to be the first object of attack, and that so early in the spring as to prevent the enemy from using the whole of the naval force that he is preparing.

With this view of the subject we should require to be built this winter two vessels that would insure our ascendency, even if the enemy should have ready at the breaking up of the ice in the spring the two vessels that are the most forward.

But, on the other hand, if it should be determined to act on the defensive until our troops are collected and disciplined, the additional naval force required upon this lake may be better built in the spring than now, and, I presume, 20 per cent. cheaper. Moreover, the transportation of stores from New York at this season of the year would not only be attended with difficulty, but a vast expense.

The enemy is collecting a considerable force at Kingston, and no doubt will push forward a part of it to the neighborhood of Fort George, and when an opportunity offers he will attempt and probably succeed in recovering that fortress, in which case he will re-occupy Fort Erie and the whole of the north side of the Niagara frontier, which will expose the four vessels that are on shore at Buffalo to be burnt by him, unless a small force should be stationed there. I have, however, directed Captain Elliott that in case he could not get the vessels off, to dismantle them and deposit the stores a few miles from Buffalo.

Whether the enemy will extend himself as far as Malden will, I presume, depend much upon the disposition of the Indians to second his views by reuniting their force with his. If he should re-occupy Malden, the two prize ships at Put-in-Bay I consider in a dangerous situation, and the force left with them quite inadequate to their defense. If the enemy should be in sufficient force to defend these ships, it would be his policy not to destroy but preserve them, and by building attempt to regain his ascendency on the lake. I have directed Captain Elliott to apply to the commanding officer at Detroit for an additional guard for those vessels. Would it not be advisable to order them destroyed in preference to their falling into the enemy's hands?

Captain Perry has never made a return to me of the prisoners taken upon Lake Erie, or said one word to me on the subject; and I am still ignorant of the number or grade or in what manner they were disposed of, and I am almost as ignorant of the prizes, as no particular return of them has ever reached me.

I shall lose no time in having the prizes valued, agreeably to your instructions, and transmit the valuation to the Department.

I directed Captain Perry, in October last, to transmit to me correct muster lists of the officers and men upon Lake Erie. These lists I received a few days since from Captain Elliott, which I will transmit to the Department as soon as copied, together with muster rolls of the officers and men on this station.

I shall continue to make all the necessary preparations here for building, and collect all the timber that will be first required, but shall recommend to Dr. Bullus to detain the ship carpenters in New York until he receives further instructions from you upon the subject. I adopt this course lest we might incur expense that by a little delay might be avoided.

Lieut.-General Drummond to Sir George Prevost.

ST. DAVID'S, December 18th, 1813.

SIR,—I have the honour to report to Your Excellency my arrival here on the 16th, and to acknowledge the receipt, this day, of Your Excellency's letter of the 10th instant.

I am concerned to say that my opinion relative to the exaggerated accounts of the disasters which were reported to have befallen Commodore Chauncey's squadron has proved but too just, the *Madison* only having sustained some damage by being ashore for 48 hours. But she is now, as well as the other vessels of the enemy's fleet, in safety at Sackett's Harbour. I have directed Major-General Vincent to proceed to Kingston without delay, he having been this day relieved of the command of the Right Division by Major-General Riall. But as the Major-General is extremely anxious to avail himself of Your Excellency's indulgence already granted, I have, in consequence, to request Your Excellency will permit Major-General Stovin to leave Montreal as soon as convenient.

I propose that Major-General Procter should remain in command at York (it being a post of little importance at present) until Your Excellency's pleasure is known.

On the arrival of the marines at Prescott, may not the entire battalion be drawn from thence to Kingston and their place supplied by the men of the Glengarry Regiment, in consideration of their great ability in controlling the conduct of the seamen, and as it will in some degree meet Your Excellency's wishes relative to the Glengarry Corps moving toward the Lower Province?

I have forwarded Your Excellency's letter to Capt. Norton.

The evacuation of this frontier will now afford ample means to the Commissariat Dept. in the supply of provisions and forage to the troops of this division.

Conceiving the present a favorable opportunity for making an attack on the enemy's Fort Niagara, I have placed a force under the command of Colonel Murray, Inspecting Field Officer, for that purpose. I had intended that the troops should have crossed the river last night, but the batteaux which were ordered from Burlington to the Four Mile Creek having been, in the first instance, considerably impeded in their progress by a gale of wind upon the lake, and afterwards, notwithstanding the unremitting exertions of Capt. Eliot, Assistant Deputy Quartermaster General, in landing them by a very heavy surf, and thence by a tedious land conveyance on slays to the place selected for the embarkation of the troops at Two Mile Run, it became too late to carry the design into execution at that time. This night, however, I propose they should be crossed over and the fort attempted by assault. Major-General Riall will follow immediately with the reserves and the Indians, (under Col. Elliott,) to act in support of Colonel Murray as circumstances may demand, independent of which I propose that an attack shall be made upon Lewiston for the purpose of destroying some works which the enemy have been throwing up at that place with the avowed intention of destroying from thence the town of Queenston. In both these attempts I have sanguine hopes of success.

I have seen a Mr. Muirhead, who this day arrived from Buffalo. He had, with the principal part of the respectable inhabitants of this part of the country, been carried off, though not in arms, by the enemy some time since. He reports that the enemy is in great apprehension of an attack and they are in consequence sending to the interior all their effects and endeavoring to collect the militia and Indians from all directions. The *Caledonia* is lying in the river opposite to the stores at Black Rock, said to have but one gun on board and in otherwise an indifferent state of equipment. Four or five other vessels are said to be ashore between Buffalo and Presqu 'Isle. General McClure was at Buffalo, Colonel Wilcox had gone to Washington.

I have directed a letter to be written to General McClure, calling upon him to state, unequivocally, whether the atrocious act of the burning of the town of Fort George had been authorized by his Government, or whether it was the unauthorized act of an individual.

Captain Barclay, Royal Navy, is at Queenston and, I am happy to say, his wound is mending daily.

(Canadian Archives, C. 681, p. 240.)

General McClure's Address to the Inhabitants of Niagara, Genesee and Chautauqua.

The present crisis is alarming. The enemy are preparing to invade your frontier and let their savages loose upon your families and property. It is now in your power to avoid that evil by repairing to Lewiston, Schlosser and Buffalo. Every man who is able to bear arms is not only invited, but required, to repair to the above rallying points for a few days or until a detachment of militia arrives. The enemy are now laying waste their own country. Every man who does not take up arms, or who are disposed to remain neutral, are inhumanly butchered, their property plundered and their buildings destroyed.

Information has just been received that six or eight of their most respectable inhabitants, between Queenston and Fort George, have fallen victims to their barbarity. Every man in the province is required to take up arms and he that refuses is inhumanly butchered. What then, fellow-citizens, have you to expect from such an enemy, should they invade your frontier? Think of the consequences; be not lulled into a belief that because you live a few miles from the river that you are secure; no, fellow-citizens, the place to meet them is on the beach; there you will have it in your power to chastise them; but should they be suffered to penetrate into the interior with their savages, the scene will be horrid. If, then, you love your country and are determined to defend its rights; if you love your families and are determined to protect them; if you value your property and are determined to preserve it, you will fly to arms and hasten to meet the enemy should they dare to set foot on our shores.

Since the above was prepared, I have received intelligence from a credible inhabitant of Canada, (who has just escaped from thence), that the enemy are concentrating all their forces and boats at Fort George and have fixed upon to-morrow night for attacking Fort Niagara—and should they succeed they will lay waste our whole frontier. In that case our supply of arms, which are deposited at Niagara, will be cut off. Therefore, all who have arms and accoutrements will do well to bring them; and all who have horses will come mounted.

GEORGE McCLURE,
Brigadier-General commanding Niagara Frontier.
Headquarters, Buffalo, 18th December, 1813.

From the Buffalo Gazette 21st Dec., 1813.

To the Editor of the Buffalo Gazette:

SIR,—Having heard from several sources illiberal and erroneous statements of the force at Fort George when that post was abandoned, and that great quantities of arms and ammunition were destroyed, we consider it a duty we owe to the commandant, General McClure, to undeceive the people and convince them of the policy of the measures that were pursued. The period for which the militia had been drafted having expired, the General held out every inducement in his power for them to remain but for a short time. He offered a bounty, but neither the love of country nor the shame of abandoning him when the enemy were advancing, could prevail on them to remain, in consequence of which he was left with about sixty effective men to maintain Fort George. The British, knowing the period when the militia term of service would expire, availed themselves of that moment to endeavor to retake the frontier and advance from Burlington Heights. The General called a council of the remainder of his officers, when it was unanimously agreed that the fort was not tenable with the small remaining force. All the public property of every description that was of any value, except three twelve-pounders, which he had not sufficient physical force to carry away (and these were spiked, their carriages burnt and buried in the ruins of the fort,) was taken across the river to Fort Niagara—nor was there a musket left or a cartridge of powder more than was necessary to blow up the works. A considerable quantity of property belonging to individuals friendly to us was also taken across and so near was the enemy that eight or ten prisoners were taken in assisting them to get their property away.

As relates to the burning of the village of Newark, however disagreeable to the General, the act was not unauthorized, but at the same time he conceived it necessary for the protection of our frontier, that the enemy might not have it in their power to quarter with their Indian allies in the village and maraud and murder our citizens.

Twelve hours' notice was given to the few inhabitants that remained to secure their household property and every measure that could be taken to alleviate their situation was done; three or four houses were left for those that chose to remain; others who might wish to go across the river the General ordered rations and quarters to be provided for. For their own immediate protection the General has ordered out *en masse* the militia of Niagara county.

JOHN A. ROGERS,
Capt. 24th, U. S. Infantry.
JOHN WILSON,
Brig. Major of Militia.
DONALD FRASER,
Lt. 13th Inf. V. A. D. C.

Kingston Gazette, Saturday, December 18, 1813.

Few regiments have evinced greater zeal than the 104th, commanded by Lieutenant-General Hunter, under whose auspices it was raised this war. It was no sooner complete to its establishment of 1000 men than it unanimously volunteered for general service. Being ordered to Canada, this regiment actually marched on snow shoes from New Brunswick to Quebec, a distance of about 260 miles, when the thermometer was twenty degrees below the cypher, a circumstance which astonished even the Canadians. Scarcely had the men recovered from being frost-bitten (which most of them were), than the regiment was ordered to the frontiers of Upper Canada, being 450 miles. The fatigue and difficulty of such a march at the most inclement season of the year cannot be well imagined. It was performed with the greatest cheerfulness and the regiment had the good fortune to reach Upper Canada in time to take a distinguished share in the recent operations in that quarter. On the whole the conduct of this regiment does credit to the province it was raised in and shows that the spirit of the old American Loyalists still exists in their sons.—Quebec Mercury.

Lieut.-General Drummond to Sir George Provost.

FORT NIAGARA, 19th December, 1813.
Half past 5 o'clock a.m.

DEAR SIR,—I have the satisfaction to inform you that the Fort of Niagara fell into our hands at 5 o'clock this morning. It was carried in a most gallant manner by assault at the point of the bayonet by the troops, as per margin, I had selected and placed under the command of Colonel Murray. The enemy have suffered some loss in killed; that on our part is comparatively small. There have been taken about 150 prisoners, amongst whom is Capt. Leonard, the commandant, and several officers. I regret to say that Lt. Nowlan of the 100th Regt. has been killed and that Colonel Murray has been wounded severely in the wrist.

<small>Grenadier Co'y Royal Scots Regt.
Flank Companies 41st
100th Regt.
Royal Artillery</small>

There are several pieces of ordnance mounted in the fort and about 3,000 stand of arms, a large quantity of clothing, salt and other stores.

It is satisfactory to remark that the capture of this place has been the means of relieving from confinement 5 or 6 respectable inhabitants of the Niagara District, who had been shamefully dragged from their families, and a few Indians.

I have not time to enter further into detail, as I am proceeding towards Lewiston, to which place Major-General Riall, with the remainder of the troops and the whole of the Western Indians, is advancing.

I will transmit to Your Excellency an official account of this affair as soon as I receive Colonel Murray's report.

(Canadian Archives, C. 681, p. 244.)

Colonel John Murray to Lieut.-General Drummond.

FORT NIAGARA, 19th December, 1813.

SIR,—In obedience to Your Honor's commands directing me to attack Fort Niagara with the advance of the army of the Right, I resolved upon attempting a surprise. The embarkation commenced on the 18th, at night, and the whole of the troops were landed three miles from the fort early on the following morning in the following order of attack:—Advance guard, one subaltern and twenty rank and file, Grenadiers, 100th Regiment, Royal Artillery with grenades, five companies 100th Regiment under Lieut.-Colonel Hamilton, to assault the main gate and escalade the works adjacent. Three companies

100th Regiment, under Captain Martin, to storm the eastern demi-bastion. Captain Bailey, with the Grenadiers Royal Scots, was directed to attack the salient angle of the fortification, and the flank companies of the 41st Regiment were ordered to support the principal attack. Each party was provided with scaling ladders and axes. I have great satisfaction in acquainting Your Honor that the fortress was carried by assault in the most resolute and gallant manner, after a short but spirited resistance.

The highly gratifying but difficult duty remains of endeavoring to do justice to the bravery, intrepidity and devotion of the 100th Regiment to the service of their country, under that gallant officer, Lieut.-Colonel Hamilton, to whom I feel highly indebted for his cordial assistance. Captain Martin, 100th Regiment, who executed the task allotted to him in the most intrepid manner, merits the greatest praise. I have to express my admiration of the valor of the Royals Grenadiers, under Captain Bailey, whose zeal and gallantry were very conspicuous. The just tribute of my applause is equally due to the flank companies 41st Regiment, under Lieut. Bullock, who advanced to the attack with great spirit. The Royal Artillery, under Lieut. Charleton, deserve my particular notice. To Captain Eliot, Deputy Assistant Quartermaster General, who conducted one of the columns of attack and superintended the embarkation, I feel highly obliged. I cannot pass over the brilliant services of Lieut. Dawson and Captain Fawcett, 100th, in command of the advance and grenadiers, who gallantly executed the orders entrusted to them by entirely cutting off two of the enemy's picquets and surprising the sentries on the glacis and at the gate, by which means the watchword was obtained and the entrance to the fort greatly facilitated, to which may be attributed, in a great degree, our trifling loss. I beg leave to recommend these meritorious officers to Your Honor's protection. The scientific knowledge of Lieut. Gaugreben, Royal Engineers, in suggesting arrangements previous to the attack and securing the fort, afterwards, I cannot too highly appreciate. The unwearied exertions of Quartermaster Pilkington, 100th Regiment, for bringing forward materials requisite for the attack, demand my acknowledgements. Captain Kerby, Lieuts. Ball, Servos and Hamilton of the different provincial corps deserve my thanks. My staff adjutant, Mr. Brampton, will have the honor of presenting this dispatch and standard of the American garrison; to his intelligence, valor and friendly assistance, not only in this trying occasion, but on many others, I feel most grateful.

Our force consisted of about five hundred rank and file. Annexed is a return of our casualties and the enemy's loss in killed, wounded and prisoners. The ordnance and commissariat stores are so immense that it is totally out of my power to forward you a correct statement for some days, but twenty-seven pieces of cannon of different calibres are on the works and upwards of three thousand stand of arms and many rifles in the arsenal. The storehouses are full of clothing and camp equipage of every description.

Canadian Archives, C. 681, pp. 249-51.)

RETURN of the killed and wounded in an assault on Fort Niagara at daybreak on the morning of the 19th December, 1813:—

General Staff—One officer wounded.
Royal Artillery—One staff officer wounded.
41st Regiment—One rank and file wounded.
100th Regiment—One lieutenant, 5 rank and file killed, 2 rank and file wounded.

Total killed—One lieutenant and 5 rank and file; 2 officers and 3 rank and file wounded.

Names of officers killed and wounded:—

Killed—Lieutenant Nowlan, 100th Regiment.
Wounded—Colonel Murray, commanding, severely not dangerously; Assistant Surgeon Ogilvie, Royal Artillery, slightly.

J. HARVEY, Lt.-Col., D. A. G.

RETURN of the enemy's loss in killed and wounded and prisoners who fell into our hands in an assault on Fort Niagara on the morning of the 19th December, 1813:—

Killed—Sixty-five.
Wounded—One lieutenant, one assistant surgeon and 12 rank and file.
Prisoners—One captain, 9 lieutenants, 2 ensigns, 1 surgeon, 1 commissary, 12 sergeants and 318 rank and file.
Total in killed, wounded and prisoners—One captain, 9 lieutenants, 2 ensigns, 1 surgeon, 1 assistant surgeon, 1 commissary, 12 sergeants and 395 rank and file. The whole belong to the artillery and line.

J. HARVEY, Lt.-Col., D. A. G.

(Canadian Archives, C. 681, p. 257.)

Major-General Phineas Riall to Lieut.-General Drummond.

LEWISTON, December 19th, 1813.

SIR,—According to your instructions I crossed the river this morning, immediately after the advance under Colonel Murray had passed over, with the Royal Scots and 41st Regiments, accompanied by a large body of Indians, and marched upon Lewiston, which the enemy had, however, abandoned upon our approach, leaving behind them a 12 and 6-pounder with travelling carriages and everything complete. I found in this place a considerable number of small arms, ammunition, 9 barrels of powder and also a quantity of flour amounting, I believe, to 200 barrels. I regret the troops had not the opportunity of coming in contact with the enemy, as I am convinced they would have acquired your fullest approbation.

(Canadian Archives, C. 681, p. 264.)

General Order.

HEADQUARTERS, Upper Canada, Dec. 19, 1813.

Lieutenant-General Drummond congratulates the troops under his command upon the brilliant success which has crowned the attack made this morning on Fort Niagara. It was assaulted an hour before daylight and after a short but severe conflict it was carried with a very slight loss on our part; that of the enemy was 65 killed and 15 wounded, all by the bayonet. The remainder of the garrison, to the number of about 350 regular troops and artillery, were made prisoners. 27 pieces of ordnance were found in the fort. Our loss does not exceed 5 killed and 3 wounded. Lieutenant Nowlan of the 100th Regiment, a very promising young officer, was the only officer killed. The Lieutenant-General has to regret that a severe wound which Colonel Murray has received is likely to deprive the army of the service of that gallant officer for some time. The troops employed on this occasion were the 100th Regiment, the grenadier company of the Royals and the flank companies of the 41st Regiment. Their instructions were not to fire, but to carry the place at the point of the bayonet. These orders were punctually obeyed, a circumstance that not only proves their intrepidity, but reflects great credit on their discipline. Colonel Murray expresses his admiration of the valor and good conduct of the whole of the troops, particularly of the 100th Regiment, which led the attack. He also bestows his particular thanks on Lieutenant-Colonel Hamilton and Captain Martin of the 100th Regiment, Captain Bailey of the Royals, Lieutenant Bullock of the 41st Regiment and

Lieutenant Charleton of the Royal Artillery, Captain Eliot, deputy assistant quartermaster general, and to Captain Kerby and Lieutenants Ball, Servos and Hamilton of the militia, of the brilliant service of Lieutenant Dawson of the 100th, who led the forlorn hope, and Captain Fawcett of the 100th Grenadiers, in entirely cutting off two of the enemy's picquets and surprising the sentries on the glacis and at the gate, by which means the watchword was obtained and the entrance into the fort greatly facilitated, the Colonel speaks in terms of the highest and most deserved praise.

Lieutenant-General Drummond will perform a most grateful duty in bringing under the notice of His Royal Highness the Prince Regent, through His Excellency the Commander of the Forces, the admirable execution of this brilliant achievement on the part of every individual concerned. The useful services of the militia volunteers in launching the boats and rowing the troops across the river were not unnoticed by the Lieutenant-General.

The Lieutenant-General has received from Major-General Riall a very favorable report of the zeal and alacrity of the detachment of the Royal Scots, under Lieut.-Col. Gordon, and the 41st battalion companies, under Major Frend, who advanced under the Major-General's command to dislodge the enemy from the heights of Lewiston. Their steadiness and regularity under circumstances of great temptation were highly creditable to them. Nothing could more strongly indicate their anxious wish to meet the enemy, and the Lieutenant-General has only to regret that his rapid retreat from Lewiston Heights did not afford to Major-General Riall an opportunity of leading them to victory.

Lieutenant-General Drummond begs that Major-Generals Riall and Vincent will accept his acknowledgements for the assistance he has obtained from them in making arrangements for the late operations.

Lieut.-Col. Hamilton, 100th Regiment, is appointed to command Fort Niagara and the Lieutenant-General will recommend that the same command money be annexed to it as was granted at Fort George.

A board of survey, composed of Lieut.-Col. Hamilton, commandant, president, Major Holcroft, commanding the Royal Artillery, and a captain of the 100th Regiment, members, will assemble as soon as possible in Fort Niagara for the purpose of taking an exact account and inventory of ordnance, stores, arms, provisions, clothing, &c., captured in that place.

J. HARVEY, Lieut.-Col., D. A. G.

Handbill Printed at Montreal, 28th December, 1813.

("Canadian Courant" Extra.)

Extract of a letter from an officer of high rank in the army to a friend in this city, dated Queenston, December 19th, 1813:—

I have the happiness to acquaint you that Fort Niagara was taken by assault an hour before daylight this morning. Colonel Murray commanded the storming party, which consisted of the 100th Regiment (the Prince Regent's Own Irish heroes,) the grenadiers of the 1st Royals and flank companies 41st. Our loss has been but trifling: Lieut. Nowlan of 100th Grenadiers, killed; Colonel Murray wounded through the wrist, and perhaps half a dozen other casualties. The quantity of ordnance stores, provisions, &c., found in the place is very great; 3,000 stand of arms, £500,000 worth of clothing, are among the articles. The remainder of the troops, with the whole of the Western Indians, who had been passed over to support the attack, immediately after ascertaining the success of Colonel Murray's column, moved towards Lewiston to attack the heights, on which the enemy had planted some heavy guns, avowedly for the purpose of laying Queenston in ashes. Both the heights and Lewiston were, however, precipitately abandoned on the advance of General Riall's column. A whoop from 500 of the most savage Indians (which they gave just at daylight, on hearing of the success of the attack on Fort Niagara,) made the enemy take to their heels and our troops are in pursuit. We shall not stop until we have cleared the whole frontier. The Indians are retaliating the conflagration of Newark. Not a house within my sight but is in flames. This is a melancholy but just retaliation.

(From the *United States Gazette* of Philadelphia, 12th January, 1814, file in Philadelphia Library. Also in New York *Evening Post* of same date.

Deposition of Robert Lee.

Robert Lee, late of Lewiston, in the county of Niagara and State of New York, gentleman, of the age of forty-two years, being sworn on the Holy Evangelists, deposeth and saith, that some seven weeks immediately preceding the 19th of December last, he, this deponent, resided in Fort Niagara for the purpose of attending to private business, that about four o'clock in the morning of the 19th the said fort was attacked or entered by the British. The garrison was not alarmed when the enemy entered the gates of the fort. Some firing took place after they entered the works, particularly between the guard at the south-east blockhouse, and the sick in the hospital at the red barrack on the part of the Americans with the enemy. This deponent is positive that there were about four hundred men of all descriptions in the fort immediately before it was taken, and that three hundred and fifty of that number were able and willing to bear arms in that way, viz., firing on the enemy from the blockhouses, &c. The principal resistance the enemy met with was from the sick in the red barracks and the guard at the south-east blockhouse before mentioned. The sick in the red barracks, as this deponent is informed and from what he saw, he believes were nearly all slaughtered. The British force that took possession of the fort were in number about four hundred, commanded by Colonel Murray, who was wounded in the arm in entering the gate and was succeeded in command by Colonel Hamilton. From the British order of congratulation that issued on the same morning, it appeared that the Americans had lost sixty-five killed and fifteen wounded, which wounds were principally by the bayonet as expressed in the order, but the above order was issued very soon after they took possession of the fort and did not include a number that were afterwards found bayoneted in the cellars of the houses. This deponent thinks that our loss in killed in the whole amounted to at least eighty. It was a matter of frequent conversation and exultation among the British non-commissioned officers and soldiers, while this deponent was under guard, that they bayoneted the Americans notwithstanding their crying out for quarter. A subaltern officer and about twenty privates made their escape from the fort by scaling the pickets. Captain Leonard, the American commander, was, at the time the fort was taken, at his farm, about two miles distant, and, hearing the attack, made towards the fort, and at no great distance from it was made prisoner by the enemy and was kept in close confinement for two days and a half and how much longer this deponent does not know. The American soldiers were kept two days in close and miserable confinement, without the use of provisions, and with a very scanty supply of wood and water; at the expiration of which the citizens and soldiers were crossed over the river and lodged in a part of what had been the British magazine at Fort George, the residue in open plank and board huts: in both situations it was impossible to lay down. The magazine was so filthy that many of the prisoners became infested with vermin and in that situation remained seven days. The citizens were then removed to a brick building, up near Queenston, where they were so much crowded that no kind of comfort was to be taken either by day or night. The supply of provisions was not only scanty, but of the very worst kind; beef of the most inferior and repulsive character, and bread, the quality of which cannot be described. The water that they used, both there and at the magazine, they had to purchase. This deponent believes that, through the influence of an individual in Upper Canada, himself, together with ten other American citizens, were permitted on the 13th instant to cross to the United States. The residue of the citizens, to the amount of about seventy, were marched, on the 12th, under a strong guard, to Burlington Heights, and this deponent was informed that from thence they would be sent to Kingston. The women and children taken at and near Lewiston were stripped of their clothing and taken across the river. And further this deponent saith not.

[Sgd.] ROBERT LEE.

Sworn to and subscribed this 18th day of January, 1814, before me.
J. HARRISON,
Master in Chancery.

(American State Papers, Military Affairs, Vol. I., p. 488.)

THE CAPTURE OF FORT NIAGARA.

By one Who Served in 1814, (Lieut. Driscoll, 100th Regt.)

This post was very strong, for a fort in that part of the country, for its *Enceinte*, besides being of regular construction and mounting many guns, included three stone towers at the west, south-west and south angles of the fort, in addition to a long and strong barracks on the north face, the whole having flat roofs mounted with cannon. It was accordingly, in December, 1813, determined to attempt its capture, and the attempt was made on the night of the 19th December.

The force destined for the purpose was composed of the 100th Regiment, the grenadiers of the 1st, the flank companies of the 41st, and some artillerymen, the whole under the command of Colonel Murray, of the 100th, a better man than whom could not have been chosen.

Batteaux having been secretly conveyed overland from Burlington to a point about four miles up the British side of the river, the troops silently left their cantonments about 10 o'clock at night, concealing their march under cover of the adjacent wood, embarked without noise and landed undiscovered on the opposite side, whence they descended cautiously towards the fort.

There lay between them and their destination a small hamlet, called Youngstown, about two miles, or somewhat less, from the fort, to which it served as an outpost, where it was known lay a detachment from the garrison.

It was necessary to surprise it without alarming the fort.

A chosen body was therefore sent in advance, while the main body followed at a convenient distance.

When arrived near it, some of the former crept stealthily up to a window and peeped in. They saw a party of officers at cards. "What are trumps?" asked one of them. "Bayonets are trumps!" answered one of the peepers, breaking in the window and entering with his companions, while the remainder of the detachment rapidly surrounded the house, rushed into it and bayonetted the whole of its inmates, that none might escape to alarm the fort. Not a shot was fired on either side, the American sentries having retired from their posts into a building to shelter themselves from the cold, there was no time for resistance.

The assailants performed their work of human destruction in grim silence—a lamentable but necessary act.

Resuming their march, they drew near the fort—not a word is spoken—the muskets are carried squarely, that the bayonets may not clash—the ice crackles audibly under their tread, but the sound is borne to their rear on the continuous gusts of a north-east wind—when lo! the charger of Colonel Hamilton (who, having lost a leg in Holland, could not march, and would not stay behind,) neighs loudly, and is answered by a horse in a stable not far from the fort. What a moment! The force instantly halts, expecting to hear the alarm suddenly given, the sound of drums and bugles and of the garrison rushing to their posts. But all remains quiet, the sentries, crouching in their boxes, take the neigh of the charger for that of some horse strayed from a farm-house or the neighboring hamlet. They feel no inclination for leaving their shelters to explore, shiveringly, the thick darkness of a moonless winter night.

It can be nothing. The approaching force, drawing freer breath, puts itself in motion, shuffles hastily and silently forward, and the the crisis is near.

The forlorn hope is commanded by Lieut. Dawson and led by Sergeant Andrew Spearman.

He halts at the distance of about 25 yards from the gate, towards which the sergeant (a tall, stalwart man) strides, and, strange to say, finds the wicket open.

The sentry, hearing some one approach, issues from his box, protrudes the upper part of his body through the doorway, and asks, "Who come there?"

Spearman, imitating the nasal twang of the American, answers, "I guess, Mister, I come from Youngstown," quietly introducing at the same time his left shoulder through the half open wicket.

The sentry stares at him, perceives by his accoutrements and his actions that he is an enemy, turns round and runs inward exclaiming "The Brit . . . !" He says no more, Spearman's bayonet is in his side.

The sergeant returns and calls in a subdued tone to the forlorn hope, which swiftly enters, followed by the column. The light company of the 100th makes a rapid circuit and escalades the wall; the attacking force has entered.

Had the assailants been discreetly silent, they might have effected the capture without loss to themselves or the enemy, but, their blood being up, they uttered a terrific yell, which roused the sleeping garrison and occasioned some resistance.

A cannon, turned inwards, was fired from the roof of the south-western tower, followed by a slight pattering of musketry.

To prevent repetition of the former, Lieutenant Nolan of the 100th, a man of great personal strength and ardent courage, rushed into the lower part of the tower, regardless of what foes he might find there, and by what friends he might be followed. Next morning his body was found, the breast pierced by a deep bayonet wound, at the bottom of which were a musket ball and three buckshot.

But he had not died unavenged. One American lay at his feet, whom he had killed by a pistol shot, while the cloven skulls of two others attested his tremendous strength of arm and desperate valour.

Some of his men, however, who had seen him plunge into the darkness, followed him, and though too late to save him, had taken the tower, slaying the defenders to a man. This resistance exasperated our men, who rushed wildly about into every building, bayonetting every American they met. The carnage, indeed, would have amounted to extermination if the British officers had not zealously exerted themselves in the cause of mercy.

Lieut. Murray of the 100th particularly distinguished himself by his humane endeavours, for, finding the tide of fugitives set towards the southern angle, where a sally-port had been burst in, he made them lie down, protected them, and thus saved many. In half an hour the fort was fully captured and was quiet, and the panting victors sought to drown their excitement in sleep. . . . .

Lieut. Dawson was promoted to a company, while Spearman remained a sergeant and never, as far as known, received any reward for his gallantry but the esteem of his officers and comrades. If he be still alive he lives in Richmond, U. C., (near St. Thomas,) where the 100th after its disbandment received lands and settled.

(From MSS. Memoirs of Colonel John Clark, pp. 185-193, in possession of Dr. T. Clark Catharines.)

From the Diary of Thos. McCrae, Sr.

Sunday, 19th Dec., 1813.

Some of the American light horse passed here this evening, the army encamped at the Widow Dolsen's. I have not heard the number.

Monday, 20th Dec., 1813.

A detachment of the American army arrived here to-day under the command of Major Langham. They camped all round the house. The Major authorized me to swear the inhabitants here by administering an oath of neutrality.

Tuesday, 21st Dec., 1813.

The American army started this afternoon on their way to Detroit.

Wednesday, 22nd Dec., 1813.

The Am. burnt a great many rails, altho' we hauled wood for them.

Friday, 24th Dec., 1813.

Most of of the inhabitants above this have been down to take the oath. Barret, Dorsey, Willett and some others are all starting for the States, being afraid of another British party coming to take them off.

Lieut.-General Drummond to Sir George Prevost.

Fort Niagara, 20th Dec., 1813.

Sir,—Conceiving the possession of Fort Niagara to be of the highest importance, in every point of view, to the tranquillity and serenity of this frontier, immediately on my arrival at St. David's, I determined upon its reduction, if possible without too great a sacrifice There being, however, but two batteaux on this side the water, I did not think proper to make the attempt until a sufficient number should be brought from Burlington, at this season of the year a most difficult undertaking. But, by the indefatigable exertions of Captain Eliot, Deputy Assistant Quartermaster General, every difficulty, particularly in the carriage of the batteaux by land for several miles, notwithstanding the inclemency of the weather (the ground being covered with snow, and the frost severe,) was overcome ; they were again launched, and the troops, consisting of a small detachment of the Royal Artillery, the grenadier company of the Royal Scots, the flank companies of the 41st and the 100th Regiment, amounting in the whole to about 550, which I had placed under the immediate orders of Colonel Murray, Inspecting Field Officer, were embarked. The enclosed report of that most zealous and judicious officer will point out to you the detail of their further proceedings.

At 5 o'clock a.m. the fort was attacked by assault, at the point of the bayonet, two picquets, posted at the distance of a mile and of a mile and a half from the works, having previously been destroyed to a man by the same weapon, and in half an hour afterwards this important place was completely in our possession.

By this gallant achievement 27 pieces of ordnance (mounted on the several defences,) 3,000 stands of arms, a number of rifles, a quantity of ammunition, blankets, clothing, several thousand pairs of shoes, &c., have fallen into our hands, besides 14 officers, and 330 others, prisoners, and 8 respectable inhabitants of this part of the country, who had been dragged from the peaceful enjoyment of their property to a most unwarrantable confinement, were released, together with some Indian warriors of the Cocknawaga and Six Nation tribes. The enemy's loss amounted to 65 in killed and to but 12 in wounded, which clearly proves how irresistible a weapon the bayonet is in the hands of British soldiers.

Our loss was only 5 killed and 3 wounded. I have to regret the death of a very promising officer, Lieutenant Nolan, of the 100th Regt.

I beg leave to bear the highest testimony of the active and meritorious exertions of Col. Murray, who, I regret to say, received a severe though not dangerous wound in the wrist (which I hope will not, at this critical period, deprive me for any length of time of his valuable services,) and to Lieut.-Colonel Hamilton, of the 100th Regt., and the officers, non-commissioned officers and soldiers who so gallantly achieved this most daring and brilliant enterprise.

The militia came forward with alacrity and assisted much in launching and transporting the batteaux across the river, in a very rapid current, for which service they are deserving of the highest praise.

Captain Norton, the Indian chief, volunteered his services and accompanied the troops.

And I beg to recommend in the strongest terms to the favor and protection of His Royal Highness the Prince Regent, Captain Eliot, of the 103rd Regt., Deputy Assistant Quartermaster General, whose conduct on this, as on every other occasion, has been so distinguished, as also Lieut. Dawson of the 100th Regt., who commanded the forlorn hope, Captain Fawcett, of the same regiment, who immediately supported him with the Grenadiers, and Captain Martin who with three companies gallantly stormed the eastern demi-bastion.

My best acknowledgements are due to Major-Generals Riall and Vincent for the cordial and zealous assistance I received from them in making the arrangements, to Lieut.-Colonel Harvey and to the officers of my personal staff.

I have the honor to forward to your Excellency the American colors taken on this occasion by Captain Foster, my aid-de-camp, who, being in my fullest confidence, will give Your Excellency such further information as you may require.

(Canadian Archives, Q. 127, p. 14.)

Lieut.-General Drummond to Sir George Prevost.

ST. DAVIDS, 20th December, 1813.

SIR,—I have the honor to transmit the copy of instructions to Colonel Murray relative to the attack upon Fort Niagara, as also a letter to Lieut.-Colonel Elliott, of the Indian Department, by which letter will be perceived how anxious my endeavors were to prevent any act of violence being committed by the Indians on the expedition to the enemy's frontier, and a letter to Brigadier-General McClure demanding an unequivocal declaration from him by what authority the unprecedented outrage of the burning of the town of Niagara by the American troops, previous to their evacuation of it, was committed, to which I have as yet received no reply.

(Canadian Archives, C. 681, pp. 262-3.)

Lieut.-General Drummond to Sir George Prevost.

QUEENSTON, December 20th, 1813.

SIR,—The enemy having established a force and erected some batteries at Lewiston, with the avowed intention of destroying the town of Queenston opposite, I determined to dislodge him thence and with that view the 1st Battalion of the Royal Scots and the 41st Regiment with the whole body of the Western Indians were crossed to the American frontier under the command of Major-General Riall in batteaux immediately after the landing of the force under Colonel Murray. The enemy retired on the approach of our troops and permitted thereby two guns, a twelve and a six pounder to fall into our hands.

From Major-General Riall's report of the good conduct of the troops employed on this service I am convinced that if an opportunity had offered they would have equally distinguished themselves with those at Niagara.

I am, however, extremely concerned to state that notwithstanding my most positive orders and their own assurances made to me through Lieutenant-Colonel Elliott in a council of their chiefs that they would refrain from outrage, several acts of violence were committed by the Indians.

(Canadian Archives, C. 681, pp. 265-6.)

Brigadier-General Timothy Hopkins to Governor Tompkins.

SIR,—I would respectfully represent to Your Excellency that on the morning of yesterday the enemy crossed over a little below Lewiston. They have burned Lewiston and every house from that place to within two and a half miles of Schlosser, and the Tuscarora village is also burnt.

The last express stated the enemy were fortifying on the mountain below Schlosser. The force of the enemy is differently represented. It is stated to be from four to eight hundred regulars and six hundred Indians. It is further stated that the enemy are still crossing. The force the enemy can bring is not precisely known. It is probably from 1,500 to 3,000, including regulars, militia and Indians. Our force is about 200 regulars at Fort Niagara and about 150 near this place. I have ordered out my brigade to repel the invasion. I am in hopes of success, with the assistance of the militia of Genesee. But I have to represent that the men of my brigade are unwilling to come under the command of General McClure, who is near Buffalo and assumes the command. His conduct since he has been out on the lines has disgusted the greater part of the men under his command and they have no confidence in him.

On his arrival at Buffalo, after evacuating Fort George and burning Newark, he requested me to invite volunteers for the defence of this frontier, and this too under the impression that the enemy contemplated an immediate attack on Buffalo and other parts of the frontier. I have met with no success. The militia of this county have stood so many drafts and have been so much absent from their homes and business that it will be very difficult to keep them out any length of time after the enemy are routed, and unless a sufficient regular force is marched to this frontier or the militia ordered out by the Commander-in-Chief the whole frontier will be a ruin. We anticipate great danger at this place, especially so soon as the ice affords a bridge for the army to cross Lake Erie. I am not disposed to censure the conduct of men placed in command, but we have reason to fear that the destruction of Newark and the retreat of General McClure from Canada have incensed the people of Canada and inspired them with courage to such a degree that nothing will save any part of this frontier but a respectable force.

I feel it a duty which I owe my country and this frontier to make the foregoing statement and earnestly solicit Your Excellency's interposition for our safety.

Dated, Head Quarters, Buffalo, December 20, 1813.

P. S.—Since writing the above the order, a copy of which is hereunto annexed, has been delivered into my hands.

[A Copy.]

HEAD QUARTERS, MAJOR MILLER'S, Dec. 20, 1813.

General Timothy Hopkins will take the command of the militia that is or may assemble at Buffalo while I go with the regulars to relieve Fort Niagara, which is in imminent danger. You will notify me of your movements and that of the enemy from time to time and co-operate with me as circumstances may require.

GEORGE McCLURE, B.-Genl.,
Commanding Niagara Frontier.

(Tompkins Papers, Vol. IX, pp. 8-9, New York State Library.)

General McClure to Governor Tompkins.

HEAD QUARTERS, BUFFALO, NEW YORK.

20th December, 1813.

DEAR SIR.—I am sorry to inform you that the enemy have invaded our country in great force on the night of the 18th inst. at Lewiston. I had a small detachment stationed there, consisting of about sixty men of Colonel Grieves' regiment and about forty Indians. The enemy's allies appeared in great numbers and surrounded our people. Some fought their way through and those who have not come in I presume are cut to pieces. The enemy is said to be 3,000 strong. Major Mallory being stationed at Schlosser with Colonel Wilcox's corps of Canadian Volunteers advanced to Lewiston. He attacked their advance guards and drove them in. I have not heard from him to-day and have my fears of their being cut off. I have used every exertion in my power to call forth the militia of the neighboring counties *en masse*. About 400 militia have arrived, but they are more engaged in taking care of their families and property by carrying them into the interior than helping us to fight. I leave General Hopkins to command at Buffalo while I go with 100 regulars and some Indians to cut our way if possible into Niagara. That post is in imminent danger. There is not 200 men in that fort and all our arms, ammunition and public stores of every description are deposited there. When shall I expect relief? Will not the Government roused to a sense of their duty and send an overwhelming force at once and drive the rascals round the lake? The last campaign has been conducted in such a manner that I shall beg leave to retire as soon as I can be relieved, as nothing but disgrace can await a commander let his exertions be what they may. My whole force is not a major's command. The Secretary at War is now sensible that the information in relation to the enemy's force at Burlington was correct.

Permit me, sir, to urge the necessity of sending on a sufficient force of some description and exterminate the enemy or at least drive them from our soil.

I had neglected in the fore-part of my letter to state that the enemy are fortifying on Lewiston Heights. I refer you for particulars to Captain Price. The enemy have burnt Lewiston and the Indian village belonging to the Tuscaroras and are massacreing and laying waste the whole country. The situation of the inhabitants at this season of the year is truly deplorable.

P. S.—Please to give the substance of this letter to the Secretary of War.

I this day ordered Colonel Chapin into confinement for treason and mutiny. There is not a greater rascal exists than Chapin, and he is supported by a pack of *tories* and enemies to our Government. Such is the men of Buffalo. They don't deserve protection. Time will not permit of my giving you the particulars. Captain Price can inform you.

(Tompkins Papers, Vol. IX, pp. 10-11, New York State Library.)

From a Diary in Handwriting of Charles Askin.

Monday, Dec. 7, 1813.—Rode to   k's in Glandford and returned again that night to Hamel's. Some rain fell and the roads very bad.

Tuesday, 8th.—Joined the commissariat, left Mr. Hamel's and rode to Stoney Creek, where I staid all night.

Wednesday, 9th.—Went to the 40 Mile Creek, whereto our army had advanced. Snowed and was very stormy.

Thursday, 10.—Part of the forces under Col. Murray moved down to Ball's Mills. The sleighing began to be tolerable good. Capt. Hamilton Merritt with some dragoons was down this night and brought off some flour from there. Went in the evening up to John Pettit's.

Friday, 11th.—Rode down in company with Mr. Coffin and A. Hamilton to Runchy's, where the 100th Regt. and some Indians under Col. Elliott had advanced. Sleighing good. Met sleigh taking flags to the party at Allan's. Went in evening to the 15 Mile Creek. Staid over night at Mr. Clark's.

Saturday, 12th.—Rode up to Lyon's Mills in Mr. Clark's sleigh. Passed a number of teams to take flour from Ball's to the Forty. Engaged some hay and oats, also cattle for Gov't. Returned to Mr. Clark's and from that to Ball's Mills, where I learned the troops had moved toward Fort George. I mounted and followed them to Bassy's (Bessey's?) Ten Mile Creek, where I staid till daybreak. Was told by several people that a great light was seen last night and was supposed to be town of Niagara on fire, and that it was consumed and the enemy had left Fort George.

Sunday, 12th.—Left Bassy's before day. Staid at Reed's a short time, then rode to Queenston, where I found Col. Elliott, who had come up from Fort George, which the enemy had evacuated. Col. Murray, with the 100th Regt., some militia, Indians and dragoons, marched in at midnight last night. Breakfasted at Mr. Dickson's, where I saw poor Commodore Berkly [Barclay] of the Royal Navy. After breakfast went to Fort George, which has undergone such an alteration I hardly knew any part. It's now very strong but there are no barracks in it. A large quantity of shot was left in it. Dined at Mr. Dickson's in company with Col. Murray and Commodore Berkley. Rode up to Emmett's after dinner.

Monday, 13th.—Went to 12 Mile Creek for a flag to hoist in Fort George, then to Beaver Dams, where I did not get until night, as I stopped at a number of places to buy cattle and forage.

Tuesday, 14th.—Staid last night at Mr. Hill's. Went and took an inventory of Asa Baker's cattle, who fled to the enemy; from that returned to Queenston, where they were preparing to cross the river, but were disappointed in getting troops, and, much against Col. Murray's wish, had to be given up. Heard that seven pieces of cannon had been found buried near Fort George, and some few prisoners were taken on Sunday morning at Niagara and Fort Erie.

Wednesday, 15th.—Rode to Ball's Mills to send down flour from there, where I staid all night.

Thursday, 16th.—Went up to 20 Mile Creek. Passed a number of sleighs to take flour and some whiskey down from Ball's Mills to St. Davids. Rode down to Queenston on Saturday, the 18th. About 10 o'clock at night our troops began to cross the river from near Count De Puysay's to the Five Mile Meadow. The 100th crossed first, then part of the 41st Regt., after which the Royals and the remainder of the 41st and last the Indians and militia. Some few militia went over in the first boats, among whom was Capt. Kerby, who was the first person who landed on the other side. The grenadiers of the 100th Regt. pushed on toward Fort Niagara, surprised the enemy's picket at Youngstown, where they killed several men. Capt. Fawcett advanced with the grenadiers to the gate of the fort and fortunately got there just while the guard were relieving the sentinels, by which they got in at the wicket, as they had got the countersign from two sentinels whom they had taken. Mr. Dawson of the 100th Regt. led the forlorn hope, but Capt. Kerby of the incorporated militia was in the fort before any other officer. While the grenadiers got in in front the light company of the 100th, under Capt. Martin, scaled the works in the rear and got in nearly at the same time as the others. Capt. Elliott, Qr. Mr. General, was with Capt. Martin. Fortunately most of the garrison were sleeping and were so completely surprised that we lost but six men in taking it, among whom was Mr. Nowlan of the 100th Regt. The enemy made as good a defence as could be expected considering the situation they were caught in, and lost sixty-five men, most of whom were bayoneted. Col. Murray, who commanded the storming party, was unfortunately wounded. Capt. Leonard, the commanding officer of the fort, was [visiting] with his family. He came very early to the garrison in the morning, but was much surprised to be challenged by a British sentinel, who made prisoner of him. Upward of three hundred men were made prisoners, a number of whom were of the 24th Regt. Just as the first boat load of Indians had reached the other shore, the news of the fort being taken reached them. They immediately pushed off for Lewiston, and General Riall with the Royals and 41st marched to the same place. There were but about sixty artillery at that place, who took to their heels as soon as they heard the yells of the Indians. About 12 or 13 of the enemy were killed at Lewiston, several of them inhabitants of the place. Unfortunately there was liquor in most of the houses, and, notwithstanding the exertions of the officers of the Indian Department, the Indians soon got intoxicated and were outrageous. Several men of the regular troops got drunk also. The Indians plundered the houses, then set fire to them. The poor inhabitants, men, women and children we were obliged to keep a strong guard over to prevent them being killed by the Indians, one of whom killed a young boy. Indeed, the Indians got so drunk that they did not know what they were about; two of their own Indians were killed by them and one of the 41st Regt. Mr. Caldwell was shot through the thigh by one of them and young McDougall had his arm broke by another, who struck him with a tomahawk. Indians, regulars, militia were plundering everything they could get hold of. Immense quantities of things were brought over from that place to Queenston. At Youngstown there were one or two stores from which everything was taken by the plunderers. I have never witnessed such a scene before and hope I shall not again.

(Historical Collections of the Michigan Pioneer and Historical Society, Vol. XXXII., pp. 513-5.)

Captain W. H. Mulcaster to Sir James Lucas Yeo.

His Majesty's Gun-Vessel, *Nelson*,

Coteau du Lac, December 20th, 1813.

SIR,—You are aware that after the enemy's sudden flight to the Salmon River they were inclosed with ice, but a partial thaw gave us an opportunity of trying to burn them. The American flotilla, six miles up a narrow river, or rather creek, were protected by three encampments of 1,500 men back within half musket shot of the boats, and a blockhouse directly over them with about 50 pieces of cannon around it. It was impossible for the gunboats to proceed up the river and I therefore determined to have their destruction attempted by means of carcasses conveyed in a canoe. Mr. John Harvey (midshipman), immediately volunteered his services with George Barnet (seaman), proceeded up the river, passed the several posts and having placed a carcass in one of the gunboats was on the point of firing it when the ice breaking about the boat unfortunately discovered them to the sentinel, and the alarm being given they were compelled to relinquish the attempt.

A few days after several deserters came over and from their information I was induced to believe the enemy's magazine, situated in the middle of their encampment, might be blown up. Messrs. Harvey and Hawkesworth (midshipmen) and George Barnet (seaman) directly offered to proceed on this desperate service, were supplied with combustible matter and landed on the American shore. After remaining for several days watching an opportunity (in the woods) to effect their purpose they found the magazine more strongly guarded than had been supposed, but Mr. Harvey, unwilling to relinquish the enterprise, went into the American camp in disguise, where he remained two days undiscovered, obtained correct information and would infallibly have succeeded had not his conductor betrayed him to General Brown, who would certainly have executed him but for the adroit manner in which he effected his escape, which can only be equalled by his previous determined resolution.

On the whole Mr. Harvey's conduct justly claims my warmest praise and I beg leave to recommend him to your notice and protection.

(Canadian Archives, M. 389-6, pp. 78-80.)

General Order.

Captain Mulcaster has represented to me that Mr. Harvey (midshipman) volunteered and made a very gallant attempt to blow up the enemy's magazine *in the centre of their encampment*, as also to blow up their gunboats in Salmon River.

I feel particular pleasure in thus publicly making known my high approbation of this gallant young officer's conduct, and with a wish to reward his meritorious exertions I have promoted that officer to the rank of lieutenant.

Mr. Hawkesworth and George Barnet (seaman), who accompanied Mr. Harvey, have evinced a zeal highly creditable to themselves.

I take this opportunity of assuring all the officers of this squadron that their promotion will depend on their *zeal, exertions,* and *good conduct,* as in all my appointments I shall be solely guided by the officers who in my opinion have the most merit.

Given under my hand on board His Majesty's ship *Wolfe* at Kingston this 1st day of January, 1813.

JAMES LUCAS YEO,
Commodore.

(Canadian Archives, M. 389-6, pp. 81-82.)

From a Memorial by Mrs. Dawson.

Mrs. Dawson begs leave to state for the information of Lord Bathurst that her son, Captain Irwin Dawson, of the 3d Garrison Battalion, late of the 100th (now the 99th Regiment) led the forlorn hope at the storming of Fort Niagara on the 19th December, 1813. One hour before daylight, in the advance, two pickets were surprised and cut off before they could give any alarm; the sentries on the glacis at the gate were killed or taken. From one of them the countersign was obtained. Before the enemy were apprised of the situation the gates were forced and the fort immediately carried, the Upper Province was saved, the Right Division relieved from the privations they had sustained and upwards of a million sterling, consisting of munitions of war, provisions, &c., &c., &c., were secured for the Government in consequence of the brilliant service and success of this young officer.

He also attacked with one company of the 100th Regiment [in] three gunboats, the *Eagle* and *Growler*, sloops of war mounting twenty-six guns, which he carried in less than three hours without the loss of a man, reference to the *London Gazette*, letter from Sir James Yeo, dated 3rd June, 1813.

(Canadian Archives, Q. 147, p. 136.)

(New York Evening Post, Tuesday, January 11th, 1814.)

Extract of a letter from Erie to the editor of the Pittsburg *Gazette*, dated,

ERIE, December 21, 1813.

The United States brig *Caledonia* arrived here yesterday morning from Buffalo, which she left about 8 o'clock the evening before. The officers that arrived in her informed that shortly after the evacuation of Fort George by our troops the enemy marched their whole force from Burlington Heights and took possession of the strait from Lake Ontario to Lake Erie. They collected in the militia on their route and their number in regulars, militia, and Indians amounted to 3,000 men. On the morning the *Caledonia* sailed (Sunday, the 19th,) the enemy crossed the Niagara river at Lewiston with 2,000 men, which place they burned and marched up to Schlosser above the falls, burning and destroying every house on their route. The inhabitants of Buffalo had all cleared out with their property, expecting certainly the destruction of that place also, as there could not be collected more than 300 or 400 men to oppose the enemy. There was no intelligence whether any part of the enemy's force had been turned towards Fort Niagara, but I think it is certain that place will be reduced, as there are not more than 300 men to defend it.

This all arises from the wanton and abominable act of General McClure in burning Newark after he and his militia abandoned Fort George, and indeed it will give a new aspect to the war, which will no doubt be carried on after this more to satiate the revengeful feelings of commanders and individuals than to obtain any great national benefit from it.

General Order.

ADJUTANT GENERAL'S OFFICE,
QUEBEC, 21st December, 1813.

General Order.

His Excellency the Governor-in-Chief and Commander of the Forces has received a despatch from Major-General De Rottenburg transmitting a letter from Major-General Vincent, containing an official report from Colonel Murray of his having taken possession of Fort George, Niagara, on the 12th instant without opposition. The Colonel states that having received intelligence of its being the enemy's intention to plunder the adjacent country and to carry off the loyal inhabitants of that district, he immediately made a forced march with a small detachment of the advanced corps under his command, consisting of a party of Royal Artillery with two field-pieces, about forty light cavalry and 340 of the 100th Regiment under Lieut.-Colonel Hamilton, the whole amounting to 379 rank and file, together with about 20 volunteers and 70 western Indians under Colonel Elliott, and notwithstanding the inclemency of the weather succeeded in arriving in time to frustrate the enemy's predatory design, who abandoned the fortress with such precipitation on the approach of the detachment that his tents were left standing, nor had he time to injure the works of the place, which have been restored to a respectable state of defence by the enemy and would have required a regular siege to reduce.

The enemy succeeded in crossing over his ordnance and stores previous to his flight, which has been marked by eternal infamy and disgrace in the wanton conflagration of the town, which, in defiance of the common rights of humanity and in direct violation of the reiterated protestations of the American commander to respect private property, has at this inclement season been reduced to a heap of ashes. By the judicious and prompt movement of Colonel Murray the Niagara frontier has been rescued from its invaders and a fruitful and extensive district preserved from meditated plunder, and its loyal inhabitants from further outrage and imprisonment, which neither the pledged faith of the American commander nor their patient submission to the imperious will of the lawless invaders would have secured them from suffering.

EDWARD BAYNES,
A. G. N. A.

Lieut.-General Drummond to Sir George Prevost.

St. Davids, 22d December, 1813.

Sir,—Having received information that the enemy was assembling a force of militia for the purpose of protecting Porter's Mills and rope-walk and the stores at Slosser's, I directed Major-General Riall to move from Lewiston yesterday morning with the Royals and 41st Regiment and a small party of Indians for the purpose of dispersing this force and of destroying or bringing off the stores, &c.

The enemy retreated on the approach of the troops, having first fired upon Major-General Riall's advance guard and afforded it an opportunity of making an officer and eleven men prisoners. One of their officers was also killed. He is said to have been a lieutenant on his parole. The country being deserted and no means of removing the stores within Major-General Riall's reach, the mills, rope-walk, with its machinery and stores, containing a considerable quantity of flour, grain, hay, iron, cordage, &c., were destroyed. A barrack at Slosser's was also destroyed, together with some scows and batteaux, which were frozen in and could not be launched.

I am happy to report to Your Excellency that the quantity of stores of every kind captured in Fort Niagara is far greater than I had at first any conception of. The enclosed memorandum will convey some idea of their value and description.

(Canadian Archives, C. 681, pp. 267-71.)

Memorandum.

Arms, about 4000 stand, with capital accoutrements, principally new, to the same amount. An immense quantity of musquet ammunition. 7150 pairs of shoes. The clothing of the Kings and 49th Regiments. An immense quantity of American clothing of every description, and also necessaries in equal abundance. Many thousand pairs of blankets and great coats. Camp equipage, medical stores, wine, tea, forges with armourer's tools, salt, spirits, beef, flour, paper, &c. The value of the captured property, including the guns and their stores, it is supposed, cannot amount to less than from £150,000 to £200,000. Independent of the stores found in the fort several boat loads of valuable articles were taken at the 4 Mile Creek, where they had been sent the day before the assault.

(Canadian Archives, C. 681, pp. 269-70.)

Copy of Address to the Indians by General McClure.

December 21st, 1813.

To the Chiefs and Warriors of the Six Nations of Indians who are friendly to the United States:

BROTHERS,—I am about to take leave of you for a short time. I cannot depart without expressing my satisfaction for the faithful services rendered your Great Father the President, for your faithful observance of orders and willing obedience to my commands.

BROTHERS,—Many of your white brothers deserted me in the hour of difficulty, which you know, and which is the cause of our disaster. You have been faithful in the hour of danger, when your white brothers were in a state of rebellion against me. You spurned indignantly at their mutinous conduct; love of country was your chief object and willing obedience your greatest pride.

BROTHERS,—I have represented to your Great Father your good conduct; he will reward you. Your agent, Colonel Granger, tells me he finds no difficulty in getting you to obey my commands. He has done his duty to you and to your Great Father. Continue to obey him. I have fulfilled his promises to you and will continue to do so.

BROTHERS,—Major Frazer, whom you all know, and by whom your Great Father sent you money, wants to fight with you. He is very fond of his Red Brothers. I have sent him and he will assist you and Colonel Granger, too.

BROTHERS,—Your Red Brothers and the British, who live on the other side of the Niagara River, have invaded your country; they have massacred in cold blood unoffending women and children; they have murdered or taken prisoners the two sons of your friend and interpreter Capt. (Horatio) Jones; they have laid waste the village of your Red Brothers the Tuscaroras, and carried off all their property. I have restrained you from this kind of warfare; I will no longer restrain you. Avenge yourselves on the authors of such barbarities, and all whom you find in arms against you, but show mercy to unoffending women and children. The enemy pay no attention to private property. You are at liberty to follow their example. Invite your Red Brethren every where to join you and drive them from our soil. There is no safety in remaining at home.

BROTHERS,—When I join you again I will bring regulars and militia who will never desert you or myself. Meanwhile I send to join you all the regular troops I can collect at present under a brave Chief, Major Riddle.

BROTHERS,—Your Red Brothers, the Tuscaroras, have lost all their huts, produce and property. I will administer to their relief and represent their distress to our Great Father the President. Adieu for the present, and the Great Spirit protect you is the prayer of your friend,

GEORGE McCLURE,
Br. General commanding

Brig.-Gen. McClure to Lt.-Col. E. Granger.

MILLER'S TAVERN, 7 o'clock p. m., 21st Dec., 1813.

DEAR SIR,—Judge Clark was here this evening and informed me that the militia of Genesee County have been ordered out *en masse*. Cols. Davis and Churchill's Regt. will meet me tomorrow night 22 miles from this place, with say 1000 men. It is highly necessary that you should accompany me with your Indians. You will therefore follow me in the course of the day. I trust Chapin has no power over them or you.*

NOTE—Gen. McClure marched out of Buffalo Dec. 21st, 1813, and halted the first night at Miller's Tavern, now standing at Cold Springs, just opposite the street car barns. Judge Granger lived on his homestead a short mile further out.

(MSS. of Colonel James N. Granger.)

Lieut.-General Drummond to Sir George Prevost.

ST. DAVID'S, 22 December, 1813.

SIR,—I have the honour to acquaint Your Excellency that I am endeavouring to get boats across the portage from Queenston to Chippawa, but owing to the severity of the weather and the backwardness of the militia so much delay and difficulty is experienced in this movement that I fear the enemy will have time to collect a considerable force at Buffalo before my preparations for an attack on that place are completed. The destruction of the vessels* and stores at that place are objects of such importance that I shall not be induced to relinquish them on light grounds. At the same time I ought not to conceal from Your Excellency that the weather has been so severe within these few days that, unprepared as the

*Chippewa, Schooner.
Ariel, do
Tripp, Sloop.
Little Belt, do

troops were in point of warm clothing, &c., to meet its rigors—all of them without fur caps and mitts and some of them actually without great coats—however willing and anxious they are to be led against the enemy, humanity will scarce suffer me to yield to their wishes.

Fortunately during the operations against Fort Niagara the weather was comparatively mild.

I have directed Lieutenant Gaugreben of the Engineers to use every exertion in putting Fort Niagara in the best state of defence that circumstances and our means will permit. He is also ordered to complete a new frame barrack which we found nearly finished, and put the rest of the buildings into a state of repair for the reception of troops. Nothing can be in a more wretched state both as to the defences and the cover than Fort Niagara at the time of its capture. Even if it is put into complete repair it will require a garrison of at least 500 effective infantry, exclusive of a strong company of artillery. The present garrison consists only of the 100th Regiment. I have appointed Lieutenant-Colonel Hamilton to the command and have directed that the same command money shall be attached to it as formerly to Fort George, viz.: 7/ per diem, which I hope will meet Your Excellency's approbation. A Fort Major being also necessary, I beg to recommend Lieutenant McCarthy, of the 10th R(oyal) Veteran Battalion, for that situation. The Assistant Commissary General has been ordered to lay in a supply of provisions and fuel equal to two months' consumption for 1,000 men. As the enemy will make an effort in the spring (if not sooner) for the recovery of this important fortress, as there are at present no heavier guns than 18-pounders mounted on the fort, and conceiving 24-pounders to be indispensably necessary to oppose the heavy guns which will no doubt be brought against it, as well by the lake as by land, I have to request that at least six long guns of that calibre may be sent up as soon as possible, one of which must be placed on the heights of Queenston.

With regard to Fort George I conceive it advisable that it should be put into a respectable state of defence, which, as the works are not materially inpaired, can be done in the spring without much labor or expense. In the meantime some cover must be erected for a small garrison of (say) 150 men and the batteries aimed towards the opposite bank, as they completely command the approach to Fort Niagara.

It will be necessary to erect a good-sized blockhouse at Chippawa where, moreover, as the proper right of the whole position, a considerable detachment of troops must always be kept. A martello tower at Fort Erie with a couple of heavy guns will be sufficient, and perhaps an intermediate blockhouse would be desirable to keep up the communication.

I have desired Colonel Elliott to send off an express to Michilimackinac to announce our success in this quarter and at the same time to assure the Indians that we shall shortly revisit them IN POWER.

Recent information from Detroit represents the enemy's force in that country as not exceeding 500 militia. The Indians there remain true to our interests. They are in want of powder, which I have invited them to come to us for. I am convinced that Detroit and the whole of the western country might be re-occupied by us at any moment without difficulty, provided we had it in our power to detach a force for that purpose. By this movement Mackinac would be preserved to us. The present is the season most favorable for such an enterprise, as it affords the greatest facilities for transport. It must be remembered, however, that *troops* alone (even if I had them) are not sufficient for the purpose. The corps, however small, should be completely equipped with field-train, engineers and artificers, commissariat, barrack and every other department. This measure appears to me the only means of getting rid of the Western Indians, who, when their presence here ceases to be useful, will be an intolerable burthen.

Before I close this subject I beg to suggest that the corps to be sent on such a service should be one which is completely effective and well appointed, and which has not been harassed and disorganized as, I am sorry to remark, is very much the case with all those at present on this frontier. Such a one, for instance, as the 13th Regiment, which, if it could be spared, it has occurred to me, might, in the event of my receiving such accounts from Sackett's Harbour of the enemy's force at that place as to hold out a rational hope of the success of an attempt upon that important depot, be employed on that service (in conjunction with other troops) on its way upwards. It is unnecessary for me to call Your Excellency's attention to an object to which it has doubtless been unremittingly directed, and which, should it be attained, would in all probability go far towards putting an end to the war as far as it relates to this Province, by depriving the enemy of the means of continuing it.

While I am upon the general subject of the means of defence of the Province, I beg to recommend that the whole of the batteaux should be placed in the charge of the Civil Commissioner of the dockyard, who alone has the means of keeping them in repair. I should also recommend that at all other stations except Kingston the batteaux should be in charge of the officers of the Quartermaster General's Department instead of the Commissariat. Moreover, it appears to me that the construction of the batteaux, particularly such as are to be used on the lake, might be very much improved with respect to size, lightness, safety, facility of rowing and managing, etc. I shall desire the Commissioner to construct one on the principles he recommends and send it down for Your Excellency's inspection.

Feeling it of infinite importance to bring forward as many troops as possible to this frontier, and fearing it may not be in Your Excellency's power to spare me any addition to the regular regiments, I propose relieving the 89th at Prescott by the five companies of the Glengarry Light Infantry and bring up the former corps to this point without delay. I shall also be glad, as soon as circumstances will permit, to be enabled to bring the 2d Battalion of Marines up to Kingston.

P. S.—I reported to Your Excellency that the Indians who advanced with Major-General Riall's force on the morning of the 19th had committed great excesses in consequence of intoxication, and had burnt the greatest part of the houses at or near Lewiston. I have now the honour to state that on withdrawing the troops from Lewiston yesterday I thought it advisable, the inhabitants having in general quitted their houses, to direct the remainder of them to be set on fire in order to deprive the enemy of cover for troops that might be sent for the purpose of destroying the opposite town of Queenston.

From every information I have been able to collect the destruction, not only of the town but of the houses along the whole of the (British) frontier of Niagara was a measure resolved on and its execution ordered by the American Government, and that nothing but the rapid advance of the troops prevented this atrocious purpose. Indeed the inhabitants themselves (of the American frontier) universally admitted the justice of the retaliation upon Lewiston and execrated their own Government as the sole cause of their sufferings.

(Canadian Archives, C. 681, pp. 272-283.)

Donald Fraser, Volunteer Aide-de-Camp to Brigadier-General McClure, to Lieut.-Colonel Harvey.

HEADQUARTERS OF THE AMERICAN ARMY ON THE NIAGARA FRONTIER, BUFFALO, December 22, 1813.

SIR,—Your communication dated York, 14th December, has been received. I have to state in reply, by order of Brigadier-General McClure, that he is only accountable to his own government for any act or procedure of his while commanding. As it respects the atrocity of the act of burning Newark, (as you are pleased to call it,) it is certainly, you'll allow, not without a precedent, and it is hardly necessary to remind you of *Havre de Grace* and *Frenchtown*, &c., &c., long previous to the late conflagration at Newark.

Should Lieutenant-General Drummond require a more explicit answer he will do well to present his communication through some other source to the American Government.

(Canadian Archives, C. 681, p. 303.)

Parole.

We, the undersigned, do certify upon our honors as gentlemen and officers, that we will not bear arms or act in any military capacity against the United States during the present war, neither will we give any information directly or indirectly whereby the enemies of the United States may take advantage.

Given under our hands at Buffalo the 22d day of December, 1813.

A. NELLES, Capt.
G. ADAMS, Capt.
WM. LYONS, Capt.
G. B. STEPHENSON.

(Canadian Archives, C. 682, p. 16.)

Brigadier-General McClure to the Secretary of War.

HEADQUARTERS, BUFFALO, Dec. 22, 1813.

SIR,—I regret to be under the necessity of announcing to you the mortifying intelligence of the loss of Fort Niagara. On the morning of the 19th inst., about four o'clock, the enemy crossed the river at the Five Mile Meadows in great force, consisting of regulars and Indians, who made their way undiscovered to the garrison, which, from the most correct information I can collect, was completely surprised. Our men were nearly all asleep in their tents: the enemy rushed in and commenced a most horrid slaughter. Such as escaped the fury of the first contest retired to the old mess-house where they kept up a destructive fire on the enemy until a want of ammunition compelled them to surrender. Although our force was very inferior and comparatively small indeed, I am induced to think that the disaster is not attributable to any want of troops but to gross neglect in the commanding officer, Captain Leonard, in not preparing, being ready and looking out for the expected attack.

I have not been able to ascertain correctly the number of killed and wounded. About 20 regulars have escaped out of the fort, some badly wounded. Lieutenant Beck, 24th Regiment, is killed, and it is said three others.

On the same morning a detachment of militia, under Major Bennett, stationed at Lewiston Heights, was attacked by a party of savages, but the Major and his little corps by making a desperate charge effected their retreat, after being surrounded by several hundreds, with the loss of six or eight, who doubtless were killed, among whom were two sons of Captain Jones, Indian interpreter. The villages of Youngstown, Lewiston, Manchester and the Indian Tuscorora Village were reduced to ashes, and the inoffensive inhabitants who could not escape were, without regard to age and sex, inhumanly butchered by savages headed by British officers painted. A British officer who is taken prisoner avows that many small children were murdered by their Indians.

Major Mallory, who was stationed at Schlosser with about 40 Canadian volunteers, advanced to Lewiston Heights and compelled the advanced guard of the enemy to fall back to the foot of the mountain. The Major is a meritorious officer; he fought the enemy two days and contestted every inch of ground to the Tonewanda Creek. In these actions Lieutenant Lowe, 23d Regiment of the United States army, and eight of the Canadian Voluntees were killed. I had myself, three days previous to the attack on the Niagara, left it with a view of providing for the defence of this place, Black Rock and other villages on this frontier.

I came here with the troops and have called out the Militia of Genesee, Niagara and Chautauqua counties *en masse*.

This place was then thought to be in imminent danger as well as the shipping, but I have no doubt is now perfectly secure. Volunteers are coming in in great numbers; they are, however, a species of troops that cannot be expected to continue in service for a long time. In a few days 1000 detached militia, lately drafted, will be on.

(American State Papers, Military Affairs, Vol. I., p. 487.)

From the National Advocate, New York, Dec. 31, 1813.

Extract of a letter from a gentleman at Canandaigua, in the *Albany Gazette* of Dec. 27, dated Dec. 22:

Newark we have burnt. Lewiston and Schlosser the British have burnt. Buffalo is secure but Fort Niagara is gone. The inhabitants on our frontier are massacred and butcheries unparalleled are practised. The Indians and British are in the full tide of successful retaliation; 300 families (says Captain Parish, Indian agent,) are now on their way to this place, and the most miserable sufferers, and many children without either stockings or shoes. All here is alarm and commotion. *O horrida bella! horrida bella!* Porter's mills at Schlosser are burnt. Two sons of Benjamin Barton, Esq., are killed.

(New York Society Library.)

Sir George Prevost to Lieutenant General Drummond.

HEADQUARTERS, QUEBEC, 22d December, 1813.

SIR,—I have the honour to receive your letter from York of the 13th instant, and I regret to observe by it that the defences of that post are so incomplete, and that the two block houses, already in a state of forwardness, have been placed in an unfavorable site and are of too slight materials. I have called upon the officer commanding Royal Engineers to explain these circumstances and he has reported to me that the present exposed situation of the two block houses will be remedied when the proposed works to protect them are complete. I approve, however, of your having directed the third block house to be constructed upon a more retired position and of more substantial materials.

(Canadian Archives, C. 681, pp. 284-5.)

Sir George Prevost to Earl Bathurst.

HEADQUARTERS, QUEBEC, 22d December, 1813.

No. 116.

MY LORD,—

I have the honor to transmit to Your Lordship Colonel Murray's report to Major-General Vincent of his having taken possession of Fort George at Niagara on the 12th instant without opposition.

In consequence of my having directed a forward movement to be made by the advance of the Right Division of the army serving in the Canadas for the purpose of checking a system of plunder organized by the enemy against the loyal inhabitants of the Niagara District, Colonel Murray was directed to march with two 6 pounders, a small detachment of light dragoons and 350 rank and file of the 100th Regiment, commanded by Lieutenant-Colonel Hamilton, together with 70 of the Western warriors under Lieutenant-Colonel Elliott of the Indian Department, and, notwithstanding the inclemency of the weather, this force arrived in the neighborhood of Fort George in time to frustrate the enemy's predatory designs and to compel him to effect a precipitate retreat across the Niagara river, having previously sent his ordnance and stores to his own side and stained the character of the American nation by the wanton conflagration of the town of Newark, reduced at the most inclement season to a heap of ashes in direct violation of the reiterated protestations of the American commanding general to respect and protect private property.

I have much satisfaction in adding to my report that the promptitude with which Colonel Murray executed this service has been the means of rescuing a fertile and extensive district from premeditated plunder and its loyal inhabitants from further outrage and captivity.

(Canadian Archives, Q. 123, pp. 105-6.)

Governor D. D. Tompkins to the Secretary of War.

ALBANY, Dec. 24, 1813.

SIR,—Upon my arrival in this place to-day I was met by an express bringing despatches of which I send you a copy.

The express further informs that on his arrival at Batavia he learned from Major Allen, (the contractor's agent at Niagara,) and from Lieutenant Loomis, who, with two or three others had made their escape, that Fort Niagara had been taken by the British. The garrison was surprised. Captain Leonard, (1st Regiment of Artillery), had the command, but it is rumored he was not in the fort at the time but with his family some miles off. What became of the rest of the garrison those who escaped do not know.

In consequence of this information Major-General Hall has been ordered to repair to that frontier with as many of his division as may be necessary to expel or destroy the invaders. The British have with them a number of Indians and continue to sanction their massacres.

(From the *National Advocate* of New York, 31st December, 1813.)

Governor Tompkins to Brigadier-General McClure.

ALBANY, Dec. 24, 1813.

SIR,—I have this moment arrived from New York and have received your communication detailing the disastrous state of things on the Niagara frontier. With my letter of the 26th November last you were furnished with an order on Major-General Hall to detach from his division such numbers as you should judge sufficient to garrison Forts George and Niagara and to protect the inhabitants of the Niagara Frontier. Upon my arrival here I learn for the first time that the former has been destroyed, the village of Newark burnt and Fort Niagara made the depot of all the cannon, military stores and equipments on that frontier, with but a handful of men to garrison it. I was not apprized of the intention to evacuate Fort George or to destroy Newark, or otherwise I should most assuredly have given direction to have that frontier supplied with a considerable force to guard against the consequences of the irritation and disposition to retaliate which the burning of Newark would naturally excite on the west side of the Niagara river.

Major Bomford has forwarded the following articles:
350,000 musket cartridges.
14,000 flints.
500 muskets and a quantity of ammunition for field pieces.

Should any further supplies be required they shall be forwarded immediately. The articles in the State arsenals at Canandaigua and Batavia are already subject to the orders of the militia generals. I understand Major General Hall has gone out. He will, of course, have the command and I have therefore addressed a communication to him containing authority to call for additional numbers of men and to repel the invasion promptly and effectually. I have also written to the Secretary of War and will communicate the answer and instructions of the President so soon as they may be received. I hope you will have been able before the receipt of this to have expelled if not destroyed the invading force.

(From Niles's Weekly Register, Baltimore, Md., February 12, 1814, Vol. V., p. 395.)

Captain Alexander Stewart, Royal Scots, Commanding the London District, to Major-General Vincent.

DOVER MILLS, 25th December, 1813.

SIR,—I beg leave to acquaint you that a party under the command of Lieutenant Medcalf of the militia, who were detached from this post some time since towards the River Thames for the purpose of collecting cattle, surprised a party of the enemy on the morning of the 15th instant, and have taken the whole of them prisoners, consisting of 3 officers and 35 non-commissioned officers and privates belonging to the 26th Regiment of the line. Great praise is due Lieutenant Medcalf and his small party, consisting of not more than 25 men, for the gallant manner in which this service was performed. After a fatiguing march of twenty miles they gained the enemy's position at daybreak, immediately attacked it and in a few minutes compelled them to surrender.

I am happy to add that this service was performed without the loss of a man on our part. The enemy had four men wounded, three of them severely. The party have not been able to collect any of the cattle. They deemed it proper to retire, as the enemy had sent for reinforcements. They will arrive here to-morrow with the prisoners.

(Canadian Archives, C. 681, pp. 288-9.)

Lieut.-Henry Medcalf to Lieut.-Colonel Bostwick.

DOVER, 25th December, 1813.

SIR,—Agreeably to orders received from Lieut.-Colonel Stewart on the 8th inst., I proceeded with a party consisting of twelve volunteers from this place and a sergeant and 6 men of Capt. Coleman's

Provincial Dragoons to the westward, for the purpose of securing some cattle which were reported to be at the Rondeau. On my arrival at Port Talbot I was joined by Lieut. Rice and Ensign Wilson and seven of the Middlesex Militia, who had volunteered their services. With this party I immediately proceeded to the Rondeau. Not finding, when I arrived there, that the report as to the cattle was correct, and understanding that a party of the enemy had posted themselves for the purpose of collecting the resources of that part of the country and compelling the inhabitants to take an oath of neutrality, I determined instantly on crossing the country and endeavour to surprise them. This, I have the greatest satisfaction in informing you, was completely effected without any loss on our part. The enemy was posted at Mr. McCrae's, about 15 miles from the mouth of the Thames, consisting of three officers and thirty-six men of the U. S. Infantry. After ascertaining the position and being joined on the river by Lieut. McGregor and seven men, we advanced in the night with all possible expedition and arrived at the house about an hour before day. The house was instantly surrounded and a discharge of musquetry from us into the house was the first intelligence they had of our approach. They made but a feeble resistance and surrendered, five of them being wounded.

When I consider the great distance through the wilderness, the badness of the weather and the difficulty of securing substance, I am really astounded at the perseverance of the gallant band I had with me, and cannot sufficiently praise them for their uniform good conduct, their patience under almost indescribable fatigue, and their gallantry and bravery in assaulting the house which contained of the enemy several more than our party consisted of. To give you an idea of the fatigue they underwent I will only inform you that the day and night previous to the surprise we marched more than sixty miles, the greater part thro' the wilderness. Some of the men before they reached the house were so completely exhausted that they actually fell down useless while marching. After we had secured the prisoners, etc., I left the place without any delay, understanding that a reinforcement of the enemy was expected up the river that morning, and have arrived with the prisoners with the exception of two men who escaped from us on the way. The five wounded men were left and paroled, and the arms I distributed among the militia of that place. The ammunition was very much damaged.

To Lieut. McGregor I am under particular obligations for his zeal and assistance; his local knowledge of the country greatly facilitated the execution of the enterprise; also to Lieut. Rice and Ensign Wilson, Sergeant Douglas of the dragoons and Roderick Drake for the assistance I received from them. Indeed I cannot sufficiently thank every individual of the party, and I trust their truly meritorious conduct will be duly appreciated. You will perceive that the whole party that assaulted the house consisted of but thirty-three including myself, and that amongst that number there were but seven bayonets. The enemy were well armed.

The consequences of this expedition will, I trust, prove beneficial to the loyal inhabitants on the River Thames, as it will, I presume, check any further advance of the enemy into the country and relieve the people from being obliged either to abandon their houses or subscribe an oath which they detest.

(Canadian Archives, C. 682, p. 44.)

General McClure to the Secretary of War.

(Extract.)

BATAVIA, 25th December, 1813.

It is a notorious fact that on the night on which Fort Niagara was captured Captain Leonard was much intoxicated and left the fort about 11 p. m. I am assured that he has since given himself up; that he and his family are now on the Canadian side of the strait. It was not without some reluctance that I left him in immediate command of the fort, but there was no alternative as he outranked every other officer. His uniform attachment to British men and measures, added to the circumstances of his not effecting his escape when in his power, strengthened me in a suspicion there was a secret understanding with regard to this disgraceful transaction.

Permit me to suggest to you, Sir, that unless regular troops are sent to this frontier immediately the enemy will penetrate into the interior of the country and lay waste all before them. The militia will do to act with regulars but not without them. In spite of all my exertions to ensure subordination my late detachment ultimately proved to be very little better than an infuriated mob. It was not, however, the fault of the privates but of such officers as were seeking popularity, and who on that account were afraid of enforcing subordination and introducing strict discipline.

I have collected from the different recruiting rendezvous about one hundred and twenty soldiers and put them under the command of Lieutenant Riddle of the 15th United States Infantry, an excellent and deserving officer.

I cannot conclude this communication without reporting the conduct of Doctor Cyrenius Chapin, (late Lieutenant-Colonel of volunteers.) To him in a great measure ought all our disasters to be imputed. His publications in the Buffalo *Gazette* that the enemy had abandoned Burlington I fear had the desired effect. I have found him an unprincipled disorganizer. Since dismissing him and his marauding corps he has been guilty of the most outrageous acts of mutiny if not of *treason*. When I came to Buffalo, accompanied only by my suite, he headed a mob for the purpose of doing violence to my feelings and person, and when marching to the Rock at the time of an alarm, five or six guns were discharged at me by his men.

(American State Papers, Military Affairs, Vol. I., p. 487.)

Brig.-General McClure to Lieut.-Colonel Granger

BATAVIA, 25th December, 1813.

COL. GRANGER.

DEAR SIR,—I have received a letter from Major Mallory in which he states Buffalo to be still in danger. I should say there was at least 1200 men now at that place. I believe that the reason the enemy is concentrating their forces at Fort Erie is that they are apprehensive of your attacking them, or why come up to pass over when they have the convenience of the river below? I have requested Major-General Hall to take command of the volunteers and other troops at Buffalo a few days until I can organize a detachment of militia. I will send all the troops as fast as they arrive. The officers commanding the regulars will not return to Buffalo unless compelled by a positive order. I should not urge them unless the place is in positive danger. I could not prevail on them to stay at 11 mile creek nor was it safe for me or any that accompanied me to stay there or travel on the road. The numerous mob we met cried out: "Shoot him down, shoot him." This mob is countenanced by many of the inhabitants of Buffalo, and I must be well convinced that they will treat me in a different way before I can agree to make that my headquarters. I am under many obligations to you, Colonel, for your stable friendship to me. I am publishing a hand bill which I will send you and will be pleased to distribute it. It is a narrative of facts which will justify me in the eyes of every impartial man. The detachment of militia will be in Buffalo in a few days, after which I presume the volunteers will return home. I have wrote the Governor that a detachment of 1000 men more would actually be necessary this winter, or regular soldiers. I am obliged to stop short; accept assurances of my highest consideration and esteem and believe me, sincerely,

GEORGE McCLURE.

Kingston *Gazette*, Saturday, 25th Dec., 1813.
Newfoundland Regiment.

The whole of the Newfoundland Regiment that belongs to the Right Division of the Army of Upper Canada, consisting of the Light Infantry company and the skeleton of two battalion companies, which, under the command of Captain Mockler, had shared in everything which took place in the Western District since the beginning of the war, were, with the exception of two or three sick men that were left on shore at Amherstburg, all embarked on board our fleet on Lake Erie and shared in the arduous struggle of the 10th of September, on which occasion they had one officer killed, viz., Lieut. James Garden of the light company, and four sergeants and thirty-two rank and file killed and wounded. Let Capt. Barclay's words speak for them: "The conduct of the soldiers serving on board as marines has excited my warmest thanks and admiration."

Governor Tompkins to Major-General Hall.

ALBANY, Dec. 25th, 1813.

SIR,—On the 26th November last an order was issued for a sufficient detachment from your division to secure the inhabitants of the Niagara Frontier during the winter. The number was left blank with directions for General McClure to fill it and deliver the order to you. It was presumed that as he had commanded on the frontier during the fall he was the best judge of the quantum of force requisite for the above purpose. I was therefore much surprised on my return from New York this day to learn the weak and disastrous state of that frontier. The express informs me that you had proceeded or would proceed to the lines in consequence of that information. The whole of your division is placed at your disposal for the purpose of repelling the invasion and driving the enemy from our State. You are charged with the command of that frontier for that purpose and will exert yourself to the utmost to put a prompt and effectual stop to the incursions and depredations of the enemy by expelling and, if possible, destroying them.

350,000 musket cartridges, 14,000 flints, 500 muskets and ammunition for field pieces have been forwarded by Major Bomford to Canandaigua where they will be subject to your order. The nature of the service to be performed on this occasion cannot give rise to any questions about the liability of militia to perform it, as the resistance of invasion is the only object. You will consider yourself vested with liberal power and authority to effect that object, and you will doubtless be zealous to accomplish it.

If there be no other quarters you can take possession of the houses and other buildings at Buffalo and Black Rock, which, I am informed, are principally abandoned, and of the huts at Williamsville. You will keep a good look out on the Ridge Road and prevent the enemy from destroying the arsenal and stores at Batavia.

The public property delivered out and not used under your orders is to be returned and secured before the militia be dismissed. There was great negligence and waste with respect to the military stores at Niagara in November and December, 1812, and in the beginning of 1813.

The contractor's agent, Major Allen, ought to be notified of the quantity of provisions which may be required, and you will permit me to suggest that unless you can arm all the militia that may arrive and be unarmed, you had better dismiss them or send them into the interior until they can be armed, as without arms they will not add to your force, but exhaust your provisions and deprive the frontier inhabitants of the means of support during the winter.

(From Niles's Weekly Register, Baltimore, Md., February 12, 1814, Vol. V., p. 393.

General McClure to the Public.

The late descent of the enemy on our frontier, and the horrid outrages committed on our defenceless inhabitants by the British allies being laid to my misfortune as commanding officer of the American forces on the frontier, and although my conduct has been approved by the Secretary of War, the Commander-in-chief of this State, and by General Harrison before his departure, still I deem it a duty which I owe to my own reputation, in order to put a stop to the evil reports which are propagated against me without knowing my orders or the means which I had in my power to execute them, to give a brief statement of my most prominent acts since I had the honor of so important a command. On my arrival at Fort George and previous to the departure of General Wilkinson with his army from that post, I suggested to the General the necessity of marching out against the enemy at the Cross Roads and Four Mile Creek, that his army with my militia were sufficient to take or destroy all the British forces in the neighborhood, which would leave nothing more for the militia to do than to protect and keep in order the inhabitants of that part of the Province, as otherwise our frontier would be liable to be invaded. This proposition, however, was not agreed to, as the General's instructions were of a different nature.

The General left with me Colonel Scott and 800 regulars, who were to remain until I considered my force sufficient to hold the fort without them, when they were to march for Sackett's Harbor.

About the 12th of October the British army commenced their retreat towards the head of the lake. I issued orders for my militia to pursue, which was promptly obeyed. We advanced as far as the Twelve Mile Creek and within a short distance of the enemy's rear guard, when Col. Scott sent an express requesting me to return and said he would abandon the fort next day and march with his troops for Sackett's Harbor, and at the same time detained my provisions and ammunition waggons, which compelled me to abandon the further pursuit of the enemy and induced them to make a stand on the Heights of Burlington. I was then left with about one thousand effective militia in Fort George and two hundred and fifty Indians, a force not more than sufficient to garrison the post. On the arrival of General Harrison's army I was elated with the prospect of uniting our forces, of driving the enemy from Burlington, taking possession of that post and giving peace to the upper province and our frontier.

We were prepared to march in twenty-four hours when the arrival of Commodore Chauncey, with orders for that excellent officer, Gen. Harrison, to repair immediately with his army to Sackett's Harbor, frustrated it. I remonstrated against his going off, as will be seen in a correspondence between the General and myself, but in vain.

By this movement all my expectations were blasted, and I foresaw the consequences unless a reinforcement was immediately sent on to supply the place of the drafted militia, whose term of service would shortly expire. I considered my force, which had then become ungovernable, as insufficient to go against the enemy. The object of the last expedition to Twenty Mile Creek is fully explained in a general order which I issued on my return.

For six weeks before the militia were discharged I wrote, and continued writing to the Secretary at War, of the necessity of sending on a detachment of militia and regular troops, that I found it impossible to retain the militia in service one day beyond their time; I also stated from the best information the enemy's forces. I offered a bounty of two dollars a month for one or two months, but without effect. Some few of Col. Bloom's regiment took the bounty and immediately disappeared, and I was compelled to grant a discharge to the militia and volunteers, which left me about sixty effective regulars of the Twenty-fourth United States Infantry under Capt. Rodgers to garrison Fort George. I summoned a council of the officers and put the question: "Is the fort tenable with the present number of men?" They unanimously gave it as their opinion that it would be madness in the extreme to attempt to hold it, and recommended its evacuation immediately, as the enemy's advance was then within eight miles. I accordingly gave orders for all the arms, ammunition and public stores of every description to be sent across the river, which was principally effected, (though the enemy advanced so rapidly that ten of my men were made prisoners,) and ordered the town of Newark to be burnt. This act, however distressing to the inhabitants and my feelings, was by order of the Secretary at War, and I believe at the same time proper. The inhabitants had twelve hours' notice to remove their effects, and such as chose to come across the river were provided with all the necessaries of life. I left Capt. Leonard in command of Fort Niagara with about one hundred and fifty effective regulars, and pointed out verbally and particularly in a general order how he should prepare for an attack, which would certainly take place. I stationed Col. Grieve's artillerists, consisting of about twenty men with two pieces of artillery, at Lewiston under command of Major Bennett and made them a present of four hundred dollars for volunteering their services three weeks, but before the place was attacked they nearly all deserted except the officers, who bravely defended themselves and cut their way through the savages. The Canadian volunteers, about forty in number, under Major Mallory, an officer of great merit, I stationed at Schlosser and went myself to Buffalo to provide for the safety of that place and Black Rock, which I trust are out of danger, having called out the militia *en masse*.

The public are now in possession of some of the leading facts which have governed my conduct in the discharge of the trust assigned me, and I appeal to the candor of all dispassionate men to determine with what justice to my feelings as a citizen and pride as a soldier have been wounded and my character aspersed. If insubordination to the orders of superiors are justifiable then possibly I may have failed in my defence. If to have suppressed the risings of mutiny is reprehensible, then also I am not justified. If to have enforced the disciplinary laws of camp is a proceeding unwarranted, then have I been in error. But, fellow citizens, I do not think so meanly of you as to credit the monstrous supposition that you deliberately advocate such a strange hypothesis. Your prejudices against me have been the result of feeling misled by the acts of my enemies, and not the result of your own sober judgment operating upon facts and principles. Those facts are now before you. By them judge me in candor and I will abide the decision.

GEORGE McCLURE.

Lieut.-General Drummond to Sir George Prevost.

HEADQUARTERS, ST. DAVIDS, 26th Dec'r, 1813

DEAR SIR,—

I have to acknowledge the receipt of your two letters of the 17th Dec'r, and immediately on my return to Kingston shall not fail to give most close consideration to the plan of Sir James Yeo for the destruction of the enemy's fleet on Lake Erie, and will transmit to you my opinion as to the probability of our being enabled to effect so very important an object.

I am exceedingly glad to find that you propose sending a reinforcement to Mackinac and request to be informed what proportion of provisions will be required from York, that I may take steps to have it forwarded by Yonge Street to Lake Simcoe, to be in readiness to proceed on the first moment of the opening of the navigation.

I have found it indispensably necessary to order up half the company of marine artillery from Prescott until you can send me the requisite number of Royal Artillery to place Fort Niagara in a state of security. I have also ordered the remainder of the King's Regt. from York.

The troops at present occupy Chippawa and in advance of it, and to-morrow I move my quarters there. With the greatest difficulty I have been able to collect ten boats and a scow, with which I hope to cross over the troops to-morrow or the following day and effect the destruction of the enemy's vessels, public buildings, stores, etc.

Immediately after the movement on Lewiston the Indian warriors retired on Burlington and are collecting but slowly towards Chippawa, but by to-morrow or the following day I am in hope a considerable number will join us.

At Black Rock I am informed there are 360 men, and at Buffalo a large force of militia under command of Brigadier-General Hopkins. This force is stated to be very badly armed. Brigadier-General McClure wiith about 200 regulars and some Indians is said to be at the 11 M le Creek, to which a great part of the public stores have been conveyed, and, indeed, I understand that all the inhabitants have moved from Buffalo with their property. The following are the names of some non-combatants taken away from their homes by Genl. Dearborn, who have just returned on parole:

Names.
Andrew Heron,
John Grier,
H. Skinner,
— McFarlane,
— Lyons,
Geo. Adams,
Abraham Nelles.

I transmit a copy of that given by the two latter gentlemen, which appears to me to be most unjustifiable, on which subject Your Excellency may wish to have a communication with the American Government.

I have found it necessary to make the following appointments until Your Excellency's pleasure shall be made known, viz: Mr. Duff, late barrack master at Amherstburg, to the same situation at Fort Niagara: Capt. Wilson, of the Indian Department, to issue provisions to the Indian warriors with the pay of 7s per day, and one or more issuers, under the responsibility of the head of the Indian Department. A surgeon in the American army, taken in Fort Niagara, is at present employed in attending the sick and wounded of the enemy. I request to know what steps Your Excellency would wish to be taken respecting him, when his services as medical officer shall be no longer required. It would perhaps be advisable to permit him to return to the United States, as I am told the enemy have not considered our medical officers who have fallen into their hands as prisoners of war.

I transmit the copy of a letter from Brigr. General McClure in answer to one which I directed Lieut.-Col. Harvey to address to him, (a copy of which was forwarded to Your Excellency,) for the purpose of ascertaining whether the burning of Newark was an act authorized by their Government or merely that of an individual.

N. B.—I have recommended Captain Eliot, Dy. Asst. Qr. Mr. General, and Capt. Foster, my aid-de-camp, be appointed by the Right Division of the army as joint prize agents for the property captured on the Niagara frontier.

(Canadian Archives, C. 682.)

John C. Spencer to Governor Tompkins.

CANANDAIGUA, Dec. 26, 1813.

SIR,—I have been driven home by an alarm that the British had arrived at Genesee River and were approaching this place. A levy *en masse* of the militia is ordered as far east as Cayuga, and our court martial, then in session at Auburn, was broke up. Before I set out to-morrow for Ithaca, where we next meet, I feel it my duty to communicate to you the situation of this frontier, although I write in great pain from a wound in my right hand.

That the enemy has landed at Lewiston and invaded our country perhaps ten or twelve miles in extent, you are probably informed.

A report has prevailed that Fort Niagara is taken, but at present I disbelieve it, as there is no authentic or direct intelligence. This night's mail will either confirm our accounts, or if it contains nothing will convince me that the fort is yet ours.

In Buffalo nothing but disorder and confusion prevails. The infamous Chapin has obtained the command of a company of militia who refused to consider themselves under the authority of the officer commanding the frontier. He was soon put into confinement for mutiny and treason, but was released by force by the Buffalo tories. General McClure then removed the regulars and Indians to 11 Mile Creek, eleven miles from Buffalo. At Lewiston Colonel Grieves' regiment was stationed. They fled on the approach of the enemy and are now scattered through the country in every direction. Such are the details. The general aspect of affairs here is much worse. I have heretofore expressed to you my opinion of General McClure. I still think him in many respects a good officer. But a more intimate acquaintance with him has convinced me that he is wholly incompetent to the command of this frontier during such times as the present. At all events, you may rest assured that he is universally detested by the inhabitants; that his soldiers have no confidence in him, and that his officers unanimously concur in the opinion of his unfitness to command. These facts I state upon my own personal knowledge. Under these circumstances it will not be difficult for you to judge of the efficiency of any force under his command. Our frontier is dreadfully exposed; the enemy is full of indignation; our brethren are flying in every direction, and, to complete the picture, the militia will not serve under General McClure, or if they do it will be with the utmost reluctance. In this situation I cannot be silent, and truths, however unpleasant, must be told. There are but two ways of saving the frontier from destruction. The one is for yourself personally to come out with all the force you can collect, drive the enemy to Canada, pursue them as far as they can go and cut them to pieces. Governor Shelby's example is before you; the crisis is greater than that which called him out.

If this cannot be done there is still another course: let a man fit for the station and with popular talents be appointed to the command of this station. Peter B. Porter is the man and the only one. If he can be appointed a Major-General, McClure's feelings would be saved and the service benefited beyond measure. Should that be done, by all means let him have powers to receive ten thousand volunteers under State authority and push instantly for Burlington, York and Kingston, and, my head for it, these places will fall in two months. The State of Kentucky raised a large militia force without waiting for our general government. Let us do the same and drive the war from our border forever.

My feelings and our exposed situation must be my only apologies for the freedom of this letter.

P. S.—There are neither arms nor ammunition here. The mail has not arrived, but accounts received since I wrote the above go to confirm the general opinion that the fort is taken. At all events something must be done immediately. The militia called out have returned home because the enemy were not at Genesee River. The draft of 1000 men goes on very slowly; 600 men will not be mustered. So we go.

(Tompkins Papers, Vol. IX, pp. 14-16, New York State Library.)

The Secretary of War to Governor Tompkins.

DEAR SIR,—

I have just received your letter enclosing those of Hopkins and McClure. The abandonment of Fort George and burning of Niagara and Lewiston were bad enough, but what shall we say of the surprise of Fort Niagara. The very worst possible sentence must be passed upon it and its commander. McClure had not, (as you seem to suppose,) authority for doing anything he did. If he could not hold Fort George destroy it, but then let him take care of his principal fortress. This was very peculiarly his business. But away he runs to Buffalo and then finds the enemy at Lewiston, and Fort Niagara in danger. He hints that Newark was burnt by my orders. This is a great error. My orders were to burn it if necessary to the defence of Fort George, not otherwise. But he does not defend Fort George, then burns Newark. My order was given on the report of the General, that the attack of Fort George might be covered by Newark. Relieve this man. But what is Hall? Of him the report was formerly not good. No movement below can be made which will have the effect you suggest. Our force at Sackett's Harbor and French Mills and Plattsburg is at neither place more than what is wanted and cannot move now. The invaders must be expelled by the militia of the west, and if it be not done shame light upon them! Why should Virginia, Georgia, Tennessee and Kentucky men so far outact and outshine us.

26th Dec., 1813.

(Tompkins Papers, Vol. IX., p. 16, New York State Library.)

Major-General Amos Hall to Governor Tompkins.

BUFFALO, Dec. 26, 1813, evening.

SIR,—On my receiving information of the enemy's crossing the Niagara River and taking the fort, I immediately set off for the frontier. On my arrival at Batavia I found a number of volunteers assembled. I tarried one day at that place to forward them on to the frontier and make arrangements for those who should follow.

I this day arrived at Buffalo and assumed the command of the troops, (being all volunteers,) now on this station. The whole number here and at Lewiston, etc., may amount to 2000 of all descriptions. The enemy have made their appearance opposite Black Rock and an invasion is to be expected.

The troops now out can be kept but a few days. The troops called out on Your Excellency's last requisition cannot all arrive at this place until the middle or last of this week.

The order did not reach me until the evening of the 16th inst.

Our loss in the capture of Niagara has been immense. What number of brave men have been sacrificed we have not yet been able to learn. It must have been great.

Several inhabitants have been killed at Lewiston, etc., among whom it is not ascertained there are any women and children.

(Tompkins Papers, Vol. IX., p. 17. New York State Library.)

Extract from a Letter to the Editor of the Albany Argus.

BUFFALO, Dec. 26, 1813.

On Sunday morning last the British troops crossed the river about four miles above Fort Niagara. Two companies of regulars proceeded and took possession of the fort by surprise or treachery without opposition. The Indians then began their hellish work by burning the buildings and plundering, killing and scalping the inhabitants. On the river and from six to eight miles on the ridge road they have not left a house from the fort to Schlosser except one owned by Mr Fairbanks, a Federalist of the Boston stamp. On Friday I proceeded with thirty mounted volunteers to Lewiston. The sight we here witnessed was shocking beyond description. Our neighbors were seen lying dead in the fields and roads, some horribly cut and mangled with tomahawks, others eaten by the hogs, which were probably left for that purpose, as they were almost the only animal found alive. It is not yet ascertained how many were killed, as most of the bodies were thrown into the burning houses and consumed. We found the bodies of Wm. Gardner, Deputy Sheriff, John M. Low and Ezra St. John, (whose family cannot be found,) Attorneys, Dr. Alvord and six others whose names I have forgotten.

We have now about 3000 militia with some Indians, and in three days we shall be 5000 strong, all determined to cross.

National Intelligencer, Washington, D. C., January 4th, 1814.

NEW YORK, December 31, 1813.

The British and Indians had been seen in force at Fort George for several days, and the inhabitants on our side, apprehending an attack, had generally prepared for flight.

Our informant was in the fort on Saturday night, and on Sunday morning a little before daylight it was taken by surprise, as he was told by persons who escaped from it after it was entered and in full possession by the British. About four cannon only were fired and a roar of firearms succeeded, when, after an interval of ten or twenty minutes, a royal salute of 22 guns was heard. The British crossed in boats they had brought from Burlington Bay.

The inhabitants evacuated the country for a distance of 14 miles from the river with such of their effects as they could bring off, and their houses were burnt by the enemy to the extent of seven miles back from the river, without that general abuse of the inhabitants which was at first reported.

We are particularly happy to learn by our informant, who is a gentleman of intelligence and had been an officer in the detached militia, that no indiscriminate massacre of the inhabitants had taken place, to his knowledge. Mr. Mullineux, one of the persons said to be killed, was in his sleigh, and he saw Mr. Barton and the son of his who was reported to be killed. The other son was in the fort.

Great numbers of citizens were met on the road to Buffalo, for the defence of that place. The Tuscarora Indians bravely repulsed a party of the enemy. The number of buildings burnt may possibly amount to 100.

National Intelligencer, January 22d, 1814.

Letter dated January 20th, 1814, signed "An Officer in the Army:"

When the enemy, stationed at Burlington Heights, were informed that the militia under the command of General McClure had returned to their respective homes and that no force remained at Fort George except Captain Willcocks's corps of Upper Canada Volunteers and about 70 of General Harrison's regular troops, he immediately commenced a line of march upon the road leading from Burlington to Fort George. This movement of the enemy was communicated to General McClure in a very short time after it commenced, and upon receiving it he sent a confidential person from Newark to reconnoitre the motions of the enemy and to find out if possible the real object of his movement. This person had not proceeded more than 12 miles when he discovered that the vanguard of the enemy had advanced to the 12 Mile Creek, and that his object was not only to recover Fort George but to cross the river and possess himself of Fort Niagara. The moment General McClure received this news he called a council of war of all the officers then under his command, at which council it was unanimously resolved that it was utterly impossible to maintain Fort George against such superior numbers as were then approaching, and that it ought to be immediately abandoned and destroyed. General McClure then related to the council that he had directions from the Secretary of War purporting "that in case Fort George should at any time be attacked by the enemy, to burn Newark, provided that by so doing he would be enabled to hold the fort." But it seemed to be the decided opinion of the council that the burning of the town could not tend in the remotest degree to preserve Fort George, as there were not a sufficient number of men to hold it under the existing circumstances. It was, however, suggested by one of the members of the council that as the enemy was approaching with all his force, and also bringing on a number of boats from Burlington, the probability was that the great object was to cross the river and take possession of Fort Niagara as had been stated, in which case the destruction of Newark became a matter of the first necessity, inasmuch as the enemy would have no shelter in that quarter to prepare himself for an attack on Fort Niagara and that he would be compelled by his complete and unavoidable exposure to severity of the weather, (at that time severe frost and snow,) to return to his encampment at Burlington without being able to accomplish his object. This suggestion met the general concurrence of the council, and it was then unanimously agreed that the General ought to destroy the town the moment he found the enemy approaching it, which he accordingly did.

General Order.

ADJUTANT GENERAL'S OFFICE,
HEADQUARTERS, QUEBEC, 27th December, 1813.

General Order.

The Commander of the Forces has received a despatch from Lieutenant General Drummond containing a supplementary report from Colonel Murray, dated at Fort George 13th December, correcting his statement of the preceding day respecting the enemy having passed over his cannon, stores, etc., having since discovered in the ditch of the fortifications one long eighteen pounder, four twelve and several nine pounders, together with a large supply of shot. Some of the temporary magazines, with a proportion of fixed ammunition, have been secured, and camp equipage for 1500 men has fallen into our possession.

The new barracks erected in the vicinity of Fort George and at Chippawa have, from the precipitancy of the enemy's flight, escaped being burnt.

EDWARD BAYNES,
Adjutant General, North America.

Sir George Prevost to Earl Bathurst.

HEADQUARTERS, QUEBEC, 27th December, 1813.

No. 118.

MY LORD,—I do myself the honor to acquaint Your Lordship that since my despatch, No. 116, of the 22d inst., I have received a communication from Lieutenant General Drummond containing a supplementary report from Colonel Murray, dated Fort George the 23d (13th?) December, correcting his statement of the preceding day respecting the enemy having passed over the river all his cannon and stores, having discovered in the ditch of the fortification one long 18 pounder, four 12 and several 9 pounders, together with a large supply of shot. Some of the temporary magazines, with a proportion of fixed ammunition, have been saved, and camp equipment for fifteen hundred men has fallen into our possession.

The new barracks erected in the vicinity of Fort George and at Chippawa have, from the precipitancy of the enemy's flight, escaped being burnt.

(Canadian Archives, Q. 123, pp. 114-5.)

Earl Bathurst to Sir George Prevost.

Downing Street, 27th Dec'r, 1813.

SIR,—I have this day received through a private channel your General Order, containing an account of an affair which took place in Upper Canada between the American army, under the command of Genl. Wilkinson, and a small British force under the orders of Lt.-Col. Morrison, which appears to have moved from Kingston. The result has been such as the uniform good conduct of the troops under your command would have led me to anticipate, and the enemy have again experienced that superiority of numbers is not alone sufficient to ensure the success of their operations.

It will, however, be very prejudicial to the success of your future operations if Genl. Wilkinson has been allowed to establish himself in Cornwall.

You have long looked for an opportunity of meeting the enemy, and the advantage gained over Genls. Hampton and Wilkinson must have so clearly evinced the commanding superiority of the British troops that I trust you have not delayed collecting your troops before the enemy could have had time to entrench themselves or to open a communication with General Hampton.

(Canadian Archives, C. 681, p. 301.)

Earl Bathurst to Sir George Prevost.

Downing Street, 27th December, 1813.

Sir,—Since I had the honour of addressing you, on the 5th inst., I have received your farther despatches to No. 106 inclusive, with the exception only of No. 95, and I have submitted the most material of them to the consideration of the Prince Regent.

His Royal Highness has observed with the greatest satisfaction the skill and gallantry so conspicuously displayed by the officers and men who composed the detachment of troops opposed to Genl. Hampton's army. By the resistance which they successfully made to the enemy, so vastly disproportionate, the confidence of the enemy has been lowered, their plans disconcerted and the safety of that part of the Canadian frontier ensured. It gives his Royal Highness peculiar pleasure to find that His Majesty's Canadian subjects have had the opportunity, (which His Royal Highness has long been desirous should be afforded them) of disproving by their own brilliant exertions in defence of their country that calumnious charge of disaffection and disloyalty with which the enemy prefaced his first invasion of the province.

To Colonel Salaberry in particular, and to all the officers under his command in general, you will not fail to express His Royal Highness' most gracious approbation of their meritorious and most distinguished services.

His Royal Highness has commanded me to forward to you by the first safe opportunity the colours which you have solicited for the Embodied Battalions of the Militia, feeling that they have evinced an ability and disposition to secure them from insult, which gives them the best title to this mark of distinction.

On the subject of the disaster which appears to have befallen the force under the command of General Procter, I am precluded by the absence of details from expressing any opinion. But whatever may have been the causes which led to it, it is at least satisfactory to observe that it has not influenced the conduct of our Indian allies, nor given to the enemy any advantage beyond that of which they were already in possession.

The safe arrival of the Marine Battalions, the seamen, the 70th Regt. and detachments which accompanied it, will have placed at your disposal, most opportunely, a considerable force to be applied to that part of the frontier which you may deem most liable to attack. In addition to this reinforcement you will receive in the spring a further supply of seamen and other regiments specified in my despatch, No. 41, of the 13th of August.

(Canadian Archives C. 681, p. 306.)

Lieut.-General Drummond to Sir George Prevost.

ST. DAVIDS, 28th December, 1813.

SIR,—Herewith I have the honor to transmit a report from Captain Stewart of the Royal Scots (stationed at Long Point) giving an account of an enterprise, the conduct of which appears to me to reflect great credit on the officer, (Lieutenant Metcalf,) and the party of militia employed.

I have found it requisite to confer on Captain Stewart the temporary rank of Lieutenant Colonel while employed in the London District.

(Canadian Archives, C. 681, pp. 286-7.)

District General Order.

CHIPPAWA, 28th December, 1813.

D. General Order.

The troops will hold themselves in readiness to embark on the service for which they have been assembled. The embarkation will take place to-morrow night under such arrangements as will be made by Major-General Riall, who will command the whole of the troops about to pass to the enemy's shore.

Lieutenant-General Drummond has great satisfaction in reflecting that the troops to be employed on this occasion are corps which have always been distinguished by their discipline and gallantry. The Lieutenant General, having personally served in each of them, may be allowed to feel a more than common degree of interest in their success. The service they are going upon is an arduous one, for, tho' the enemy they will have to encounter be undisciplined and consisting almost wholly of militia, yet he is numerous and highly exasperated. The troops must therefore wholly depend, not only for their success but even for their safety, on their bravery and discipline,—a relaxation in the latter may be as fatal as even a deficiency in the former quality.

The Lieutenant-General most strongly enjoins the troops never to *throw away their fire.* When they do give it let it be with regularity and consequently with effect, but the bayonet is the weapon most formidable in the hands of a British soldier, and he earnestly hopes that on it they will place their principal dependence on the present occasion.

By the successful accomplishment of the present service the enemy will be deprived of all means of offering any further annoyance, and the troops will be suffered to enjoy a well earned repose during the remainder of the winter.

Army horses taken from the enemy are immediately to be given up to the artillery officer for the service of the guns, to be transferred by him to the Commissariat Department for the benefit of the captors.

Any soldier leaving his ranks for the purpose of plunder is liable to be shot on the spot. The captured property belongs not to any individual but to all.

Intoxication in the presence of an enemy, let it be remembered, is not only the most disgraceful but the most dangerous crime which a soldier can commit. The man who wilfully disqualifies himself from meeting the enemy, by whatever means, cannot be considered as a brave man

J. HARVEY, Lt.-Col.,
D. A. Genl.

(Canadian Archives, Q. 341, pp. 211-3.)

Brigadier-General McClure to Lieut.-Col. Granger.

BATAVIA, 28th of Dec., 1813.

DEAR SIR,—I propose visiting my family after giving the command of the militia to Col. Davis with orders for him to repair to Black Rock. Being the senior Colonel, he, in my absence, will have the command of the regulars, the volunteers and all other species of troops, except the volunteer militia and Generals Hall and Hopkins, and while they remain to be subject to Gen. Hall's orders. The gross insults which I have received from many at Buffalo will apologise for my absence. When I return again with the regular troops I will be able to do myself justice. I have sent that able officer, Major Frisbie, to assist you in the Indian department. By him I have sent a talk to the Indians and request you to send me their answer. I have written to the President in their behalf, and recommended their good conduct in the strongest terms. I have ordered the needy among them some blankets, which are at this place. I shall be happy to hear from you at any time.

Lieut.-Colonel Harvey to Major-General Riall.

HEADQUARTERS, CHIPPAWA, 29th Dec., 1813.

SIR,—Finding that the enemy is assembling a large force on the opposite frontier, the object of which can only be to attempt the recovery of the fort of Niagara, or the prosecution of his atrocious system (began at Fort George) of laying waste our peaceful frontier, Lieutenant General Drummond has considered it his duty to pass over to the opposite shore the disposable troops for the purpose of dispersing this force and destroying the villages of Buffalo and Black Rock in order to deprive the enemy of the cover which these places afford.

The Lieutenant General desires that you will accordingly take under your command the troops now assembled on this line, and in conjunction with the whole body of the Indians proceed to execute the service above mentioned by crossing the river in the course of this night, so as to be ready to commence the attack on Black Rock at daylight to-morrow morning. You will make such arrangements for crossing and such distribution of the troops as may appear to you most advisable for the successful performance of the service. The Lieutenant General recommends that at least two-thirds of the whole force should be landed, (under your personal direction,) below Squaw Island, the remaining third to cross either directly on to Black Rock on a concerted signal, or a little *above* it, so as to turn that position whilst attacked in front by the troops from below. The first troops which cross should have directions to secure the bridge on Conjunckaty Creek, to prevent the enemy from destroying it, and if possible to capture the picquet stationed there. In moving upon Buffalo the centre road should be avoided, while the principal part of the troops gain the road leading to the Eleven Mile Creek, and the Right Column moves by the beach so as to reach Buffalo as nearly as possible at the same moment. If you find that the enemy has a force in your rear at the Eleven Mile Creek not a moment should be lost in moving in that direction to attack him as soon as his troops at Buffalo and Black Rock have been defeated, taken or dispersed.

The destruction of these places should be deferred to the last moment in order that the troops may avail themselves of their shelter as long as it may be necessary to keep them on the other side. You will be particularly careful to secure all provisions and flour, and if possible to have them removed to this side. Such other stores as cannot be moved must be destroyed.

Finally, I am instructed to repeat the Lieutenant General's earnest request that you will use your best exertions and require all under your command to do the same in restraining the savage propensities of the Indian warriors and to give protection to the persons and property of such of the inhabitants as may remain in their houses. All liquor should be destroyed to prevent it falling into the hands of the Indians or troops.

I have omitted to the last calling your attention to an object of primary importance, and which not a moment must be lost in endeavoring to effect, viz.: The destruction of three of the enemy's armed schooners on shore high and dry on the beach—two below the Buffalo Creek and one above it. It would be advisable to appoint an intelligent and experienced officer with a party of select militia expressly for the performance of this important service.

The passage of the troops across the river and the operations against Black Rock will be covered as far as possible by the fire of the field guns, and it is also proposed to send a light piece or two across if found practicable.

(Canadian Archives, C. 681, pp. 315-18.)

District Order.

CHIPPAWA, 29th December, 1813.

D. Order.

Agreeably to the District General Order of yesterday, the troops which have been placed under Major-General Riall's command for the purpose of attacking the enemy on his own shore will commence their embarkation in the following order at ——— o'clock this evening, viz.:

The King's Regiment and the 89th Light Company with 25 Militia Volunteers and a party of Indian warriors, the whole under the command of Lieut.-Colonel Ogilvie, 1st embarkation.

The 41st Regiment, grenadiers of the 100th Regiment, with 25 militia volunteers and a party of Indian warriors, under Major Frend, 2nd embarkation.

Third embarkation wholly of Indian warriors.

Fourth embarkation, Royal Scots with the remainder of the militia volunteers and the Indian warriors, under the command of Lieut.-Colonel Gordon.

Major Simons of the Incorporated Militia is appointed to command the armed militia and volunteers.

Officers commanding corps with the senior officer of the Indian department and the officer commanding the militia will meet the Major-General at Palmer's at 3 o'clock this afternoon.

The Deputy Assistant Quartermaster General will also attend.

J. H. HOLLAND, Capt., A. D. C.

(Canadian Archives, Q. 341, pp. 214-5.)

Major-General Hall to Brig. General McClure.

BUFFALO, Dec. 29th, 1813.

SIR,—Enclosed is a letter received yesterday by flag. Not knowing but there might have been something that would have been important to be immediately known to the commanding officer, I took the liberty to open it and found it contained an answer to your letter to Gen. Vincent, and a printed General Order of the Commander in Chief of the Canadas.

We have now on the frontier, including Lewiston, &c., about 2000 volunteers. I had an inspection and review yesterday at Buffalo. The troops appeared extremely well and all equipped. We have been able to bring a little order out of confusion, which, to be sure, was very great when we arrived. I this day review the troops at the Rock.

I have ascertained that no women or female children have been butchered in the late affair at N(iagara) and Lewiston.

The detachment you will please to order on as expeditiously as possible, for it will be absolutely necessary to keep at least 2,000 men on the frontier. The enemy make considerable movements on the opposite shore and (we) keep strict watch by night by sentinels and patrols. I, however, do not believe they will attempt to cross unless they find our force is wasting, which will of course be the case in a few days unless the detachment should supply their places.

(From Publications of the Buffalo Historical Society, Vol. V., pp 32-3.)

Captain Heman Norton to Governor D. D. Tompkins.

BUFFALO, 29th December, 1813.

SIR,—I am instructed by Major-Gen. Hall to enclose you a return from the Asst. D. Q. M. Genl. at this station, of the ordnance stores on hand. I am further instructed to state to Your Excellency that the forces now on the frontier are mostly composed of volunteers who have left their homes under the impression that the tour would be short, and cannot be retained consistently for a long period. The force of the enemy in regulars and Indians are, from correct sources, ascertained to be about 2,000, of which 800 are Indians. No doubt can exist in the mind of the Major-General of the determination of the enemy to retain possession of Fort Niagara; that they are equally determined on the destruction of this part of the frontier, is derived from recent information direct from the other side.

The militia of the enemy are ordered out and are now collecting and their boats have been removed up to Chippeway. Under these circumstances, with only 1,500 troops at this station and these poorly supplied with ammunition, the Major-General feels confident that no time will be lost by Your Excellency in forwarding succors of every description. The troops, however, I believe, will meet the enemy with spirit should they invade our territory.

The troops of the enemy are commanded by Lieut.-Genl. Drummond. The expedition against Fort Niagara was commanded by Major-Genl. Riall. No officer killed on the side of U. S. A.

(From Publications of the Buffalo Historical Society, Vol. V., pp. 33-4.)

From Colonel John Murray to Lieut.-General Drummond.

FORT NIAGARA, 22d Dec'r., 1813.

SIR,—

I take the liberty of bringing before your honor's notice Volunteers John Frazer and Allan McNab, two young gentlemen attached to the 100th Regt. They were amongst the foremost during the attack of the picquets and the assault of Niagara on the morning of the 19th inst., and conducted themselves with great bravery and zeal—also Volunteer Thos. Pigot, 89th Regt., whose zeal and intrepidity were equally conspicuous. The latter gentleman guided the grenadiers when embarking.

(Canadian Archives, C. 19, p. 239.)

General Order.

HEADQUARTERS, BUFFALO, Dec. 29, 1813.

The Major-General returns his thanks to the corps of militia under his command on the Niagara frontier, as well for their civil deportment and soldier-like conduct since arriving on the frontier as for their patriotism in leaving their homes at this inclement season to meet an invading enemy and repel a violence (that) threatened the lives, property and safety of their fellow citizens. Their alacrity in flying to arms at the first alarm of danger merits and will no doubt receive the thanks of their country. At least they will have the consolation of reflecting that they have done their duty, although others may have forgotten theirs.

The Major General cannot too much applaud the martial appearance and good conduct of the troops in Buffalo during the review of yesterday, and flatters himself with the conviction that should opportunity present they will prove that their bravery is not exceeded by their patriotism.

The General is aware that the troops now on this frontier, having left their homes on a moment's call, are not prepared to remain any considerable length of time. It cannot reasonably be expected of them. It is hoped that the necessity for their absence from their homes and families will be short. A few days will determine it. Detachments are making and marching to the frontier. Notice has been given to the Governor of our situation, and it is confidently expected that adequate provision will in a few days be made to guard our frontier, when the patriotic citizens now in service can return to their families and repose themselves in the confidence of safety.

The General will not delay for a moment to make known to his fellow soldiers the period when they may return to their homes in safety, until which time he entreats their patient endurance of those privations incident to their situation.

The General gives it in strict orders to the several commandants of corps to restrain all irregular firing. He requests his fellow soldiers to bear in mind that powder and ball are the means of attack and defence; if they waste them in idle sport their continuance on the frontier is worse than useless.

The several commandants of distinct corps will cause this order to be read at the head of their several corps.

By order of Major General Hall.

GEO. HOSMER, A. D. C.

(From Publications of the Buffalo Historical Society, Vol. V., pp. 31-5.)

Major J. B. Glegg to Colonel Talbot.

BURLINGTON HEIGHTS, 30th December, 1813.

DEAR COLONEL,

During the last two days I have been so much indisposed as to be incapable of doing anything. The application of a blister to my chest has relieved me a good deal and will, I hope, equal Dr. Kerr's expectations, but my arm is of little use to me. I did hope it would have been in my power to send you an acceptable bulletin by Lieut. Medcalf, as Lieut.-Colonel Harvey wrote me on the 27th that the army were to cross the river that night for the purpose of advancing against General McClure, who, it was expected, had taken up a position at the Eleven Mile Creek beyond Buffalo. On the landing Buffalo and Black Rock were to be reduced to ashes. I hope in God their hearts did not fail them, for such an expedition, consisting of one thousand regulars and eight hundred Indians, could not fail meeting with success. I hope you and others received the letters I sent on a few days ago, that to Lieut.-Colonel Stewart containing bills for paying the militia.

I sent them in the first instance after you to S. Hatt's, but you were gone. Do let me have the earliest intelligence if there is any truth in a report of an enemy being on the Thames.

You may rely on hearing punctually from me when there is any good news to relate and my health enables me to write. I can scarcely now hold my pen. I have written in very strong terms to Lieut. General Drummond respecting the merits of Lieut. Medcalf and Ensign McGregor.

P. S.—General Vincent and Barnard are here waiting anxiously for snow.

(From the Talbot Papers.)

Lieutenant-General Drummond to Sir George Prevost.

BUFFALO, 30th December, 1813.

DEAR SIR,—
  I have the satisfaction of acquainting Your Excellency that the attack which was made at daylight this morning on the enemy's troops at Black Rock has been completely successful, Major General Riall having in the most gallant style defeated, after a short but severe contest, a body of upwards of 2,000 men advantageously posted. The corps employed on this service were detachments of the Royals, King's and 41st Regiments with the flank companies of the 89th and 100th. After having driven the enemy from Black Rock Major General Riall immediately pursued them towards Buffalo, from whence after a few rounds from his field guns he again rapidly fled towards the Eleven Mile Creek. The number of the enemy killed and wounded was very great. Our loss has been severe. Not having as yet received any official report I can only say generally that the conduct of the troops, not only in the field but in their patient suffering of great privation, &c., was above all praise—that the circumstances of carrying on military operations in such a climate is sufficient proof of the zeal of the troops.

  I enclose a copy of my instructions to Major General Riall. It will be my endeavor in transmitting the Major General's despatch to point out to Your Excellency the great merit of the Major General, the officers and the troops, in the execution of this arduous service.

  Very few prisoners were made except such as were wounded, a circumstance which marks very clearly the rapidity of the enemy's flight. About seventy prisoners are in our hands, amongst whom is the famous Dr. or Colonel Chapin, whom, in consequence of his former escape, I have sent off towards Quebec by an officer and two dragoons.

  We have taken seven pieces of ordnance of different calibres and destroyed four of the enemy's armed schooners and sloops. The town of Buffalo has been burnt, as well as that of Black Rock previous to its evacuation by the troops. Many valuable stores have been taken.

  (Marginal note)—Lieutenant-Colonel Ogilvie and Captain Fawcett are the only officers wounded, with about 50 or 60 men, and perhaps half that number killed.

(Canadian Arch.ves, C. 681, p. 321-2.)

Major-General Hall to Governor Tompkins.

HEADQUARTERS, NIAGARA FRONTIER,
December 30th, 1813, 7 o'clock p. m.

SIR,—

I have only a moment to acknowledge the receipt of your letter of the 25th inst. and to add that this frontier is wholly desolate. The British crossed over, supported by a strong party of Indians, a little before day this morning near Black Rock. They were met by the militia under my command with spirit, but overpowered by the numbers and discipline of the enemy the militia gave way and fled on every side; every attempt to rally them was ineffectual.

The enemy's purpose was obtained and the flourishing village of Buffalo is laid in ruins. The Niagara frontier now lies open and naked to our enemies. Your judgment will direct you what is most proper in this emergency. I am exhausted and must defer particulars till to-morrow. Many valuable lives are lost.

(Tompkins Papers, Vol. IX., pp. 18-9. New York State Library.)

Colonel Winfield Scott to the Secretary of War.

GEORGETOWN, December 31st, 1813.

(Extract.)

I left Fort George on the 13th of October last by order of Major General Wilkinson with the whole of the regular troops of that garrison, and was relieved by Brigadier General McClure with a body of the New York Militia. Fort George, as a field work, might be considered as complete at that period. It was garnished with ten pieces of artillery, (which might easily have been increased from the spare ordnance at the opposite fort,) with an ample supply of fixed ammunition, &c., as the enclosed receipt for those articles will exhibit.

Fort Niagara on the 14th October was under the immediate command of Captain Leonard, 1st Artillery, who, besides his own company, had Captain Read's of the same regiment, together with such of General McClure's brigade as had refused to cross the river. Lieutenant-Colonels Fleming, Bloom and Dobbins of the militia had successively been in command of this fort by order of the Brigadier General, but I think neither of them was present at the above period. Major General Wilkinson, in his order to me for the removal of the regular troops on that frontier, excepted the two companies of the 1st Artillery then at Fort Niagara, and under the supposition that I should meet water transport for my detachment at the mouth of the

Genesee river, I had his orders to take with the whole of the convalescents left in the different hospitals by the regiments which had accompanied him. This order I complied with.

(Armstrong's Notices of the War of 1812, Vol. II., pp. 194-5.)

Statement of the Number of Non-Commissioned Officers and Privates of the 1st Norfolk Regiment of Militia on Active Service During the Year 1813.

From 25th December, 1812, to 24th January, 1813	25
From 25th January to 24th February, 1813	34
From 25th February to 24th March, 1813	30
From 25th March to 24th April, 1813	12
From 25th April to 24th May, 1813	47
From 25th May to 24th June, 1813	42
From 25th June to 24th July, 1813	42
From 25th July to 24th August, 1813	42
From 25th August to 24th September, 1813	34
From 25th September to 24th October, 1813	148
From 25th October to 24th November, 1813	181
From 25th November to 24th December, 1813	181

Statement of the Number of Non-Commissioned Officers and Men of the 2nd Norfolk Regiment of Militia on Active Service During the Year 1813.

From 25th December, 1812, to 24th January, 1813	42
From 25th January to 24th February, 1813	16
From 25th February to 24th March, 1813	16
From 25th March to 24th April, 1813	12
From 25th April to 24th May, 1813	50
From 25th May to 24th June, 1813	50
From 25th June to 24th July, 1813	21
From 25th July to 24th August, 1813	26
From 25th August to 24th September, 1813	53
From 25th September to 24th October	181
From 25th October to 24th November, 1813	181
From 25th November to 24th December, 1813	115

Statement of the Number of Non Commissioned Officers and Privates of the 1st Middlesex Regiment of Militia on Active Service During the Year 1813.

From 25th December, 1812, to 24th January, 1813	64
From 25th January to 24th February, 1813	15
From 25th February to 24th March, 1813	15
From 25th March to 24th April, 1813	15
From 25th April to 24th May, 1813	21
From 25th May to 24th June, 1813	20
From 25th June to 24th July, 1813	20
From 25th July to 24th August, 1813	20
From 25th August to 24th September, 1813	21
From 25th September to 24th October, 1813	22
From 25th October to 24th November, 1813	44
From 25th November to 24th December, 1813	22

(Compiled from returns in the Talbot Papers.)

Major General Riall to Lieut.-General Drummond.

NIAGARA FRONTIER, NEAR FORT ERIE,
January 1st, 1814.

SIR,—

I have the honor to report to you that, agreeably to your instructions contained in your letter of the 29th ulto., and your General Order of that day, to pass the river Niagara for the purpose of attacking the enemy's force collected at Black Rock and Buffalo and carrying into execution the other objects therein mentioned, I crossed the river on the following night with four companies of the King's Regiment and the light company of the 89th under Lieut.-Colonel Ogilvie, 250 men of the 41st Regiment and the grenadiers of the 100th under Major Frend, together with about 50 militia volunteers and a body of Indian warriors.‡ The troops completed their landing about 12 o'clock, nearly two miles below Black Rock. The light infantry of the 89th, being in advance, surprised and captured the greater part of a picquet of the enemy and secured the bridge over Conguichity Creek, the boards of which had been loosened and were ready to be carried off, had there been time given for it.

I immediately established the 41st and 100th Grenadiers in a

Royals	370
King's Regiment	240
41st	250
89th Light Infantry	55
Grenadiers, 100th	50
Militia	50
Indians	400

position beyond the bridge for the purpose of perfectly securing its passage. The enemy made some attempts during the night upon this advanced position, but were repulsed with loss.

At daybreak I moved forward, the King's Regiment and light company of the 89th leading, the 41st and grenadiers of the 100th being in reserve. The enemy had by this time opened a very heavy fire of cannon and musketry upon the Royal Scots under Lieut.-Colonel Gordon, who were destined to land above Black Rock for the purpose of turning his position while he should be attacked in front by the troops who landed below. Several of the boats having grounded, I am sorry to say this regiment suffered some loss and was not able to effect the landing in sufficient time to fully accomplish the object intended, tho' covered by the whole of our field guns under Captain Bridge, which were placed on the opposite side of the river. The King's and 89th having in the meantime gained the town, commenced a very spirited attack upon the enemy, who were in great force and very strongly posted. The reserve having arrived on the ground, the whole were shortly engaged. The enemy maintained his position with very considerable obstinacy for some time, but such was the spirited and determined advance of our troops that he was at length compelled to give way, was driven through his batteries, in which were a 24-pounder, three 12s and one 9 pounder, and pursued to the town of Buffalo about two miles distant. He here shewed a large body of infantry and cavalry and attempted to oppose our advance by the fire of a field piece posted on a height which commanded the road, but finding this ineffectual he fled in all directions, and betaking himself to the woods further pursuit was useless. He left behind him one 6-pounder brass field piece, one iron 18 and one iron 6-pounder, which fell into our hands.

I then proceeded to execute the ulterior objects of the expedition. I detached Captain Robinson of the King's with two companies to destroy the two schooners and sloop, (a part of the Lake Erie squadron,) that were on shore a little below the town, with the stores they had on board, which he effectually completed. The town itself, (the inhabitants having previously left it,) and the whole of the public stores, containing considerable quantities of clothing, spirits and flour, which I had not the means of conveying away, were set on fire and totally consumed, as was also the village of Black Rock on the evening it was evacuated.

In obedience to your further instructions I then directed Lieut.-Colonel Gordon to move down the river to Fort Niagara with a party of the 19th Light Dragoons under Major Lisle, a detachment of the Royal Scots and the 89th light company and destroy the remaining cover of the enemy upon his frontier, which he has reported to me has been effectually done.

From every account I have been able to collect the enemy's force opposed to us was not less than from 2,000 to 2,500 men. Their loss in killed and wounded I should imagine from 3 to 400, but from the nature of the ground, being mostly covered with wood, it is difficult to ascertain it precisely; the same reason will account for our not having been able to make a greater number of prisoners than 130.

I have great satisfaction in stating to you the good conduct of the whole of the regular troops and volunteer militia, but I must particularly mention the steadiness and bravery of the King's and 89th light infantry. They were most gallantly led to the attack by Lieut.-Colonel Ogilvie of the King's, who, I am sorry to say, received a severe wound, which will for a time deprive the service of a very brave and intelligent officer. After Lieut.-Colonel Ogilvie was wounded the command devolved on Captain Robinson, who, by a very judicious movement to his right with the three battalion companies, made a considerable impression on the left of the enemy's position.

I have every reason to be satisfied with Lieut.-Colonel Gordon in command of the Royal Scots, and have much to regret that the accidental grounding of the boats prevented me from having the full benefit of his services, and I have also to mention my approbation of the conduct of Major Frend, commanding the 41st, as well as that of Captain Fawcett of the 100th Grenadiers, who was unfortunately wounded. Captain Basden of the 89th and Captain Brewster of the King's light infantry conducted themselves in the most exemplary manner. Lieut.-Colonel Elliott, on this as well as all other occasions, is entitled to my highest commendation for his zeal and activity as superintendent of the Indian Department, and I am happy to state that thro' his exertions and those of his officers no act of cruelty, as far as I could learn, was committed by the Indians towards any of their prisoners.

I cannot close this report without mentioning in terms of the warmest praise the good conduct of my aide-de-camp, Captain Holland, from whom I have received the most able assistance throughout the whole of these operations. Nor can I omit my obligations to you for acceding to the request of your aide-de-camp, Captain Jervois, to accompany me. He was extremely active and zealous and rendered a very essential service. I enclose a return of the killed, wounded and missing and of the ordnance captured at Black Rock and Buffalo.

(Canadian Archives, C. 682, pp. 5-8.)

Return of the Killed, Wounded and Missing of the Troops of the Right Division, under the Command of Major General Riall, in the Attack on Black Rock and Buffalo on the 30th December, 1813.

Killed.	Officers	Sergeants	Rank and File
Royal Scots			13
King's Regiment			7
41st Regiment			2
89th Light Infantry			3
Volunteer Militia			3
Indian Warriors			3
Total killed			31
Wounded.			
Royal Scots		3	29
King's Regiment	2		14
41st Regiment			5
89th Light Infantry			5
100th Grenadiers	1		4
Volunteer Militia	1		5
Indian Warriors			3
Total wounded	4	3	65
Missing.			
Royal Scots			6
41st Regiment			3
Total missing			9
General total of killed, wounded and missing	4	3	105

Names of officers wounded—

King's Regiment—Lieut.-Colonel Ogilvie, severely, not dangerously; Lieut. Young, slightly.

100th Grenadiers—Captain Fawcett, severely, not dangerously.

Volunteer Militia—Captain Servos slightly.

(Canadian Archives, C. 682, p. 10.)

Return of Ordnance Captured at Black Rock on the 30th December, 1813.

1 brass 6-pounder field piece, with carriage complete.
1 iron 24-pounder.
1 do. 18 do.
3 do. 12 do.
1 do. 9 do.
1 do. 6 do.

C. BRIDGE,
Captain Royal Artillery.

(Canadian Archives, C. 682, p. 9.)

Lieutenant General Drummond to Sir George Prevost.

NIAGARA FRONTIER, NEAR FORT ERIE,
2nd January, 1814.

SIR,—
Having pushed forward the troops as nearly opposite the head of Grand Island as I could without discovering them to the enemy, I moved my headquarters to Chippawa on the 28th, and on the following day to within two miles of Fort Erie, when, having reconnoitred the enemy's position at Black Rock, I determined to attack him that night. The boats were accordingly moved up from Chippawa Creek on the evening of the 29th, and Major General Riall proceeded to execute the instructions with which I had previously furnished him and of which a copy is enclosed. As soon as the troops destined under the direction of Major General Riall to advance upon Black Rock from below had passed across the river the boats were tracked up as high as the foot of the rapids immediately below Fort Erie. In doing this, which cost much time and labor, it was necessary to observe considerable caution and the greatest silence, as the river there narrows very much and the position in particular to which the boats were brought and from whence the troops were to embark was immediately under the point blank fire of the enemy's heaviest batteries. Owing, I am sorry to say, to the backwardness of some of the militia who were to row and steer the boats, and their having been brought in the dark to a part of the beach which was shoal and full of rocks, and on which they had grounded before anything was ready for pushing off, the day appeared and at the same moment the attack on the enemy's outposts commenced by the troops under Major General Riall.

By the uncommon exertions of all the boats were got off and the Royals, after being exposed to a galling fire of musketry on their passage across, (notwithstanding the well directed fire of five field pieces with which I had directed the old batteries to be occupied,) reached the opposite shore in time to co-operate with the troops under Major General Riall in the defeat of the enemy. I beg to refer Your Excellency to the Major General's report for a detailed account of the operations of the troops, of whose gallantry and exertions he speaks in terms of the highest praise.

To the Major General himself I feel greatly indebted for the very gallant and able manner in which he has executed the service with which I have entrusted him. Of the conduct of the officers and and troops too much cannot be said; the patience and fortitude with which they have borne the privation of almost every comfort, and the severity of a most rigorous climate at this advanced season of the year, reflects the highest credit on all. Nothing in fact can more strongly evince their anxious desire to meet the enemy. Their conduct when he was met, the result of the action, as well as the report of the gallant officer by whom they were led, sufficiently prove.

The conduct of Captain Robinson, King's Regiment, and of Captain Holland, aide-de-camp to Major General Riall, were particularly conspicuous, and I beg leave to recommend those officers to the favorable notice of His Royal Highness the Prince Regent.

All the objects proposed in my letter of the 27th ultimo., and in fact all that are at this moment attainable, having thus been completely accomplished by the destruction of the whole of the cover on the opposite frontier, and by the infliction of a severe retaliation for the burning of the town of Niagara, the justice of which the enemy himself most fully admits, the troops have been placed in cantonments along the frontier in the manner which appears to me best calculated to secure its security and their comfort and repose.

To Lieutenant Colonel Harvey, Deputy Adjutant General, I am much indebted for the able assistance he has afforded me through this arduous service. The exertions of Captain Eliot, Deputy Assistant Quartermaster General, in directing the preparation of the boats and in assisting at the embarkation of the troops were unremitted.

To Captain Bridge, Lieutenants Armstrong and Charlton of the Royal Artillery, and Captain Cameron of the Militia Artillery, whose zeal and exertions in transporting the heavy ordnance were conspicuous, great praise is due.

Lieutenant Colonel Baby, Assistant Quartermaster General of Militia, and Major Simons of the Incorporated Militia, were useful and indefatigable in embarking the troops. Lieutenants Putman, Davis and Anderson and several other officers of the militia very handsomely volunteered in piloting the boats across the river, a service of considerable difficulty and importance, owing to the great rapidity of the current.

I beg leave also to mention the great assistance I received from the officers of my personal staff.

This despatch will be delivered to you by Captain Jervois, my aide de camp, who was in the action and particularly distinguished himself. I beg to recommend him to the favorable notice of His Royal Highness the Prince Regent. He is perfectly qualified to give Your Excellency any further information you may require.

(Canadian Archives, C. 682, pp. 1-4.)

Militia General Order.

HEADQUARTERS, ST. DAVIDS, 2nd January, 1814.

His Honor Lieut. General Drummond has been pleased to make the following promotion :—
1st Regt. Kent Militia:
Lieut. Henry Medcalf to be captain, 2nd January, 1814.

ÆNEAS SHAW,
Adjt. Genl. Militia.

District General Order.

HEADQUARTERS, ST. DAVIDS, 4th January, 1814.

D. G. O.

The good conduct and bravery of the officers and soldiers of the advance corps of the Right Division having been crowned by the most complete success by the capture of Fort Niagara, with all the enemy's guns and stores, and the destruction of four armed vessels, together with the cover along his whole frontier from that fort to Buffalo Creek, a measure dictated not only by every consideration of military policy but authorized by every motive of just retaliation, it only remains for Lieutenant General Drummond to thank the troops for their exertions and to express his admiration of the valuable qualities they have displayed in the course of this short but severe service, in which they have cheerfully borne the absence of almost every comfort and the rigors of a climate for which they were far from being prepared. The immediate reward of their gallant conduct, the Lieutenant General trusts, will be felt in the repose which they have so well earned for themselves by depriving the enemy of all present means of annoyance. The more remote recompense of their exertions will be found in the approbation which their services will doubtless meet with from their King and country.

J. HARVEY, Lt. Col., D. A. G.

(Canadian Archives, C. 682, p. 20.)

From the Kingston Gazette.

Wednesday, January 5, 1814.

The following "GOOD and GLORIOUS NEWS" was received in town yesterday by express:

"The enemy defeated at Black Rock—one hundred and sixty of them killed; one hundred prisoners and seven pieces of cannon taken. Their army fled to the interior. Five vessels destroyed. Every building at Black Rock destroyed. Buffalo burnt down. We lost about 20 men killed."

Buffaloe at night, 30th Dec., 1813.

We are informed that the famous, or rather infamous quack, Doctor Chapin, is among the prisoners.

Several of the American officers taken at Fort Niagara arrived in town yesterday. More are momently expected.

We regret, says the Cincinnati *Gazette*, to inform our readers of the loss of the Chippeway, her crew and baggage, in a gale on Lake Erie. The Chippeway was a schooner carrying two guns and taken by the gallant Perry from the British. She was sailing from Put-in-Bay to Detroit, having on board 60 souls, among them three lieutenants, the baggage of two regiments and a large sum of money for the 24th United States Regiment, all drowned and lost by the staving of the vessel.

From the New York Evening Post, Tuesday, January 11th, 1814.

Extract of a letter from Canandaigua, Sunday evening, January 2nd, 1814:

Amidst the general confusion, such facts as I can collect are as follows:

The British are in possession of Buffalo, which is not hurt. They have not advanced further on that road. General Hall's headquarters are at Batavia, but we have troops at 11 Mile Creek. Our volunteers fled soon after the attack, and are all coming home in droves. I have just learned that Mr. ——— has written that on the Ridge Road they had advanced 17 miles this side of Niagara. There is no regular force and the militia are dispirited. Few arms, little ammunition, no confidence, general complaints, no one at the head of affairs but Hall, who, however, has behaved very well and seems to be meriting the public confidence.

This will be a very distressed country before spring. We shall certainly have continual alarms and shall know experimentally the success of burning and plundering.

From the New York Evening Post, January 12th, 1814.

(From the Geneva Gazette of January 5th.)

The following statement is derived in part from a person who was detained in the fort as a prisoner three days after its capture and then released, and other sources.

It seems that General Drummond, with between 1000 and 1100 regulars, 200 militia and about 300 Indians, landed soon after midnight at the Meadows. After landing preparations were made for attacking the fort at dawn of day, and Colonel Murray was sent towards the fort to reconnoitre with 5 or 600 regulars. Instead of returning with intelligence by daylight in the morning, as was expected, Colonel Murray sent word to General Drummond that he had taken the fort. It appears that a British officer advanced towards the centinel at the outmost gate and when challenged for the countersign, under pretence of giving it, seized his bayonet and before he could give the alarm threw him down and by threats compelled the centinel to communicate the countersign to him, by which means the enemy immediately entered the fort, meeting with little opposition, it being a complete surprise. The British state the number killed on our part to be about 60, and their own loss at 6 or 7. No Indians were at the taking of the fort, they having gone up to Lewiston after landing. The reports that the garrison and invalids at Youngstown were massacred were entirely without foundation. Our informant states that the prisoners in the fort were well treated after the surrender.

Not a house is left standing at Lewiston. Among those killed by the savages at that place the following persons are named: Dr. Joseph Alvord, Mr. Wm. Gardner, Deputy Sheriff, Mr. Gillett and the family of Mr. Pitcher. Mr. Collins, stated last week to have been killed, was only wounded. The enemy advanced on the lake to 18 Mile Creek and burnt the mills at that place and all buildings between that and the fort.

From the Ontario Repository of Canandaigua, January 4th, 1814.

BATTLE AT BLACK ROCK. BUFFALO DESTROYED.

The following information is obtained from Major H. Norton, an aide to General Hall, who was in the battle:

On Wednesday night last, about 11 o'clock, our patrol guard was fired upon by a small party of the enemy about a mile below Conjockety Creek. This was the first notice of the enemy approaching our shore. The alarm was immediately communicated to Major

General Hall, who was at Buffalo with 1200 men, the residue of our force, 200, being at Black Rock, and all were soon under arms.

Colonel Chapin with 400 men marched against the enemy, who were supposed to be landing between Grand and Squaw Islands, and met their advance at Conjockety Creek and in possession of the Sailors' Battery. They had repulsed our troops at Black Rock after exchanging a single shot, which so alarmed the militia under Colonel Chapin that all save 30 fled, and he in vain attempted to rally them to face the foe. Colonel Blakeslee's Regiment of Ontario volunteers, with Captain R. McKay's company from Caledonia, marched to relieve Colonel Chapin and his brave few, but before they reached the spot they received orders to repair to Black Rock, to which point a division of the enemy's boats were now discovered to be steering. The order was promptly obeyed, and as the boats made the shore they received a most destructive fire. In one of the boats every man save one was killed or wounded, and this one taken prisoner. The enemy now commenced throwing shells and hot shot from the opposite shore to annoy a reinforcement going down to the Rock, while at the same time their regulars attacked from below and their Indians commenced a cross fire from the adjacent field and woods. In this situation our troops sustained the action in a most gallant manner for 20 or 30 minutes, when they were compelled to retreat, which was made in great disorder and exposed to the fire from pursuing Indians.

Our loss is not known but is believed not to exceed 30. The names of the officers who are missing, as far as we can learn, are Colonel P. Gardner of West Bloomfield, Colonel Boughton of Avon, Captain Rowley and Lieut. Lusk of Victor, Captain Tyler of Honeoye, Lieut. Harris of East Bloomfield, and Captain W. Hull of Buffalo. Some, it is ascertained, were killed. Colonel Chapin of Buffalo was taken prisoner. The activity and bravery of the Major General and of most of his officers was conspicuous throughout the affair, and had the whole of the militia been firm the issue of the battle would have been very doubtful and perhaps very different.

The loss of the enemy, as near as can be ascertained, is at least twice as great as ours. We took 5 prisoners. Their force on the day before was estimated at 1500 regulars, 500 militia and 800 or 1000 Indians, under command of Major General Riall. Major General Hall had been but three days in Buffalo previous to the action. His force was 1500, of which about 300 men on guard and patrol duty and engaged in making cartridges. In the engagement the average number of cartridges was only about 12 per man. Each British soldier had 60.

The enemy followed up their success and soon after entered the village of Buffalo. Here all was confusion, alarm, distress—the inhabitants who remained in the village were got off as well as possible, and we have heard of but one outrage on the defenders. Mrs. Lovejoy, wife of Mr. Joshua Lovejoy, was killed in her house by an Indian. The reader must picture to himself, for language cannot describe the horror which prevailed. The fate of the place was known to be fixed. Buffalo was to be sacrificed to the vengeance of the foe, and the whole of this pleasant flourishing village has been laid in ashes.

Such is the horrid character which this war has assumed—a war of plunder and of burning.

We lost the following pieces of cannon: One 32-pounder, four 9-pounders, one 6-pounder, also 1,500 barrels of flour with some pork, &c.

No vessels lay at Black Rock at the time. Private losses in property are numerous and heavy. Many enterprising men are ruined.

Our force is now at 11 Mile Creek, i. e., 11 miles this side of Buffalo. Detached militia and volunteers are joining them. Colonel Caleb Hopkins's Regiment in the northwestern part of this county is assembling on the Ridge Road.

Every house from Buffalo to this side of Batavia is evacuated.

A meeting was held in this town last evening and a committee appointed to do such things as the present alarming situation of the country requires for the general safety.

(File in the Wood Library, Canandaigua, N. Y.)

From the New York Evening Post, January 15th, 1814.

A letter from the postmaster at Warren to J. Johnson, Esq., postmaster at Pittsburg, dated Warren, January 3rd, 1814, states:—

I am informed by the postmaster at Lower Sandusky that a party of 40 men, commanded by Lieuts. Larwell, Fisk and Davis, who were sent by General Cass to reconnoitre on the river La Tranche, were attacked by the British, three killed, two made their escape and the rest were taken prisoners.

From the New York Evening Post, January 15th, 1814.

To the Commandant at Erie or to whom it may concern:

The British this morning landed about 3000 regulars, militia and Indians at Black Rock, and after a severe engagement with the militia under the command of General Hall, forced them to retreat to the village of Buffalo, and about sunrise to surrender themselves prisoners of war. The houses in the villages were immediately committed to the flames, and about three o'clock this afternoon almost entirely consumed. At the same time two large vessels lying above Black Rock were set on fire and consumed. It is the avowed object of the British, as received by good authority, to proceed in a short time to Erie for the purpose of burning the vessels in that port, and, as an inducement to the Indians to aid and assist them in this nefarious plan, full liberty is given them to plunder for their own benefit wherever they go. As the communication from this place to the eastward is entirely interrupted by the said Indians, and as it is important for you to have the earliest information of the above, we recommend to you every exertion to be in readiness in case of an attempt to burn as aforesaid, and request of you some assistance in men, arms and ammunition, as we have but few arms and no ammunition. The time is alarming; destruction is the order of the day.

On the retreat from Buffalo, 30th December, 1814.

    ISAAC BARNES, Major,
      Commanding Militia near Buffalo.

Nathaniel Sill to General Peter B. Porter.

        LIMA, 3rd January, 1814.

DEAR SIR,—

Last Thursday morning the British made an attack at Black Rock. Their plan of operation was so well concerted that they could not fail of succeeding. From the best information I could get it would seem that our officers were apprised of the design and in consequence took measures to repel the attack.

The enemy first landed a detachment below the navy yard, which caused an alarm and drew the attention of our whole force to that quarter, at which time their main force was discovered to be approaching our shore near the warehouse. Our whole force was then ordered to oppose this landing. It is said they fought well, but by the time they found themselves well engaged the detachment of the enemy which first landed, fell upon our rear with such impetuosity as broke the line, threw the whole force, (about five hundred,) into confusion, and those who escaped, escaped by flight.

The enemy then marched to Buffalo, a detachment taking the road to Granger's Mills. Chapin with a few volunteers fought with a field piece til his men mostly deserted their post, when he surrendered. Our army retreated to Eleven Mile Creek and left the enemy in possession of the whole country beyond that. We have as yet been able to obtain but a very imperfect account of the affair. We suppose our loss must have been severe. What the fate of the women and children must have been who remained at Buffalo is not yet known. We must have lost all our goods. They were deposited at Mr. Atkins's. Joseph (Sill) was with them. I have this morning heard from him that he was trying to save such articles as he could, but I think he could save but few. The inhabitants were flying from Batavia. We know that the whole country as far as this place is in imminent danger. It is full of men who would defend it but they are destitute of arms and ammunition. One thousand horsemen would burn Canandaigua and return with little loss. The event rests only in the counsels of the all-wise Governor of Worlds.

(From Ketchum's History of Buffalo, Vol. II., p. 386.)

From the Manlius Times, January 4th, 1814.

BUFFALO BURNED.

This distressing occurrence, which has been anticipated ever since Niagara was taken by the enemy, took place last Thursday forenoon. We have seen no official account of this affair but have conversed with the express, Mr. Landon, who passed through this village on Saturday morning last, and since with several gentlemen who have left Williamsville since that time, from whom we have obtained the following particulars:

On Thursday morning about one o'clock it was discovered that a detachment of the enemy had landed just below the Navy Yard, about a mile from Black Rock. A skirmish immediately commenced with our Indians and a body of militia who were stationed there as a corps of observation, which lasted several hours. Towards daylight a body of regulars, from eight hundred to one thousand, with cannon, etc., landed at the mouth of Buffalo Creek, directly above the village, when by a signal made the party below commenced a violent attack on the advance. Our men, finding themselves attacked on both flanks, immediately retreated, or rather fled through the woods on to the road near Major Miller's. Here General Hall rallied them and conducted them towards Buffalo, where they met the enemy and considerable hard fighting took place. But what availed courage or numbers. Our troops were not organized—had no cannon. Their muskets could not be depended on and few had but four rounds of ammunition when they took the field. They were soon put to flight. It is said that General Hall continued upon the field until he was almost entirely deserted, when he was obliged to retire. The village was then burnt, with the exception of a few houses which are probably destroyed before this time. The village of Black Rock is also destroyed. The enemy are said to be in the vicinity of Black Rock. The inhabitants are scattered in every direction. Most of them have come off to Williamsville, eleven miles this side of Buffalo, where our force is assembled. No particulars of our loss in this affair have been received, but it is believed to be considerable. Amongst the slain is Colonel Boughton of the Ontario Dragoons.

A gentleman in high standing in the quartermaster's department informs that the loss the United States must have sustained in the capture of Niagara cannot be less than two million five hundred thousand dollars. There were in the fort when taken ten thousand stand of arms and two hundred and seventy tierces of clothing.

BATAVIA, January 8th, 1814.

To the want of discipline, of subordination and proper concert is to be attributed the fate of Buffalo and Black Rock. Our forces were not only sufficient to have repelled but to have captured the invaders. Our frontier from Buffalo to Niagara now presents one continued scene of ruin. The buildings that now remain in Buffalo are the jail, (built of stone,) and a small wooden dwelling belonging to the widow St. John, who had the address to appease the ferocity of the enemy so far as to remain in her house uninjured.

Since our last publication the enemy have evacuated Black Rock. Their last detachment crossed the river on Tuesday, since which time the alarm so generally spread through this section has in a great measure abated, and a degree of calmness succeeded that of bustle and confusion. Previous to evacuating Black Rock the British fired every building in that place but three. Two of these, a stone dwelling house belonging to Peter B. Porter, and a storehouse on the bank of the river, were blown up by a quantity of powder placed in them for that purpose. A log house, in which some women and children had taken refuge, was suffered to remain. This is an act of humanity in the enemy not to be expected after the barbarous assassination of about twenty of our wounded, who had been carried into a barn near that place. We have not been able to procure a list of the names of our men who have been made prisoners. Of the killed thirty-three have been found, but being stripped of their clothing few of them have been recognized. This number, together with the wounded said to be inhumanly butchered at the Rock, swells the list of killed to upwards of fifty.

The schooners Ariel, Little Belt, Chippawa and sloop Trippe, lying near Buffalo Creek, fell into the enemy's hands and are probably destroyed.

(From Ketchum's History of Buffalo, Vol. II., p. 387.)

From the United States Gazette of Philadelphia, 17th January, 1814.

Extract of a letter from an American officer in the Northern army to his friend in the city, dated at Canandaigua, January 7th, 1814:

I was slightly wounded in the battle of Buffalo in endeavoring to rally the militia. Our loss is about 40 killed, 60 or 70 wounded and 100 prisoners. The loss of the British was 60 killed, upwards of 100 wounded, and 8 or 10 prisoners. Their force consisted of the Royal Scots Regiment, (which suffered most,) 89th, 100th, the remains of the 41st and one company of the 8th or King's Regiment. The number of their Indians I do not know. Our force was about 2,200 including militia, and 70 Indians.

(File in Philadelphia Library.)

From the New York Evening Post, January 19th, 1814.

CANANDAIGUA, January 11.

AFFAIRS ON THE NIAGARA.

The enemy recrossed into Canada on Saturday, the 1st inst., having completed the work of destruction in a way rather more satisfactory to themselves than to us. They left no buildings standing at Black Rock and Buffalo except they are a blacksmith's shop, used as an armory, and a small house of a Mrs. St. John. They came out of Buffalo about two miles and burnt all as far as the brick house of Mr. W. Hodge inclusive, in which were 6 or 8,000 dollars worth of goods that were also lost.

Of the Americans killed at Black Rock the bodies of 35 have been found. The enemy have also in their possession 69 prisoners. A list of their names we have not room to publish in this paper. It may be seen at this office.

The schooners Ariel, Little Belt, Chippawa and sloop Trippe, lying near Buffalo Creek, fell into the enemy's hands and are probably destroyed.

The tavern house of Major Miller at Cold Springs and the house of Lieut.-Colonel Granger at 4 Mile Creek are not burnt as reported.

The conduct of a portion of our militia during the awful scenes at Buffalo is reported as more rapacious than that of the enemy, (excepting perhaps the British Indians.) Many of them have been seen engaged in plundering our unfortunate sufferers of what the enemy did not take.

Lieut.-Colonel Harvey to Major T. G. Simons.

1st January, 1814.

Dear Major,—

I enclose a requisition for the articles of clothing, etc., required for the American prisoners of war. You will get them either at Mr. Dickson's at Queenston or at Fort Niagara.

It is the General's wish that every attention in your power should be paid to the wants and comfort of the prisoners: at the same time they must be vigilantly guarded.

(Canadian Archives, Q. 311, p. 215.)

Memorial of Colonel Titus Geer Simons.

To His Excellency Sir Peregrine Maitland, K. C. B., Lieutenant Governor of the Province of Upper Canada, and Major General commanding His Majesty's forces therein:

The Memorial of Colonel Titus Geer Simons, now commanding the Second Regiment of Gore Militia,

Most respectfully sheweth:—

That Your Excellency's Memorialist, during the campaign of 1812, (the commencement of the late war with the United States of America,) served as major and commanded the flank companies and the Second Regiment of York Militia on the Niagara frontier, as Your Excellency will perceive by the Adjutant General's certificate, marked No. 1.

That in March, 1813, he received orders to recruit for a majority in the Incorporated Militia, and completed his quota of men forthwith, as the document marked 2 will shew to Your Excellency, and he served with that battalion until June, 1814, when he rejoined his former regiment, the 2nd York Militia.

To the notes and General Orders from the Major General commanding, from Lieut.-Colonel Harvey, Deputy Adjutant General of the forces, and from other officers, marked 3, 4, 5, 6 and 7, your Memorialist respectfully begs leave to refer Your Excellency for some account of his services in the year 1813, and to which he begs leave to add that he aided in the capture of the American Fort Niagara and was consulted relative thereto before the division under the command of Lieut.-Colonel Murray left Burlington on that expedition, as Your Excellency will perceive by referring to the document marked 8.

Your Memorialist commanded all the volunteer armed militia in the successful attack on Black Rock and Buffalo in December under Lieutenant General Drummond and Major-General Riall. He adds

District Orders Nos. 9 and 10 to shew it, and on the 1st January, 1814, he left Black Rock with 279 prisoners for York, as Your Excellency will perceive by Colonel Harvey's letter, marked 11.

That he unceasingly experienced the favorable and valuable attention of Lieut.-Colonel Harvey, now Sir John Harvey, the Deputy Adjutant General in Upper Canada, and respectfully begs leave to refer Your Excellency to document No. 13.

Your Excellency's Memorialist annexes also an extract of the District General Order marked 12, issued by Sir George Prevost and Lieutenant General Drummond on occasion of the victory at Lundy's Lane on the 25th July, 1814, by which it will be partly seen how the regiment under his command suffered in that action, and in which he received a severe wound from a grape shot passing thro' his right arm near the shoulder, which has deprived him of the use of it, and for which he has since received a pension of two hundred pounds per annum.

But Your Excellency's Memorialist being now informed that under these circumstances he is by His Royal Highness the Prince Regent's orders entitled to the pension of a major commanding, he therefore humbly prays that Your Excellency will be pleased to recommend him to the favorable consideration of His Majesty's Government for the pension of a major commanding, and Your Excellency's Memorialist, as in duty bound, will ever pray.

TITUS G. SIMONS,
Flamboro West.

25th September, 1826.

(Canadian Archives, Q. 234-1, pp. 201-4.)

From "A Statement of the Services of Major General Richard Say Armstrong, R. A."

19th December, 1813. Assault and Capture of Fort Niagara, State of New York. The assaulting force was 580 men; the American garrison 429; 65 of the enemy killed; 14 officers, 12 sergeants and 318 rank and file taken prisoners, including wounded. About 20 made their escape over the walls of the fort. We captured 27 pieces of ordnance and 3,000 stand of arms. On 25th December, 1813, I was sent with two guns to destroy two of the enemy's vessels under Black Rock, and forced them to run ashore. On 27th December Lieut. Gen. Drummond moved up to the ferry opposite Black Rock with a force of 1,300 men under Major General Riall. On the night of the 30th the troops crossed the Niagara River under cover of the fire of the artillery under Captain Bridge, and as soon as their landing was effected we likewise crossed. The enemy's force was from 2,000 to 2,500 men. They fled from Black Rock to the town of Buffalo, about 2½ miles distant. We followed in close pursuit. The enemy again fled, followed by all the inhabitants of Buffalo. I received orders from General Riall to burn the town of Buffalo in retaliation for the burning of Newark, which, with one gun detachment, I did, with the exception of one detached house which we left standing because there was a female in it badly wounded, who must have perished if she had been removed out into the snow, and who I afterwards had the satisfaction of hearing had recovered, although she had been shot through the body and tomahawked in the head by an Indian. The United States ships of war "Chippewa," "Little Belt" and "Trippe" were burned by the infantry. On our return to Black Rock I was ordered to burn it, which was done. We took 130 prisoners and six guns. Our killed, wounded and missing, 113.

From the National Intelligencer of Washington, D. C., January 27th, 1814.

Extract of a letter from Colonel John McMahon, dated at Cattaraugus, 2nd January, 1814, to Colonel J. C. Wallace at Erie, Pa.

I am under the necessity of asking your assistance in men and ammunition: if it is possible to furnish us with 3000 cartridges or powder and lead we can make them. I need not give you a detail of what has taken place, as you must have been informed of it before this. I am rallying that part of my regiment that retreated this course at this place and will collect the remainder as soon as possible. At 8 o'clock yesterday I left the beach 12 miles this side of Buffalo.

The fire around where Buffalo stood was kindled afresh. Yesterday 100 Indian warriors tendered their services. They are in want of ammunition. The families are all moving off below Cattaraugus. I have seen a number of women and children running away half naked.

I cannot give you a correct account of the number of the enemy, but I believe they do not exceed 1,100 or 1,200. Our force at Buffalo previous to the attack consisted of about 2,000. I think not more than 400 were in the action.

The day previous to the attack an American prisoner made his escape and informed us that Black Rock would certainly be attacked that night, and that he knew and had heard of a plan to visit Presqu' Isle in the following manner:—

Whenever the ice would admit 100 sleighs, each carrying 6 men, to start and reach that place in one night, burn the vessels and town, if they should sacrifice their whole force. The first part of this information has come to pass. I hope the latter will fail.

[From the Northern Centinel.]

From the National Intelligencer, Washington, D. C., February 8th, 1814.

Killed at Black Rock in the battle of the 30th ult., Col. Seymour Boughton, aged 44. His remains have been removed to his late residence in Avon and interred. Col. Boughton was much esteemed by numerous acquaintances for his integrity and amiable character and he has ended his life in defence of his country.

On the 1st inst. (Jan., 1814,) in a skirmish with the British near Buffalo, Joshua B. Totman, formerly of Colrain, Mass., lieutenant and adjutant in Col. Willcocks' corps of volunteers. He was brave and worthy.

At Schlosser on the 21st ult., fighting in defence of his country, John M. Lowe, Esq., 1st lieutenant in the 23rd United States Infantry.

From the Ontario Messenger of January 25th, 1814.

Taken by the British in the battle of Black Rock and belonging to the the militia of the State of New York, under the command of Major-General Hall. Besides those named below there are a number of others in the hands of the enemy, among them Col. C. Chapin, of Buffalo.

Lieut.-Colonel Peregrine Gardner, (flesh wound in the thigh), Captain J. Rowley, Ensign Ebenezer Stewart, Lieut. John Lusk, Reuben Pierce, Eli Shattuck, John Putnam, S. Fowler, John Armsden, John Elgor of Bloomfield, Lieut. John Campbell, Asa Woodford, Abner Kitray, John Conant, Samuel Clark, John Richardson, Amos Thompson, David Palmer, Socrates Swift, wounded in the belly; Benjamin Barrett, wounded in the body, of Livonia; Wm. Lyon of Honeoye, Lazarus Church, Dennis Frost, wounded in the shoulder; Wm. Miller, wounded in the cheek; Jared Wheedon, Seth Chapin, Anson Merry, Samuel Burgess of Avon, Jacob L. Loomis, Wm. Hickox of Canandaigua, Hezekiah Parmalee of Victor, Jesse Warren, wounded in the thigh, of Phelps; Jabez Smith, wounded in the thigh, of Ontario County; Almon H. Millard, aid de camp to Brigadier General Hopkins; Robert McKay, Levi Boughton, Wm. Martin, Thos. Grant, wounded in thigh, badly; Wanton Brownell, wounded in hip; Chester Narramorn of Caledonia, Levi Farnum, Willis Buel, Wm. G. Hathaway of Leroy, James Lyon, Joel Allen, Sylvester Blodgett, Asahel Martin, Apollo Fordham, Anson Bristol, Levi Wright of Batavia; Hiram Wilcox, Matthew Park, Sergt. Lodowick Champlin, Jr., Jacob Jackson, flesh wounds in both thighs, of Sheldon, Genesee County; Ensign Wm. Martin of Ellicott, Wm. Hutchinson, Holden Allen of Black Rock, George Stow, Daniel Perry, wounded in head, of Buffalo; Benjamin Russell, Henry Downing, John Harris of Clarence, Niagara County; Friend Johnson, Oliver Hitson of Chautauqua, Daniel G. Gould, Daniel S. Cole of Pomfret, Chautauqua County.

PROCLAMATION.

By His Excellency Sir George Prevost, Governor General and Commander-in-Chief over His Majesty's North American Provinces.

A PROCLAMATION.

It having been represented to His Excellency the Commander of the Forces that in consequence of the adoption by the Government of the United States of the novel and unjustifiable principle of making prisoners of war and paroling the unarmed and peaceable citizens of this Province, several subjects of His Majesty have under such circumstances been deterred from accepting employment in their different callings as mechanics or otherwise, or from aiding in any other manner the public service, under an apprehension of exposing themselves to the resentment of the enemy for having violated their parole, His Excellency takes this public opportunity of declaring that such a principle is not sanctioned by the usages of war amongst civilized nations and that no parole thus extorted from peaceable citizens not taken in arms can be considered as binding upon them or as exempting them from military or other duties which they may be called upon to perform.

The only legitimate objects of capture on land during war as recognized by the laws of nations are those who are actually engaged in military service or who are found with arms in their hands. Beyond these two descriptions of persons it has never been the practice of modern nations of Europe to consider any other as liable to be carried away as prisoners of war or subject to be paroled.

It was reserved for America, who has last assumed a rank among the nations and for those acting under its authority, unnecessarily to increase the calamities of war by making peaceable and unoffending citizens subject to its rigors and by exacting from them engagements, the nature of which is to preclude them from gaining their subsistance by their honest and ordinary callings if exercised in support of the government which protects them. In order to remove from the minds of such persons who, having fallen into the power of the enemy, have been obliged to enter into engagements of this nature all apprehension with regard to the consequences of violating them His Excellency deems it necessary thus publicly to declare that a parole, even lawfully taken, can only extend to the military service in arms, either in the garrison or in the field, of the persons giving it, and cannot preclude them from performing their ordinary duties as subjects or from the exercise of their usual civil occupations. And His Excellency here further declares that should the enemy still persist to act upon the unjust principle before mentioned and should any persons (who have been paroled as aforesaid and shall again fall into the hands of the enemy) be treated with severity in consequence of of their having been employed in the public service in any other manner he will not fail immediately to avail himself of the means within his power of removing from the American frontier such of their citizens as shall be within his reach and of retaliating upon them all the severity and rigor which shall have been practiced towards any of His Majesty's subjects under the foregoing circumstances.

His Excellency at the same time feels it incumbent to declare that as he has strong reasons to believe that in several instances the paroles thus taken have been sought for by the persons as giving them the means of evading their militia and other duties and as others, notwithstanding the present declaration, may from similar or worse motives be induced to withhold their aid in carrying on public works, His Excellency will feel himself compelled forthwith to send all such useless and disaffected characters out of the country to the enemy, to whom they consider themselves as belonging as prisoners of war, there to remain as such until regularly exchanged.

Given under my hand and seal at arms, at Kingston, this fourth day of September, one thousand eight hundred and thirteen.

GEO. PREVOST,
Commander of the Forces.
By His Excellency's command,
E. B. BRENTON.

Certificate by Major-General Hall.

This may certify that Cyrenius Chapin of Buffalo was, on the twenty-fifth and up to the thirtieth of December, 1813, inclusive, in the service of the United States on the Niagara Frontier, commanding a corps of volunteer infantry, containing 136 men, as per return, raised in and about Buffalo. That the said Chapin was acting as Lieutenant-Colonel, having a short time previous been brevetted to that rank by Major-General Wilkinson, by the hands of General McClure, under which appointment he acted on the thirtieth December, 1813, and was in the action opposing the British and Ind-

ians at their crossing at Black Rock, on the aforesaid 30th of December, 1813.   A. HALL,
Lately Major-General, New York Militia,
and commanding on the Niagara Frontier at that time.
[Original in Library of the Buffalo Historical Society.]

Memorandum of Killed and Taken Prisoners at Black Rock, 30th December, 1813.

	Killed	Taken Prisoners
Lt.-Col. Boughton's Regt.	2	2
Lt.-Col. Blakesley's Regt.	11	32
Lt.-Col. Churchill's Regt.	8	17
Lt.-Col. Warren's Regt.	7	2
Captain Seeley's Company	3	
	31	51
Lt.-Col. McMahon	1	2

[Original in Library of the Buffalo Historical Society.]

Militia General Order.

HEADQUARTERS, ST. DAVIDS, 5th January, 1814.

His Honor Lieutenant-General Drummond is pleased to confer on Thomas Dickson, Esq., the rank of Lieutenant-Colonel of militia.

Lieutenant-Colonel Dickson will be pleased to take charge of the 2nd Regiment Lincoln Militia, during the absence of Lieutenant-Colonel Clark.

By order of His Honor the President.
J. HARVEY, Lt.-Col.,
Deputy Adjt. Genl. of the Forces.

General Order.

ADJUTANT GENERAL'S OFFICE,
HEADQUARTERS, QUEBEC, 6th January, 1814.

His Excellency the Commander of the Forces has received a report from Lieutenant-General Drummond, communicating the report of Captain Stewart of the Royal Scots, of a spirited and judicious attack made by Lieutenant Medcalf, in command of a party of militia, consisting of 25 men, at McCrae's house on the river Thames, by which a party of the enemy, consisting of three officers and thirty-eight soldiers of the 26th United States Regiment, were surprised and taken prisoners. Four of the enemy were wounded, but none of Lieut. Medcalf's party received any injury. The prisoners have been brought in.

E. BAYNES, Adj. General, N. A.

Major-General Hall to Governor Tompkins.

HEADQUARTERS, NIAGARA FRONTIER, Jan. 6th, 1814.

DEAR SIR:—

The confusion into which everything was thrown by the events of the 30th December and the imperious necessity of taking precautionary measures against the advance of the enemy, put it out of my power to furnish at an earlier period a detailed account of the operations on this frontier during my hitherto unfortunate and embarrassing command. Add to this the extreme difficulty of collecting facts relative to our loss, since the forces under my command were of that multiform description which they necessarily were, being composed almost wholly of volunteer militia and exempts hastily and confusedly assembled in the moment of alarm and dissipated by the events of the battle.

The storming of Fort Niagara and the burning of Lewiston presaging further devastation, threw the whole country into the most violent agitation. On the moment and without any previous preparation I hastened to Batavia with a view to take such measures as might be within my power to repel the enemy and protect the frontier. I hastily collected from the militia and volunteers of Genesee County and the brigade of General Wadsworth in Ontario, a considerable force, but generally deficient in arms and ammunition, and the necessary conveniences of a camp.

In the evening of the 22nd December General McClure with the regulars under command of Major Riddle arrived in Batavia and on the morning of the 23rd signified by letter his desire that I would take the command during the moment of general alarm. I accordingly proceeded to organize in the best manner in my power the forces then at Batavia, and with the arms and ammunition collected from different sections of the country and what little could be procured from the arsenals at Canandaigua and Batavia, I was enabled to get under march on the 25th, for Lewiston, a body of infantry about 150 strong, under Lieutenant-Colonel Lawrence, supported by one company of cavalry under command of Captain Marvin, with orders to proceed to join a corps of militia, said to be 200 men under command of Lieut.-Colonel Achinson, which was stationed at Forsyth's, on the Ridge Road, 15 miles east of Lewiston, to collect and save all the ammunition in his power, which had been moved from the arsenal at Lewiston and was then dispersed on the road and in different parts of the country, and with instructions to act as circumstances and the nature of his force would permit against the enemy, and, if practicable, to effect a junction with the main force at Buffalo, by the way of Manchester, Schlosser, and thence up the river to Black Rock, leaving as a reserve the corps under Colonel Achinson at the station near Lewiston. I then ordered the remainder of the troops to Buffalo, with the exception of the regular forces, over whom I assumed no command. On the morning of the 25th I proceeded to Buffalo, leaving General McClure at Batavia with instructions to organize such detachments of volunteers as might arrive, and direct their march for Buffalo. I arrived in Buffalo on the morning of the 26th and there found a considerable body of irregular troops of various descriptions, disorganized and confused. Everything wore the appearance of consternation and dismay. On the same day I issued an order to the several commandants for a return of the number of effective men under their command and an order to Captain Camp, Assistant Deputy Quartermaster General, for a return of the ordnance and ordnance stores in the quartermaster's department, a copy of which return I have heretofore had the honor to forward Your Excellency and which sufficiently exhibits the destitute condition of that department. On the 27th I ordered a review of all troops under my command at Buffalo and Black Rock, when I found my force to be as follows:—

At Buffalo, Lieut.-Colonel Boughton, of the cavalry and mounted volunteers, 129; Lieut.-Colonel Blakesley, of the Ontario exempts and volunteers, 433; Lieut.-Colonel Chapin, of the Buffalo militia, 136; Lieut.-Colonel Mallory, of the Canadian volunteers, 97; Major Adams, of the Genesee militia, 382. At the Rock were stationed, under the command of Brigadier General Hopkins, 382 effective men, composed of the corps commanded by Lieut.-Colonel Warren and Lieut.-Colonel Churchill, exclusive of a body of 37 mounted infantry, under command of Captain Ransom, 83 Indians, under command of Lieut.-Colonel Granger, and one piece of field artillery, a six pounder, and 25 men commanded by Lieut. Seeley, making my aggregate force on the 27th to be 1,711 men. Add to this a regiment of Chautauqua militia, under the command of Lieut.-Colonel McMahon, which arrived at Buffalo on the 29th, about 300, swells my force to 2,011, which was reduced on the morning of the alarm to less than 1,200, and so deficient were my supplies of ammunition that a greater part of the cartridges of Lieut.-Colonel McMahon's regiment were made and distributed after they were paraded on the morning of the battle.

The movements of the enemy already indicated their intention of attacking the village of Buffalo or Black Rock, which left me not a moment from the arduous duty of preparing the most effective means in my power of meeting the enemy with the crude force under my command. On the 28th I was so fortunate as to procure information as to the enemy's movements, from a citizen who made his escape from Canada, as to leave me no doubt as to his intentions.

In the evening of the 29th, at about 12 o'clock, I received information that our horse patrol had been fired on a short distance below Conjockatie's Creek, and one mile below Black Rock. Lieut. Boughton, an enterprising and brave officer, had his horse shot under him. The enemy advanced and took possession of the Sailors' Battery, near Conjockatie's Creek. The troops were immediately paraded and stood by their arms. I was yet uncertain as to what point the enemy would attack me, the darkness of the night was not favorable for making observations. I was apprehensive the enemy designed to make a feigned attack below Black Rock, for the purpose of drawing off my force from the village of Buffalo, preparatory to landing above the village, intending thereby to take it by surprise. At the same time being anxious to anticipate the enemy's landing and meet them at the water's edge, I gave orders that the troops at the Rock, commanded by Colonels Warren and Churchill, (General Hopkins being at that time absent from camp,) attack the enemy and endeavor to dislodge them from the battery and drive them to their boats. The attempt failed through the confusion the militia were thrown into at the first fire of the enemy and the darkness of the night. They were dispersed and not again embodied under their proper officers through the day. I then ordered the corps under Major Adams and the corps under Colonel Chapin to make the attack. This was attended with no better effect. The men were thrown into confusion by the enemy's fire and after skirmishing a short time, fled and were not again embodied during the day. I then ordered the corps under command of Colonel Blakeslee to advance to the attack, and at the same time I put the remainder of my troops in motion for the same point and proceeded by the hill road to Black Rock. On approaching the village of Black Rock, I discovered a detachment of the enemy's boats crossing to our shore and bending their course to the rear of General Porter's house. The day was now beginning to dawn. I immediately countermanded the order given to Colonel Blakeslee to attack the enemy's left and directed him to form and attack the enemy's centre at the water's edge.

I now became satisfied as to the disposition of the enemy and their object, which I ascertained to be as follows:—

Their left wing, composed of about 800 regular troops and the Incorporated Militia and 150 or 200 Indians, were disposed below Conjockatie's Creek and had been landed under cover of the night. With this force the enemy designed to cover their left, outflank our right, and cut off our retreat by the woods. With their centre, consisting of about 400 Royal Scots, commanded by Colonel Gordon, the battle was commenced. Their right, which was purposely weak, was landed near our main battery under cover of a high bank and was merely intended to divert our force from the principal attack. The whole, under the command of Lieut.-General Drummond, conducted to the attack by Major General Riall. I therefore ordered the enemy's left wing, which was discovered to be wheeling upon our right, to be attacked by the Indians, under command of Lieut.-Colonel Granger, and the Canadian Volunteers, under command of Col. Mallory, at the same time I posted the regiment under command of Col. McMahon, at the battery, as a reserve, to act as emergencies should require. The attack was commenced by a fire from our six-pounder under Lieut. Seeley, below General Porter's house, and one 24 and two 12-pounders at the battery, under command of Lieut. Farnum of the 21st United States Infantry, acting as a volunteer. At the same time the enemy opened a heavy fire from the batteries on the other side of the river, of shells, spherical shot, and ball. The regiment under command of Colonel Blakeslee, about 400 strong, were regularly in the line, together with detached bodies from other corps, amounting, according to the best estimate I can make, in all about 600 men. These few but brave men commenced the attack with musketry upon the enemy in their boats and poured upon them a most destructive fire. Every inch of ground was disputed with the steady coolness of veterans and at the expense of many valuable lives. Their bravery at the same time it casts a lustre over their names reflects equal disgrace on those who fled at the first appearance of danger, and who neither entreaties nor threats could turn back to the support of their commanders. Perceiving that the Indians, on whom I had relied for attacking the enemy's flank, were offering no assistance, and that our right was endangered by the enemy's left, I gave directions for the reserve under Colonel McMahon to attack the enemy in flank, but terror had dissipated this corps and but few of them could be rallied by their officers and brought to the attack. Of this corps there are some who merit well of their country, but more who covered themselves with disgrace. The defection of the

Indians and of my reserve, and the loss of the services of the cavalry and mounted men, by reason of the nature of the ground on which they must act, left the forces engaged exposed to veteran and highly disciplined troops, overwhelmed by numbers and nearly surrounded, a retreat became necessary to their safety, which was accordingly made. I then made every effort to rally the troops, with a view to renew the attack on the enemy's columns on their approach to the village of Buffalo. But every effort proved ineffectual and experience proves that with militia retreat becomes a flight, and, a battle once ended, the army is dissipated. Deserted by my principal force, I fell back that night to 11 Mile Creek and was forced to leave the flourishing villages of Black Rock and Buffalo a prey to the enemy, which they have pillaged and laid in ashes. At the 11 Mile Creek I collected between 200 and 300 who remained faithful to their country; with those I preserved the best show of defence in my power, to cover the flying inhabitants and check the advance of the enemy. The enemy have gained but little plunder from the public stores. The chief loss has fallen upon individual sufferers. Eight pieces of artillery fell into the hands of the enemy, of which but one was mounted on a travelling carriage. What little remained of the public stores capable of being removed is preserved through the exertions of Captain Camp of the quartermaster's department, whose bravery is only equalled by his zeal for the public service. It is not in my power to give a particular account of our loss in killed and wounded, as the wounded were generally got off by their friends and taken to their houses, and our dead mostly buried by the enemy. But from the best information I can collect, our loss is about 30 killed and perhaps 40 wounded. In prisoners our loss is ascertained to be 69, twelve of whom are wounded. The enemy's loss must be much greater, as many were killed in their boats before landing. Their loss may reasonably be presumed in killed and wounded at not less than 200. Lieut.-Colonel Boughton of the light dragoons is among the slain. He was a good officer and a valuable citizen. I regret that it is not in my power to do justice to all who were engaged on this day. The veteran Blakeslee and his corps were pre-eminently distinguished. There were of the broken remains of other corps many officers and soldiers whose bravery and conduct merits my warmest praise, but having fought irregularly and in detachments I cannot designate them to do them that justice they deserve. The good conduct of Lieut. Seeley and Lieut. Farnum, who had charge of the artillery, was particularly noticed. The cavalry under Colonel Boughton, and mounted volunteers under Major Warren receive my thanks for their prompt obedience of orders and the valuable services rendered in the fatiguing duties of patroling, and it is a matter of regret that the nature of the ground on which we contended deprived me of that support which I might confidently expect of their bravery. To Lieut. Frazer of the United States Infantry I tender my thanks for the valuable services he rendered me as one of my staff. To my two aides de camp, Majors Hosmer and Norton, I cannot withhold my warmest thanks for their cool deliberate bravery and alacrity with which they executed my orders from the first movements of the troops in the morning to the close of the day.

(Tompkins Papers, Vol. IX., pp. 21-6. New York State Library.)

James Wadsworth to Governor Tompkins.

GENESEO, January 6, 1814.

SIR,—

When I heard that General Hall had removed his headquarters to Batavia and that 11 Mile Creek was abandoned, I thought it high time to rally. I sent out circulars to put in motion a thousand men, started myself, met General Hall returning to Bloomfield. He thought the frontiers were safe and disapproved of volunteers going on irregularly. The convictions of my mind were very different, but I instantly acquiesced and sent expresses to stop the volunteers. I continued on myself.

The enemy recrossed the Niagara River Saturday and Sunday except about sixty men, who were sent to burn all before them between Black Rock and Lewiston. Dr. Brown, who went with a flag to dress our wounded, was informed that the force which crossed the river consisted of six hundred regulars and 50 Indians.

There are about 200 men at 11 Mile Creek and about the same number at Batavia. Colonels Davis and Brooks are good citizens but feeble men. Major Mallory, (I think his name is,) of the Canada Volunteers, being more efficient, has in effect the command of our frontier. In fact the consternation of the militia is so great that they cannot be reduced to tolerable (order) for some time. A hundred regulars and fifty Indians would now march to Batavia without serious opposition. The frontier is now dependent for its safety on the clemency of the English, Butler's Rangers and the Indians.

General Hall is detaching and organizing fifteen hundred militia. You will be deceived if you expect any effective service from them. General McClure (who is a mere coxcomb) by his bad management and the disaster at Buffalo, has spread fright and consternation among all ranks, broken down the ardor and spirit of the militia, and it will require some time for it to recover. The frontier will remain defenceless until a regiment of regulars is sent on.

I have just returned much fatigued and write this sketch in haste. I deemed it essential you should be apprized of the real situation of the frontier, this is my apology for addressing (you.) I beg you to consider this letter as confidential and not to be communicated to any person. Most of the inhabitants have left Batavia. The population west of Batavia are flying in all directions in great distress.

(Tompkins' Papers, Vol. IX., pp. 33-4. New York State Library.)

General Order.

HEADQUARTERS, BATAVIA, Jan. 6th, 1814.

The A. D. Q. Master-General is directed to cause forty thousand rations of bread and meat to be transported from Batavia and deposited at or near Forsyth's, on the Ridge Road, for the use of the troops in that quarter.

By order of A. HALL, M. Gen'l.

(Publications of the Buffalo Historical Society, Vol. V., p. 37.)

Sir George Prevost to Earl Bathurst.

No. 121.   HEADQUARTERS, QUEBEC, 6th January, 1814.

MY LORD,—

Having ascertained the enemy's force at Forts George and Niagara and on that frontier to have been considerably reduced for the purpose of strengthening the division of the American army under Major-General Wilkinson, now acting against Lower Canada, I directed Lieut.-General Drummond, on the 3rd of last month, to hold the right division of the army in the Canadas, placed under the immediate command of Major-General Riall, in so perfect a state of preparation, as to be enabled to act with promptitude when required to take advantage of the weakness or negligence of the enemy, and I feel a high satisfaction in having the honor of transmitting to Your Lordship the Lieut.-General's letters, containing the reports of the capture of Fort Niagara on the morning of the 19th of December, and of the flight of the enemy's force from Lewiston on the approach of the corps commanded by Major-General Riall.

The arrangements of Lieut.-General Drummond and the brilliant manner in which they were executed, have excited my warmest applause and afford me infinite satisfaction in the communication I now make to Your Lordship.

I request to call the gracious consideration of His Royal Highness the Prince Regent to the various officers who have distinguished themselves on the occasion, more especially to Colonel Murray, who has availed himself of this favorable opportunity to confirm my opinion of his zeal, intelligence and military talents.

After the dispersion of the enemy's force at Lewiston and the destruction of that village, Major-General Riall's brigade proceeded forward towards Black Rock and Buffalo, and on its march obtained possession, after a feeble resistance, of the mills and ropewalk of General Porter, one of the principal contractors for the supply of the American army, which were destroyed.

On this occasion an American officer and a few privates were killed, and one officer and eleven privates taken prisoners, but not a British soldier suffered.

The bridge over the Tonawanda Creek having been destroyed by the enemy, the progress of Major-General Riall's brigade has been impeded until the arrival of a sufficient number of boats at Chippawa, to enable the troops intended to co-operate with it in the destruction of the vessels and stores at Buffalo to cross the river. When the last accounts left Fort George, the weather had not then become too severe to render the movement impracticable. I therefore hope to be able to report its success to Your Lordship by the next opportunity, as the enemy appears in great consternation, and without plan or organization for defence.

Having been under the necessity of employing the Western Indians, who had retreated with General Procter from Amherstburg, as well as those inhabiting near the Niagara Frontier, in conjunction with the force acting under Major-General Riall, I have not failed strongly to enjoin upon Lieutenant-General Drummond to restrain by every means in his power any excesses or cruelties on their part which might give just cause of complaint to the American Government or attach disgrace to His Majesty's arms.

The enemy set an example in his retreat from Fort George, by firing the town of Newark, that has produced calamitous consequences to himself since the theatre of war has been transferred to his own territory.

Painful is such retribution, to those who execute it. I have felt the authority most repugnant, and I sincerely hope it may not again be excited.

I have sent my aide de camp, Captain Cochrane, overland to Halifax as the bearer of my despatches to Your Lordship. He carries with him a stand of colors taken in the fort of Niagara, to be laid at the feet of His Royal Highness the Prince Regent, and I beg leave to refer Your Lordship to him for such information as you may require respecting this command.

(Canadian Archives, Q. 127, pp. 9-13.)

General Order.

HEADQUARTERS, NIAGARA FRONTIER, Jan'y 7th, 1814.

A flag is ordered to proceed by the way of the new State road, south of Batavia, to Buffalo and Black Rock, and there to cross to the Canada shore, for the purpose of landing in Canada Wm. Dickson, Esquire, barrister-at-law; Joseph Edwards, Esquire, justice of the peace; William Ross of the commissariat department; John Baldwin, merchant; and John Crooks, merchant, prisoners, under safe conduct on their parole. Lieut.-Colonel Walter Grieve of the N. Y. S. Artillery, and Major James Ganson, are assigned to bear the flag.

By order of MAJOR-GENERAL HALL.
GEO. HOSMER, A. D. C.

(Publications of the Buffalo Historical Society, Vol. V., pp. 37-8.)

Major-General De Rottenburg to the Military Secretary.

KINGSTON, 7th January, 1814.

SIR,—

I have the honor to acknowledge the receipt of your letter of the 31st ultimo, covering a plan of Sackett's Harbor, which, in obedience to the directions of His Excellency the Commander of the Forces, I shall deliver over either to Lieutenant-General Drummond, or to the general officer who may relieve me before his arrival.

Our beef contractor, who has just returned from Albany, informs me that about ten days ago a thousand men have been detached from Sackett's Harbor to reinforce the enemy's position at Salmon River, where they apprehended an attack. This intelligence has been communicated to the officers commanding at Cornwall and Coteau du Lac. Two vessels are on the stocks at Sackett's, equal in size to the Pike and Madison. I have sent to Sackett's a confidential man from here, and another from Cornwall.

(Canadian Archives, C. 682, pp. 14-5.)

Major-General Hall to Governor Tompkins.

BLOOMFIELD, January 7th, 1814.

SIR,—

Enclosed is a report of the action at Black Rock, fought on the 30th December, ulto. Viewing the singular and extraordinary situation in which I was placed, I could not, in justice to myself and my volunteers, refrain from giving a detailed account of our situation previous to the engagement. We were in want of everything, and I was but three days in Buffalo before the action, a time too short to make much preparation. I therefore took the liberty to make the report more lengthy than I would have done under other circumstances.

I have ordered out 1,700 infantry since receiving Your Excellency's letter of the 23rd ulto. They will march to 11 Mile Creek and towards Lewiston as soon as possible. The arms, &c., you mentioned in your letter, have not yet arrived at Canandaigua, and unless an additional supply arrives we shall not be able to arm the detachment.

The enemy have recrossed the river, but the inhabitants west of Batavia are still alarmed. It will be impossible for me to guard and protect our western frontier, so various will be the duties to be performed, without public funds, and at present I have none at command. Your Excellency will see the propriety of making some arangement in that respect.

(Tompkins' Papers, Vol. IX., pp. 20-1. New York State Library.)

Major-General Wilkinson to the Secretary of War.

MALONE, Friday morning, Jan. 7th, 1814.

SIR,—

The mail route by Burlington has become dilatory and uncertain. I therefore send this to Utica by express to advise you that we are still safe from the enemy, and I understand snug from the weather, but our troops die at the French Mills owing, as all ranks avow, to the bad quality of the flour, medicines and hospital stores.

This circumstance and the precarious dependence to be placed in the contractor, apparently from his own letter recently received, although it manifests a very commendable zeal and much anxiety for the interests of the service, and the silence of his agent, Mr. Thorne, who left this place the 21st ultimo for the country about Utica expressly to provide a prompt supply of flour, have compelled me, most reluctantly indeed, to order the deputy quartermaster, Major Brown, his principal being absent, to remedy the defect with all possible expedition; the troops at the French Mills being reduced to about seven days rations and those at Chateauguay to less than three, the restraints and precautions imposed on this purchase will prevent any interference with the measures of the contractors, and the flour which may be purchased will be delivered to them for issue.

My personal feelings, which have not been at ease under the obloquy I have suffered from the mal-conduct of others, are silenced by the unlooked for results of Major-General Harrison's campaign and the catastrophe at Niagara; to counteract as far as I can the effects of our disappointments and misfortunes, I contemplate to give the enemy near me a "contre coup" which shall reach to the bone, but the accomplishment of my views will depend on the following contingencies:—

    1st.—The co-operation of Governor Tompkins with a mere show of militia to cover Sackett's Harbor, which I do not consider in danger, to enable me to draw eight hundred or a thousand men from that place.

    2d.—The adherence of the enemy to their proper occupancies.

    3d.—The increased health of our troops.

    4th.—The accumulation of a competent stock of sound flour.

    5th.—The procurement of the means of protection to the ears, fingers and feet of the men, without which they cannot operate under the frosts of the climate, and

    6th.—The depth of snow which may fall.

    I think the provisions depending on myself and those I command may, with our support, be reasonably accomplished; I have no reason to believe the enemy will materially change his ground; I shall either steal an interview with Governor Tompkins or send to him a citizen of his confidence, and as to the elements, which at present are entirely favorable, we must rest on Providence.

    And now permit me briefly to submit my project to you for your consideration and opinion, which I beg to receive with as little delay as possible. I propose to march on the 3d or 4th of next month a column of two thousand men from Chateauguay and the same from Plattsburg, with the appropriate attirail and the necessary sleighs for transport; the first to move by the route of General Hampton to sweep the enemy to the St. Lawrence, then to turn to the right and march for St. Pierre, while the second will march by the route of Hemmingford and La Tortue to form a junction at St. Pierre, from which point the united corps will proceed against the posts of St. Philip, L'Acadie and St. John, and, having beaten, routed, or captured the detachments at these defenceless cantonments, shall be governed by circumstances whether to occupy their quarters and hold the country and reduce the Isle aux Noix or return to our cantonments.

    Simultaneous with these movements four thousand men from the French Mills will cross the St. Lawrence, attack Cornwall, capture or rout the corps of the enemy's regular troops in that vicinity, disperse the militia, fortify and hold possession of the village, and then effectually cut off the intercourse between the two provinces.

To secure a favorable issue to these enterprises without much loss of blood, the demonstrations heretofore made of fear and alarm on our part will be continued by more than ordinary means of military deception, in which you may be able to assist me powerfully through the medium of the prints known to be friendly to the war; the recent alarm at Plattsburg, of which I have made much, has enabled me to bring on the cavalry and other troops from Burlington capable of hardy service without exciting the smallest suspicion on the part of the enemy, and the defences projected and put up at our three posts the caution, vigilance, and extensive excursions of our outlaying patrols and scouts, and the deception of his spies and impositions of my own, it is believed, may continue the enemy in the security they appear to indulge; in fine, we shall march in force to justify the most favorable expectations, and in case of disappointment shall have the same ground to retire upon over which we had advanced from our fortified cantonments, where we shall have guards and where in any extremity we shall be able to defend ourselves against any force the enemy can at present command.

Should the double operations proposed be deemed too hazardous, then will you be pleased to point out that which may be preferred, either to take possession at Cornwall or to break up the posts or cantonments in our front; we are certainly competent to either, and I am desircus the troops under my command should not eat the bread of idleness.

(Wilkinson's Memoirs, Vol. III., Appendix XLVIII.)

General Order.

Adjutant General's Office, Headquarters, QUEBEC,
8th January, 1814.

His Excellency the Commander of the Forces has the satisfaction of announcing to the troops that he has received a despatch from Lieutenant General Drummond reporting the complete success of an attack that had been made at daybreak on the 30th of December on the enemy's position at Black Rock, where he was advantageously posted with upwards of 2,000 men, and after a short but severe contest the enemy was repulsed in the most gallant manner and pursued to Buffalo, where he attempted to make a stand but on receiving a few rounds from the British fieldpieces he abandoned that post also and fled with precipitation to the 11 Mile Creek on Lake Erie, leaving seven fieldpieces and four schooners and sloops, with a considerable quantity of ordnance and other stores, which have fallen into our hands. The enemy suffered severely but from the rapidity of his flight 70 prisoners only are taken, among whom is Dr. or Lieut. Colonel Chapin.

The corps under Major General Riall consisted of detachments of the Royal Scots, 8th (or King's), 41st, and the flank companies of the 89th and 100th Regiments, the whole not exceeding 1,000 men.

The Lieutenant General bestows the utmost praise upon the undaunted courage and patient submission of the troops, in contempt of the inclemency of the weather and the hardships to which they were exposed.

No British officer has fallen on this occasion. Lieut. Colonel Ogilvie, 8th (or Kings), and Captain Fawcett, 100th Grenadiers, were wounded and it is supposed our loss does not exceed 25 killed and 50 wounded.

Black Rock and Buffalo were burnt previous to their evacuation, together with all the public buildings and the four vessels, a considerable quantity of stores having been sent away before the conflagration.

EDWARD BAYNES, Adjt. General N. A.

Lieut. General Drummond to Sir George Prevost.

YORK, 9th January, 1814.

DEAR SIR,—

Your Excellency's letter of the 27th December met me on the route to this place yesterday evening, and I take the opportunity of replying to it by Lieut. Colonel Harvey, who leaves this immediately for Kingston, with my permission to proceed from thence to Quebec. I shall pay every attention to the points touched on by Your Excellency respecting the strengthening and retaining possession of Fort Niagara, which will be without doubt an object of the highest importance in the prosecution of the war with the United States. With this view Lieutenant Gaugreben has been constantly employed since the capture of the place in repairing and adding to such parts of the defences as appear most immediately to require it. The picketting from Fort George has been taken up and made use of for the above purpose until more adequate means can be provided. I entirely agree with Your Excellency in regard to the necessity of establishing both a tower at Mississaga Point, to command the entrance to the river, and also a heavy battery opposite to that side of the fort which it is proposed to weaken. I shall therefore have occasion to remove from York the two 24 pounders to that situation, and intend replacing them by 18 pounders, which I hope will be found to answer every purpose. I shall also forward the two mortars from hence the moment the roads are in a state to admit of their transportation. I have to request, as mentioned in a former letter, that Your Excellency will order up more guns of heavy calibre as they will be essentially requisite at many points. It gives me much satisfaction to learn that Colonel Bruyeres is coming to this Province and I hope to reap every advantage from his services. An enclosed battery with a heavy gun on the Heights at Queenston will be absolutely necessary, and I have ordered a log barrack for 200 men to be constructed in the hollow where the huts formerly stood. I propose re-establishing the barracks at Fort Erie. The distribution of the troops will be as follows:—The King's Regiment will garrison Fort Niagara. The 100th Regiment and light company 89th Regiment will occupy Chippawa, Fort Erie, and the intermediate line; the Royals, Queenston and Fort George and the 41st Regiment will be concentrated at York.

I enclose a copy of Captain Nelles, Adams, and Lyons parole omitted in my letter of the 26th ulto.

The Receiver General not being able to procure money from the Commissary here upon the warrant for £8,000 in his hands, I have authorized him to draw upon the Commissary General for that amount, payable at Montreal, which I hope will meet Your Excellency's approbation.

(Canadian Archives, C. 682, pp. 17-9.)

General Order.

Adjutant General's Office, Headquarters,
QUEBEC, 9th January, 1814.

His Excellency the Commander of the Forces has received from Sir Sidney Beckwith a report from Captain Barker of the Frontier Light Infantry, stating the complete success of an expedition committed to the charge of that officer against the enemy's post at Derby, in the State of Vermont, which was taken possession of at daybreak on the 17th of December. An extensive barracks for 1,200 men, lately erected, were destroyed, together with the stables and storehouses, and a considerable quantity of valuable military stores has been brought away.

Captain Barker mentions Captain Curtis and Taplin, Lieuts. Messa and Bodwell and Ensign Boynton of the the Township Battalions of Militia, as having been most active in the execution of this judicious and spirited enterprise.

EDWARD BAYNES, Adjt. Gen. N. A.

Captain George Hosmer to Lieut. Colonel Hopkins.

Headquarters, BATAVIA, Jany 10, 1814.

SIR,—

Yours of instant date rec'd and I am instructed by the Major General to offer you his thanks for your intrepidity and bravery displayed in a successful attack on the enemy's picket on the 8th inst. The General approves of your sending the prisoners to Canandaigua. At the same time he would caution you against rashness of enterprise in the present weak state of your forces. A detachment of 1,900 men is ordered out, but cannot be expected on the frontier under 10 or 12 days at the shortest. A supply of arms and ammunition has arrived at Canandaigua and has been ordered on to this place, and he flatters himself that our situation will in a few days be such as to enable you to present an imposing front to the enemy and justify bolder movements.

(Publications of the Buffalo Historical Society, Vol. V., pp. 3+9.)

Lieut General Drummond to Sir George Prevost.

KINGSTON, January 10th, 1814.

SIR,—

In reference to Your Excellency's letter of the 2d inst., I have the honor to state that Major General Stovin arrived at Burlington on his way to Turkey Point on the 31st ulto. The Major Genl. reports that he had fully expected that Lieut. Colonel James had proceeded towards the westward, but found he had not, from want of sleighs and the roads having become impassable for that mode of proceeding by a heavy thaw, the project of endeavoring to surprise the enemy's advanced party of foragers at Camden has necessarily been abandoned for the present, but Lieut. Colonel James has been directed by Major General Stovin, immediately on the roads being again fit for sleighing, to set out upon the expedition should the enemy not have previously retired to Detroit.

A person lately escaped from thence reports that the enemy has made Detroit extremely strong. The fort of Malden is heavily picketted all round. Twenty-two pieces of ordnance are in the place, five 18 pounders, two brass 12s, 2 9s, and one mortar being mounted.

(Canadian Archives, C. 682, p. 21.)

Major General Hall to Lieut. Colonel Swift and Lieut. Colonel Hopkins.

BATAVIA, Jany 11, 1814.

GENTN.—

Your letter advising me of the approach of the enemy on your lines I have this moment received. Esquire Edy, to whom you referred me for further particulars respecting the enemy's forces, has not arrived, but I have only to direct that, should you not be able to meet the enemy in fair fight, that you give him every annoyance in your power, covering your retreat in the best manner your force will warrant.

A company of cavalry left this place yesterday morning to join your corps. The detached troops that have arrived at this place have been marched to Williamsville.

But a large reinforcement is ordered out and will very soon be in arms, when we shall be able to meet any force the enemy can command.

You will (send) me the earliest information of the enemy's movements and of your situation. I shall give you every assistance in my power.

N. B.—I shall come out to your cantonment as soon as I return from Williamsville. It may be two or three days.

(Publications of the Buffalo Historical Society, Vol. V., p. 39.)

PROCLAMATION.

PROVINCE OF UPPER CANADA.

Gordon Drummond, Esquire, our President administering the Government of our said Province, and Lieutenant General commanding our Forces within our said Province.

To all to whom these presents shall come.

GREETING.

Whereas by an act of the Parliament of this Province passed on the thirteenth day of March in the year of Our Lord one thousand eight hundred and thirteen and in the fifty-third year of His Majesty's reign, intituled an act to authorize the Governor, Lieutenant Governor, or person administering the Government of this Province, to prohibit the exportation of grain and other provisions, and also to restrain the distillation of spirituous liquors from grain, it was among other things enacted that from and after the passing of the said act it should be lawful for the Governor, Lieutenant Governor, or person administering the government by and with the advice of His Majesty's Executive Council of this province, from time to time, and when and so often as should be judged expedient, to prohibit by proclamation generally for a limited time after the first day of May next ensuing and now last past, the distillation of spirits, strong waters, and low wines, from any wheat, corn, or other grain, meal, or flour, within the same. Now know ye, that finding such prohibition at present expedient and necessary, I do hereby, by and with the advice of His Majesty's Executive Council for the affairs of this Province and under the authority of the said act, prohibit the distillation of spirits, strong waters and low wines, from any wheat, corn, or other grain, meal, or flour, within this Province, from the expiration of five days after the date of this proclamation in the Home District and of ten days in every other district of this Province, to the first day of March next ensuing, unless the next session of the Provincial Legislature shall sooner terminate, under the penalties and forfeitures by the said act imposed. And I do for that purpose issue this my proclamation, declaring the provisions and restrictions of the said act, so far as respects the distillation of spirits, strong waters, low wines, from wheat, corn, or other grain, meal, or flour, within this Province, be in force from the time and for the period above mentioned.

Given under my hand and seal at arms at York, this eleventh day of January, in the year of our Lord one thousand eight hundred and fourteen, and in the fifty-fourth year of His Majesty's reign.

GORDON DRUMMOND, President.

By His Honor's command,
WM. JARVIS, Sec'y.

Brigadier General Lewis Cass to the Secretary of War.

(Extract.)

WILLIAMSVILLE, eleven miles east of Buffalo,
January 12, 1814.

I passed this day the ruins of Buffalo. It exhibits a scene of distress and destruction such as I have never before witnessed.

The events which have recently transpired in this quarter have been so astonishing and unexpected that I have been induced to make some inquiry into their causes and progress, and, doubting whether you have received any correct information upon the subject, I now trouble you with the detail.

The fall of Niagara has been owing to the most *criminal negligence*. The *force* in it was *fully competent to its defence*. The commanding officer, Captain Leonard, it is said, was at his own house, three miles from the fort, and all the officers seem to have rested in as much security as though no enemy was near them. Captain Rodgers and Captain Hampton, both of the 24th, had companies in the fort. Both of them were absent from it. Their conduct ought to be strictly investigated. I am also told that Major Wallace of the 5th was in the fort. He escaped and is now at Erie.

The circumstances attending the destruction of Buffalo you will have learned before this reaches you. But the force of the enemy has been greatly *magnified*. From the most careful examination I am satisfied that not more than *six hundred and fifty men* of regulars, militia, and Indians landed at Black Rock. To oppose these we had from *two thousand five hundred to three thousand* militia. All except very few of them behaved in the most cowardly manner. They fled without discharging a musket. The enemy continued on this side of the river until Saturday. All their movements betrayed symptoms of apprehension. A vast quantity of property was left in town uninjured, and the Ariel, which lies four miles above upon the beach, is safe. They continue in possession of Niagara and will probably retain it until a force competent to its reduction arrives in its vicinity.

(American State Papers, Military Affairs, Vol. I., pp. 187-8.)

Lieut.-General Drummond to Sir George Prevost.

KINGSTON, January 12th, 1814.

SIR,—

I have the honor to acquaint Your Excellency that my latest reports from Major-General Stovin state that the enemy had passed Arnold's mill (near Dolson's) in number about 130 on their return to Detroit, on the 20th ultimo, followed by their cavalry, about 60, on the 22d. They took off with them all the flour and grain in that direction for the purpose of depositing it with the rest of the provisions they had seized at Detroit. They burned Arnold's barn on retiring.

The roads from Delaware town are stated to be in a most impassable degree bad, so that Lieut.-Colonel James could not have made his intended movement with that rapidity which would have ensured surprise even had the enemy remained at Camden, and had the attempt been made sooner the roads were in such a condition as to have precluded all hope of success.

It has also been reported to me from a person who crossed over at Fort Erie ferry on Saturday last, that the enemy have brought on to Buffalo 15 pieces of cannon and that they intend taking possession of Fort Erie again as soon as the weather permits; that they are raising two regiments of colour, and that Sergeant Powell of the 19th Light Dragoons is at Eleven Mile Creek in a most deplorable state, extremely anxious, either by exchange or parole, to be permitted to come to Canada.

(Canadian Archives, C. 682, p. 24.)

From the Diary of Thomas McCrae.

RALEIGH, Wednesday, 5th January, 1814.

Eight or nine Indians with young Walker came up from Detroit on some expedition. A detachment is on its way up here; it is said 400.

Friday, 7th January.

About 200 Americans passed on their way upwards to-day, commanded by Major Smiley.

Monday, 10th January.

The American troops went down on the other side of the river. It is said they are going to remain some time at Mr. Jacob's to collect the wheat that is on the river.

Tuesday, 11th January.

The Americans got 100 bushels of wheat from me.

Wednesday, 12th January.

A party of American soldiers with Lieut. Watson took my harness and cariole.

Friday, 14th January.

The American army started down from Mr. Jacob's to-day.

Sir George Prevost to Earl Bathurst.

No. 123.   Headquarters, QUEBEC, 12th January, 1814.

MY LORD,—

I have great satisfaction in transmitting to Your Lordship the copy of a letter I have received from Lieutenant-General Drummond, containing a report of a successful attack made on the enemy's position of Black Rock and Buffalo, by a brigade of His Majesty's troops, under the command of Major-General Riall, on the 30th ulto.

In this brilliant affair, as in that of the capture of Fort Niagara, the officers and men engaged have acquitted themselves with determined bravery, and are distinguished by their devotion to the service of their country under peculiar hardships and privations.

Eight pieces of ordnance and one hundred and thirty prisoners have fallen into our possession, and the towns of Black Rock and Buffalo have been totally destroyed, the inhabitants having previously abandoned those places.

Four of the enemy's armed sloops and schooners have also been burnt.

I beg Your Lordship's indulgence in submitting to the gracious consideration of His Royal Highness the Prince Regent the officers who are particularly mentioned by the Lieutenant-General as having acted with great gallantry upon this occasion.

Captain Robinson, who commanded the King's Regiment after Lieutenant-Colonel Ogilvie was disabled, and to whose judicious and prompt execution of a flank movement, much merit and great advantage have been ascribed. Captain Fawcett, of the 100th Regiment, who was wounded, and Captain Jervois, aide de camp to Lieutenant-General Drummond, and Captain Holland, aide de camp to Major General Riall, appear to have been very forward in zealous performance of their respective duties, and present themselves as objects entitled to my commendation.

(Canadian Archives, Q. 127, pp. 30-1.)

Major-General Hall to Governor Tompkins.

Headquarters, BATAVIA, Jan'y 13, 1814.

SIR,—

Since my last communication there has not anything of importance transpired on this frontier materially affecting us. On the 8th inst. a detachment under the command of General John Swift, (a volunteer,) and Lieut.-Colonel C. Hopkins, with about 70 men, surprised a party of the British who were procuring wood about half a mile from the fort, fired upon them, killed four of the enemy, lost one of their own men, and took eight prisoners, subsequent to which a large force of the enemy was observed to be in motion, which induced our troops on that station to fall back 4 or 5 miles to a more defensible position. The affair ended here and all is quiet.

In consideration of our feeble force, I have cautioned the commandant on that station against indulging too much in rash enterprises until our reinforcements shall have arrived, which may be expected here in 7 or 8 days. I have ordered on to the arsenal at this place a sufficient supply of arms and ammunition for the forces now on this frontier and those expected to arrive, so that I flatter myself that within a few days I may be able to pronounce this frontier safe against any encroachments of the enemy.

I regret to add that our loss in killed on the 30th ulto. proves to be greater than I had supposed. On repossessing the ground we found that our dead were yet unburied. There have already been collected about 50 bodies and probably there are some yet undiscovered in the woods. The cannon were not removed by the enemy (except the 6-pounder), nor are they materially injured. The enemy admit their loss in killed and wounded to be 300.

P. S.—Messrs. Dixon, Edwards, Ross, Baldwin and Crooks, citizens of U. Canada, prisoners of war, have received permission from the Commissary of Prisoners to proceed to Canada. Their passports were granted anterior to the late disturbances and changes on this frontier. I have detained them a few days until our reinforcements shall have got on. I shall be happy to learn Your Excellency's opinion whether they should be permitted to pass over at this place. I do not myself perceive any serious objection to their being permitted to pass. General Dearborn will know the men.

(Tompkins' Papers, Vol. IX., pp. 35-6. New York State Library.)

PROCLAMATION.

By His Excellency Sir George Prevost, Baronet, Commander of His Majesty's Forces in North America, &c., &c., &c.

To the inhabitants of His Majesty's Provinces in North America:

A PROCLAMATION.

The complete success which has attended His Majesty's arms on the Niagara Frontier having placed in our possession the whole of the enemy's posts on that line, it became a matter of imperious duty to retaliate on America the miseries which the unfortunate inhabitants of Newark had been made to suffer on the evacuation of Fort George.

The villages of Lewiston, Black Rock and Buffalo have accordingly been burned.

At the same time that His Excellency the Commander of the Forces sincerely deprecates this mode of warfare, he trusts it will be sufficient to call the attention of every candid and impartial person, both amongst ourselves and the enemy, to the circumstances from which it has arisen to satisfy them that this departure from the established usages of war has originated with America herself, and that to her alone are justly chargeable all the awful and unhappy consequences which have hitherto flowed and are likely to result from it.

It is not necessary to advert to the conduct of the troops employed on the American coast in conjunction with His Majesty's squadron under Admiral Sir John B. Warren; since they were neither within the command nor subject to the control of His Excellency their acts cannot be ascribable to him, even if they wanted that justification which the circumstances that occasioned them so amply afford.

It will be sufficient for the present purpose, and to mark the character of the war as carried on upon the frontiers of these Provinces, to trace the line of conduct observed by His Excellency and the troops under his command since the commencement of hostilities, and to contrast it with that of the enemy.

The first invasion of Upper Canada took place in July, 1812, when the American forces under Brigadier-General Hull crossed over and took possession of Sandwich, where they began to manifest a disposition so different from a magnanimous enemy, and which they have since invariably displayed, in marking out as objects of their resentment the loyal subjects of His Majesty and in dooming their property to plunder and conflagration.

Various instances of this kind occurred, both at Sandwich and in its neighborhood, at the very period when His Majesty's standard was waving upon the fort of Michilimackinac and affording protection to the persons and property of those who had submitted to it. Within a few weeks afterwards the British flag was also hoisted on the fortress of Detroit, which, together with the whole of the Michigan territory, had surrendered to His Majesty's arms.

Had not His Excellency been actuated by sentiments far different from those which had influenced the American Government, and the persons employed by it, in the wanton acts of destruction of private property, committed during their short occupation of a part of Upper Canada, His Excellency could not have failed to have availed himself of the opportunity which the undisturbed possession of the whole of the Michigan Territory afforded him of amply retaliating for the devastating system which had been pursued at Sandwich and on the Thames.

But strictly in conformity to the views and disposition of his own Government and to that liberal and magnanimous policy which it had dictated, he chose rather to forbear an imitation of the enemy's example in the hope that such forbearance would be duly appreciated by the Government of the United States, and would produce a return to the more civilized usages of war.

The persons and property therefore of the inhabitants of Michigan Territory were respected and remained unmolested.

In the winter of the following year, when the success which attended the daring and gallant enterprise against Ogdensburg, had placed that populace and flourishing village in our possession, the generosity of the British character was again conspicuous in the scrupulous preservation of every article which could be considered as private property, such public buildings only being destroyed as were used for the accommodation of troops and for public stores.

The destruction of the defences of Ogdensburg and the dispersion of the enemy's force in that neighborhood laid open the whole of their frontier on the St. Lawrence to the incursions of His Majesty's troops, and Hamilton as well as the numerous settlements on the banks of the river might at any hour, had such been the disposition of His Majesty's Government or of those acting under it, been plundered and laid waste.

During the course of the following summer, by the fortunate result of the enterprise against Plattsburg, that town was for several hours in the complete possession of our troops, there not being a force in the neighborhood which could attempt a resistance.

Yet even then, under circumstances of strong temptation, and when the recent example of the enemy in the wanton destruction at York of private property and buildings not used for military purposes must have been fresh in the recollection of the force employed on that occasion, and would have justified a retaliation on their part, their forbearance was strongly manifested, and the directions His Excellency had given to the commander of that expedition, so scrupulously obeyed, that scarcely can another instance be shown, in which, during a state of war and under similar circumstances, an enemy so completely under the power and at the mercy of their adversaries had so little cause of complaint.

During the course of the same summer Forts Schlosser and Black Rock were surprised and taken by a part of the forces under the command of Major-General de Rottenburg, on the Niagara Frontier, at both of which places personal property was respected and the public buildings alone were destroyed.

It was certainly matter of just and reasonable expectation that the humane and liberal course of conduct pursued by His Excellency on these different occasions would have had its due weight with the American Government, and would have led it to have abstained, in the further prosecution of the war, from any act of wantonness and violence, which could only tend unnecessarily to add to its ordinary calamities, and to bring down upon their own unoffending citizens a retaliation, which, though distant, they must have known would await and certainly follow such conduct.

Undeterred, however, by His Excellency's example of moderation, or by any of the consequences to be apprehended from the adoption of such barbarous measures, the American forces at Fort George, acting, as there is every reason to believe, under the orders or with the approbation of their Government, for some time previous to the evacuation of that fortress, under various pretences, burned and destroyed the farm houses and buildings of many of the respectable and peaceable inhabitants of the neighborhood. But the full measure of this species of barbarity remained to be completed when all its horrors might be more fully and keenly felt by those who were to become the wretched victims of it.

It will be hardly credited by those who shall hereafter read it in the page of history, that in the enlightened era of the 19th century and in the inclemency of a Canadian winter, the troops of a nation calling itself civilized and Christian, had wantonly and without the shadow of a pretext, forced 400 helpless women and children to quit their dwellings and to be mournful spectators of the conflagration and total destruction of all that belonged to them.

Yet such was the fate of Newark on the 10th of December, a day which the inhabitants of Upper Canada can never forget, and the recollection of which cannot but nerve their arms when again opposed to their vindictive foe. On the night of that day the American troops under Brigadier General McClure, being about to evacuate Fort George, which they could no longer retain, by an act of inhumanity, disgraceful to themselves and to the nation to which they belong, set fire to upwards of 150 houses, composing the beautiful village of Newark, and burned them to the ground, leaving without covering or shelter those "innocent, unfortunate and distressed inhabitants" whom that officer by his proclamation had previously engaged to protect.

His Excellency would have ill considered the honor of his country and the justice due to His Majesty's injured and insulted subjects, had he permitted an act of such needless cruelty to pass unpunished, or had he failed to visit, whenever the opportunity arrived, upon the inhabitants of the neighboring American frontier the calamities thus inflicted upon those of our own.

The opportunity has occurred, and a full measure of retaliation has taken place, such as, it is hoped, will teach the enemy to respect in future the laws of war, and recall him to a sense of what is due to himself as well as to us.

In the further prosecution of the contest, to which such an extraordinary character has been given, His Excellency must be guided by the course of conduct which the enemy shall hereafter pursue. Lamenting, as His Excellency does, the necessity imposed upon him of retaliating upon the subjects of America the miseries inflicted upon the inhabitants of Newark, it is not his intention to pursue further a system of warfare so revolting to his own feelings and so little congenial to the British character unless the future measures of the enemy should compel him again to resort to it.

To those possessions of the enemy along the whole line of the frontier which have hitherto remained undisturbed, and which are now within His Excellency's reach and at the mercy of the troops under his command, His Excellency has determined to extend the same forbearance and the same freedom from rapine and plunder which they have hitherto experienced, and from this determination the future conduct of the American Government shall alone induce His Excellency to depart.

The inhabitants of these Provinces will in the meantime be prepared to resist with firmness and with courage, whatever attempts the resentment of the enemy, arising from their disgrace and their merited sufferings, may lead them to make, well assured that they will be powerfully assisted at all points by the troops under His Excellency's command, and that prompt and signal vengeance will be taken for every fresh departure of the enemy from that system of warfare which ought to subsist between enlightened and civilized nations.

Given under my hand and seal at arms at
Quebec, this 12th day of January, 1814.
GEORGE PREVOST.

By His Excellency's command, E. B. BRENTON.

Kingston Gazette, February 22nd, 1814.

Extract of a letter dated Sackett's Harbor, January 13:

"We have every probable reason to expect, and I have not the least doubt of an attack here during the winter. Report says that the enemy are making every necessary preparation for that purpose at Kingston. A short time since several detached companies of troops, amounting to about 800 men, were marched from this place to French Mills, leaving this place nearly destitute of troops. There remains at the Harbor only about 700 or so of Harrison's men. Our fleet is moored to the best advantage, but at the best they can only operate as batteries."

Another letter states that Mr. Eckford was there and had about 400 ship carpenters at work, and that all the forces were employed in cutting and drawing timber and erecting blockhouses.

Commodore Chauncey is proceeding from Washington to Sackett's Harbor.

Major J. B. Glegg to Captain W. H. Merritt.

BURLINGTON HEIGHTS, 14th January, 1814.

DEAR MERRITT,—

I received yours of the 11th, enclosing a *long looked for* return of your troop, which I regret to find continue so weak. Provided you station two of your men at the 12, the communication will be complete, and stands as follows: Henry's, Pettit's, (church at the 40,) Stoney Creek, Beasley's, and Price's, across the creek—at the two former are civilians, and the three latter are carried by your and Coleman's men. Kilute (Canute?) was so ill provided in necessaries, and not having a *saddle*, I gave him a pass to join his headquarters, and Kerr will proceed on the same route to-morrow, his activity on the public service having drawn upon him the ill-will of several disaffected characters on the mountain. From what has already passed, I don't like to expose him to further risk, he having been beat severely a few evenings since by a gang of ruffians. Deacon will remain across the creek at Price's, and is the only remaining man of your troop on this side the 12. Do recollect to have two stationed there, for a sad delay is often reported in consequence of there being no person there to forward the bag.

I have so far recovered from my late fall as to begin to think of returning to the Niagara Frontier. I will either call or send to your father's house when I arrive at the 12. I am well aware that when your men are not within a few hours' ride of a post a difficulty may arise respecting rations, as it is not likely civilians will furnish them for so small a sum as sixpence each. To obviate this inconvenience I keep your men at the points contiguous to the ensuing posts, from whence they can draw rations, and their horses have been shod at the government forge.

I saw Ingersoll a few days since, on his way down with the *late commandant* of Niagara.

(Merritt MSS.)

Captain George Hosmer to Major Riddle.

Headquarters, BATAVIA, Jan. 14, 1814.

SIR,—

You are directed to march the regular troops under your command towards Buffalo. You will station yourself at or near Major Miller's, wherever you can find convenient quarters for your forces. You will keep a patrol from your camp to Buffalo and Black Rock, and will report yourself to Brig.-Gen. Hopkins, commanding at Williamsville, whose orders you will respect. In your march you will keep your men embodied and subject to orders. Circumstances require that your march be commenced very early to-morrow morning and conducted with expedition.

Should you discover any movements of the enemy causing an alarm, you will communicate the intelligence to Gen. Hopkins.

(Publications of the Buffalo Historical Society, Vol. V., pp. 41-2.)

Major-General Hall to Governor Tompkins.

BATAVIA, Jan. 14, 1814.

SIR,—

I have nothing to communicate worth remark since my letter of yesterday. Everything remains quiet at present on this frontier.

There is one thing I omitted to mention, I believe, in my last, which is of much consequence. There is very little camp equipage for the troops already in service, and the quartermaster's department gives little encouragement of any being provided. It will be impossible for the troops to remain in service without cooking utensils. The detachment, now mustering of 1,900 men, will want at least 300 camp kettles. I know not how they are to be obtained. They are not in our country. I am in hopes there have been some fowarded which will arrive in season.

Col. Lamb will be able to give you the particulars of our situation more fully than I can write.

(From Niles's Register, Baltimore, Md., February 12, 1814, Vol. V., p. 397.)

Captain George Hosmer to —— ——

Headquarters. BATAVIA, Jan. 15, 1814.

SIR,—

I am directed to reply to your communication, to say that the Major-General cannot recognize Col. Mallory as an officer in the U. States service, his brevet not having emanated from a legitimate source, nor being predicated upon any prior regular commission. The case has been communicated to His Exc'y the Commander in Chief for his direction and advice. At present you are considered the senior commanding officer of that corps. It is not a little singular that two, and these all the commissioned officers in the regular service on this frontier, should be stationed at one recruiting rendezvous, and no one should be left to command the troops on detachment; it is desirable that you will adjust the difficulty with Capt. Scott, so that some one may take command of the troops, and that in the meantime there be no delay in marching the troops to the station assigned, where they can be of any service to the Government.

(Publications of the Buffalo Historical Society, Vol. V., pp. 42-3.)

Edward McMahon to William Jarvis.

KINGSTON, 16th January, 1814.

DEAR SIR,—

Your note of the 10th came to hand yesterday, enclosing a letter addressed to Messrs. Gerrard, Youmans & Co., which, with great pleasure, I shall put in the way of being forwarded by the first express. I most cordially congratulate with you on the fortunate result of our operations on the Niagara frontier, and I trust that not only for the general quiet, but more particularly for that of the inhabitants of the Niagara District, who have already experienced their share of distress and tribulation the enemy will not find it either practicable or convenient to bring another army on that frontier. In the navy department here the greatest exertion is making, and little doubt can be entertained of the superiority which that exertion must ensure on the lake next summer. I have heard Captain O'Conor, the Commissioner, say that both the vessels will be ready for launching before the ice will be out of the harbor. One of them will be much larger than any frigate in the British navy. It will be found necessary to carry sixty heavy guns, and the other will carry forty-four. I have been over at the yard yesterday myself to see them, and the progress made in last week is truly astonishing. I cannot but think that they will be nearly finished in the course of the ensuing month. There are no less than fifteen hundred men employed in the yard, five hundred of whom are carpenters and artificers. At Sackett's Harbor it is said two 36's are on the stocks. The guns for our ships are coming up in brigades of six each, the first of which has just now arrived here. Until last night, during which we had a fall of two or three inches of snow, the roads were quite bare and I have been told that they were not much better between this and Montreal. I hope, however, that the fall last night has been general. We have been in the hourly expectation this day or two past of the arrival of General Drummond. Of when or where parliament meets, I have not as yet had the least intimation. Although it would cause me no small journey, yet I would rather it would meet at York than here.

(Militia Papers, S. P. Jarvis Collection, Toronto Public Library.)

Sir Gordon Drummond to Sir George Prevost.

YORK, February 15th, 1814.

SIR,—
I have the honor to acknowledge the receipt of your letter of the 5th instant, transmitting a communication from Col. Chapin of the United States army, and in reply thereto have to acquaint Your Excellency that considering the circumstances under which that officer was captured, as reported to me by Gen. Riall on my arrival at Buffalo, I conceive that his detention as a prisoner of war was fully justifiable.

It appears that he was not only extremely active during the action at Black Rock on the morning of the 30th December, but afterwards retreated with the American army to Buffalo, where I understand he assumed command of the force that remained there, and having taken a commanding position in front of the town, considerably annoyed our troops with round and grape shot from a six-pounder, whilst they were advancing; and I have been informed it was not until he found that his exertions to arrest their progress were without effect that he came out of Buffalo as a self-constituted flag of truce, at a time when our forces were in full pursuit of the American army. It was not until some time after Buffalo had been taken possession of that, Major-General Riall having mentioned to me that he had ordered Col. Chapin to remain in arrest at his own house until he was made acquainted with my intentions with regard to him, that I directed the Major-General to send him across the water in charge of an officer, considering him a prisoner of war.

(Ketchum's History of Buffalo, Vol. II., pp. 166-7.)

Colonel Cyrenius Chapin to the Public.

The distressing scenes exhibited on the Niagara frontier last fall and winter having excited many painful reflections and anxious inquiries for the causes which led to those disgraceful disasters, have induced me to lay before the public some of the most conspicuous actors of those base exploits.

While the American regular forces continued at Fort George nothing occurred to affect our security till that strange phenomenon, George McClure, appeared. He, with much pomp and parade, however, kept out of harm's way by riding up and down upon the east side of the streights of Niagara till I had, with a small body of volunteers, militia and Indians, routed the enemy from his encampment at the Four Mile Creek. Then this mighty man crossed the river with all the wind of a Hull or a Smyth (aided by the fœtid breath of a J. C. Spencer,) who burst forth with terror and rage upon the defenceless inhabitants of Canada. These terrible heroes, however, very cautiously avoided any engagement with the enemy. They conceived it sufficient for them to war with women and children; to lay waste their dwellings, "to burn up the d——d rascals" was their favorite motto.

Their march from the Beaver Dam to Queenston will be long remembered by the distressed victims of that march. Property of almost every description was plundered and buildings burned under his own eye. This, however, was a mere prelude to the tragedy he was destined to enact.

The ill-fated town of Newark was burnt, under his orders, the night of the 10th of December, 1813. Here was exhibited a scene of distress which language would be inadequate to describe. Women and children were turned out of doors in a cold and stormy night; the cries of infants, the decrepitude of age, the debility of sickness, had no impression on this monster in human shape; they were consigned to that house whose canopy was the heavens and whose walls were as boundless as the wide world. In the destruction of this town he was aided by the most active exertions of Joseph Wilcox, who had for a number of years resided in this pleasant village and had been patronized far beyond his merits; and at that time, when it became his duty as a man of justice and as a subject of His Majesty, whose government he had sworn to protect and defend, he, like a cowardly sycophant, deserted the cause of his country and actually led a banditti through the town, setting fire to his neighbors' dwellings and cursing every American—applying the epithet of tory to everyone who disapproved of this act of barbarity. It will be remembered that this town was burned when the British forces were not in any considerable force within a distance of thirty miles.

The General next selected the American side of the river for the theatre of operations. He took up his quarters at Buffalo. A small force of about two hundred regulars was called from Canandaigua, which we should have supposed ought to have been sent to the protection of Fort Niagara, as that place was menaced by the enemy. Instead of this the General ordered them to remain at Buffalo. Fort Niagara was taken on the morning of the 19th of December, 1813. The day previous the General was informed by a citizen who had made his escape from Canada, that an attack would be made on Fort Niagara at the time it was made. Here then is something very remarkable in the conduct of General McClure: instead of despatching an express with this very important intelligence he omitted it, if not altogether, until it was too late for the express to get there.

As soon as the capture of that fort was known at Buffalo, the General removed himself and men from Buffalo to Cold Springs, a distance of two miles. This movement appeared to be made that the redoubtable General should have time to retreat without hearing the whistle of British balls, which, by-the-bye we suppose would have been very unpleasant to the General's organs of hearing, as he was totally unused to such sounds. Here he remained for a few days, but finding from intelligence which he received from Canada that the enemy were preparing to attack Buffalo, he took up his line of march to Batavia, a distance of forty miles, no doubt conceiving that a place of greater safety, as there he could not hear the report of the enemy's guns. From Batavia I was told he made good his retreat to his own home in Steuben County, having covered himself and his associates with laurels of disgrace. As to his assertion that he was fired upon by men who he said were under my command, I believe it to be utterly false. The inhabitants of Buffalo all felt deeply interested in the protection of that place, apprehending full well the consequences of an invasion of it by an enemy whose character had been marked by acts of outrage and cruelty, and who was now stimulated to the most desperate measures of retaliation by the conduct of McClure in the burning of Newark. They repeatedly requested him to afford them the necessary protection. The ruins of the Niagara frontier, the tears of the widows and the cries of orphan children, still testify to his cowardice and villany. As it regards myself and the command I held in the army while it was under General McClure, I think proper to state the principal reason that induced me to resign, after having been repeatedly exposed to much danger by his orders, especially when he ordered me to Forty Mile Creek in Upper Canada, and while I remained there under his orders, with about forty men, he said in presence of Mr. Curtiss, whose affidavit I procured, "that he regretted that I had not been taken by the enemy, that he wished I had been and that he hoped the damned rascal would be." Now the public will observe that I was acting under the orders of Gen. McClure and had taken a commanding position at that place. He ordered Col. Hopkins to command the men in rear of me, who were twelve miles from that place. I was ordered to remain at the Forty Mile Creek until I was reinforced, but, contrary to the assurances which McClure gave me, Colonel Hopkins was ordered to remain twelve miles in rear of me. Should any person concerned reply to these observations further facts will be developed; meanwhile the public are requested to peruse the subjoined documents. Others are in my possession and will be published next week.

JUNE 13th.   CYRENIUS CHAPIN.

NIAGARA COUNTY:

Benjamin Caryl of Buffalo, being duly sworn, deposes and says that he, in company with Captain Frank Hampton of the 24th Regiment of United States Infantry, on or about the third day of January last, at Batavia, then and there heard the said Hampton declare that he most cordially rejoiced at the burning of the village of Buffalo—that he regretted the loss of two or three of the inhabitants only; and in the same conversation he heard him say he wished he had the power of the Almighty, he would exercise the same in damning the greater part of the inhabitants of Buffalo to all eternity. Further this deponent saith not.

BENJAMIN CARYL.

Sworn to this 14th day of March, 1814, before me, Samuel Tupper, First Judge of Common Pleas for Niagara County.

STATE OF NEW YORK,
NIAGARA COUNTY:

Asa Ransom, of the town of Clarence, in the said county, being solemnly sworn, deposeth and saith that on the 23rd or 24th of December last past, he (this deponent) was at the house of Frederick Miller, near the late village of Buffalo. Brig Gen. McClure and his Aides and several gentlemen from Buffalo and elsewhere were there. In a conversation with Erastus Granger, Esq., this deponent heard Gen. McClure publicly declare that he would take away the regulars and was going away himself. Judge Granger asked if he meant to take away the ammunition. Gen. McClure answered that he did. Judge Granger observed, "for God's sake don't do that for we shall all be destroyed. Buffalo will be burned and we shall have nothing to defend ourselves with." Gen. McClure said, "I will stay and defend you if the inhabitants will arrest and bind that d——d rascal (Chapin) and bring him to me; if they will not do that they may all be destroyed and I don't care how soon." And this deponent further saith that he had understood that McClure and Chapin had quarrelled violently about the burning of Newark and that he believed that animosity continued to exist up to the time of McClure's departure from Buffalo, which was on or about the day above mentioned. And further this deponent saith not.

ASA RANSOM.

Sworn, &c.

NIAGARA COUNTY:

Dudley Frink and Jacob L. Fort, being duly sworn, say that on or about the 23d of December last they were in company with Captain John A. Rodgers of the Twenty-fourth Regiment of United States Infantry, then acting aide to Gen. McClure, at Key's tavern, in Batavia; these deponents heard the said Rogers solemnly declare, in the presence of a number of other gentlemen, that he wished to God Buffalo was burned, and that he would give one hundred dollars to any person who would bring him information that Buffalo was actually burned. And further these deponents say not.

DUDLEY FRINK.
JACOB L. FORT.

Sworn, &c.

STATE OF NEW YORK,
COUNTY OF NIAGARA :

Nehemiah Seeley, late a resident of the village of Buffalo, being duly sworn, says that on the 22d or 23d day of December last, this deponent had a conversation at the house of Frederick Miller, with Donald Frazer, a lieutenant in the regular service, who was then acting as aide to Gen. McClure, in which conversation the said Frazer said that if Buffalo should be burned he had no doubt that the inhabitants would be remunerated by government; that he believed it would be an advantage to the country to have it burned; it would make hundreds of soldiers; it would stimulate men to enlist—to prosecute the war with more vigor; he said if he had a house in Buffalo he should be glad to see a firebrand in it in two minutes. And further saith not.

NEHEMIAH SEELEY.

Sworn, &c.

NIAGARA COUNTY:

Reuben B. Heacock, late of Buffalo, in the County of Niagara, on oath saith : That on the third or fourth day of January last past he saw Captain Hampton of the Twenty-fourth Regiment of United States Infantry four miles east of Batavia in the County of Genesee, and heard the said Hampton say he rejoiced that Buffalo was burned; that he did not regard the loss of any except one, and all he regretted was that some of the inhabitants were not burned in the village. And further deponent saith not.

R. B. HEACOCK.

Sworn, &c.

NIAGARA COUNTY:

Edmund Raymond being sworn saith : That on or about the 23d day of December, at Porter's tavern in Clarence, he fell in with

Gen. McClure and Capt. John A. Rogers, the General's aide, on their march with the regular troops from Buffalo to Batavia, at which time and place he heard Capt. Rogers say, (in the hearing of Gen. McClure,) that he hoped Buffalo would be burned, and that if he could save it by holding up his hand he would not do it, at which remark the General made no reply.

E. RAYMOND,

Sworn, &c.

NIAGARA COUNTY:

Frederick Miller in the County of Niagara, being sworn, deposes and says: That on the 21st or 22d day of December last, Gen. George McClure was at the house of this deponent, and while he was at his house this deponent heard him say that he hoped to God the village of Buffalo would be burned by the British, and that he would march the regular troops to Batavia. And this deponent further says that Gen. McClure marched the regular troops from Buffalo to the house of this deponent on the 19th day of December last, and marched the said troops from this deponent's house to Batavia on the 22d day of December. And this deponent further says that at the time Gen. McClure ordered the said troops to Batavia it was not ascertained whether the enemy were proceeding up this side of the river towards Black Rock and Buffalo or remained at Schlosser, as this deponent understood and verily believes.

FREDERICK MILLER.

Sworn, &c.

STATE OF NEW YORK:

Mosely W. Abell, late a resident of the late village of Buffalo, being solemnly sworn, deposeth and saith: That a few days previous to the burning of Buffalo by the enemy he saw Gen, McClure with his aides at Porter's tavern in Clarence; they were then on their march from Buffalo towards Batavia with regular troops; that he heard Capt. Rogers, one of the aides of Gen. McClure, publicly declare that he believed that the village of Buffalo would be destroyed and he hoped it would be, for the inhabitants were all a pack of d———d rascals; that he hoped that would wake them up. Gen. McClure was at the same time standing by the side of Rogers, and observed that he did not know but of one d———d rascal and that was Chapin. And this deponent further saith that there was a number of militia present who were on their march to the frontier and heard the above mentioned declaration. And further this deponent told Rogers he ought to be arrested for his conduct. And further saith not.

M. W. ABELL.

Sworn, &c.

STATE OF NEW YORK.

NIAGARA COUNTY:

William T. Miller of the town of Buffalo, of the age of twenty-two years, being solemnly sworn, deposeth and saith: That Lieut. Riddle of the United States service came into the house of Frederick Miller, (father of the deponent,) after the discharge of the alarm guns at Black Rock on the night of the 29th December last past; that the said Riddle called for a brandy sling and drank part of it. He then went to sleep in his chair before the fire in a room adjoining the bar-room. After the said Riddle had slept some time, on this deponent's going into the room he woke up and began to pull bank notes out of his coat sleeve: this deponent believes he pulled out to the amount of eighty or a hundred dollars, and observed that he won so much that night at playing cards. This deponent believes that he again drank of his sling, lay down on the floor and went to sleep. He continued to sleep until nearly or quite daylight when he awoke, drank the remainder of his brandy sling, mounted his horse and started for the Eleven Mile Creek after his men. And this deponent further saith that the said Riddle did not return from the Eleven Mile Creek with the regulars on the morning of the 30th of December till after the British had entered Buffalo village. This deponent further saith that the said Frederick Miller did then (and still continues to) keep a tavern two and a half miles from the village of Buffalo. And further saith not.

WILLIAM T. MILLER.

(Ketchum's History of Buffalo, Vol. II., pp. 405-11.)

Major General Wilkinson to the Secretary of War.

WATERFORD, Sunday evening, January 16th, 1814,

SIR.—

I left Chateauguay the 10th and arrived here this morning, having been detained a day and a half at Plattsburg; on my route I fell in with Mr. Anderson, the contractor, whose prospects for a supply of flour from the borders of Lake Champlain and this quarter of the country are so faint that we must, until the opening of spring, depend for that article on the western parts of this state, not only for the posts of French Mills and Chateauguay, but I fear in some measure for that of Plattsburg also. Our distance from the settlements of Black River, the Oswego and Mohawk, to which we are to look for support, combined with other causes depending on the season, leave us no expectations of being able to accumulate such magazines as may justify our taking post within the territory of the enemy as heretofore proposed; indeed my personal observations and enquiries made on the road I have travelled, and reports just received by General Swartwout from the westward, justify the apprehension that we shall be barely able to subsist the troops from day to day.

In this situation, instead of advancing on the enemy we are in danger of being compelled to retrograde for want of subsistence, and as it would almost destroy the troops to erect second cantonments at this inclement season, with the approbation of government I will endeavor to find quarters for them in Prescott and Kingston, which I consider practicable to a corps of hardihood and resolution aided by the facility of movement to be derived from sleds.

Charge me not with caprice for thus suddenly varying my plan of operations, since it is caused by posterior information, which presents an insuperable obstacle to the execution of the project submitted in my despatch of the 7th instant. The object now presented had not escaped my mind, but it was opposed by my repugnance to give ground to the enemy and to sacrifice our boats, the infallible consequence of its execution. Reduce Prescott and Kingston and the occupancy and maintenance of these posts would be secured by our proximity to our own resources and our distance from those of the enemy.

You are sensible that I dare not enter upon this expedition without permission, and also that the lapse of the season renders a prompt decision necessary on the part of the executive. I shall therefore expect your answer as soon as may be convenient, and in the meantime will put the troops in the best condition for the enterprise my means may permit.

Should the President sanction the plan now proposed, I shall remove the sick, the convalescent and every article of useless baggage, together with the artillery and munitions of war for which I shall have no occasion, to Plattsburg: shall destroy our boats and break up our cantonments at the French Mills and Chateauguay; and whilst I keep the enemy in expectation that these precautions are preparatory to the attack of their posts and cantonments in my vicinity, I shall detach a thousand selected men to steal a march and take Prescott by surprise or storm, whither I shall follow that detachment with the main body a few hours after it marches, and having everything in readiness for the movement, by its rapidity and the feints of some light parties, I shall prevent the enemy from penetrating my real design until I have gained my first point.

Examining the abstract of our forces, which accompanies this letter, you will perceive a very considerable part of it reported sick in quarters, but of these we are to calculate on three-quarters being competent to any stationary service with arms, and amongst them one-third of the whole number for any duty of a soldier: I therefore think I shall be able to march five thousand five hundred men, which, with the co-operation of the corps at Sackett's Harbor, will, I expect, give us a force of seven thousand five hundred non-commissioned officers and privates, to which, if necessary, I hope Governor Tompkins, (whom I shall see to-morrow,) may consent to add two thousand volunteers or militia.

The blow which I desire to give warrants great sufferings, much hardship and continual hazard, because, if successful, we shall destroy the squadron of the enemy at Kingston, kill and capture eventually four thousand of his best troops, recover what we have lost, save much blood and treasure to the nation, and conquer a province.

I anticipate the difficulties in my way, and know that disease, tempests and snow storms may forbid the attempt and baffle all my hopes, but I remember what General Montgomery accomplished under circumstances more unfavorable, and we may reasonably expect the elements will not always be unpropitious.

(Wilkinson's Memoirs, Vol. III., Appendix XLVIII.)

Brigadier John S. Gano to Major General Harrison.

HEADQUARTERS, O. M. LOWER SANDUSKY,
January 17, 1814.

DEAR GENERAL,—

The disagreeable news from below causes me to have great anxiety for the vessels in Put-in-Bay. I proceeded a few days ago to Portage in order to cross to see their situation; the ice prevented me going by water and was not strong enough to bear. I have, however, been relieved by a visit from Lieutenant Champlin and Doctor Eastman of the navy, who came up the night before last and returned yesterday; they came over on the ice though it was very thin in places. The lieutenant informs me that he has ten seamen and forty soldiers and has his vessels and guns so prepared that in case of an attack he can bring about forty to bear from on board and a small blockhouse on a rocky point of land near the vessels. I shall by his request and my own opinion of the necessity of the measure send a reinforcement of about thirty of the regulars from Seneca as soon as the ice is strong enough to bear them. At the fort at Portage I have about one hundred militia, which may render them some assistance if necessary. My troops are very much scattered, and I believe every post is in a tolerable state of defence. The troops have had immense fatigue since they have been out. They are now more healthy and seem in better spirits since two months' pay has come on, though nothing will induce them to continue more than their term of service, which expires the last of next month. Majors Vance and Meek arrived three days ago from Detroit, and have an exalted opinion of the vigilance and arrangements of Colonel Butler. The officers, Captains Holmes and Hill, commanding Malden and Sandwich, have put themselves in the best possible state of defence. A detachment under the command of Major Smiley has gone up the River Thames. The militia at Detroit are discontented, some sick, some dead, &c. I have been between hawk and buzzard as to supplies—the commissary and contractor—and I fear that with all the exertions that can be made some of the posts must suffer; at Meigs no flour, and two or three other posts in nearly the same situation. I called on the contractors and urged the necessity of immediate supplies, but I cannot rely on their promises. The want of forage has destroyed nearly all the transport on this line. I have urged Captain Gardner to supply the agent of that department at this place with funds for that purpose, but to no effect. I have lately been very unwell, but have recovered except a lame ankle. As it is uncertain when this will meet you, I shall not give a detailed account until I know where you are, and will then write more fully and send you a report of the troops under my command.

P. S.—Six o'clock p. m. An express from Erie have just arrived here, a naval officer with a letter from General Cass and a request from Captain Elliott for a reinforcement for Put-in-Bay of two hundred men. I have ordered Lieutenant McFarland from Seneca with all his effective regulars, about thirty able to march, being all the disposable force I have, except a small command at Portage erecting a fortification there, from which I will detach a part, though the whole cannot make more than a third of the number required. From information there is not the least doubt but an attempt will be made to take or destroy the vessels. It is the opinion of Lieutenant Packet and General Cass also. Will it not be proper to send on some regular troops or militia from the interior without delay?

(American State Papers, Military Affairs, Vol. I., p. 656.)

Lieut.-General Drummond to Sir George Prevost.

KINGSTON, 17th January, 1814.

DEAR SIR,

In reference to that part of Your Excellency's letter of the 10th inst. on the subject of Your Excellency's intention of issuing a proclamation declaratory of your desire to forbear from making any further example in retaliation than what had already been inflicted so severely but so justly on the Niagara frontier, and desiring me to take all necessary steps for the prevention in future of any violence being committed against private property, I have the honor to acquaint Your Excellency that I propose issuing a District Order fully explanatory of your instructions on this head, which will, I doubt not, have the effect required as far as regards the British troops, and I trust that the American Government will see in a just point of view the humane and liberal intentions of Your Excellency. Such of the prisoners of war taken on the Niagara frontier as have been capable of undertaking so long a march, I have directed Major General Riall to forward on their route to Quebec by suitable divisions. Several have already passed through this place and others are expected.

(Canadian Archives, C. 682, pp. 25-6.)

Militia General Order.

HEADQUARTERS, KINGSTON, 18th January, 1814.

The Adjutant General having obtained His Honor Lieutenant General Drummond's permission to retire, the state of his health not permitting him to discharge the active duties of his situation, his additional pay and allowances will cease from the 24th instant.

His Honor the Lieutenant General and President having been pleased to appoint Lieutenant Colonel Nathaniel Coffin to be Adjutant General to the militia, all communications on militia matters will in future be addressed to him at headquarters.

By order,
ÆNEAS SHAW,
Adjutant General Militia.

Major General Hall to Major General David Mead, at Erie, Pa.

HEADQUARTERS, BATAVIA, Jan. 18, 1814.

SIR,—

Yours of the 11th inst., enclosed in a letter of Lt. Elliott of the 14th, was received on the 17th at evening. I am happy to learn that you are on your guard against supposed movements of the enemy threatening Erie and the fleet stationed in that harbor, and at the same time regret that it will not be in my power to lend you any material aid in the event of an attack. The forces under my command are small and barely sufficient for covering the frontier and quieting the apprehensions of the inhabitants. Large detachments and those frequent have been made from my division, and the militia in this quarter are now exceedingly harassed with duty. I shall take care to apprise you by express of any information that may be in my possession relative to the enemy's movements which may be material for you to know. As at present advised, I think there is some reason to apprehend an attack on your post should the ice become sufficiently strong and your post not be strongly guarded.

I presume you have through your Executive or directly communicated to the Sec'y at War your situation, and that thereby the Government are possessed of a knowledge of the critical situation in which you are placed. It would give me great pleasure to have such a force under my command as would enable me to co-operate with you in the meditated plan of defence and attack, without at the same time exposing the frontier to further devastation.

I beg you will show this to Lieut. Elliott, who will see in it an answer to his communication, and that you will at the same time assure him of my respect and esteem.

(Publications of the Buffalo Historical Society, Vol. V., pp. 43-4.)

Lieut. General Drummond to Sir George Prevost.

KINGSTON, January 19th, 1814.

SIR,—

I am concerned to have to report to Your Excellency a circumstance of an unpleasant nature which occurred at Fort Niagara, and which Major General Riall states may be principally attributed to the want of exertion, or, as indeed he believes, he should more properly say to the neglect of the commissariat in not throwing a supply of that indispensably necessary article, fuel, into that place.

A party that was sent out on the morning of the 9th to cut wood, under protection of a sergeant's covering party, was attacked by a body of the enemy, reported to consist of about 150 men, and driven in. The sergeant was severely wounded and nine men of the working party, it is supposed, taken prisoners, for no account was received of them so long after as the following night. It appears very extraordinary that any individuals of so small a fatigue party should not have been able to effect their escape, and particularly as it appears they were not furnished with arms to assist the covering party in repelling the attack or in effecting a slow and cautious retreat. I shall take care that proper orders be issued on this head to guard against future accidents of a similar nature.

Major General Riall also states to me that the troop of Provincial Dragoons commanded by Captain Merritt have become extremely unserviceable from the wretched state of their horses, and that the most effective means of getting them in order for service in the coming spring would be by the appointment of an Inspecting Field Officer of Provincial Cavalry from the line and of known experience to visit their several posts frequently and issue such instructions as would ensure a certain if not speedy amendment in so useful a body. If the line of expresses could also be included in this officer's duty it would prove, I conceive, a matter of much benefit. For although he might not be invested with the power to order the owners of express horses any particular mode of treatment, he could offer salutary advice, and report such neglect and inattention as too frequently occur.

If this appointment meets Your Excellency's approbation I beg leave to recommend Brevet Major Lisle of the 19th Light Dragoons for that situation, with such pay and allowances as Your Excellency may deem suitable.

(Canadian Archives, C. 682, pp. 29-31)

Lieut. General Drummond to Sir George Prevost.

KINGSTON, 19th January, 1814.

DEAR SIR,

In reply to Your Excellency's letter of the 2d inst., marked private, I beg to assure you that I have lost no time in giving ample instruction relative to the supply of troops and provisions to be forwarded to Michilimackinac by Lakes Simcoe and Huron, as also with regard to the building of gunboats at Penetanguishene Bay for their conveyance thither.

In fact I had, prior to the receipt of Your Excellency's letter, ordered two of the latter description of boat to be constructed at that place for the transport of the provisions and stores for some time since deposited at Machedash, and also for 100 bbls. of flour and 50 of pork, which I had ordered, in addition, before I left York.

I found it totally impracticable to push the troops of the Right Division beyond Buffalo, and fortunately I did not even attempt it, for with every exertion I had only sufficient time to repass them across the river previous to it being blocked up with ice. With regard to Sackett's Harbor any information I have received from thence has been so unsatisfactory that I cannot form any just opinion of the practicability of any attempt upon it at present, but Your Excellency may rest assured that I will not lose sight of any favorable opportunity that may offer of aiming a heavy stroke at so vital a spot of the enemy's resources in this neighborhood. Your Excellency is at the same time well aware of the inadequacy of the force I can command in this vicinity for an operation of any magnitude.

(Canadian Archives, C. 682, p. 27.)

Major General Hall to Governor Tompkins.

BATAVIA, January 20, 1814.

SIR,—
Nothing important has occurred since I last wrote you. Our scouting parties from the camp near Lewiston occasionally approach within musket shot of Fort Niagara. It is ascertained the enemy keep no guards without the fort. The garrison from the best information that can be obtained, consists of 250 or three hundred men commanded by Colonel Young of the 8th Regiment. There has been but little appearance of force seen of late opposite Black Rock and Buffalo. The whole force of the enemy, from information recently received, and their disposition were as follows:—

Say, 200 at Burlington Heights—Major Clegg.
300 at Ft. Niagara—Colonel Young.
300 at Queenston Heights—Col. Hamilton.
1,200 from Chippawa to Erie.
300 or 400 Indians of the Six Nations.
800 or 1,000 Indians commanded by Colonels Elliott and Claus; the whole said to be under the command of Major General Riall.

There are no militia now in service on the British side of the Niagara River, according to late accounts from that side.

It is reported that Lieut. General Drummond has gone to Lower Canada, accompanied by Colonel Murray, who commanded at the capture of Fort Niagara and received a wound in the wrist. I have recently received letters from Major General Mead of Meadville and Captain Elliott commanding the navy at Erie, stating the apprehension of an attack at the latter place as soon as the ice becomes sufficiently strong to pass over, which generally happens by the 10th of February. They have requested me to co-operate with them by stationing a force at Chautauqua. In answer I was obliged to state that my force on this station will be small and barely sufficient to guard the frontier and quiet the fears of the inhabitants. My force may be calculated as follows:—

1st detachment of 1,000, at most 600.
2d detachment of 1,900, say 1,000, possibly 1,200, making at most 1,800 men.

This force will be stationed at Williamsville and near Lewiston, and nearly equally divided. There are about 150 regulars, (such as they are,) on this frontier without officers, except a Lieutenant Riddle, who, I am informed by himself, is ordered to superintend the recruiting service at this place. But Major Malcomb arrived this evening with orders from General Wilkinson for those troops to join their several regiments at French Mills, &c. The second detachment of militia is coming in daily, and as fast as they can be organized are marched to Williamsville and the cantonment near Lewiston.

(Tompkins Papers, Vol. IX, pp. 39-40. New York State Library.)

General Order.

HEADQUARTERS, Jan'y 20, 1814.

The detachment of the militia from the 7th, 38th and 6th Brigades will be organized into companies of 100 men each, officers inclusive. The Brig. Gen. will cause them to be mustered by Major Riddle, who is appointed to that duty. As soon as the muster is completed the men will be furnished with arms, &c., and camp equipage. They will march under the direction of officers of companies to the cantonment quarters of Gen. J. Swift on the Ridge Road near Lewiston, where they will report themselves to the commanding officer on that station.

The officers commanding companies will be held responsible for damages done by their soldiers on the march, and they are strictly charged to keep their men in order and not suffer any of them to leave their places in the ranks without permission. Every attention will be paid by the officers to the men; they will see that their quarters are the best that can be provided while on the march. The practice of disorderly firing, which has been the subject of much complaint, and is seriously to be regretted, by militia heretofore called into service, from the good conduct and orderly appearance of the present detachment, the Major-General flatters himself, will in no instance happen. One company of the detachment from the 24th and 39th Brigades will be supplied with arms, etc., and commence their march as soon as they have been mustered for Williamsville, under the direction of the commanding officer of the company, who will be accountable for the orderly and good conduct of the men.

They will not be suffered to stroll, but will march in order. The captain will report himself and the company to the commanding officer at Williamsville on his arrival.

A. HALL, Maj.-Gen. Comm'd'g Niagara Frontier.

(Publications of the Buffalo Historical Society, Vol. V., pp. 44-5.)

Anthony Lamb to Governer Tompkins.

ALBANY, Jan. 20th, 1814.

SIR,—

Agreeably to Your Excellency's orders, I left this city on the 4th inst. and proceeded with all possible despatch to the Niagara Frontier. On my arrival at Bloomfield in the County of Ontario, I met Gen. Hall, who was on the point of returning to Batavia to collect the troops who had been detached, under Your Excellency's order of the 26th November, which amounted to one thousand, which he had ordered out on authority subsequently given him.

On my arrival at Batavia I found that the inhabitants of that place and the country west as far as Buffalo on the main road had, on receiving information of the landing of the enemy, fled and left their homes, but were generally returning. I proceeded to Buffalo and found that flourishing village totally destroyed. The only buildings remaining in it are the gaol, which is built of stone, a small frame house, and an armourer's shop. All the houses east of Buffalo on the Batavia road for two miles, excepting log houses, are also destroyed, and almost every building between Buffalo and Niagara along the river had, I was informed, shared the same fate.

The enemy had with him at Black Rock and Buffalo a number of Indians, (the general opinion in that country is about two hundred,) who pursued their accustomed mode of horrid warfare, by tomahawking, scalping, and otherwise mutilating those who fell into their hands. Among the victims of their savage barbarity was a Mrs. Lovejoy of Buffalo, who was tomahawked and afterwards burnt in her own house. The conduct of these savages has struck the minds of the people on the Niagara frontier with such horror as to make it absolutely necessary that a more efficient force than ordinary militia of the country be employed for its protection, to prevent its becoming entirely depopulated.

There was, when I left Batavia, between five and six hundred militia at Williamsville and its vicinity, under command of General Hopkins, and about the same number on the Ridge Road, near the arsenal, under the command of Col. Hopkins. It was the intention of Gen. Hall, who was at Batavia, to make up the number at each of these stations to one thousand men. There was also at Batavia about one hundred regulars under the command of Major Riddle, who had received orders to march to Williamsville.

As the enemy had recrossed into Canada, leaving no part of his force in our territory except the garrison at Fort Niagara, I did not think it necessary for me to remain in the country, or to exercise the plenary powers with which you were pleased to invest me, especially as the authority given to Gen. Hall appeared to me to be amply sufficient to enable him to give a temporary protection to that frontier. I am decidedly of opinion, however, that it is absolutely necessary that a force of a more permanent substantial nature should be provided with as little delay as possible.

(Ketchum's History of Buffalo, Vol. II., pp. 398-9.)

The Secretary of War to General Wilkinson.

WAR DEPARTMENT, Jan. 20, 1814.

SIR,—

I have the orders of the President to inform you, that under a full consideration of your present position on Salmon River, in relation as well to present safety as to future operations, it is his direction that you abandon that position, and that, after detaching General Brown with two thousand men and a competent proportion of your field and battering cannon to Sackett's Harbor, you will fall back with the residue of your force, stores and baggage, &c., to Plattsburg. Means should be immediately taken to cover the men in huts or barracks, and, to promote this object, orders will be directly sent from this office to the officers commanding at Plattsburg and Sackett's Harbor to put into activity, by hired labor and fatigue duty, all the resources within their respective commands. This will not, however, supersede any auxiliary measures or orders going to the same object which your judgment and experience may suggest.

The sick and wounded of the army should be sent to Burlington.

(Wilkinson's Memoirs, Vol. III., Appendix XLIX.)

General Order.

Headquarters, BATAVIA, Jan. 21st, 1814.

By permission of the High Sheriff of Genesee County a room in the gaol of the said county is to be the provost guardhouse at this station, and Capt. N. Marvin will furnish a corporal and four men for provost guards. The provost guards will take into custody ——— Burgess, charged with holding correspondence with the enemy, and keep him safely until further orders.

By order of Maj.-Gen. A. Hall,
WILLIAM H. ADAMS, Acting A. D. C

(Publications of the Buffalo Historical Society, Vol. V., p. 45.)

Major-General Hall to Major-General Mead, at Erie, Pa.

BATAVIA, Jan. 21st, 1814.

MAJOR-GEN'L MEAD,—

SIR,—This will accompany my letter in answer to yours of the 11th inst. I was not informed until last evening that the express who brought your letter was waiting for an answer. I was at that time on the northern part of the frontier and your express came no further than Williamsville. I had ordered an express to go through Erie, to start this morning, but shall send this by your express.

I have nothing new to inform you of respecting the movements of the enemy, nor can I ascertain to my satisfaction whether their main force is gone on any secret expedition or not. The following is the latest, and I believe the most correct, account to be obtained, except the forces said to be above Chippawa. . . . .

(Publications of the Buffalo Historical Society, Vol. V., p. 45.)

Lieutenant-General Drummond to Sir George Prevost.

KINGSTON, January 21st, 1814.

SIR,—

Your Excellency's letter of the 17th ultimo, directing me to give my opinion of the practicability of an attempt being made for the destruction of the enemy's vessels and craft on Lake Erie, I have the honor to acquaint you that I have had, since my return to Kingston, frequent communications with Commodore Sir James Yeo and with Colonel Nichol, Quartermaster General of Militia, whose local knowledge renders him competent to afford the most correct information on this important subject.

The security of the right flank of the army and the preservation of the intercourse with and influence over the Western Indians being objects of the very first importance, it is proposed to undertake an expedition against Detroit and the enemy's vessels in that quarter as the only means by which these ends can be obtained.

In making arrangements for the service due regard must be had to the immediate security of the Niagara frontier, the force which the enemy has at Detroit, and the means necessary to transport and provision the force which it may be thought necessary to employ.

From the destruction of the enemy's boats and craft on the Niagara, no apprehension of an attack need be entertained on any part of that line below Fort Erie, and a very small force will suffice to prevent their crossing on the ice. By blocking up the roads leading from Sugar Loaf and from Haun's, all the routes except that immediately on the bank of the river, will be closed, and therefore our line of defence will be shortened and greatly strengthened. Under these circumstances, I should consider twelve hundred men as amply sufficient for the defence of this line, which will leave a sufficient number for performing the other service.

I am not correctly informed as to the strength of the enemy at Detroit, but, from the information I have received, it cannot be very great, and I understand it is not in their power to subsist a very large force in that country, it having been greatly exhausted during the last campaign, and the enemy having no other resource but to bring their provisions from the State of Ohio on pack horses and in waggons, which is a most tedious, expensive and difficult mode of supply. I should not, under the circumstances just mentioned, estimate the force of the enemy at more than six hundred effective men. Of these I suppose four hundred to be in garrison at Detroit, the remainder at Amherstburg, Sandwich and other outposts.

The force I should propose for this service would be:—

100th Regiment		500
Light company, Royal Scots		100
Do	41st Regiment completed to	100
Do	89th Regiment	50
		750
Marines, if to be had		100
		850
Marine artillery, with two six-pounders and one 5½ inch howitzer		40
Militia		250
Western Indians		400
Capt. Coleman's Provincial troop		20
Seamen		200
		1,760

The detachment of seamen would be of the greatest service in the attack on the vessels in Put-in-Bay.

The next consideration is the moving and provisioning this force, which, from the state of the country, must be marched in separate columns and probably by the following routes:—

Light Infantry and part of the militia, by the Talbot Road.

100th Regiment, &c., and guns, through Oxford. Indians, from Point aux Pins to Point Pelee, followed by light infantry and part of the militia through the woods.

A road at this season of the year, the ground being frozen, may be made with facility through the woods from the Thames to Amherstburg, without going round, and by moving by this last mentioned route to the new settlements on the lake, with the aid of the militia of that country, all communications with the islands will be prevented and Amherstburg will immediately be secured with such resources as the surrounding country can supply, while the rapid advance of the troops by the Thames will prevent the enemy from detaching, either to support Amherstburg or to reinforce their post at the islands.

In some instances it will be necessary for the troops to sleep out, but, being sheltered by the woods and with large fires, it is hoped they will not suffer much.

The troops should be provided with bill-hooks or light hatchets, and the militia with each a good axe, exclusive of his musquet or rifle, and the whole to be supplied with creepers.

The provisions necessary to subsist this force may be calculated at 2,500 rations per diem, weighing, including contingencies, two and a half pounds each, or 6,250 lbs. A sleigh may be calculated to carry (1,000 lbs.) one thousand pounds weight, so that for 21 days' provisions 132 sleighs would be requisite. It is, however, proposed to take 300 sleighs, as in moving the troops forward they might (as it is called) ride and tie, that is, suppose a column of 500 men on the march, 250 might make 12 or 15 miles without halting, while the other 250 went on in sleighs. After the end of this march, the party in sleighs, having refreshed themselves, would proceed on foot, leaving the sleighs for the party in rear, who would get into them and overtake the party in advance in the evening, by which means they might proceed thirty miles per day.

To procure the necessary number of sleighs, active young officers from the militia should be selected, viz.: one in each township, who would procure even twice the number if wanted.

On arriving at Amherstburg the movements of the troops would altogether depend on the information received. But I should think that the capture of Detroit would be indispensable, previous to any attack upon the vessels, unless they were in Detroit river, as were Detroit left in the enemy's possession the vessels at the islands could not be maintained without running a very great risque.

The river Detroit during the winter may be crossed in several places, though seldom immediately opposite the town. And in Lake St. Clair and at Bar Point, below Amherstburg, it may be crossed in most seasons as late as the middle of March.

The distance from Amherstburg to Put-in-Bay, where two of the enemy's vessels are said to be, is about forty miles, all the way on the ice.

Should the expedition be determined upon, the sooner it is undertaken the better, as the enemy will doubtless make great exertions to reinforce and provision Detroit, which delay on our part will perfectly enable them to effect.

As much biscuit as possible should immediately be baked, on which subject I have called the attention of the commissariat at Niagara and York.

I need scarcely observe to Your Excellency the necessity of the commissariat being furnished with four or five thousand pounds in specie and small bills for this occasion.

Should this proposed outline of operations meet Your Excellency's view, I shall lose no time in putting matters in train for carrying them into execution, altho' the state of the roads through the want of snow, from the Bay of Quinte upwards, renders any movement of such a nature at present totally impracticable.

I am aware there are several minor arrangements to be made, but which easily can be, provided the general plan be approved of.

I propose moving with this expedition myself, and Commodore Sir James Yeo has expressed his intention to accompany me. I shall be most happy to avail myself of his services if it meets Your Excellency's approbation.

(Canadian Archives, C. 682, p. 32.)

Colonel R. H. Bruyeres to Sir George Prevost.

YORK, 23d January, 1814.

SIR,—

I have to report to Your Excellency my arrival here yesterday. I was detained some days at Kingston, waiting the arrival of Gen'l Drummond, as I was apprehensive of passing him on the road. I have made every inquiry since I have been here, respecting the practicability of building four gunboats in Penetanguishene harbor on Lake Huron, for the purpose of communicating from thence to the island of Michilimackinac as early as the opening of navigation will permit. The total want of resources in this part of the country renders any public undertaking extremely difficult and uncertain. I have seen the only person that could be competent for this service (Mr. Dennis, late master-builder at Kingston.) He is at present unemployed, but from the conversation I have had with him he is unwilling to engage in this business owing to the impossibility of procuring workmen here for the purpose. Captain Barclay, whom I have seen on this subject, very strongly recommends a Mr. Bell, who was master-builder at Amherstburg. He is now at Kingston and I have written to Gen'l Drummond to endeavour to engage him for this service, and to procure 12 shipwrights to accompany him. I have stated fully all that will be necessary, and I still hope that this business may be accomplished.

The total want of artificers and laborers of every description has retarded the progress of all the public works here, and unless some efficient means are taken to procure men nothing effectual can be done towards the defence of the place. Kitson has exerted himself to the utmost, but personal exertion is of no use without assistance. Only 13 carpenters are now employed, whereas four times the number are required. The want of snow has also retarded the supply of materials being brought, but the roads are now more practicable and I have directed requisitions to be made for all that is necessary.

Mr. Crookshank, the commissary, is now at Lake Simcoe, where, I understand, he is gone to make arrangement for the building of five bateaux, to convey provisions that were left on the communication to be sent to Michilimackinac.

I proceed this day towards Niagara, and will make every arrangement in my power, on my arrival there, for the security of that frontier, but I am informed the want of workmen is fully as severely felt as in this place, and in some instances worse, but I will do the best that can be devised for the public service.

(Canadian Archives, C. 732, p. 10.)

General Order.

Headquarters, BATAVIA, Jan. 23d, 1814.

Lt.-Col. Jno. Harris will proceed to Hardscrabble, to the cantonment now occupied by the troops under the command of Col. Swift, and take charge of the detachment to the command of which he was assigned by Division Orders of the 8th inst., marched and marching to their station. The troops under the command of Lt.-Col. Harris will be quartered in as compact a manner as the nature of the ground and the present barracks will admit, and Col. Harris will make the proper provision for quarters by building huts as soon as may be. Lt.-Col. Harris, being on the exterior post, will be vigilant in providing against surprise, by sending patrols to Lewiston, by keeping a picquet at Hustler's and such other place and places as his discretion shall direct, and by causing patrols to Schlosser, Manchester, and as near the enemy as he may deem practicable. The strictest attention will be paid to the comfort and convenience of the men, to the preservation of their arms, &c. No parties will be allowed to sally out or stroll from the camp, nor will any scouts be suffered but by the particular order of the commanding office. The commanding officers of the companies will be held responsible for the safe-keeping of the arms, accoutrements and ammunition, and see that no waste be committed. Morning reports will be required. Some house in the rear will be assigned as a hospital and particular attention paid to the sick. The commanding officer will pay attention to provision returns and see that they correspond with morning reports.

From the talents and experience of Col. Harris, the Major-General has the strongest confidence that the important post to the command of which he is designed and the regulation and discipline of the troops will be such as to reflect honor on the officers and soldiers.

WILLIAM H. ADAMS, A. D. C.

General Order.

Headquarters, BATAVIA, Jan. 23d, 1814.

Brig.-Genl. Burnett will repair to the cantonment at Williamsville, (Eleven Mile Creek,) and take command of the troops on that station and vicinity. Genl. Burnett will cause the detachment under his command to be quartered in the barracks already existing at the cantonment, as far as those barracks will accommodate them and as near as may be. Should there not be a sufficient number of huts to accommodate the whole detachment, no time is to be lost in building, taking care that the troops are quartered in a compact and regular manner. Genl. Burnett will be vigilant in providing against surprise, by causing picquets, patrols, etc., at such places and in such directions as his discretion shall direct. No troops are to be stationed in advance of the cantonment but by detachment and the countersign, etc., will emanate from cantonment quarters. No men will be allowed to stroll from camp, nor any scouts be suffered but by particular orders of the commanding officer. The commandants of companies will be responsible for the arms, accoutrements and ammunition of the men and see that no waste be committed.

The zeal of Genl. Burnett in defence of our common country, as well as the promptitude and decision, which has characterized him in the detachment and organization of troops, are a sure pledge to the Major-General that the cantonment committed to his charge and the troops under his command will be in such a state of regularity and efficiency as to meet the expectation of an anxious and exposed country.

By order,

WILLIAM H. ADAMS, Acting A. D. C.

(Publications of the Buffalo Historical Society, Vol. V., pp. 47-3.)

Lieut.-General Drummond to Sir George Prevost.

KINGSTON, 23d January, 1814.

DEAR SIR,—

Since addressing to Your Excellency the proposed outline of operations against Detroit and the enemy's vessels on Lake Erie, it has struck me that you might consider it advisable to send part of the reinforcements destined for Michilimackinac with the Detroit expedition instead of by the route of Penetanguishene Bay, as they would serve, in the first instance, to increase the strength of the assailing force, and might afterwards, in the event of success, easily be transported from Detroit to their ultimate destination. Your Excellency will perhaps favor me with your opinion on this subject.

(Canadian Archives, C. 682, p. 41.)

New York Evening Post, 29th January, 1814.

HARRISBURG, January 24, 1814.

Accounts from the westward received here this evening, as the general opinion at Erie, that the British were preparing to attack Erie and the fleet. A letter dated January 4th at Cattaraugus, from Colonel John McMahon to Colonel J. W. Wallace at Erie, states that as soon as the ice would admit of it, 100 sleighs, each with 6 men, were to proceed to Erie, to burn that place and the fleet, at the risk of sacrificing his whole force. The *Trippe, Little Belt* and *Chippewa* were burnt at Buffalo—the *Ariel* escaped.

From the Diary of Thomas McCrae.

RALEIGH, Monday, 24th Jany, 1814.

Tom Johns, Norton & Chambers were here this evening on their return to Detroit.

Sunday, 30th January, 1814.

Some of the Am(erican) light or heavy horse came up the (last) night and it is said some of them were surprised and taken to-day by a party of the British at Richardson's.

Monday, 31st January, 1814.

It is only a false report about the British taking the party at Richardson's.

Wednesday, 2d February, 1814.

The Am(erican) party went down this afternoon. They took down John Dolsen, Fran. Baby, old Cun. Springer, old Brigham and some unknown person. They were here hunting Billy and James McGregor.

A list of men on duty at the house of Andrew Westbrook, in Delaware, from the 22d January to the 1st February, 1814, under command of Captain Daniel Springer:
Benjamin Schram.
Joseph House.
William Dingman.
William Schram.
David Dingman.
John McClemings.
John Davy.
John Chamberling.
John Crandall.
Frederick Shineck.
Samuel Stiles.
Frederick Stroback.

(From the Talbot Papers.)

Major-General Hall to Major-General Swift.

BATAVIA, Jan. 24, 1814.

SIR,—
I have this moment received your letter of 8 o'clock last evening. I regret very much that you have not a force equal not only to meet but to hunt the enemy back to the fort. There are four companies of 100 men each on their way to your relief, one of which must undoubtedly arrive this morning, another in the course of this day, probably two. That will give you a handsome reinforcement. One other company will march to-day and Col. Harris will move this morning. They are all well equipped. I have no doubt that you will do everything to repel the enemy, should they attempt to attack you, that your force would justify. Your judgment will direct your immediate operations. I have to request that you would stay with Col. Harris a few days after his arrival, if possible. You will be of great service to him.

(Publications of the Buffalo Historical Society, Vol. V., pp. 48-9.)

Brig. General Gano to Major-General Harrison.

Headquarters, O. M., LOWER SANDUSKY,
January 25, 1814.

DEAR GENERAL,—
Yours of the 16th I received this day and directed my brigade major to make the enclosed report, by which you will see the situation of the troops under my command. I have issued orders as per enclosed copies. The difficulty in forwarding provisions, owing to the impossibility of transportation by land, has been and is severely felt. The troops at Meigs have been obliged to take flour from Winchester themselves, there being no other means of transport, and are now but scantily supplied. I have urged the contractors on this head, but have received nothing but fair promises until my patience is entirely exhausted, and I have directed Mr. Oliver to supply. A man from Put-in-Bay left here this morning. He informs me the detachment I sent on had not been able to cross on the ice but are waiting at the point of the peninsula and will cross as soon as possible. I have ordered Major Crooks with some militia to cross, which will make the force there as follows:—Sailors, twenty-two; Atkins' command, forty-two, all now there; McFarland with twenty-eight regulars on the march, and Crooks with Captain Howel's company, say forty, which is one hundred and thirty-two, and I have one company at the fort at Portage. I fear that the provisions at the island are not sufficient to support them until the ice will break up to afford water transportation to them, and at Portage they depend on this place for flour, which is scarce; they have, however, meat enough there. Thus you see, as before I observed to you, we are between hawk and buzzard—the contractor and commissary. I am told the detachment that returned to Detroit from the Thames did not succeed in getting the quantity of provision expected. I am also informed by some officers from Buffalo that the British are preparing a secret expedition, their destination unknown. I am happy to inform you that every exertion has been made at Detroit, Sandwich and Malden to defend those places to the last extremity, and the commanding officer, since General Cass left there, deserves great credit. Neither of those places will be given up without some fighting; the officers commanding are in high spirits and have great confidence in their ability to defend their posts. Some artillery officers have passed on to Detroit, and I am of opinion that some active regular officers are wanting there, as many have left it. The militia have been very much reduced there, as you will see. I must inform you I have lost a number of my militia out of the few I had here, I buried at this place fifteen or sixteen, which is as great a proportion as they have lost at Detroit, and one other small part of a company

has lost seven. I have never mentioned this part of the subject before, as I thought it best to keep it close. I am informed some Canadians attempted to cross from Long Point to Put-in-Bay, their object not known. I assure you I have and will continue to use every exertion for the good of the service. I have had the arms, &c., that the Kentuckians threw away at Portage collected, and the principal part brought to this place, and the cattle and some horses have been taken and converted to public use. There is plenty of ammunition at Fort Meigs but it is scarce on this line. I sent for powder to Meigs but our means of transportation was such that we only received two hundred pounds, half cannon, but I am informed there is a large quantity on board the vessels, fixed and unfixed, and six thousand five hundred stand of arms, some field carriages, &c., which I have ordered to be brought over as soon as the ice will permit. The roads are so very bad it has been impracticable. I am well satisfied I have not been ordered to Detroit, and particularly as General Cass appeared to be opposed to it, and I have had immense trouble in regulating my different posts and quieting the murmurs of my militia. They are very good, but not such as I used to take the field with when we were first acquainted in the former Indian wars

. . . .

P. S.—You will see a great diminution in my force, many being sick and absent, and I having discharged two companies by your order to escort the prisoners, &c. My first report was two thousand one hundred and thirty-four, and the amount ordered to Detroit was near six hundred. You see now the number of effectives there are amazingly reduced.

(American State Papers, Military Affairs, Vol. I., p. 656.)

Lieut. General Drummond to Sir George Prevost.

KINGSTON, Jan'y 25th, 1814.

SIR,—

I have already had the honor of communicating to Your Excellency in my letter of the 23d ultimo, the gallant conduct of Lieut. Medcalf of the volunteer militia of the Western District, in surprising and capturing a detachment of the enemy on the river Thames early in the last month. I have now the honor to transmit that officer's own report on the subject.

I consider it to reflect so high credit on Lieut. Medcalf's loyalty, gallantry and indefatigable zeal that I have conferred on him the provincial rank of captain in consequence.

(Canadian Archives, C. 682, p. 43.)

Lieut. General Drummond to Sir George Prevost.

KINGSTON, January 25th, 1814.

SIR,—
I have the honor to acquaint Your Excellency that I have received a report from Major General Riall dated the 14th inst., stating that two militia men, Isaac Ryan and Andrew Hearn, taken prisoners about 7 months since, had arrived at Niagara, having made their escape from Greenbush, where they had been confined with about 320 other regular and militia soldiers.

They passed through Sackett's Harbor last Thursday week.

They confirm the account of the march of troops from that place to Salmon River and say that there are no troops at Sackett's Harbor but the seamen and carpenters employed in building three brigs, as they were told, and they declare there is no other force than what they mention.

About 50 or 60 other prisoners made their escape from Greenbush at the same time by undermining the prison.

I beg leave to communicate the substance of other intelligence I received this day, viz:—

That sleighs are collecting at Sackett's Harbor to the number of 200 and to rendezvous there on Saturday at an early hour for the purpose of loading provisions for the army at Salmon River, at least such was the report. But better informed persons believe that they were collected for some military movement and think it more than probable that the evacuation of the position at French Mills is in contemplation, and that the troops and stores will be sent from thence to Sackett's Harbor to secure the ships to be built there.

The effective force at the former place is said to be about 2,000, at the latter it does not exceed 600 men.

(Canadian Archives, C. 682, pp. 49-51.)

PROCLAMATION.

By His Honor Gordon Drummond, President, administering the Province of Upper Canada, and Lieutenant General commanding His Majesty's Forces in the same.

A PROCLAMATION.

Whereas by a Proclamation issued by the late President, Major General Francis de Rottenburg, bearing date the twenty-second day of November last, Martial Law, so far as related to the procuring of provisions and forage, was thereby declared to be in force in the Eastern and Johnstown Districts, and whereas that measure being no longer necessary, I do therefore by virtue of the power and authority in me vested hereby declare the said proclamation no longer to be in force.

Given under my hand and seal at arms at Kingston this twenty-fifth day of January, one thousand eight hundred and fourteen, and in the fifty-fourth year of His Majesty's reign:

GORDON DRUMMOND,
Lieut. Gen. and President.

Lieut. General Drummond to Sir George Prevost.

KINGSTON, January 26, 1814.

SIR,—

I have the honor to acquaint Your Excellency that, agreeable to directions, I had given to Major General Riall before leaving Niagara, that officer has reported to me that he met several of the most respectable inhabitants of that part of the country for the purpose of enquiring into the resources the country possesses for providing the Right Division during the ensuing summer. The general opinion was that though the crop last year was much short of what it had been for several preceding years, yet from the measures that had been adopted, (according to a proclamation I had found necessary to issue to that effect,) of preventing the distillation of grain, a sufficient supply is still in the country, *provided the resources in the neighborhood of Long Point are collected in due time,* to last until the harvest of the present year is got in, but it is also the opinion that a scarcity of flesh meat is to be apprehended, as the black cattle are already a good deal exhausted and very little pork has been cured, from the difficulty of procuring salt and the small number of hogs which has been put up to fatten in consequence of the failure of the spring crops.

Such being the state of resources for provisioning the Right Division of the army and Mr. Dance, the Assistant Commissary General, having made a calculation that he had not nor could he procure a greater quantity of meat than would be sufficient for 7,000 men for 86 days, I beg to draw Your Excellency's attention most strongly to the case and to request that the Commissary General may be directed to send up a supply of pork the very first opportunity practicable.

The opinion with respect to grain is formed upon the supposition that the issue of rations may amount to between 7,000 and 8,000 daily.

I had already endeavored to diminish this number by sounding as delicately as possible the disposition of the Grand River Indians to return to their homes. But to this measure they objected, as they had no means of supporting themselves and families, from their provision grounds having been altogether neglected during the last season.

Major General Riall has also reported to me an opinion of these gentlemen, and in which I am in some degree induced to concur and to which, if it should meet Your Excellency's approbation, I will turn my more minute attention, namely, that it would prove a matter of much economy to Government and of great public benefit and convenience that a corps of waggoners be attached to the Commissariat Department, as it (would) permit the farmers to remain at home and afford them the means of pursuing their agricultural avocations, whereby the resources of the country would be considerably increased, and when an occasion did exist of calling upon them for the public service their horses and carriages would be in good order, they would give much more willingly and would do twice as much work in the same portion of time as they now do, from being constantly jaded and harassed.

The carriage of flour now from the Forty Mile Creek to Niagara costs four dollars per barrel, the sleighs being obliged to travel around by the mountain, as there is no snow by the lower road, and this to go and return requires four days.

I am happy notwithstanding to acquaint Your Excellency that the necessary quantity of flour and fuel is getting into Fort Niagara with tolerable expedition.

(Canadian Archives, C. 682, pp. 52-5.)

Secret Information.

I am well informed that five hundred sleighs were to assemble at Sackett's Harbor on Friday night last for the purpose of carrying troops to make a descent or diversion against Canada. The object cannot be known certainly. Rumor says Kingston or Prescott. I think the latter. They are to take about 3,000 troops; 1,500 are of Harrison's army, and 500 are dragoons armed with pikes, scaling ladders, &c.

From a letter.

A true copy lately in my possession.

THOS. OSBORNE, D. A. C. Gen.

(Canadian Archives, C. 682, p. 56.)

Lieut Colonel Thomas Fraser to ———

PRESCOTT, January 26th, 1814.

SIR,—

Last night two men from Hamilton who have been employed

this some time in procuring information of the movements of the American army have informed me that 500 sleighs, assembled at Sackett's Harbor or near there for the purpose of transporting troops either to Kingston or Prescott, but generally supposed the latter, 500 of dragoons who were with Wilkinson's army, armed with long pikes, and 1,500 of Harrison's army, and a number of troops from Sackett's Harbor and elsewhere, amounting in all to 3,000.

(Canadian Archives, C. 682, p. 56.)

Lieut. General Drummond to Sir George Prevost.

KINGSTON, January 27th, 1814.

SIR,—

. . . .
. . . .

I am concerned to say that nothing has been as yet done at Fort Erie or Chippawa and little at Fort Niagara, in consequence of the confinement from opthalmia of Lieutenant Gaugreben ever since I left the frontier and the illness of Major Holcroft, Royal Artillery.

The inefficiency of these two officers at the present juncture is particularly inconvenient. But I trust should Lieutenant Gaugreben's indisposition prove likely to continue for any considerable length of time that Lieutenant Colonel Bruyeres will see the necessity of there being an active and intelligent officer to supply Lieutenant Gaugreben's place at that post.

Major General Riall acquaints me that Major Holcroft has received instructions from Your Excellency to station 50 artillerymen in Fort Niagara.

(Canadian Archives, C. 682, pp. 61-2.)

Lieut. General Drummond to Sir George Prevost.

KINGSTON, January 27th, 1814.

SIR,—

I have the honor to enclose herewith for Your Excellency's information the copy of intelligence I received this day relative to the enemy's movements in the neighborhood of Sackett's Harbor.

I have already directed the utmost vigilance to be preserved at Cornwall, Prescott and Gananoqui, and particularly at the two latter posts, that every individual, (officer and soldier,) should sleep within the fort and blockhouse, excepting of course the necessary picquets.

Lieut. Colonel MacBean in transmitting me the enclosed did not mention in what state the ice was in the neighborhood of Prescott. I know that the river was open a few days ago.

(Canadian Archives, C. 682, pp. 57-8.)

Lieut. General Drummond to Sir George Prevost.

KINGSTON, January 28th, 1814.

SIR,—

I have the honor to acquaint Your Excellency that I received a communication from Deputy Assistant Commissary General Crookshank, at York, on his return from Lake Simcoe, where he had been to make arrangements for forwarding the supplies to Michilimackinac.

He informs me, that from the authority of several credible persons, and likewise from Mr. Wilmot, the surveyor who had been employed in running the line from Lake Simcoe to Penetanguishene Bay, that it is impracticable to transport anything by that route previous to a road being cut upwards of thirty miles in length, and that it was calculated to take 200 men for at least three weeks before it could be made passable, and in case of deep snow it could not be done at all. In consequence of the delay and the difficulty attending such a measure, Mr. Crookshank has made arrangements for forwarding the supplies to Nottawasaga Bay, on Lake Huron, a distance of only 20 miles from Penetanguishene.

The opening of the road to the river leading to Nottawasaga Bay will take but 12 men for 10 days, and in the course of a few days, as soon as a shed can be erected on the other side of Lake Simcoe, he will commence sending the stores across it, should a thaw not prevent.

As Mr. Crookshank found it almost impossible to procure hands to build boats, and altogether so a person to contract for the whole, or even a part, I have had a communication with the Commissioner of the Navy here, who says he could furnish 30 workmen, with an able foreman, that would ensure the measure being completed in a given time, contracts at once for the building of as many as should be required, and they could set out from hence at a day's notice, well furnished with tools and oakum and every other requisite for the occasion.

This mode of proceeding would undoubtedly prove somewhat expensive, but I see no alternative, and as there would be some check on the work of the new ships here, unless it was thought proper to send up an additional number of workmen to supply the place of those otherwise to be employed, I have to request Your Excellency's instructions on this head as soon as convenient.

P. S.—Since writing the foregoing I have received a letter from Lt.-Col. Bruyeres, from York, corroborating that part of Mr. Crookshank's letter relative to the inability of procuring persons there to build at Penetanguishene, and asserting that the only way this object can be accomplished is by sending up builders with the necessary materials of pitch, ironwork, &c., from Kingston.

(Canadian Archives, C. 682, p. 67.)

Brig.-General Gano to Major-General Harrison.

LOWER SANDUSKY, January 27, 1814.

DEAR GENERAL,—

Captain Payne has called on me to sanction his drawing funds for his department. I have thought proper to refer him to you. I am informed a good supply of corn may be had near a mill forty miles from this. Will it not be advisable to have three or four hundred of meal forwarded on to the army? The flour the contractor's agent promised should have been here ten days ago but has not arrived, and, owing to the disappointment, we are reduced in that article at this post, to nineteen barrels; Seneca, 17; Portage, ———. I sent four barrels there yesterday. At Meigs they are very short; at Winchester they have two or three hundred barrels, but short of meat. I must confess I have been completely deceived and disappointed by them, they having stated it was on the road. I gave them notice the 24th December to have three months' rations at the different posts for the number specified. Captain Payne knows the situation. You will please give him such directions as you think proper on this subject. He certainly exerted himself much to my satisfaction in forwarding provisions and clothing to Detroit. You know him. If he could get leave to settle his accounts it may be best. Excuse this suggestion. If you had not arrived in your district I was determined to have sent in every direction and purchased provisions, at all events for the troops in service and those that were to relieve, but I am happy the arrangement has fallen into your hands, for I think *I would hang half of the quartermasters and all the contractors if I was to remain in service much longer,* and I am astonished how you have managed with them to effect the objects you have, for there seems no system of regularity with any of them. I have ordered one company more to this place from Findlay, and one sergeant, two corporals and twelve men from Upper Sandusky to that post, which is all the force I can order from this and the centre line. This day's report is eighty sick at Meigs. I am happy to inform you the troops at Detroit are recovering, for you see we can afford them but little aid. If a successful attempt is made at Put-in-Bay, (which God forbid, and I think impossible,) we may have a visit from them. We will endeavor to give a good account, for my men are in high spirits and I have added much to the strength of this place. We are not well supplied with ammunition, but have sent for some from the shipping and Franklinton.

(American State Papers, Military Affairs, Vol. I., p. 657.)

Major General Wilkinson to Sir George Prevost.

PLATTSBURG, January 28th, 1814.

SIR,—

I am commanded by the Executive of the United States to disavow the conduct of Brigadier-General McClure of the militia of the State of New York in burning the town of Newark and in irrefragable testimony that this act was unlicensed to transmit to Your Excellency a copy of the order under color of which that officer perpetrated a deed abhorrent to every American feeling. From this testimonial Your Excellency will perceive that the authority to destroy the village was limited expressly to the defence of Fort George, a measure warranted by the laws of modern war and justified by precedents innumerable.

The outrages which have ensued the unwarrantable destruction of Newark have been carried too far and present the aspect rather of vindictive fury than just retaliation, yet they are imputed more to personal feeling than any settled plan of policy deliberately weighed and adopted, and I hope I shall receive from Your Excellency an assurance that this conclusion is not fallacious, for although the wanton conflagrations on the waters of the Chesapeake are fresh in the recollection of every citizen of the United States, no system of retaliation which has for its object the devastation of private property, will ever be resorted to by the American Government but in the last extremity, and this will depend on the conduct of your royal master's troops in this country.

(Canadian Archives, C. 682, p. 83-5.)

From Sir George Prevost to Lieut.-General Drummond.

Head Qrs., MONTREAL,

Secret. 29th Jany, 1814.

SIR,—

I waited the arrival of Sir James Yeo to reply to your letter of the 21st, containing your opinion upon the practicability of an attempt to destroy the enemy's vessels and craft on Lake Erie. The Commodore's sentiments respecting this highly important service appeared to me to fully accord with your own. The consequences which would result from the complete success of such an expedition are obvious, in fact that feat only seems wanting to the brilliant issue of the campaign, as it would place us in the proud attitude of again reoccupying the widely extended frontier of the Canadas, an event exceedingly to be desired.

Unless a sudden change should occur in the enemy's disposition of his force, the troops you propose to remain would give sufficient security to the Niagara frontier, and the force intended for the proposed service seems adequate; still there are obstacles of magnitude to be encountered, but the principal arise from the very advanced state of the season, the little time left to mature preparations, and which, were they even now complete, the impossibility of advancing for the want of snow.

These considerations, with the uncertainty of the western shore of Lake Erie being sufficiently frozen to render their ships in Put-in-Bay assailable, and the thorough conviction on my mind that to give a chance of success the possession of Sandwich and Amherstburg should be obtained by the 24th Feby, and the destruction of the five vessels, reported by the Commodore, accomplished by the 25th.

I consider such serious embarrassments as rendering doubtful the attainment of what is proposed, and the more so if either Amherstburg or Detroit must previously be reduced. The delay which would be caused by this operation would, I apprehend, render the subsequent and all important attack upon the remote vessels impracticable, from the decay and insecurity of the ice at a later period.

It is allowed that in all great enterprises some risk must be run and something left to fortune. In this instance success depends on a sufficiency of snow and the expeditious assemblage of the force to be employed, and the possibility of obtaining the number of sleighs for conveying it rapidly to the point of attack accompanied by an ample supply of provisions.

Should circumstances so far favor you as to permit the whole to move from Burlington or Ancaster by the 12th of Feby, and the snow on the ground at that time be sufficient, there appears a reasonable expectation of accomplishing a part of this important plan, but all depends on its being carried into execution with promptitude, celerity and secresy.

I am apprehensive the resources of the country you will have to traverse have rather been exaggerated by Lt. Colonel Nichol, and that the scarcity of provisions which has prevented the enemy from maintaining a sufficient force at Detroit will inevitably affect your ulterior movements and may compel you to retrograde as soon as the service has been executed.

Your wants shall be attended to as respects moneys and Lt.

Colonel McDouall will take with him £3,000 in specie and some small bills. The several other equipments, including provisions, blankets, billhooks and axes must be obtained in Upper Canada.

Whilst the enemy continues to concentrate a large disposable force near the frontier of Lower Canada, situated between Lakes St. Francois and Champlain, thereby indicating his intention that the pressure of the approaching campaign should fall upon that Province, you must be sensible of my total inability of augmenting your present force.

I give you this information that you may regulate your measures accordingly.

I conclude you have sought for information from Colonel Talbot respecting the state of things at Amherstburg and on the Detroit. From him you may obtain correct intelligence of the enemy's force and resources, and of the number and description of vessels which have wintered there. Such previous information must be considered as essential to your ulterior arrangements.

(Canadian Archives, C. 1222, pp. 32-5.)

From the Military Secretary to Lieut. General Drummond.

Head Qrs., MONTREAL, 30th January, 1814.

SIR,—

The Commander of the Forces has directed me to acknowledge his receipt of your letter of the 26th and two of the 27th instant, which arrived this morning. I have his commands to acquaint you, in reply to those communications, that the measures you have adopted for ascertaining the resources of the country appear calculated to ensure for the use of the troops and Indians during the ensuing season a supply of provisions to the extent that the part of the Province to be occupied by the Right Division will afford. The attention of the Commissary General will be immediately called to this important subject, that arrangements may be made for supplying the deficiency of flesh meat. The Commissary General will at the same time be required to consider and report upon the suggestion of the formation of a corps of waggoners in this department in Upper Canada.

Sir George Prevost approves of your having ordered the claims of individuals for supplies furnished to Government to be investigated by Major General Riall, and those that are equitable being settled without delay.

His Excellency regrets exceedingly the inconvenience you represent to exist in Upper Canada for the want of small moneys; he is aware that such a difficulty must occasion injury to the public service, and to remedy it is an object he has some time had in view. The measures now in operation by the Provincial Assembly of this Province for the issue of a large supply of small notes, not redeemable in cash, it is hoped will produce the effect.

His Excellency desires that of the specie sent forward yesterday in charge of Lt. Colonel McDouall you will order £1,500 to be appropriated to the subsistence of the corps, to be applied exclusively for the settlement of the balance of those Regts. which you state to have been so long unpaid. This sum will be replaced from Montreal by the first conveyance.

The command money for the post of Michilimackinac when placed in charge of a field officer is, by His Excellency's desire, to be increased to the same as that for Fort Niagara.

No command money is to be paid for Chippawa and Fort Erie until those posts are placed in a footing equal to their former establishment when that allowance was granted.

(Canadian Archives, C. 1222, pp. 35-7.)

From the Buffalo Gazette.

To the Editor of the Buffalo Gazette:

WILLIAMSVILLE, January 29th, 1814.

SIR,—

From the different statements which have appeared in the public prints it appears to be the prevailing opinion that the scarcity of arms and ammunition was the prime cause of the disaster which has befallen this part of the frontier. As those statements are calculated to poison and mislead the public mind and to keep from the public the real causes of our present situation by attaching the whole blame to Government or some officer whose duty it was to make the necessary provision for the defence of the frontier, when, in fact, the blame must and will rest alone on the disorganized and cowardly conduct in a great proportion of the troops who were on the frontier at that time, who deserted their ranks on the first appearance of the enemy.

I must beg to state the following facts: On the morning of the 30th December, after having furnished to all who applied both arms and ammunition, upwards of seven thousand rounds of musket cartridges remained in my possession, a great proportion of which was ordered to the Rock for distribution when required, but none being applied for it was ordered back after the principal part of the troops had retreated, or rather deserted from that place. Upwards of fifty stand of arms were on hand and from twenty to thirty were daily repaired; in fact no one appeared who was not furnished. Upwards of three hundred stand of arms, (which but a day or two before had been furnished to the militia,) were burnt in the different houses they had occupied as quarters, they having deserted both the village and their arms on the first assurance of the enemy having crossed. At the house of Mr. Haddock, in which only one small company was quartered, upwards of twenty of this brave company left their arms for the use of their friends or any other persons who might wish to use them, they having deserted. Such, Sir, are the men whose complaints are daily appearing in our newspapers of Government not affording them the common means of defence, when, if one-half of the troops that were on duty the day previous to the action had made use of half the means Government had provided for them the villages of Buffalo and Black Rock would still have been flourishing and afforded sufficient shelter not only for the troops who would have captured the invading foe, but for many distressed families who are at this time living on the charity of their friends.

I would not be understood as wishing to censure the citizens of Buffalo and Black Rock in the retreat that morning, for many of them, to my personal knowledge, fought while any probability remained of saving either of these villages.

I am respectfully, Sir, your humble servant.

JOHN G. CAMP, Dep. Q. M. Gen.

Colonel Matthew Elliott to Major J. B. Glegg.

(BURLINGTON) BEACH, 31st January, 1814.

SIR,—

The Indian messengers I had sent westward arrived to-day at 12 o'clock, just as I received your letter.

They brought a speech on wampum from their brethren expressing their joy at our success and their anxious wishes for our speedy arrival among them, telling their Father that they have only taken the Big Knife by *his fingers end* and have spoken to them from the lip outwards, and that they are always ready to obey their Father's order so soon as given. They are more afraid of the French inhabitants, who are all armed, than of the American troops, because if they hear of their having received messages from this place they will seize their wives and children and put them in confinement.

The messengers report that the inhabitants have made the Indians believe that the Americans had cleared all before them to Quebec, and that the small remnant was shut up in Quebec living on dogs and horses.

The Americans we suppose are in expectation of a reinforcement at Detroit, as a vast number of hogs and cattle are daily killed and the store kept full. The *Detroit* with about a hundred shot holes in her, is at Amherstburg and all the other vessels at Presqu' Isle. This we will be more certain of when Captain Caldwell arrives. Our friends to the westward make a demand for arms and ammunition and wish us to send about forty men loaded with the articles. Arms also and gunpowder are wanted for the people here. Of the first I secured some from Kingston and you can supply the latter. The stores here will otherwise answer all demands.

The Saukies and Foxes, as they intend to go to their own country on arriving at Detroit, will take their families with them, but as there are not many of them the expense will not be considerable. The other tribes leave their families here, and six hundred warriors if wanted are ready to co-operate with the troops and only wait the call.

Upon this point the Lieut. Genl's further directions are requested.

Altho' desirous of manifesting in the name of H. R. H. the Prince Regent his desire to maintain a perfectly good understanding with the Western Indians and to protect them from the encroachments of the U(nited) States upon their territory, I am disposed to relinquish that wish provided Lt. Gen. Drummond is satisfied that the reasons alleged are just and ought to be attended to.

It is my opinion that at present it would not be proper for us to meddle with young Techkumtha; he is very young and it might disgust his nation. He has yet time to show his nation whether they would take him as their chief.

I had almost forgot to mention that I received, a few days ago, a letter on the subject of the projected expedition from His Honor Lieutenant General Drummond, requiring my opinion about employing only the Delawares and Munseys, and also his desire that no useless consumer of provisions should be allowed to go along. I certainly am of his and General Riall's opinion as to the last, but I stated to him on the subject of the Munseys and Delawares that it appeared to me impolitic and might occasion jealousies, and I proposed a selection from all the tribes, amounting to the number that might be required, as a step that I was sure would give general satisfaction.

I am now recruiting slowly and I hope in a few days to be able to undertake any service General Riall may wish to be performed.

(Canadian Archives, C. 682, p. 150.)

Lieut. General Drummond to Sir George Prevost.

KINGSTON, February 1st, 1814.

SIR,—

I have the honor to acquaint Your Excellency that I have received a report from Major General Riall that the enemy had erected a small work at Black Rock, and opened a fire with one gun from thence on the 27th ultimo.

The Major General had attempted to dislodge them by the fire of a 5½ inch howitzer but could not effect it.

The Major General also states that the communication between Fort George and Fort Niagara had been stopped for nearly a week by the quantity of ice in the river.

(Canadian Archives, C. 682, pp. 88-9.)

Return of Persons who are Reduced to Great Distress by the War.

NIAGARA DISTRICT, Feb'y 2d, 1814.

Names.	Remarks of circumstances which occasioned their distress:
Mrs. Hannah Frey,	Widow of the late Captain Bernard Frey, who was killed in the town of Niagara by a cannon shot and his house in town burned by the enemy, the crop and fences at the Four Mile Creek Cross Roads destroyed by the British encampment last summer and the materials, such as boards, brush or lime, made use of in the encampment, and that she is thereby become destitute of any support or house to live in.
Mrs. Eliza Lawe,	Wife of Captain George Lawe of the Lincoln Militia, and Assistant Engineer, who was wounded on the 27th of May last when the enemy landed at Fort George, and now prisoner with the enemy. His house has been burned by the enemy and Mrs. Lawe is left without a house or any income to support her and two children during Mr. Lawe's absence.
Mrs. Heward,	A widow. She has maintained herself for many years past by teaching school in the town of Niagara and its vicinity, which employment has failed by the war and she has lost nearly all the property she had.
Sarah Lawrence,	Wife of George Lawrence, who is now prisoner

	with the enemy. What little he was able to gather of the crop on his farm last summer the enemy took away after the British army retreated from the Cross Roads, and Mrs. Lawrence and family were thereby reduced to want and distress.
Gerritt Slingerland,	Who lived in the town of Niagara and was taken prisoner by the enemy across the river, where he remained for six weeks before he could make his escape, during which time his house and barn were burned by the enemy. He has lost everything he had. Mr. Slingerland served the King during the American Rebellion and is now old. Has a numerous family of nearly all small children and not a shilling left to support them.
Larkin Perrish,	Lived in Niagara, lost his property by the war; says he served His Majesty during the Rebellion in America, is now old and not able to do much labor. Is reduced to great distress.
Michael Benninger,	Near Niagara, had his barn burned, his house robbed of all the money he had and other property. Is reduced to great distress.
Mary Grass,	Widow of the late George Grass, a private in the First Regiment of Lincoln Militia, was wounded on the 27th of May last in opposing the enemy's landing near Fort George; he died on the 29th following of his wounds. Mrs. Grass had two children when her husband died and one born since, on the 14th of October. Her husband was a poor man; she is consequently left without support.
Elizabeth McClellan,	Widow of the late Captain Martin McClellan of the First Regiment of Lincoln Militia, who was killed on the 27th day of May last in opposing the enemy's landing near Fort George; his house and barn near Fort George burned and the fences carried away by the enemy. Mrs. McClellan has a family of small children and is destitute of means to support them.
Eliza Wright,	Widow of the late Charles Wright, a private in the militia artillery, who was killed on the 27th of May last in opposing the enemy's

	landing at Fort George. He was a young man just begun for himself, had little or no property, supported himself and his family by his trade as a tailor. He left a widow and one child who are reduced to want.
Phœbe Cameron,	Widow of the late William Cameron, a private in the militia artillery, who was killed on the 27th day of May last in opposing the enemy's landing near Fort George. He supported his family by his trade as a blacksmith. His widow and one child are reduced to want.
Polly Sporbeck,	Of the township of Niagara, widow, lived on the Four Mile Creek at the Cross Roads. Had her crops of grain and grass destroyed by the troops and Indians being encamped on her farm last summer, which has reduced her and two young children to want.

(MSS. of Miss Amy Ball.)

Major General Hall to Governor Tompkins.

WILLIAMSVILLE, Feb'y 2d, 1814.

SIR,—

The detachment of militia has been organized into companies of 100 men each and are now at this place and near Lewiston, amounting to 1,100 *only*. The requisition was for 1,900. This statement will show Your Excellency the impossibility of filling a requisition, and at the present time it is more difficult than usual, owing to the harassed state of the western part of my division. I have not been able to discover any late movement of the enemy, but believe a part of their force is going on a secret expedition. I have been apprehensive for Detroit, but an officer who arrived this day from Gen. Mead's army at Erie assures me that our strength at that place is sufficient to repel any force the enemy can bring against it. I sincerely hope that he may not be deceived. The troops under my command are healthy, though badly furnished with camp equipage. There is not a camp kettle nor tin pan to twenty men. I have been anxiously expecting the arrival of those necessary articles for the use of the troops, but have as yet been disappointed. I have this day rec'd letters from Maj. Gen. Mead, stationed at Erie, who states that his force is now very respectable. He is of opinion that he could give a good account of the enemy should he attempt to disturb him, tho' he still wishes a co-operation of my force in case of an attack. I have written Your Exc'y several letters since I have had the honor of receiving any from you. I trust your letters must have been detained or that your other engagements have engrossed so much of your time that you have not had leisure to answer mine.

(Publications of the Buffalo Historical Society, Vol. V., p. 50.)

From Lieut. General Drummond to Sir George Prevost.

KINGSTON, January 22d, 1814.

SIR,—

In reference to the postcript of Your Excellency's letter of the 10th ultimo, I have the honor to acquaint you that although I have not had it in my power personally to inspect the troop of Provincial Dragoons commanded by Captain Coleman, as they have been for some time past stationed in the neighbourhood of Long Point, I am perfectly satisfied of the utility of their services, from the report of Major General Vincent and other officers, and am consequently inclined to recommend the augmentation of the 10 men and cornet alluded to, and have written to Captain Coleman on the subject accordingly.

May I request therefore that clothing and additional appointments be forwarded to York as soon as possible.

(Canadian Archives, C. 704, pp. 153-4.)

From Hon. J. W. Croker to Lieut. Colonel Williams, R. M.

DOWNING STREET, 27th January, 1814.

SIR,—

I am commanded by my Lords Commissioners of the Admiralty to signify their directions to you to take the necessary measures for causing the Second Battalion of the Royal Marines, which Sir George Prevost will be directed to place at the disposal of Commodore Sir James Lucas Yeo, (excepting the Artillery Company,) to be broken up and such numbers of men from the said battalion as may be necessary for furnishing the marine complements of the ships now on the lakes of Canada or intended to be sent thither, to be appropriated to them according to Sir James Yeo's requisition, incorporating the surplus, if any, in the 1st Battalion under your command.

The staff of the Second Battalion and the captains not wanted for the lake service or belonging to the Artillery Company are to proceed, forthwith after the dissolution of the said battalion, to join Vice Admiral Sir Alexander Cochrane, Commander-in-Chief of His Majesty's ships and vessels on the North American station and follow his orders for their further proceedings.

(Canadian Archives, C. 788, pp. 9-10.)

Major General Hall to Major General Mead.

Feb'y 2nd, 1814.

I shall immediately establish my line of expresses to meet and co-operate with yours, agreeable to my former proposal............ It gives me great pleasure to be informed of the improvement of your militia, and should the enemy have the temerity to visit your post I shall not permit myself to doubt that it will end in his total overthrow. Permit me to give you a sketch of the British force from recent information. Present force:—8th, King's, 500; 41st, King's, 600; 1st Royals, 700; 100th, 500; 1st light company, 80; marine artillery, 80; 1 company black corps, 100; 1 Co. H. artillery, 80; 1 Co. dragoons, 80; 2, 740. Watteville's legion (German troops are expected up soon. Indian force, Six Nations, 400; Western Indians, 1,000; 1,400. I refer to Capt. Atkinson for further particulars.

(Publications of the Buffalo Historical Society, Vol., V, pp. 50-1.)

Lieut. General Drummond to Sir George Prevost.

KINGSTON, February 3, 1814.

I have the honor to acknowledge the receipt of your letter of the 29th ultimo, communicating your approval of my proposed attack upon the enemy's vessels on Lake Erie.

The obstacles which Your Excellency pointed out to that highly desirable and important object are no doubt numerous, but they had not escaped my observation.

And I am so sanguine as to think they could have all been by suitable energy and exertion surmounted were it not for the peculiarly uncommon mildness of the season, which has been so unusually free from cold and frost that I could not form any hope that at this late period the ice would attain a sufficient degree of strength and soundness for our purpose during the remainder of the month.

In a letter from Colonel Talbot I learn that even the bordage upon Lake Erie from Port Talbot to Point Pelee is at present unsafe, and from every other information I can collect there appears to be but little probability of its being much better.

As it would be highly imprudent to enter upon arrangements under the probability that the season might still prove favorable, I conceive it much better altogether to give up the expedition at once than to make a show of assembling troops without a very fair prospect of being able to continue my original intentions.

From all these circumstances, having given the subject my most serious consideration and placed every circumstance in the most favorable point of view, I feel myself under the necessity of relinquishing with great reluctance an object from the success of which such beneficial consequences must have ensued.

(Canadian Archives, C. 682, pp. 90-2.)

Governor Simon Snyder to Major General David Mead.

HARRISBURG, February 4, 1814.

SIR,—

It is a matter of regret that no mode of guarding against a sudden invasion of our lake frontier has been adopted less expensive to the State than the one pursued. Permit me to suggest a system to which, whilst danger is at so great a distance as is the enemy's force in the straits from Erie, would in my apprehension and of others be equally efficacious and save to the State an expense to which, if calls *en masse* are continued, our ordinary resources will be altogether unequal.

Let us say one hundred and fifty or two hundred men to be stationed at thirty or more miles in advance toward the straits, at a place calculated for creating the greatest quantity of obstruction to an invading army. Let a few active and enterprising individuals, mounted on good horses, be stationed in advance of the main body at places where probably the enemy might attempt an irruption, with directions on the appearance of an enemy or any movement by him indicating an attack to convey intelligence thereof to the commanding officer. Let it be his duty in such case to cause every obstruction that the face of the country affords to be created, by the tearing up of bridges and the felling of timber trees across the roads, &c. This would retard an invading force so that sufficient time would be had to bring out the neighboring militia in numbers sufficient to repel any disposable force the enemy may have on the straits. Other avenues for the approach of an enemy, (if there be any,) might be guarded in a similar manner. Standing orders to the militia of your division might be issued to hold themselves in readiness to march in a moment's warning.

This suggestion grows out of a wish, which I trust you feel equally strong with myself, to prevent a dissipation of public treasure in the pursuit of measures which appear to me of doubtful utility.

(Pennsylvania Archives, Second Series, Vol. XII., pp. 696-7.)

From the Military Secretary to Lieut. General Drummond.

Head Qrs. QUEBEC, 4th Feb'y, 1814.

SIR,—

I have the honor by the direction of the Commander of the Forces to acknowledge the receipt of your letter of the 28th ultimo, containing the substance of the report you had received from Dy. Asst. Commissary General Cruikshank after his return from Lake Simcoe, from which it would seem that the original plan for the transport of stores and provisions to Penetanguishene Bay is impracticable, while the opening of the road to Nottawasaga Bay on Lake Huron, a distance only of 20 miles from Penetanguishene, can with facility be effected. In answer to which I am desired to express His Excellency's satisfaction at your having ordered the latter route to be adopted, the former appearing to offer no hope of success.

With respect to the suggestion for sending from Kingston a foreman and such a number of artificers as might be necessary for the construction of the boats intended to be built on the shore of Lake Huron, it is a subject which has been debated upon between the Commander of the Forces and the Commodore, and the conclusion was to forward from Kingston a builder and a proportion of artificers to York, with everything required for building of the boats intended to be employed on Lake Huron, and Sir James Yeo undertook to communicate with you accordingly thereon, and this number will, if possible, be replaced from Lower Canada, tho' the demand for shipwrights, who have been recently engaged for Kingston, has been so extensive as nearly to exhaust this part of the country of that description of persons.

In reply to your second letter, of the 28th ulto., relating to the deficiency of artillery officers for the post of Kingston, and requesting to be furnished with a supply of Congreve rockets and a proportion of men who understand the use of them, to be employed as occasion may offer, I am directed to observe that His Excellency has allotted for Upper Canada a full share of the artillery subalterns at his disposal, and the garrison of Quebec, being now left with one captain and a subaltern of that corps, he is not aware of any subaltern that can immediately be spared from the posts on this side of Kingston.

His Excellency has ordered a detah't of rocketteers with sleighs containing 72 rockets to move on from Coteau du Lac to Kingston whenever circumstances have rendered them disposable.

The requisition for intrenching tools, adverted to in your third letter of the 28th Jany, will be approved by His Excellency when it comes forward, and the several articles will be supplied from hence as far as can be accomplished. At the same time the Commander of the Forces has instructed me to desire that all articles of wooden tools must be provided on the spot, as the serious and expensive operation of land transport will (not) permit the possibility of their being sent from this Province, and in any future requisition of this description the engineer must confine his demand for such tools as cannot be made or procured at the post at which they may be required.

His Excellency is induced to think that the commissariat has been burthened with duties for other departments which has impeded the service in many instances, and it is his wish to afford relief, if it were possible, by throwing the executive part of each branch of the service upon its proper dept. and leave the commissariat the performance only of the business required by its regulations. He is also aware that inconvenience is suffered by the engineers being called upon to execute the various contingent works of the barracks and other departments, and it would be desirable that it should not be done when those services could be performed by contract, which might probably in many cases afford a saving to the public, and recourse should not be had to the engineers for such service but in cases civil aid cannot be obtained and that it does not interfere with service of greater importance.

(Canadian Archives, C. 1222, pp. 38-40.)

Lieut. General Drummond to Sir George Prevost.

KINGSTON, February 5th, 1814.

SIR,—

I have the honor to acquaint Your Excellency that I received the following information this day from a person of tolerable confidence, viz., that there are about 1,000 fighting men, about 800 sailors and 300 ship carpenters, at Sackett's Harbor at present; that no movement of troops has taken place; that all the sleighs lately collected have been dismissed; that Colonel Smith commands. Three vessels are positively to be built, (their dimensions will be known by the next opportunity.) It had been generally supposed that Major Forsyth was to have crossed over at or below Cornwall to intercept some of the convoys of stores and render the guns useless. But this place it would appear has been given up for the present.

P. S.—Since writing the foregoing a young Canadian belonging to our dockyard, sent over some time since, has just returned from Sackett's Harbor, which he left on Sunday last. His information is that there are 2,000 troops there besides the sailors; that the keels of three vessels are already laid down, viz., of a ship 154 feet in length, a brig and a schooner. Seventeen vessels of all descriptions

were in the harbor, but to the best of his belief but one with three masts. The guns for the new ship are to come from New York by the turnpike road in about three weeks; 50 gunboats are contracted for at Oswego and three schooners at Catfish Creek. It was reported that Montreal was still to be attempted or Prescott taken possession of, to cut off the supplies from the Lower Province to Kingston.
(Canadian Archives, C. 682, pp. 83-6.)

Lieut. General Drummond to Sir George Prevost.

KINGSTON, February 5th, 1814.

SIR,—

I have the honor to acknowledge the receipt of your letter of the 29th ultimo.

The two companies of the Newfoundland Regiment to accompany Lieutenant Colonel McDouall, and the non-commissioned officer and 10 gunners of the Royal Artillery, have all been selected for that service, and I know the lieutenant of the Royal Navy and the sailors are likewise in readiness to proceed from hence when thought necessary they should move.

The whole will now, of course, now that the expedition to the westward has been relinquished, proceed by the same route as Lieutenant Colonel McDouall.
(Canadian Archives C. 682, pp. 97-8.)

Lieut. General Drummond to Noah Freer.

KINGSTON, February 5th, 1814.

SIR,—

In reply to your letter of the 29th ultimo I have the honor to acquaint you for the information of the Commander of the Forces, that I have given directions to Colonel Claus of the Indian Department to signify to the son and daughter of the late Shawanese Chief Tecumseth His Excellency's desire to see them in Lower Canada, together with any chiefs of the Western Indians, (as a deputation from those tribes) that may be willing to accompany them.

I have likewise given orders to the commissariat to afford them the necessary assistance on the journey to Montreal.
(Canadian Archives, C. 257, p. 211.)

General Orders.

HARRISBURG, February 7th, 1814.

In compliance with a requisition from the President of the United States, I do order into the service of the Union one thousand men, rank and file, of the Pennsylvania Militia, and a competent number of officers, to be composed of the First and Second Brigades of the Seventh Division and of the Second Brigade of the Fifth Division, designated for the service of the United States under General Orders of the 12th of May, 1812, to rendezvous at Erie on the 5th day of March, then, or as soon thereafter, to be organized into one regiment and to be officered agreeable to law.

SIMON SNYDER,
Governor of the Commonwealth of Pennsylvania.

(Pennsylvania Archives, Second Series, Vol. XII., pp. 697-8.)

Secret Information.

Camp, FRENCH MILLS, February 7th, 1814.

From the 3d to the present instant very considerable confusion has been in camp. On Sunday, the 6th instant, the 25th and 9th Regiments, (who were encamped west of the bridge near Mr. Jones's farm,) marched. Their place of destination has evidently appeared since to be Sackett's Harbor, from having sent on a quartermaster who had, as is understood, contracted for forage for about fifty miles on that route, and also from the circumstances of the officers on the moment of their march having left directions to the postmaster to forward on all letters to that place, also the last news from them, they were about 22 miles distance in that direction. A few minutes previous to their march some soldiers were cutting the masts of their flotilla, others setting fire to the barracks they were about to evacuate. This movement appeared, however, soon to be countermanded, and the cutting of masts and burning of barracks stopped. Three barracks only were consumed. On Saturday last a General Order was read on parade, stating that General Wilkinson had resumed command and that the place would soon be reinforced by 800 men, that this was a place the enemy were grappling for and that the troops must be prepared to defend it with spirit. Since which to this morning three other regiments were placed under marching orders to be ready at a moment's notice. A considerable body of troops, say 500, marched from Plattsburg destined for French Mills, but on their arrival at Chateauguay were ordered to continue their march in the direction of Sackett's Harbor. A few soldiers, however, had arrived at French Mills but were immediately ordered on in the direction of the harbor. The army still continuing to press all the sleighs they can obtain.

What is done with the artillery and small arms forwarded to Chateauguay not as yet ascertained. It is the general opinion among the officers and citizens that the army will evacuate the French Mills and march to Sackett's Harbor and Plattsburg.

(Canadian Archives, C. 682, pp. 114-6.)

Lieut. General Drummond to Sir George Prevost.

KINGSTON, February 8th, 1814.

SIR,—

I have the honor to acquaint Your Excellency that I propose setting out to-morrow for the purpose of meeting the Provincial Legislature at York on the 15th instant.

From the information I have received from Prescott, and which no doubt has been communicated to Your Excellency from thence, of the movement of the enemy's guns and stores from Salmon River, from the departure of the Newfoundland Regiment from hence, the deficiency of artillerymen and particularly of officers of that corps and the want of the 89th Regiment, which I had expected here, I consider the garrison to be so insufficient for the defence of this place that I have thought it necessary to order the effectives of the 41st Regiment from York without delay.

The garrison will be left, as well as the Centre Division, under the command of Major General Stovin, who arrived here on the 6th inst.

I regret to report to Your Excellency the great deficiency of forage in this neighborhood, particularly of oats. Although hay is abundant the Deputy Commissary General will not, I am apprehensive, without a recurrence to martial law, be able to procure a supply beyond the month of April. The farmers hold back their stock on hand so very rigidly that, although I am extremely averse to using such means, I believe I shall ultimately be under the necessity of issuing a proclamation to that effect.

With regard to provisions, I fear we shall suffer the greatest distress in spring if we do not receive a supply from below. We should feel ourselves most satisfactorily relieved if we could get rid of a considerable portion of the Indians from the Head of the Lake by some of them being employed in the Lower Province, where such as in the neighborhood of Odelltown, Chateauguay or Salmon River their services might be made extremely useful, if it meet Your Excellency's approbation to direct them to be removed to that neighborhood.

I have ordered Major General Riall to organize a small force, consisting of the light companies of the Royals and the 89th Regiment with the Kent Volunteers and a strong body of Indians and push forward to Oxford, and according to information advance thence to Delaware town or even towards the mouth of the Thames. I hope this force will be able to circumscribe the bounds of the enemy, to collect what supplies the country affords, (which I fear, however, has been well drained already,) and at all events provide for themselves and the Indians with them for a short time.

I am sorry to say that some of the inhabitants in the neighborhood of the Head of the Lake have left their farms rather than reside among such troublesome neighbors.

And how necessary it is that their numbers should be diminished I have only to state to Your Excellency that their consumption of provisions amounts to no less upon an average than 16 head of cattle and 25 barrels of flour daily.

I beg leave to call Your Excellency's attention to the inadequate supply of money usually sent to this Province. It is not so much felt at this post as at York and Burlington in particular, in consequence of the Deputy Commissary General here being able to procure a loan occasionally from the merchants, but at the latter places the want of money to defray the common expenses has been highly prejudicial to the service and prejudicial to the public credit. The sum commonly sent up is sufficient only to pay off old debts, and nothing scarcely is left to commence afresh with.

(Canadian Archives, C. 682, pp. 104-8.)

From Sir James Yeo to Sir George Prevost.

WOLFE, KINGSTON, 8th Feby, 1814.

SIR,—

I deferred writing to Your Excellency until I had communicated with General Drummond, who has no doubt made known his sentiments and decision respecting the expedition above.

I am also of opinion, and fully aware that the season is not only too far advanced but the enemy's movements on that frontier will not allow the enterprise to be undertaken with reasonable hopes of success.

From information obtained thro' two men sent from this yard, I am inclined to believe the enemy have already laid down a forty gun frigate, have the timber and keels cut for another frigate and a brig of 26 guns, the latter is named such on purpose to deceive. One of the men went on to Oswego and reports that they are building a great number of boats at that place, some for gunboats, that they have removed the sails, cables, guns, &c., of the Pike and Madison to Watertown.

Under these circumstances I feel it my duty to recommend our building another frigate of the following dimensions : Length of gun deck, 150 ft.; length of keel, 136 ft.; breadth, extreme, 44 ft.; depth in hold, 13.6; depth of water, 17 ft.

I believe that Your Excellency will agree with me that the more concentrated our force the better. She may be ready by July, when we shall most likely have sufficient seamen to man her; if not I can take the seamen out of the small vessels for so desirable a ship. The Aeolus's guns will exactly answer.

If Captain Sherwood's information is correct that the enemy are about evacuating their position at the French Mills, I beg leave to suggest to Your Excellency the propriety of suspending building more than four gun boats at the Cauto, (Coteau,) which, with those already there, will, in my opinion, be fully adequate to the service, in which case part of those shipwrights now at the Cauto could be engaged and employed on the new frigate, as four of the gun boats are in a state of forwardness at that place.

I have directed Captain Pring to divide his attention during the winter between Isle aux Noix and the Coteau du Lac, but to be ready before the navigation opens to take Lake St. Francis with the flotilla, which I have arranged in three divisions. I was most pleased with the neat arrangement, good order and discipline of the naval yard at Isle aux Noix, which reflects great credit on the officer commanding that establishment.

Mr. Edgecombe appears well qualified to fill the situation of storekeeper, and I think fifteen shillings a day a fair salary both to himself and the service.

If any more seamen can be obtained at Quebec it will be desirable to send up twenty-five for the establishment at Michilimackinac. In the meantime I have sent a very intelligent active officer, Lieut. Poyntz, with twenty prime seamen with Lieut. Colonel McDouall.

I hope you will give us a few of the rocket company with some rockets by the opening of navigation.

Will Your Excellency have the goodness to issue a warrant for the payment of the prize money, and the order to the commissary to take up the Bank of England notes.

Your Excellency may rely on every exertion being made by the naval department in this country.

(Canadian Archives, C. 732, pp. 26-30.)

From Sir George Prevost to Lieut. General Drummond.

Secret.   Headquarters, QUEBEC, 8th Feby, 1814.

SIR,—

I have directed Lt. Colonel Harvey to hasten to Kingston for the purpose of being useful to you in the final arrangements for the execution of the contemplated enterprise for the recovery of Sandwich and Amherstburg and the destruction of the enemy's vessels in and near Detroit.

I am desirous of strongly impressing upon you the necessity of making every effort during the remainder of the winter for the destruction of the enemy's naval force on Lake Erie, as the reduction of the enemy's present superiority is of high importance to the preservation of Upper Canada and for the maintenance of our relations with the Western Indians. Nothing but the impracticability of the measure from the causes alluded to in my late letter to you on this subject will justify its not being attempted.

You will have the goodness to report to me upon the possibility of immediately proceeding to a naval establishment on Lake Erie in the event of the successful termination of the expedition, in order that care may be taken to forward to the situation that you may select as best adapted to the purpose the necessary articles of naval equipment.

The Deputy Adjutant General having had an opportunity of making himself intimately acquainted with the military resources of Lower Canada, and my sentiments respecting their employment for the approaching campaign, is enabled fully to explain to you the aid you may expect from thence under circumstances removing the pressure of the war from this province to the one committed to your charge.

(Canadian Archives, C. 1222, pp. 40-1.)

From the Military Secretary to Lieut. General Drummond.

Head Qrs. QUEBEC, 8th Feby, 1814.

SIR,—

The Comr. of the Forces has directed me to acknowledge the receipt of your letter of the 1st inst., stating your having received a report from Major General Riall that the enemy had erected a small work at Black Rock and had opened a fire from thence with one gun on the 27th ultimo, and that the Major General had endeavored without effect to dislodge them by the fire of a 5½ inch howitzer.

His Excellency trusts that when Major General Riall is in possession of the two 24 pr. brass guns on travelling carriages, ordered for Queenston, and which can be moved with facility to any point with the assistance of five or six horses, he will have the means of silencing this annoyance of the enemy on that frontier, and of securing to himself perfect command of the Niagara River.

(Canadian Archives, C. 1222, pp. 41-2.)

Lieut. General Drummond to Sir George Prevost.

KINGSTON, February 11th, 1814.

SIR,—

I have the honor to acquaint Your Excellency that I have received a letter from Major General Riall stating that an American had come into Fort Niagara on the 2d instant, who says that General Hall is at a village about 7 miles in rear of Lewiston with 700 militia, and that they are erecting large barracks and that there are about 2,000 men at Batavia.

I have the honor to enclose for Your Excellency's information a letter I received this day from Colonel Elliott of the Indian Department.

(Canadian Archives, C. 682, p. 99.)

Cornet Amos McKenney to Captain W. H. Merritt.

YORK, 9th Feby., 1814.

DEAR SIR,—

I have just arrived. We drove on a little before the slays in order to get slays here before they discharged their lading from Kingston. I expect the slays in to-morrow, as they were only half a day's drive behind with your goods and saddles and bridles for 33 men complete, and we have also some gray cloth for the troop.

I think we will meet with some detention here in consequence of slays.

I got your letter to-day from Mr. Chisholm and will lose no time that can be helped in getting home. Captain Burton has just informed me of the two Stivers being in the back settlements of Yonge Street. If I have time before the goods come I will go for them.

(Merritt MSS.)

Captain Thomas Coleman to Captain W. H. Merritt.

DOVER, February 9th, 1814.

DEAR SIR,—

I was favored with your letter of the 1st inst., in answer to which, whenever you find it convenient to make a transfer of the property belonging to Mr. Holmes, I shall with pleasure take charge of it and send you a receipt for the amount.

Respecting our troops acting together, I perfectly acquiesce in your opinion of the advantage which would be derived from it and shall readily entertain any proposals for that purpose. I doubt not Genl. Riall will give every encouragement to Provincial Cavalry, who are doubtless better calculated from their knowledge of the country for the service they are generally employed upon. I shall take an early opportunity of suggesting your sentiments to Major Glegg and write you after receiving his answer.

Pray, have you received your appointments? I am recruiting the strength of my troop, but with little success at present. If you can procure me a few good recruits without interfering with your own interest, I should feel obliged. I am offering thirty dollars bounty to serve eighteen months or during the war with the United States. I am ordered to hold myself in readiness for active service, I presume to accompany the intended expedition. I wish your troop is to accompany us, it would make the Provincial Cavalry appear upon a more respectable footing, and promote a generous emulation to serve our country. I am of an opinion the United States have nearly exhausted their means of providing an army, nor would it at all astonish me if they withdrew what force they now have from the frontiers of Canada before next May. Much, however, may depend upon our energies ere that period.

(Merritt MSS.)

From Sir James Yeo to Sir Sidney Beckwith.

WOLFE, KINGSTON, 10th Feby, 1814.

SIR,—

On my arrival here I received information (thro' two men sent from this yard) that the enemy *have* actually laid down a forty-four gun frigate, have the timber and keels out for another, and a brig of twenty-six guns, the latter is named such on purpose to deceive. One of the men went on to Oswego and reports that they are building a great number of boats at that place, some for gun boats; that they have removed the Pike's, Madison's, &c., sails, guns and cables from Sackett's to Watertown.

I have therefore recommended to His Excellency building another frigate and to forward up the Aeolus's guns.

This ship, I have told His Excellency, may be ready by July, but my private opinion is she may be finished, (if we receive your able support and assistance,) in June. You must be sensible to accomplish this additional and most desirable service it will be absolutely necessary to engage every shipwright that can be procured, as, independent of those detained at the Coteau, we have been under the necessity of detaching some of the best shipwrights to construct the boats on Lake Huron.

Have you ascertained the truth of Captain Sherwood's information—if the enemy evacuate the French Mills it will remove the necessity of building a number of gun boats at the Coteau, and, in my opinion, four, in addition to those already there, will be fully adequate to the service, in which case part of the shipwrights now there might be engaged and employed on the third frigate.

I am equally anxious to have a naval force ready whenever it is most likely the enemy will strike the blow. Lieut. General Drummond agrees with me in the necessity of constructing another frigate if the enemy directs their attention to the Upper Province.

I feel persuaded that the great struggle for naval prowess and superiority will be contended on Lake Ontario. It is the only place where an equal force of the same magnitude are likely to meet. I am therefore naturally solicitous to have such a force ready as may save the country, honor the British flag and do credit to myself.

I request that you will give orders that any canvas that may be at Montreal or may arrive from Quebec for this establishment is forwarded without a moment's delay, as we have not received one-third what was demanded, and the ships cannot take the lake without sails. We are also very short of oakum and we commence calking the new ships next week.

(Canadian Archives, C. 732, pp. 3-4.)

From the Military Secretary to Lieut. General Drummond.

Head Qrs., QUEBEC, 12th February, 1814.

SIR,—

I have in command from the Comr. of the Forces to acknowledge the receipt of your communications of the 3d and 5th inst., and am instructed to express His Excellency's deep regret that circumstances uncontrollable should have compelled you to abandon the expedition from which so much advantage to the public service might have been derived, at the same time that he approves of a decided relinquishment in preference to a temporizing abandonment after extensive preparations.

The Commander of the Forces feels incredulous respecting the whole of the young Canadian's information as contained in your letter of the 5th.

(Canadian Archives, C. 1222, p. 44.)

From the Diary of Thomas McCrae.

RALEIGH, Saturday, 12th February, 1814.

Norton and Westbrook came here on their way down about noon. They had been up the river a-spying. In the afternoon five of the British Kent Volunteers passed in pursuit of them but did not overtake them.

Monday, 14th February, 1814.

The men say McGregor's company were all ordered down to Trudelle's, a report having been circulated the Americans were moving up.

Tuesday, 15th February, 1814.

A party of Americans under Lieut. Ruland came from the Round O with 40 or 45 head of cattle as far as Hitchcock's, and was there informed that the British was on the river; they then took the alarm, left the cattle and crossed over towards Baldoon. The British is gone from the mouth of the river in pursuit, also another by the road from opposite the fork at Chatham.

General Order.

Adjutant General's Office,
Headquarters, QUEBEC, 13th February, 1814.

His Excellency the Governor in Chief and Commander of the Forces has received the report of Lieut. Colonel Morrison, 89th Regiment, to Lieutenant General Drummond, announcing the complete success of an enterprise which he had sanctioned in consequence of having received information that the property belonging to British merchants, captured by the enemy near Cornwall in October last, and which had been stipulated to be returned by a capitulation entered into on the 10th of November following, by Judge Ogden and Mr. Richards on the part of the United States, and Lieut. Colonel Morrison and Captain Mulcaster on the part of the British Government, had not only been withheld contrary to the faith of that treaty but had been removed to Madrid on the Grass River and was publicly advertised for sale for the benefit of the American Government.

Lieut. Colonel Morrison availed himself of a plan submitted by Captain Sherwood of the Quartermaster General's Department for the recovery of this British plundered property, and placed for that purpose under his command as a detachment a subaltern officer, two sergeants and twenty rank and file of the Royal Marines, together with ten soldiers of the Incorporated Militia at Prescott under Captain Kerr. Captain Sherwood reports that he crossed his small party to the enemy's shore on the night of the 6th, marched through the village of Hamilton after midnight, and having taken necessary precautions proceeded fourteen miles to the interior on the Grass river where the plunder was deposited, and having on his route impressed all the sleighs and horses he could find he immediately took possession of the property, which was left in the possession of Collector Richard's son, who was secured but afterwards released.

The sleighs being loaded at half-past four Captain Sherwood returned and again passed through the village of Hamilton, of which not a single house was entered, nor did any individual suffer the slightest loss or insult in person or property, that officer having previously avowed the object of the expedition and engaged that no molestation would be experienced by the inhabitants, and so scrupulous has that officer been in the observance of the strict injunctions he received from Lieut. Colonel Morrison to adhere to the spirit of forbearance prescribed by His Excellency in his proclamation of the 12th January, that, not being provided with sufficient means to remove the whole of the property, Captain Sherwood left about twenty sleigh loads of articles of minor value and would not suffer the building which contained them to be set on fire lest any private property should in consequence be destroyed.

The party returned at two o'clock in the afternoon, where their boats awaited them under the orders of Lieut. Shaver of the Dundas militia. A few of the enemy's militia began to collect in the vicinity, but were soon dispersed by the detachment of Royal Marines and did not again make their appearance. The whole of the party and stores crossed over to Cornwall without having experienced any loss and casualty.

His Excellency the Governor in Chief and Commander of the Forces highly approves of the plan and conduct of this enterprise, as well for the judgment evinced in its arrangement as for the promptness and spirit displayed in its execution, and most particularly for the extreme good order and regularity preserved, which reflects the highest credit on the discipline of the troops and on the skill and conduct of Captain Sherwood.

EDWARD BAYNES,
Adjutant General, North America.

Major General Hall to Enoch A. Hall.

WILLIAMSVILLE, February 14, 1814.

MY DEAR SON,—

I have been about three days at this place. The troops of the detachment have mostly arrived at their places of destination. Those detached from Generals Burnett's, Wadsworth's and McClure's brigades are at 11 Mile Creek. Those from General Tillotson's, late Himrod's, (Seneca County,) and Rea's brigades are at Hardscrabble, six miles east of Lewiston. Colonels Colt's and Davis's regiments from the brigade commanded by General Burnett, Lieut. Colonels Harris and Churchill, have arrived at the places above mentioned.

Everything remains perfectly quiet here and on the ridge. I was yesterday at the Rock and down as far as Conjockities Creek and took a view of the ground where the action was. I find that the greatest part of our men were killed on the retreat. The trees are much marked on the Miller road and a little north of it. Many of our dead were found in that direction.

We keep guards and patrols at and below the Rock and at and up the lake from Buffalo. There are but few troops seen on the opposite shore.

The weather has been extreme cold for two days and the lake is frozen across, tho' not sufficient to cross over on; if it was we should not try it, nor do I think the enemy will. There being no object to induce them to venture on this side short of this place and this is too far from the river. It is expected by some that they will attempt to go to Presqu' Isle, (Erie,) but I have no idea that they will risk so much. I think their next push will be Detroit or Sackett's Harbor, either of which will be an object of the first importance to them if carried into effect.

. . . . . I have heard nothing from Colonel Gardner lately, but I understand generally that our wounded remain at what is called the blue house, opposite Grand Island. The prisoners not wounded have marched to Kingston and probably to Montreal, tho' I am inclined to believe they will be paroled at Kingston or Prescott.

(MSS. in Buffalo Historical Society Library.)

Major General Hall to Enoch A. Hall.

WILLIAMSVILLE, February 18, 1814.

MY DEAR SON,—

. . . . . I understand that the soldiers that were taken prisoners at Black Rock were exchanged at Montreal and returned home, but that the commissioned officers are as yet detained. I expect those soldiers from Bloomfield have got home. I have seen one man that belonged to N(iagara) County, who had been prisoner, on his way home. He states the enemy admit their loss in killed and mortally wounded to have been nearly 300, and that they have not lost so many men in any one action since the commencement of the war. Our loss has been greater than we at first expected. The whole number yet discovered I believe is 51 or 52. I don't learn that any of our wounded have died.

(MSS. in Buffalo Historical Society Library.)

Lieut. General Drummond to Sir George Prevost.

YORK, February 14th, 1814.

SIR,—

I have the honor to acquaint Your Excellency that in consequence of former intelligence, (February 7th, 1814,) which has already been communicated to you, relative to movements on the line from Plattsburg towards Sackett's Harbor, as also of that beneath enclosed, I have deemed it right to authorize the detention of the detachment of the Canadian Regiment by Lieut. Colonel Morrison commanding at Cornwall to be employed by that officer as circumstances may for the present require.

(Canadian Archives, C. 682, p. 117.)

Lieut. General Drummond to Noah Freer.

YORK, February 14th, 1814.

SIR,

I have the honor to acquaint you for the information of His Excellency the Commander of the Forces, that I have just received intelligence from the River Thames of the capture by the enemy of Lieut. Colonel Baby, Assistant Quartermaster General, and Captain Brigham of the militia, in that neighborhood. The enemy appeared on Monday, the 31st ultimo, in some force at Delaware, and made prisoners of Captain Springer and a small guard of militia posted at Westbrook's for the security of his property, he, (Westbrook,) having gone over to the enemy. Westbrook was with the enemy and before they retired he burned his buildings himself. It was said they were to proceed to Port Talbot, but it was not imagined they would carry their intentions into effect.

I have this day received information from a respectable person who has been specially employed in collecting intelligence in the neighborhood of Presqu' Isle, &c. He says there are six large and three small vessels at that place, and that their two largest are at Put-in-Bay, where a blockhouse has been erected for their defence. One of these latter vessels was to have been removed to Malden for repair, and is supposed to be there at present.

It was reported that if the reinforcements expected at Detroit should arrive in time a strong body of the enemy is to move in the direction of Oxford by the River Thames, at which time also another force is to cross the River Niagara above the Falls for the purpose of forming a juncture and co-operating with that from Detroit.

About two-thirds of the inhabitants in the neighborhood of Buffalo are desirous, it is thought, of peace, the remaining third declare their determination to cross again into Canada and burn and destroy everything within reach.

(Canadian Archives, C. 682, p. 111.)

Speech of His Honor the President on Opening the Third Session of the Sixth Provincial Parliament at York, on the 15th inst.

Honorable Gentlemen of the Legislative Council and Gentlemen of the House of Assembly:

Called to the Civil Administration, which the policy of His Majesty's Government has united to the military command of this Province, it is with great satisfaction I meet you here in the free and uncontrolled exercise of the legislative powers entrusted to us by our parliamentary charter.

That we are enabled so to meet at this crisis demands every sentiment of our most devout gratitude to the Divine Providence, which seems to have manifested an especial protection to the righteous cause of our defence against an enemy unprovoked and implacable, who, at the moment they were exulting in the assurances of their commander that the conquest of the Canadas was achieved, were arrested in their progress to invade our sister province, and their collective troops discomfited by a handful of British troops, who, emulous of the glorious career of their comrades in the Peninsula, drove them in dismay to seek refuge on their own shores.

With no less gallantry in another quarter a small band of British soldiers attacked and carried by storm the fortress of Niagara, the strongest and most formidable position they held on our frontier.

In advancing to this enterprise the troops beheld with indignation the smoking ruins of the town of Niagara, which an atrocious policy had devoted to the flames. Resentful of the misery brought upon the innocent but too credulous inhabitants, who had remained to the last moment under promise of protection to their persons and property, the army inflicted a severe retaliation in the entire destruction of the whole frontiers from Lake Erie to Lake Ontario, after defeating a very superior force of the enemy.

Thus the valor of our soldiers and citizens has proved what can be effected in a good cause by men who have nothing in view but their own honor and their country's safety.

I lament it is not in my power to congratulate you upon any favorable change in the health of our beloved sovereign. His government continues to be administered by His Royal Highness the Prince Regent, under whose conspicuous direction the glory of Great Britain has attained to its zenith, as well in the field as in the cabinet.

His Majesty's arms, united with those of Spain and Portugal, under the command of Field Marshal the Marquis Wellington have rescued the Peninsula from its invaders, whilst the Northern Powers of Europe, combined by the wise measures of His Majesty's Councils, have overwhelmed and destroyed his immense armies and compelled him to retire into the bosom of France.

Gentlemen of the House of Assembly:

I have directed the public accounts to be laid before you. The moneys placed at the disposal of my predecessor for the defence of the Province have, I doubt not, been wisely disbursed. However small a proportion they may bear to the requisite expenditure, you have the merit of giving all you had, and I fear the present state of the Colony does not justify an expectation that your means will increase.

Honorable Gentlemen of the Legislative Council and Gentlemen of the House of Assembly:

You must be well aware of the importance of a well organized militia for the defence of the Province. It is a subject which will require your most serious consideration. The measure which has been adopted of incorporating battalions of militia for permanent service during the war has not on trial been found to answer You will doubtless find it expedient to authorize the embodying detachments from the different regiments in no greater proportion than one-third of the corps for any period not exceeding twelve months, as the only method by which they can be furnished with clothing and appointment similar to troops of the line, without which the militia cannot be relied on as an efficient force.

During the last campaign the militia service has been greatly impeded by the neglected state of the public roads. It is an essential object that one great road through the province should be in a condition to facilitate the transport of military stores.

In your deliberations on this head justice to those who have gallantly hazarded their lives in defence of the Province will suggest the propriety of others who profit by such services, but who from religious scruples abstain from war, being called upon by legislative authority more liberally to afford their pecuniary assistance for the defence of that property which by the valor of their fellow subjects they so peacefully and with so many advantages enjoy.

It has been more a subject of regret than surprise to have found two members of the legislative body in the ranks of the enemy. This disgrace could not have been had their malignant influence in the last session failed to reject the call of the Executive Government for a suitable modification of the Habeas Corpus Act. I rely upon the good sense of the two houses so to strengthen the hands of Government as to obviate all apprehensions of the recurrence of a similar reproach.

A due regard to the interests of the loyal subjects requires that means should be adopted to punish such traitors as adhere to the enemy, by the confiscation of their estates. It may often happen, as in the instance of the two representatives of the people, that they may withdraw from the process necessary for legal conviction. To obviate this an Act of Attainder by the Legislature may subvene to the usual process of outlawry.

In submitting such a measure it is my duty to apprize you of the gracious desire of His Royal Highness the Prince Regent that all such forfeitures shall be applied to the relief of the sufferers by the war within this Province.

The authority to restrain the distillation from grain expires with the session. I fear that the necessity to prolong it still exists. In revising or continuing the statute it may be expedient to except His Majesty's military service from its provisions.

With confidence I commit to your consideration and care the other matters which may be requisite for the welfare of this Province in the present emergency.

Your attention will of course be called to such expiring acts as require to be renewed.

In the actual situation of the Province it would be superfluous to remind you that as little time should be spent in the Session as is consistent with mature deliberation on the several topics to which your attention may be called.

Provincial Parliament of Upper Canada.

To His Honor Gordon Drummond, Esquire, President administering the Government of Upper Canada, Lieutenant General commanding His Majesty's Forces within the same, &c., &c., &c.:

May it please Your Honor:

We, His Majesty's most dutiful and loyal subjects, the Commons of Upper Canada in Provincial Parliament assembled, beg leave to offer to Your Honor our humble thanks for your most gracious speech from the Throne. In recognizing the wisdom of the policy which at a crisis so momentous has united to the military the civil administration of the government in this Province, we rejoice that so important a trust has devolved on an officer to whose energetic measures we are, under Providence, indebted for some of the most splendid successes which shed so much lustre on the termination of last campaign.

We participate in the satisfaction you express at meeting us in the free and uncontrolled exercise of the legislative powers committed to us by our parliamentary charter and unite with you in devout and grateful acknowledgments to Divine Providence for its signal protection of us from an unprovoked and implacable enemy, who at the moment they were exulting in the assurances that the conquest of the Canadas was achieved were arrested in their progress to invade our sister Province, and their collective force discomfited by a small division of His Majesty's forces, who, emulous of the glorious career of their comrades in the Peninsula, drove them in dismay to seek refuge on their own shores.

The gallantry and intrepidity with which a small band of British soldiers in another quarter attacked and carried by storm the fortress of Niagara, the strongest and most formidable position the enemy held on our frontiers, have excited our admiration and gratitude and afford a convincing proof that, under the direction of able commanders, the courage and determination of the British soldiers are invincible.

In deploring, as we feelingly do, the misery and ruin brought upon the innocent but too credulous inhabitants of the town of Niagara, (who had remained to the last moment under promise of protection to their persons and property,) by the atrocious policy of the enemy, we acknowledge the justice of the severe and prompt retaliation inflicted upon him by our victorious troops, and whilst we lament the necessity which so imperiously dictated a measure so repugnant to the feelings and character of British soldiers, we hope it will have the effect of checking a system so productive of individual distress, so contrary to the established usages of war among civilized nations, be a warning to the inhabitants of this Province how they confide to the delusive promises of an enemy so profligate and unprincipled, and unite them more firmly in the defence of the just cause in which we are engaged.

We participate with Your Honor in feelings of unfeigned sorrow for the continuance of the severe indisposition under which our most gracious and beloved Sovereign has so long labored, and we acknowledge with grateful thanks to Divine Providence the ability and energy which, both in the cabinet and the field, have distinguished the administration of his government by the Prince Regent.

The splendid successes which have been achieved by His Majesty's arms, united to those of Spain and Portugal, under the able command of Field Marshal the Marquis Wellington, and which have rescued the Peninsula from its invaders, are subjects of exultation and triumph, and the unparalleled victories of the Northern Powers, combined by the wise measures of His Majesty's Councils against the common foe, have compelled him to retire into the bosom of France. On events so important, and which will, we hope, lead to an honorable and lasting peace, we offer to Your Honor our most cordial congratulations.

When the public accounts are laid before us we shall endeavor to examine them with that attention that the nature of the subject may require.

With Your Honor we are aware of the importance of a well organized militia for the defence of this Province, and shall give to that subject our most serious consideration. We individually have witnessed the brave, zealous and meritorious exertions of a very large proportion of His Majesty's subjects, and the privations and sufferings they have undergone in the defence of this Province, and shall most cheerfully co-operate in any measures for ameliorating their condition and for embodying under more efficient regulations such a proportion of the militia population as the situation of the country will admit.

We shall take the condition of the public roads into our serious consideration, as well as the propriety of calling for pecuniary assistance from those who from religious scruples abstain from war, and who by the valor of their fellow subjects enjoy their properties with so many additional advantages.

The disgraceful and traitorous conduct of two members of this house in joining the ranks of the enemy are subjects of real concern. Their infamous conduct has, we believe, been very partially followed, and while the disappointment of their hopes must lead to the misery and ruin of themselves and their misguided followers, their fate will be a warning to His Majesty's subjects in this Province and convince them that loyalty to their Sovereign and attachment to his Government are the surest foundations for their public welfare and individual happiness. We shall, however, not fail to give the subject every attention.

We shall pay every regard in our power to the interests of His Majesty's loyal subjects, and shall endeavor to frame such regulations as in our opinion may best answer for the confiscation of the property of such traitors as may have joined the enemy and who may not be within reach of legal conviction.

In the gracious desire of His Royal Highness the Prince Regent that all forfeitures of this nature should be applied to the relief of sufferers by the war in this Province we have an additional proof of the benevolence of His Royal Highness, and of his solicitude for the welfare and happiness of His Majesty's subjects in Upper Canada.

The restrictions on the distillation from grain shall receive our serious and prompt consideration.

Such other matters as shall appear to require our deliberations shall receive every consideration and we shall, fully sensible of the importance of despatch, use every diligence to bring the business of the present session to a speedy termination.

ALLAN MACLEAN,
Speaker, Commons House of Assembly,
17th February, 1814.

Lieut. General Drummond to Noah Freer

YORK, February 16th, 1814.

SIR,—

I have the honor to acquaint you, for the information of His Excellency the Commander of the Forces, that the Indian chiefs of the western tribe, whose names are herewith enclosed, together with the late Tecumseth's sister and son, and about twenty-six of the young warriors who could not be restrained from accompanying them, have arrived here and are to proceed immediately on their visit to His Excellency at Quebec.

I have afforded them every accommodation and supplied Captain Elliott, who conducts them, with money and letters (for assistance on their route,) to Major General Stovin at Kingston and Major General de Rottenburg at Montreal.

(Canadian Archives, C. 257, p. 217.)

Names of the Chiefs of the Western Nations who go to Quebec:

Chippewas—Kishkiwabik.
Ottawas—Naiwash.
Saakies—Mitass.
Foxes—Walisseka, Kenailounak.
Kickapoos—Waikitchai.
Delawares—Pamamai.
Munseys—John Gray, Wabachkweela, or White Horse.
Six Nations—Ounagechtai, Twalwa, or Isaac Peters.
Winibiegoe—Wassasskum.
And Techkumthai's sister and son, of the Shawanese.

Captain W. H. Merritt to Major General Riall.

TWELVE MILE CREEK, 16th February, 1814.

SIR,—

I beg leave to report to Your Excellency the state of my troop, and as the system is so very imperfect beg you will recommend it being put on another establishment. Our horses are furnished by the men @ 6d per diem, in consequence of which we have not more than twelve good horses in the troop. As our clothing and appointments have arrived, providing the Government will furnish twenty horses and deduct the sixpence, the troop will be effective in a very short time. I have thirty rank and file, which, if on the same establishment as Capt. Coleman's, (whose men are raised on the same terms and for the same period,) I trust will be of the most essential service the ensuing campaign, as they have a thorough knowledge of the country and their fidelity has been well tried since their first formation.

(Merritt MSS.)

General Order.

Headquarters, WILLIAMSVILLE, Feb'y 17th, 1814.

The companies of volunteers under the command of Capts. Hull and Stone in public service will be consolidated and placed under the command of Capt. William Hull, to whom is attached Lieut. James Chapin and Ensign Harris Hibbard. Captn. Hull will march with all convenient despatch to Lerche's Ferry on the Buffalo Creek and keep such a guard from thence to Buffalo as the number of his corps will warrant, subject to the orders of the officer of the day. He will make return to the officer commanding on the Niagara Frontier.

WILLIAM H. ADAMS, Acting A. D. C.

(Publications of the Buffalo Historical Society, Vol. V., p. 51.)

Major General Hall to Governor Tompkins.

Headquarters, WILLIAMSVILLE, Feb'y 17, 1814.

SIR,—

I feel it my duty to communicate for the information of Your Excellency some circumstances necessary to be known and which it is thought will require your early attention, and probably the co-operating aid of the Legislature.

In the first moment of alarm on this frontier, for the purpose of defence and to supply present deficiencies, arms and ammunition were provided by any means wherever they were to be had, of individuals or otherwise. The ammunition has in part been paid for on a requisition by the Q. Master's department of the U. States, but the arms purchased have not been nor is there any probability that they will be paid for by the U. States. Those arms have been appropriated to the use of the State and have been turned into the public arsenals; the individuals of whom they were purchased remain to be paid and are men who cannot without inconvenience remain unrenumerated. These purchases were chiefly made on the authority of Lt. Colo. Davis, and although the proceeding was not strictly warranted by law or usage yet it is presumed that Your Excellency will perceive in the correctness of the motive a fair claim on the state authority for the assumption of such contracts. The sum requisite to cover such purchases will probably amount to 10 or 1,200 dollars.

Your Excellency will recollect that immediately after my assuming the command on this frontier, a representation was made of the destitute situation of our troops as to arms and military stores, an event naturally resulting from the loss of the great depot of the munitions of war, Fort Niagara, as well as the other contingent losses of war. This representation received prompt attention and a supply, it is understood, was ordered on to the frontier. It would have relieved me of much embarrassment had there accompanied the arms, &c., a bill of them. But learning that they had arrived at Canandaigua and were placed under the care of Captain Ridgeway, a U. S. officer, an order was given to remove them to Batavia. The arms have chiefly been delivered out. It is a matter of regret that there should have been so great a deficiency of cartouch boxes; a very considerable number of arms were unsupplied in this particular. The importance will readily be perceived of supplying this deficiency. Of ammunition and flints there is a sufficiency for the present.

The camp kettles and pans so much desired have been received and distributed by the Q. M. of brigade, under the supposition it was the property of the State.

I flatter myself that Your Excellency will lose no time in ordering detachments of troops from other divisions into service to relieve those at present here. On this, so momentous a subject, it is earnestly hoped that there may be no delay; the whole number on this frontier do not exceed 1,800 men, and the term of the 1st detachment called for on the requisition of the War Department, will expire as soon as new troops can be got out. Those of the 2d detachment, having been ordered out under the State authority, it cannot be thought reasonable should be much longer detained. The harassing duty of the 7th Division call loudly for consideration, and it is hoped that those citizens more happily situated will commiserate and relieve them.

From recent information the enemy are in considerable force near this frontier and adequate security cannot be afforded without a considerable addition to the numbers now in service.

There is another subject I am constrained to press upon Your Excellency's attention: the troops which have been and now are in service under the State authority have only the promise of pay expressed in the statute book, but it is not known that any appropriations are made by law for their pay, nor is it known that the District Paymaster of the armies of the U. States will feel authorized to pay such troops without express orders from the War Department. Some uneasiness has already been manifested on this subject, and it would afford me much satisfaction to be informed by Your Excellency as to what answer I can give those who may inquire of me respecting their pay and the means which may be provided. A satisfactory assurance on this subject may be of important service.

(Publications of the Buffalo Historical Society, Vol. V., pp. 53-4.)

Major General Wilkinson to Sir George Prevost.

Headquarters, PLATTSBURG, 17th February, 1814.

SIR,—

Having received no answer to my letter of the 28th ultimo, I do myself the honor to transmit to Your Excellency a duplicate and will hope to receive a reply as soon as may comport with your convenience, as it is my duty to report copies of our correspondence to the executive of the United States; an additional motive for this application is the representation of certain acts of conflagration which have been committed near Four Mile Creek in the vicinity of Fort Niagara by the troops under your command.

(Canadian Archives, C. 682, p 119.)

From Sir George Prevost to Lieut. General Drummond.

Head Qrs., QUEBEC, 17th Feb'y, 1814.

SIR,—

In reply to your letter of the 5th inst. I have the honor to acquaint you that whenever I am enabled to augment the proportion of artillery now serving in Upper Canada I propose doing so.

Should the late movement of the enemy from their position on the frontier of Lower Canada throw sufficient light on their future designs as to remove apprehensions of a second concentration of their force for the purpose of invading this Province, I will endeavor to increase the divisions placed under your command.

With regard to the difficulties attending the maintenance of horses at Kingston, I recommend the greatest reduction being made in the Driver Corps attached to the field train at that post, and that the troop of the 19th Lt. Dragoons now there should be sent either to Cornwall or St. Davids.

Having no employment at this moment in the Lower Province for the Western Indians it would be highly impolitic under existing circumstances to place them where you suggest, to the annoyance of the Canadians and to the irritation of the hitherto peaceful American borderers.

Experience has taught me that Indians are not a disposable force and far from a manageable one when brought into action. Their cooperation is never to be relied on. From these considerations I am apprehensive they cannot be turned into an enemy's country as a free corps, there to feed themselves, while food is to be obtained.

It is therefore proper you should ascertain the correctness of my objections before you adopt any plan for removing them from their present situation.

The information you have received of the force of the enemy at Batavia and of a detachment collecting at a village near Lewiston under Major General Hall does not appear to me calculated to create any immediate apprehension for the safety of the Niagara frontier provided our troops are vigilant and that a proper spirit of discipline is cherished among them.

With regard to Lieut. Colonel Ellictt's communication relating to the disposition of the Indians respecting young Tecumseth, I am inclined to coincide to his opinion, relying on your assuring their principal warriors that I only wished to express to them in person H. R. H. the Prince Regent's commands to assure the Western Indians that H. R. H. is desirous of maintaining a perpetual good understanding with them, and also to protect their territory against the encroachments of the Government of the United States.

I have desired the Commissary General to attend to the inadequacy of the supply of money at the uppermost posts, and he has taken measures to meet the want of that article and of salt provisions.

(Canadian Archives, C. 1222, pp. 49-50.)

From Lieut. General Drummond to Sir George Prevost.

YORK, February 18th, 1814.

SIR,—

Entertaining a reasonable hope that considerable alterations and improvement will be made during the present session of the Legislature in the existing Militia Law of the Province, whereby I am led to expect that I shall be enabled to establish that body into a tolerably efficient force, particularly by its being in the power of the Executive Government to continue their services when called out for a period of one year, and being particularly desirous to form them in discipline and interior economy as much as possible like troops of the line, I propose incorporating such as shall become at my disposal into battalions of about 600 men each, and being equally anxious to assimilate their appearance to the same troops I have to request Your Excellency will be pleased to assist me in this desirable object by ordering 2,000 suits of scarlet clothing, complete, to be forwarded to Kingston immediately, for that purpose, and for the use of the present Incorporated Militia, whose clothing will become due in a very short time.

I propose collecting this latter body at one place and placing it as well as the battalions on the new system under the superintendence of officer from the line, should it meet Your Excellency's approbation, in which case it will be necessary to confer upon them the Provincial rank of Lieutenant Colonel with the pay and allowances as such.

I have selected Captain Robinson of the King's Regiment to take charge of the militia at present incorporated.

(Canadian Archives, C. 704, pp. 158-60.)

From the Diary of Thomas McCrae.

RALEIGH, Friday, 18th February, 1814.

The British detachment all passed here on their way upwards to-day.

Saturday, 19th February.

Young Walker, one of the American interpreters, was here to-day.

Wednesday, 23d February.

The wolves are uncommonly plenty this year. They are seen in droves around the neighborhood and keep a continual howling at night.

Thursday, 24th February.

A party of Am(erican) horsemen of about 80 went up yesterday. Capt. Gill of the regulars commanded them.

General Order.

President's Office, YORK, 19th February, 1814.

His Honor the President has been pleased to appoint Capt. Foster on half-pay to be Adjutant General of Militia, with the rank of Lieutenant Colonel, *vice* Shaw, deceased.

His Honor has been further pleased to appoint Captain Loring, A. D. Camp, to be his Private Secretary, *vice* Foster. These appointments to take place from the 7th instant, inclusive.

From Lieut. General Drummond to Sir George Prevost.

YORK, February 19th, 1814.

SIR,

I have the honor to acknowledge the receipt of Your Excellency's letter of the 8th inst., covering a despatch from Earl Bathurst relative to the emigration of several families into this Province from Scotland at the present crisis.

In reply to which I do not hesitate to declare my decided opinion in favor of the introduction of so valuable a portion of subjects into a country already too much inhabited by aliens from the United Kingdom, very many of whom are avowedly disaffected to the British Government, and as many more of doubtful principles.

Independent of the advantage to result from the population being thus increased by such loyal inhabitants, the ranks of the militia would be filled with a brave and hardy race of men, whose desertion to the enemy would not be apprehended.

And although the want of provisions would weigh strongly against the introduction at present of these settlers, yet I conceive it fully counterbalanced by the accession of so much military strength.

I am of the opinion therefore that these people ought to have every assistance afforded them in their passage out and for a fair length of time after their settlement here, and that they ought to be encouraged to leave home by the very earliest opportunity in the spring.

A large supply of provisions should accompany them, besides felling axes and the other requisite implements, which cannot be procured in this country, together with a suitable proportion of scarlet militia clothing, shoes, &c., complete.

The lands to be granted to these people must be from those at present unsettled, as, in compliance with the instructions contained in Earl Bathurst's letter to Your Excellency of the 11th of August last, the confiscated property of those who have gone over to the enemy (must) be appropriated to the relief of such as have suffered by the war in adhering to their allegiance.

(Canadian Archives, C. 621, pp. 1-3.)

Lieut. General Drummond to Sir George Prevost.

(Secret.) YORK, February 19th, 1814.

SIR,—

I have the honor to acknowledge the receipt of Your Excellency's letter of the 8th inst.

Your Excellency will have already perceived by my letter of the 3d instant that with very great reluctance I have found it totally impracticable, from the lateness of the season and the unusually mild weather during the entire of this winter, to make an attempt with any reasonable hope of success against the enemy's vessels upon Lake Erie and their force at Detroit.

The observations contained in Your Excellency's letter of the 29th ultimo have been realized and I have been most fully and amply justified in the reluctant decision I made at that time, by the present state of the weather. For the last four days past the thaw has been so considerable that many of the oldest inhabitants of this Province, which at all times differs so much from the lower one, are almost induced to believe that even at this early period the winter is fast breaking up. The snow has hitherto been but very thin upon the ground and the bordage upon Lake Erie never so strong or sound as to render a passage upon it to Put-in-Bay sufficiently safe.

I therefore do not hesitate in declaring to Your Excellency that any attempt against the enemy's vessels on Lake Erie or their force at Detroit is at present totally impracticable, as well from the unusual mildness of the weather as from the lateness of the season.

(Canadian Archives, C. 682, p. 120.)

New York Evening Post, 18th March, 1814.

DETROIT, February 20th, 1814.

There are a few of the enemy's light horse at or near the mouth of the Thames. They advanced the other day as far as the River St. Clair and took some of the inhabitants prisoners.

Major J. B. Glegg to Captain W. H. Merritt.

NIAGARA FRONTIER, 20th Feb'y, 1814.

MY DEAR MERRITT,—

I shall be glad if you could call upon me to-morrow, as I wish to have some conversation with you respecting the establishment of your troop. Bring with you all the documents in your possession respecting the first raising of the troop and subsequent organization by order of His Excellency the Commander of the Forces.

Elias Gillies, stationed at Queenston, reports that his horse is quite knocked up and unfit for service. Let him be immediately relieved, and there must always be two at that post, as the duty is very severe.

On recollection I shall be at Queenston to-morrow from 10 until three at a General Court Martial, and perhaps you can meet me there and we can ride home together.

I have some other business to speak about.

(Merritt MSS.)

N. B. Boileau to James Lamberton.

HARRISBURG, February 21, 1814.

. . . . The detachments are to be organized at Erie so as to form one regiment, to consist of ten companies of one hundred men each rank and file, to be officered as follows:—One colonel, one lieutenant colonel, two majors; to each company, one captain, first, second and third lieutenants, one ensign, four sergeants, four corporals and customary staff. The regiment to be divided into two battalions, each to be commanded by one major. Col. James Fenton, colonel commandant, lieutenant colonels, those designated by law .

(Pennsylvania Archives, Vol. XI. p. 705.)

Lieut. Colonel Foster to Major General Riall.

Headquarters, UPPER CANADA,
February 21st, 1814.

SIR,—

I am commanded by Lieut. General Drummond to acknowledge the receipt of your letter to His Honor, transmitting a report relative to an advance of a body of the enemy to Delaware and the outrage committed in the burning of the house and barn of Mr Westbrook at that place and the forcible seizure of Mr. Brigham and Mr. Springer, two of its most respectable inhabitants, from thence. These two gentlemen, though not in arms, were taken from the bosom of their families and the peaceable enjoyment of their properties and, together with Mr. Baby, shamefully and inhumanly tied with cords until it was found convenient to remove them to an unjust imprisonment. Such conduct being totally subversive of the customs and usages of war amongst civilized nations, and being inclined to believe that it is not intended to be followed up by the Government of the United States, having recently received a copy of a letter from Major General Wilkinson disclaiming such a system, the Lieutenant General cannot suffer it to pass without expressing his most decided disapprobation of it. I am therefore commanded to request that you will be pleased to direct Lieutenant Colonel Stewart to send a flag of truce to Brigadier General Cass or the officer commanding the United States forces at Detroit, to request that the gentlemen before mentioned be returned to their homes, and an assurance on the part of His Honor that if such conduct be persisted in, the most full and ample retaliation must unavoidably be the result on the Detroit as well as every other point where an opportunity may offer.

You will be pleased to direct Lieutenant Colonel Stewart to permit Captain Rowe of the United States militia to return to his home, for although his house contained several stands of arms yet he was himself not in the force at the time of his apprehension and was unnecessarily brought to this side of the river. Mr. Blodget, apprehended under very suspicious circumstances, must be forwarded, with papers found upon him, to York.

(Canadian Archives, C. 682, pp. 149-50.)

Lieut. General Drummond to Sir George Prevost

BURLINGTON HEIGHTS, February 21st, 1814.

SIR,—

I have the honor to report to Your Excellency my arrival here this evening.

I have received a report handed to me by Major General Riall of the arrival of the light company of the 89th Regiment with Lieutenant McGregor's Volunteers and some Indians at Tilbury, near the mouth of the River Thames, in consequence of a party of the enemy which had appeared near Chatham driving about 40 or 50 head of cattle, but which had abandoned the cattle and made a precipitate retreat, intelligence of the arrival of Captain Basden's detachment having been communicated to them by a family of the name of Hitchcock.

A Captain Rowe of the militia has been taken prisoner, and a Mr. P. Blodget apprehended, on suspicion of acting for the enemy. Twenty-six stands of arms and a thousand rounds of ball-cartridge have fallen into the hands of the pursuers.

The light company of the Royals and the troop of Captain Coleman's Canadian Dragoons have been advanced to Delaware and some militia are daily expected there.

<small>(Canadian Archives, C. 682, pp. 129-31.)</small>

George Platt to Captain W. H. Merritt.

MONTREAL, 21 Feby, 1814.

DEAR SIR,—

I rec'd your letter by Capt. Leonard, who proceeded to Quebec immediately after I had seen him. Col. Murray had the good fortune to replace your country in a state which must be cheering to the inhabitants, and I hope the enemy will never again have the power to disturb them, as the *old errors* will, of course, not again occur. Genls. Procter and Vincent are here, as also Capt. Hall, (Coleman's friend.) It is not expected they will have command in U. C. again. I trust Great Britain will now have it in her power to send reinforcements and officers to lead them on, *such* as will make Jonathan tremble, as her attention to Spain and Portugal, as well as the Continent, will now have some relaxation in consequence of the unparalleled and rapid success of the allies. Our latest accounts you will find in the enclosed handbill. The burning of Newark by the enemy must have produced a most serious and distressing loss to individuals at the season of the year in which it took place, but the measure of retaliation which followed, although it produced no relief to individuals, yet in a national point of view was most gratifying, as it will shew them they are not to commit such atrocious acts with impunity. We have not heard what they intend to do with the prisoners of war held in close confinement. I am much in the opinion that the rapid decline of their ally, Boney, will make them *sing small* and of course a peace must take place, but God forbid that any peace should be granted them until they are completely humbled. A new line also should be drawn in order that a peace should become permanent, for if they are allowed to progress and populate upon the lands next our waters then we must not count upon a lasting peace, for the St. Lawrence will be such a bone for these *Lords of the Creation* that they will forever be picking at it to our great annoyance and perhaps discomfiture in the end. You will have heard no doubt of the fate of Wilkinson's Invincibles at the French Mills where, after building barracks, &c., they found it would not be safe for them to remain, and therefore burned the most of their boats and spiked the cannon they did not take away and hide, and set fire to the huts and marched off, some to Sackett's (Harbor) and some to Plattsburg. So ended the Great Southern General's expedition to Montreal. Report says Col.

Morrison has some orders at the present moment which is in operation in the neighborhood of Prescott, particulars not yet known.

(Merritt MSS.)

Commodore Chauncey to the Secretary of the Navy

(No. 7)   SACKETT'S HARBOR, 24th February, 1814.

SIR,—

I arrived here yesterday and found the station in excellent order, and everything in a fine state of preparation. Captain Crane is entitled to very great praise for his extraordinary exertions and indefatigable industry in preparing everything for service.

The three ships first ordered are in a great state of forwardness; the largest has all her ribs up and the two smaller ones all planked and nearly half caulked, and will be ready to launch before the ice breaks up. My letter to Mr. Eckford did not reach him in time to make the alteration in the two small ships as proposed. They will be the same as the *Peacock*, as you first ordered. The larger one has been increased in the beam two feet. This vessel will be ready to launch about the first of May.

The roads are dreadful, and if the present mild weather continues we shall experience difficulty in getting on our stores. I, however, hope for cold weather yet. I will in a day or two transmit to you a view of the whole station.

From Sir George Prevost to Lieut. General Drummond.

Head Qrs., QUEBEC, 25th Feby, 1814.

SIR,—

The Military Secretary has laid before me your confidential letter of the 14th inst., containing information of the enemy's movements in the neighborhood of the River Thames, where it is reported that Lt. Colonel Baby, Captain Brigham and Springer, with a detachment of militia, have been made prisoners. I should wish that the Indians attached to the Right Division may be thrown forward, supported by militia and light troops, to check the excursions of the enemy in that direction and to re-occupy the ground recently lost.

The report you have received of the disposition of the enemy's naval forces on Lake Erie has appeared to me important and satisfactory, proving, however, that the previous intelligence of the situation of those vessels was incorrect.

I confidently trust that such precautionary measures may be adopted by our troops on the Niagara frontier as will prevent the advance of the enemy by that line of communication, and I recommend a peaceable disposition being promoted in the inhabitants of the neighborhood of Buffalo as best calculated to appease the wrath of the more violent characters amongst them, and to frustrate any attempt to carry into execution their threats to burn and destroy.

I enclose for your information the copy of some secret and valuable intelligence which has just reached me, showing that if another campaign takes place the energies of the enemy will be displayed on Lakes Ontario and Champlain.

(Canadian Archives, C. 1222, pp. 53-4.)

From Lieut. General Drummond to Sir George Prevost.

BURLINGTON HEIGHTS, February 21st, 1814.

SIR,—

I am concerned to report to Your Excellency the desertion of no less than eight men of the Royal Scots Regiment from Queenston. They were all foreigners. Three were on sentry along the river, and it is supposed the others left their quarters about an hour before daybreak and crossed over in a small boat which was in charge of one of those on sentry, as the boat was found adrift about two miles below Queenston in the morning.

I am concerned also to state to Your Excellency that four of the King's Regt. have likewise deserted from Fort Niagara.

(Canadian Archives, C. 824, pp. 35-6.)

From Sir James Yeo to Sir Sidney Beckwith.

MY DEAR SIR,—

Many thanks for your kind letter and information. His Excellency is pleased to think my information is exaggerated. Pray have you communicated to him yours. I only know that if every effort is not made they will have a very superior force.

If we can get the new boats from the Coteau it will save us much time and trouble, and all the shipwrights can be employed on the ships.

I shall transmit your information to the Commander in Chief at Halifax and request him to forward the sails, &c., of the third ship with all possible despatch.

Pray, my dear Sir, send us up all the shipwrights you can muster.

You shall hear from me by Tuesday's express in the meantime.
Kingston, 26th Feby, 1814.

(Canadian Archives, C. 732, pp. 41-2.)

Captain Leslie Patterson, 1st Regiment Middlesex Militia, to Col. Talbot.

PORT TALBOT, 26th February, 1814.

COLONEL TALBOT,
 DEAR SIR,—
   John Crawford arrived here last evening with intelligence that the enemy was at his place the evening before, where his family and the family of John Cull had everything ready for a start the next morning. There was also one Ball and two others at his place from the new settlement, when the house was surrounded by about twelve of them on horseback. They all sprung out and Crawford see two of them take hold of Cull as he was running and what come of the others he cannot say. After he got out of the woods about a mile distant he saw his house on fire, and Clark told him he expects everything in the new settlement is burned, as their orders was to kill all the cattle and burn everything they could not get with them. Corbit is with them and it is the general opinion (that) we will have a visit from them very shortly. Mitchel's family has got into this settlement and, I expect, Crawford's and Cull's if they are not carried off. Crawford requests a party to go with him and see what has come of them, and says that he and one of his sons will join the volunteers as soon as he gets his family out of the woods. Fields is one of the volunteers and came with Cull to assist him in getting his family away. I hope the Col. will be so good as to send me some advice what I am to do with these distressed families, and likewise if we are to expect any protection from these marauders. The cows came up from Defields last night and the cattle are all doing well.

(Canadian Archives, C. 682, pp. 159-61.)

From Sir James Yeo to Noah Freer, Esqr., Military Secretary.

His Majesty's Ship *Wolfe,*
 KINGSTON, February 28th, 1814.

SIR,—
   The Acting Commissioner having informed me that there is no iron of larger dimensions at Montreal than the rings already sent up, I request that orders may be given to furnish us with the articles contained in the requisition transmitted by me on the 19th inst. without a moment's loss of time, as they are indispensably necessary.

I am sorry to say that the man who was bringing in the spar for the *Regent* has by accident broke it in two, and we cannot get another before the navigation opens, but I will have the mast made in the woods to save time.

(Canadian Archives, C. 732, p. 43.)

From Sir James Yeo to Sir George Prevost.

KINGSTON, 28th Feb'y, 1814.

DEAR SIR,—

I had the honor of Your Excellency's note with the agreeable intelligence of 200 seamen being on their way.

From the information obtained thro' the Qr. Master-General, I am decidedly of opinion that the enemy will use every exertion to establish a formidable force on Lakes Ontario and Champlain. It is the only measure at this moment likely to be popular in America.

I pledge myself to Your Excellency that every exertion of my mind and body shall be devoted to defeat the enemy's views, and that the force entrusted to my command never shall surrender to the enemy while *I have life.*

I feel persuaded at the same time that Your Excellency will agree with me, that to ensure such an important object as the naval superiority on the lakes, as little ought to be left to chance as possible. I therefore request Your Excellency will urge the Commander-in-Chief or Admiral at Halifax to forward the sails, rigging and cables with all possible despatch.

I have written to Admiral Griffith and Commissioner Woodhouse on the same subject. There are only 40 32-pr. carronades and fifty-one long twenty-fours yet arrived, but suppose the remainder are on the road. No. 68's arrived.

If Your Excellency gives credit to that part of Sir Sidney's information relative to the enemy's building fifteen gun boats on Lake Champlain, I beg leave to suggest the propriety of Captain Pring being allowed to build six or eight in addition to his present force.

I have received a report of survey on the sails, cables, &c., of the *Aeolus*, by which it appears that almost the whole of them are more than half worn, and as I am certain it never could have been their Lordships' intention her coming out in that state, I have reported the same to the Admiralty.

On the opening of navigation, I have ordered Captain Creighton to send up two anchors and cables, which will answer for the third ship.

(Canadian Archives, C. 732, pp. 44-7.)

From Sir George Prevost to Lieutenant-General Drummond.

Head Qrs., QUEBEC, 28th Feb'y, 1814.

SIR,—

Adverting to your letter of the 8th inst., on the subject of the difficulty experienced at Kingston in procuring forage and provisions, I cannot but lament the precipitancy with which Major-General de Rottenburg's proclamation, partially establishing martial law in Upper Canada, was revoked, as its continuance for a few weeks more would have contributed to replenish the King's magazines, without attaching odium to yourself.

It appears to me that it need not have been repealed until the commissariat stores had derived greater advantages from its effect, as under existing circumstances a recurrence to that measure may be fraught with objections, but which, however, must yield to the imperious necessity of supplying the King's troops in Upper Canada with the food they require.

You should take into your calculation, in addition to the serious expense, difficulty and inconvenience, inseparable from the transport of provisions from Lower Canada, the uncertainty of their arriving at their destination, and make corresponding exertions to be prepared against disappointment.

I regret circumstances have compelled you to relinquish the expedition to the westward; even as regards the economy of provisions, the removal of the western warriors would have been a great advantage.

The preservation of the resources in the Long Point District should be a primary consideration at this moment, nor would I have you extend your force now acting on the defensive so as to uncover them.

As it is possible our naval ascendency on Lake Ontario may only have a short duration, the Federalists and Democrats agreeing cordially on the propriety of the exertions of the American Government to preserve their superiority on the lakes, it becomes doubly necessary that you should resort to every practicable expedient for procuring provisions.

The foregoing consideration, combined with the actual state of Lake Erie, renders it possible (in my estimation) that not only Fort Niagara may be invested, but that the residue of the Right Division may be obliged to depend on the depots and magazines, which you may have been enabled to establish previous to the opening of the campaign, for its supplies.

I have called the Commissary-General's attention to this most interesting and highly important part of his duty, and I feel assured that he will not fail in exerting a proper sensibility on the subject on the minds of the Commissariat officers serving in Upper Canada; altho' you may continue to rely on every exertion being made by me to support your endeavors for the preservation of the territory you have to defend, and to supply the wants of the army under your command, still it is requisite you should circumscribe your demands as much as possible by drawing forth the resources of the province, and by a judicious accumulation of them.

I propose removing my headquarters in the course of the next month to Montreal.

I am making arrangements for adding to your force the 103rd Regt., a very effective corps. It will arrive at Kingston shortly after the seamen. The proportion of Rocket Artillery intended for Upper Canada have left Montreal.

(Canadian Archives, C. 1222, pp. 55-6.)

The Secretary of War to Major-General Brown.

War Department, 28th February, 1814.

SIR,—

It is obviously Prevost's policy and probably his intent to re-establish himself on Lake Erie during the ensuing month. But to effect this, other points of his line must first be weakened, and these will be either Kingston or Montreal. If the detachment from the former be great, a moment may occur in which you may do, with the aid of Commodore Chauncey, what I last year intended Pike should have done without aid, and what we now all know was very practicable, viz.: to cross the river or head of the lake on the ice and carry Kingston by a *coup de main*. This is not, however, to be attempted but under a combination of the following circumstances: practicable roads, good weather, large detachments (made westerly) on the part of the enemy, and a full and hearty co-operation on the part of our own naval commander. If the enterprise be agreed upon, use the enclosed letter (No. 2) to mask your object, and let no one into your secret but Chauncey.

NO. 2 (INTENDED TO DECEIVE THE ENEMY.)

SIR,—

Colonel Scott, who is in nomination as a brigadier, has orders to repair to the Niagara frontier, and to take with him a corps of artillerists and a battering and a field train, &c.; Major Wood of the Engineers, and Dallaba of the Ordnance will accompany or follow him. Four hundred Indians and about four thousand volunteer militia are under similar orders. The truth is that public opinion will no longer tolerate us in permitting the enemy to keep quiet possession of Fort Niagara. Another motive is the effect which may be expected from the appearance of a large corps on the Niagara in restraining the enemy's enterprises westward of that place. But will a corps so constituted be able to reduce Niagara or long impose on an enemy as well informed as itself? This is not to be expected— whence it follows that the President orders you to assemble means for conveying, with the least possible delay, the brigade you brought from French Mills to Batavia, where other and more detailed orders await you. Our advices from M(ontreal) state that large detachments are under orders for K(ingston) westwardly, and that no intention exists of attacking the harbor. Should, however, new movements from M(ontreal) indicate a different design, they will be promptly known to General W(ilkinson), and will produce a counter-movement.

(Armstrong's Notices of the War of 1812, Vol. II., pp. 213-4.

From the Military Secretary to Lieutenant-General Drummond.

Head Qrs., QUEBEC, 1st March, 1814.

SIR,—

The Commander of the Forces having been pleased to grant to the Indian chief, John Norton, a commission as captain and leader of the Five Nations, Grand River Indians or Confederates, I am directed to convey to you His Excellency's request that no interference may be allowed from the officers of the Indian Department between these tribes and Captain Norton, and all communications to those tribes are to be made through the medium of Captain Norton. That Captain Norton may have it in his power to reward the faithful services of the warriors acting with him, and also to give countenance to the leading war chiefs who assist in preserving good order in the Five Nations, it is His Excellency's desire that an ample proportion of presents be put up separately for the Indians of the Five Nations, to be distributed under Captain Norton's directions.

The clerk and storekeeper of the Five Nation department is to be ordered to give to Captain Norton an acct. of the arms, ammunition and goods that he receives for the use of the warriors and their families, and he is to be required to keep a regular account of the distribution of the same under the orders of Captain Norton, that the course of the expenditure and means of supply may always be seen.

The number of the Five Nations and Delawares on the Grand River is reported to be about 400 men.

The Moravians, Delawares and Munceys on the River Thames are stated to be nearly 100. The latter joined Captain Norton when proceeding with the army under Major-General Brock for the capture of Detroit, and have since shewn their fidelity; it is the wish of the Comr. of the Forces, therefore, that the opportunity be afforded Captain Norton to protect and reward these people according to their merits.

Captain Norton leaves Quebec in a few days on his return to Upper Canada, to assume the charge of those warriors who look up to him, and His Excellency trusts that officer will fulfil the expectation entertained of his zeal, courage and activity, and it is hoped this mark of confidence and good opinion placed in him by the Comr. of the Forces will have the effect of ensuring that degree of usefulness to our cause from Captain Norton and his followers that cannot fail of being attended with the best consequences, and under these impressions I am instructed, in His Excellency's name, to recommend Captain Norton to your protection.

(Canadian Archives, C. 1222, pp. 57-8.)

From Commodore Chauncey to the Secretary of the Navy.

U. S. Ship *General Pike*,
SACKETT'S HARBOR, 4th March, 1814.

(No. 11.)
SIR,—

I have the mortification to inform you that I have this moment received information that all our heavy guns are stopped at and below Poughkepsie, in consequence of the badness of the roads, and that the teamsters have abandoned them there. I have wrote to the navy agent at New York upon the subject, and I have also directed Mr. Anderson to proceed immediately to the place where the guns are stopped, and send them to Albany, either by land or water. I presume that the latter will be the most preferable mode, as in all probability the North River will be completely open in ten days. If these guns should not arrive in Albany before the 20th of this month, I shall direct them to be sent up the Mohawk to Oswego, where I will have boats to receive them. By this route I can calculate on receiving all the guns by the first week in May. If they come by land, no calculation can be made when they can be delivered here.

From the Military Secretary to Lieut.-General Drummond.

Head Qrs., QUEBEC, 4th March, 1814.

SIR,—

The Comr. of the Forces has directed me to acquaint you that he

has given orders for half a company of Rocket Artillery, four companies of marines and the 103rd Regt. to proceed to Kingston, and that three companies of the 89th Regt., under the command of a field officer, are to be stationed at Cornwall, and the remainder of that corps at Coteau-du-Lac, where Lt.-Colonel Morrison will command and have charge of the communication to the Rapid Plat.
(Canadian Archives, C. 1222, p. 59.)

Colonel Matthew Elliott to Lieut.-Colonel Stewart.

DELAWARE, March 4th, 1814.

SIR,—

I have this day had a meeting with the Indians on the subject of carrying ammunition to their friends within the American territory. The result is that they refuse to proceed with the ammunition on the ground that our regular troops do not advance further than the settlements on the River Thames, and of course would be of no use in protecting their friends in the enemy's country. The Americans might hear of these supplies being sent to the Indians, and the consequence would be fatal, perhaps, to their whole tribes. They would, therefore, rather suffer for want of ammunition than endanger themselves or their families.
(Canadian Archives, C. 682, p. 190.)

Ensign F. Mills to Lieut.-Colonel Stewart.

LONGWOODS, March 4th, 1814.

SIR,—

I beg leave to acquaint that this afternoon, about 5 o'clock, the party commanded by Captain Basden of the 89th Regiment came up with the enemy in force of nearly 500 men, and after an action of an hour and a half, in which I am concerned to state our loss is very considerable, the troops were withdrawn in consequence of the great superiority of the enemy's numbers. I have the satisfaction to assure every man did his duty, and that we retired in perfect order.
(Canadian Archives, C. 682, p. 182.)

Captain Alexander Stewart, Royal Scots (Lieut.-Colonel Commanding London District,) to Major-General Riall.

FOURTEEN MILE CREEK, March 5th, 1814.

SIR,—

Having received a report from Captain Caldwell, late on the

night of the 3d inst., stating that he had fallen in with a party of Americans that day on his advance through the Long Wood, the flank companies of the Royals and 89th Regiment moved early yesterday morning to his support, and at 5 o'clock in the afternoon came up with them, who were posted on a commanding eminence strongly entrenched by a log breastwork. They were instantly attacked in front by the two companies of the Royals and 89th Regiment; at the same time the Kent Militia and Captain Caldwell's company of rangers made a flank movement to the right, and a small party of Indians to the left, to gain the rear of the enemy's position, and after repeated efforts to dislodge them, without effect, the troops were most reluctantly withdrawn. I regret that our loss is very considerable. I enclose a letter from Ensign Mills of the 89th Regiment, who remained in command of the troops in this affair, every other officer being killed or wounded. I was detained at Delaware several hours after the movement of the two companies, making arrangements with Colonel Elliott of the Indian Department for a particular service in which the Indians were to be employed, which, I regret, prevented my joining the troops till the close of the action. Information is just received that the Americans have retreated from their position.

I herewith enclose a return of the killed, wounded and missing.

(Canadian Archives, C. 682, pp. 184-5.)

Return.

Return of officers, non-commissioned officers and rank and file killed, wounded and missing in action with the enemy on the 4th of March, 1814:—

Royal Scots Light Company:
    One captain, nine rank and file killed; one lieutenant, 3 sergeants, 31 rank and file wounded; one bugler missing.

89th Light Company:
    One lieutenant, three rank and file killed; one captain, one sergeant and seven rank and file wounded; Volunteer Pigot wounded and taken prisoner.

Loyal Kent Volunteers:
    One lieutenant, one sergeant and five rank and file wounded.

Names of officers killed and wounded:
    Captain D. Johnston, Royal Scots, killed.
    Lieut. P. Graeme, 89th Regt., killed.
    Captain Basden, 89th Regt., wounded.
    Lieut. A. Macdonald, Royal Scots, wounded.

                        A. STEWART,
                      Capt. Roy'l Scots,
            Lieut.-Colonel, London District.

FOURTEEN MILE CREEK,
    5th March, 1814.

Lieut.-Colonel H. Butler, Commanding in Michigan Territory and its Dependencies, to Major-General Riall.

DETROIT, (M. T.,) 5 March, 1814.

SIR,—

By the return of Lieut. Jackson of the Royal Scots, who has been the bearer of your flag of truce from Delaware, (U.C.,) to this place, I have to acknowledge the receipt of your letter of the 22d ulto., accompanied by a transcript of the communication made to you by Lieut.-General Drummond on the day preceding, relative to the burning of Mr. Westbrook's barn and house, and the capture of Messrs. Baby, Springer and Brigham by a detachment of troops from my command at Detroit.

In the communication made to you by Lieut.-Gen'l Drummond, he has fallen into some errors it will be my duty to correct. The first complaint exhibited against the conduct of the detachment is for "the outrage committed in burning the house and barn of Mr. Westbrook." When it shall be known that Mr. Westbrook was a man born within the States, and retaining the attachment for his native country which a citizen ought to feel, and for which, since the commencement of the present war, he has suffered from your Government oppression, imprisonment and persecution, in fact, has been virtually outlawed, one is at a loss to imagine the source whence the extreme sensibility in regard to this man's rights should be so suddenly felt and displayed. But when it is added that Mr. Westbrook accompanied the detachment, and courted its protection in the removal of his family from Delaware, and that he was himself the principal actor in the "outrage" complained of, it is presumed that no repetition of this complaint will be heard.

With regard to Col. Baby, a few words may suffice, as his release, if intended to be demanded, is so faintly urged that we see at once his name has been used merely to augment the list. Col. Baby, who bears a commission in your service, as his papers prove, was taken in arms and under circumstances of such suspicion as regarded his designs that I should have felt justified in using much more vigorous measures towards Col. Baby than were adopted. He was, however, immediately sent on to headquarters to Major-Gen'l Harrison.

As it regards the capture of Capt. Springer and Mr. Brigham, I exercised the discretion vested in me by my Government, who have confided to that discretion an important command, nor have I by that act in anywise violated a personal right or contravened a general principle but what is fully justified by the law of nations and the usages of war.

It is presumable that Gen'l Drummond is well advised of the

customs and usages of war, and, notwithstanding he speaks so confidently on the subject in the despatch which he communicated to you on the West ulto., and (of) which you enclosed me a copy, I am still authorized in saying that the sentiments expressed by the General in relation to the right of capture and detention of your subjects conflicts with the best opinions on national law, and is, moreover, directly opposed to the conduct of your own commanders whilst the Michigan Territory was occupied by the troops of your Government. Nay, in the very communication to which I have just alluded, he acknowledges that a detachment of your force has made prisoner of Mr. Blodget within those limits that have submitted to our army, and now holds him in confinement. This Mr. Blodget is a citizen of the U. States, in no employment of its Government, either in a civil or military capacity (not even at this time incorporated with a militia company,) but merely engaged as a clerk to a mercantile firm in Detroit, to settle accounts and to make purchases for their individual advantage from citizens on the River Thames, with whom this person had some previous transactions in the way of their business. Yet he is seized, and without other reason offered for his detention than his being "apprehended under very suspicious circumstances," he has been ordered to York. With such a case as this before you, the demand for a liberation for your own subjects comes with a very ill grace. In the capture of Captain Springer, I was justified from the circumstance of his having commanded a militia company in your service and having been actively engaged against us. The other prisoner, Brigham, I had received information against, and information of a character that induced me to decide on his removal from his residence. There exists, as it relates to him at this time, no more than relates to Blodget. I shall very readily, therefore, discharge the one when the other is set at liberty. Capt. Springer is, with Col. Baby, now at headquarters. Gen'l Harrison will decide on their cases.

I could have wished that Lieut.-General Drummond had avoided in his letter, (as it seemed intended for my inspection,) the harsh epithets of "shameful and inhuman" applied to the treatment which Messrs. Baby, Springer and Brigham received. Neither of these persons would make such a charge, and I am warranted in saying the expressions were unmerited. It merely would have comported better with the attitude assumed by the General in that letter to have abstained from language that has but one character. With regard to the threat of retaliation which General Drummond has permitted himself to use, I have but one remark to make. He is altogether a stranger to the American character if he supposed for a moment it would avail him in any purpose he intended, or intimidate an officer from his duty. We are appalled neither by the scene on the River Raisin or on the Niagara frontier.

(Canadian Archives, C. 682, p. 151.)

Lieut. General Drummond to Sir George Prevost.

YORK, March 5th, 1814.

SIR,—

I have the honor to report to Your Excellency that I availed myself of an opportunity to visit that part of the district which lies to the westward, as far as Delaware town on the River Thames and Long Point and vicinity on the shore of Lake Erie.

I was much concerned to find that part of the country bordering on the River Thames entirely drained of its resources, so much so in fact as to make it almost amounting to an impossibility to support an adequate force for its protection without drawing all supplies for that purpose from the neighborhood of Long Point.

As, however, this latter country can furnish a tolerable quantity of flour and a few cattle, and as the only approaches from the lake shore all unite nearly at one point, (about 20 miles from Turkey Point,) I propose posting a considerable force, providing I am supplied with the means of so doing, in the vicinity of Mr. Culver's house, near the junction of the roads alluded to, from whence a small party may be detached to Oxford to watch the road to the westward, and small guards posted to Turkey Point, Mrs. Ryerson's and Dover.

I conceive the 100th Regt. will be most advisable to employ on this occasion, as that part of this corps stationed there before, I am much gratified in stating, conducted itself, collectively and individually, in the most orderly and correct manner during its service there, very widely different, I am [concerned to say, from the light companies of the Royals and 89th Regiment, whose behavior has been that more of a plundering banditti than of British soldiers, employed for the protection of the country and its inhabitants. Two light guns and the troop of the 19th Light Dragoons from Kingston may likewise prove of service in this direction, as the country consists of plains but thinly scattered with trees, except in a few places, almost to the borders of the Grand River.

By this river, it is true, the enemy might endeavor to advance into the interior, but the distance from the lake is so excessive that, even supposing them daring enough to hazard such an attempt, intelligence of their motions would arrive in sufficient time to prevent the retreat of our force being cut off prior to its crossing the Grand River.

I have directed Captain Stewart of the Royals to make a diversion with his and the light company of the 89th Regt. and the Kent Volunteers, under Lieut. McGregor, towards the mouth of the Thames, for the purpose of covering the passage of the River St. Clair by about 200 Indians, whom I have sent to their brethren to the westward with an ample supply of powder and ball.

I was not so much surprised, as I regretted to find when at Burlington that Mr. Dance, the Asst. Commy. General, had scarcely procured at this late season of the winter any quantity of flour, the future consumption of which, it appears to me, instead of being at this moment only contracted for should have been long since safely lodged in the commissariat magazine. The favorable season for transport has been permitted to pass, the difficulty and expense will not be consequently considerably increased. I am thoroughly convinced that such conduct would not have been pursued by any other person in that department possessed of the smallest spark of energy, activity or genuine zeal in His Majesty's service. And so little of either does it appear to me that Mr. Dance possesses that I firmly believe that it would prove of the most beneficial consequence to the army in general, and to the right division in particular, if his place were supplied by an officer of more energy and talent.

I beg leave again to draw Your Excellency's attention to the very great want of money in this Province. Mr. Dance informed me that a supply of £30,000 would scarcely more than suffice to discharge the demands upon him and carry on the service.

I am extremely concerned to state to Your Excellency that I seldom entered a house to the westward where the claims of individuals for cattle and provisions furnished, taken and destroyed by the troops and Indians in the retreat of the division from Detroit, were not numerous, as well as for provisions furnished by individuals, principally in the vicinity of Long Point and Port Talbot, on the authority of Major General Brock and Colonel Talbot, which have not as yet been paid, and which in consequence is the cause of the greatest discontent, and in many instances of persons withholding their produce altogether from sale until their former demands are satisfied. The roads in the Province have been so much neglected since the commencement of the war that during the wet weather in some parts they become totally impassable. I am induced therefore to submit to Your Excellency's favorable consideration the necessity of a communication being afforded by water between the different posts on Lake Ontario, and a recommendation that you will be pleased to sanction the building of two light and fast sailing vessels for that purpose.

(Canadian Archives, C, 682, p. 163.)

Lieut. General Drummond to Sir George Prevost.

YORK, March 5th, 1814.

SIR,—

I have the honor to transmit to Your Excellency a letter I received enclosed from Colonel Talbot, reporting that the enemy had again advanced up the Thames and crossed over to Point aux Pins, 36 miles above Port Talbot on Lake Erie, where they destroyed the settlement.

The inhabitants at Port Talbot and upon the Talbot Road are in the greatest state of alarm, it being reported it is the intention of the enemy to lay waste the entire of the settlements in that vicinity, when, if such be the case, not less than 200 families will fall a sacrifice to this infamous species of uncivilized warfare. The enemy were accompanied by a man named Corbett, who sometime since made his escape from York gaol.

When at Delaware I directed Major General Riall to return a captain of militia (Rowe) who had been brought over the River St. Clair by Lieut. McGregor's Kent Volunteers, as he was at the time not in arms but in the peaceable possession of his house, to Brigadier General Cass at Detroit, with a flag of truce which also conveyed a strong remonstrance from me against the incendiary system which appears likely to prevail to the westward, and more particularly against the burning of Westbrook's house and offices at Delaware, headed by himself, and the seizure of Messrs. Brigham and Springer from thence, who, with Lieut. Colonel Baby and another were shamefully tied with cords until the enemy found convenient to carry them away.

Your Excellency may perhaps judge it advisable to make a representation on these subjects to the Commander in Chief of the United States army or to the American Government.

(Canadian Archives, C. 682, p. 157.)

Sir James Lucas Yeo to Sir John Borlase Warren.

His Majesty's Ship *Wolfe* at KINGSTON,
Upper Canada, 5th March, 1814.

SIR,—

A deserter from the *Lady of the Lake*, American schooner, came in yesterday and has given us a statement of the enemy's naval preparation for the ensuing campaign, which, as it is corroborated by the testimony of many other people who have been lately at Sackett's Harbor, I firmly believe to be correct.

I have the honor to enclose for your information a copy of the deserter's deposition and a comparative statement of the two squadrons as they are likely to meet in battle.

You will regret with me that the enemy's preparations are so great, and yet so short a time back as the 20th January not a keel was laid at Sackett's Harbor. Now they have 400 shipwrights and two of their new ships nearly ready for launching, and a third will be ready by the 1st of May and a fourth by the end of that month.

The roads from Albany, Boston and New York are covered with ordnance and stores for these vessels, and which when added to their old squadron will be far superior to anything I can bring against them. It therefore becomes my duty to acquaint you that unless I receive *immediate* reinforcements of guns, long 24 and 32 pounders, men and stores of every description, Upper Canada will, in my opinion, be lost to His Majesty.

In the meantime I shall use every exertion to collect the shipwrights in this country and build (if possible) to be on something like equal terms with the enemy, altho' their resources are so much nearer to them than ours are to us that if they exert themselves it will be *impossible* for us to get an equal force.

You, however, may rely that this squadron will do all in its power to uphold the honor of the British flag, nor shall it ever be surrendered to the enemy under any circumstances whatever.

I have sent a copy of the information herewith transmitted to the Lords Commissioners of the Admiralty and have solicited from their Lordships immediate reinforcements, and I have acquainted them without which I cannot expect success against the enemy.

(Canadian Archives, M. 389-6, pp. 92-4.)

Copy of the Naval Part of a Deposition made by a Seaman Deserter from the United States Schooner, The Lady of the Lake, in Sackett's Harbor.

There are four vessels building at Sackett's Harbor. The first, a ship of 162 feet keel to carry 30 long 32-pounders on the main deck and thirty-two 42-pounder carronades on the spar deck. The second, the size of the *Pike*, to carry 30 long 24-pounders, and two of 124 feet keel to carry 30 long 24-pounders each. The Madison is to have long 18 pounders and the Oneida brig to have 32-pounder carronades instead of 24-pounders.

The Sylph schooner they have made a brig, and she is to mount 22 long 12-pounders. They are also building another schooner the size of the *Lady of the Lake*.

(Canadian Archives, M. 389-G, p. 96.)

From the Diary of Thomas McCrae.

RALEIGH, Friday, 5th March, 1814.

One of the Americans came down and says they have had an engagement with the British above Ward's and have defeated the latter. All the American party arrived here this evening and confirmed the above report. They brought down only two prisoners, one an officer, the other a trumpeter. They say the killed and wounded about 70; camped here all night.

Saturday, 6th March, 1814.

The Americans all started downwards this morning.

New York Evening Post, 28th March, 1814.

Extract of a letter from Major General Harrison to the Secretary of War.

CHILLICOTHE, March 5, 1814.

Colonel Baby, a militia captain, taken from the township of Delaware, and two other individuals who were supposed to be particularly mischievous, have arrived here under escort from Detroit. The militia captain denies his being in service, but was found with his uniform on, and acknowledges to have frequently served at the head of a militia company under Procter since the commencement of the war. He is a native of the County of Albany, State of New York, and emigrated to Canada in the year 1798.

This man, whose name is Springer, is also a magistrate, and of course must have been naturalized by the British Government.

Earl Bathurst to Sir George Prevost.

No. 60.   Downing Street, 5th March, 1814.

SIR,—

Captain Cochrane has delivered to me your despatches to No. 126 inclusive, and I have lost no time in laying before the Prince Regent the gratifying intelligence which they contain.

Although His Royal Highness on many occasions has had reason to express his approbation of the conduct of the army under your command, yet His Royal Highness can refer to none in which the skill and judgment of the officers and the gallantry and discipline of the men have been more conspicuously displayed than in the late operations on the Niagara Frontier. The results of these new exertions made by the army in that quarter will be to give more immediate security to the Upper Province, not only by repelling the enemy to a greater distance from the frontier, but by giving increased facility to the formation of a preponderating naval force upon Lake Erie.

You will not fail to convey to Lt. Genl. Drummond, to Major Generals Riall and Vincent, and to all the officers and men of the regular force and militia engaged, the high approbation which His Royal Highness the Prince Regent has expressed of their services on that occasion, and you will equally express to Capt. Norton and the Indians under his command, His Royal Highness's gracious acknowledgments of their exertions in the common cause.

His Royal Highness entirely approves of your having retaliated on the inhabitants of the United States the harsh measures which the American Government had adopted with respect to that part of the Canadas which had been in their temporary occupation. You will not fail to inflict a similar retaliation whenever the conduct of the enemy will render it necessary. It is, however, the anxious wish of His Royal Highness that the example which has so properly been made of the destruction of Lewiston, Black Rock and Buffalo, may be sufficient to deter the enemy from the repetition of outrage so much at variance with the practice of war as carried on between civilized nations, for nothing can be more painful to His Royal Highness than to be under the necessity of extending to unoffending inhabitants the aggravated miseries to which such a system, if persevered in on the part of the enemy, must infallibly give rise to.

(Canadian Archives, C. 682, p. 176.)

Earl Bathurst to Sir George Prevost.

No. 61.   Downing Street, 5th March, 1814.

SIR,—

In reply to your despatch, No. 126, in which you urge in the most earnest manner the necessity of a reinforcement of troops being sent to Quebec early in the approaching spring, I am happy to have it in my power to acquaint you that the expectation which I held out to you in my despatch of the 10th August, of placing at your disposal four regiments by the spring of this year, is on the point of fulfilment.

The 70th Regiment, which was one of those specified in that despatch, has long since been placed at your disposal.

By a letter from Sir J. Sherbrooke it appears that the remaining companies of the 98th reached Halifax on the 15th of December and will have therefore long since supplied the deficiency occasioned by the previous removal of the 2nd Battalion of the King's Regiment.

The 90th Regt. was expected to embark at Barbadoes about the middle of December, the transports having arrived there on the 10th of that month, and the regiment having been long waiting in expectation of their arrival.

The 7th Batt. of the 60th and the 16th Regiment, (which latter has been substituted for the 2nd Battalion of the 93d,) are now embarking at Guernsey and Cork in order to proceed with the first fleet, the former will relieve the 90th at Halifax and the latter will proceed in company with the 90th to Quebec.

The four regiments which will therefore be actually placed under your orders are the 70th, the 2nd Batt. of the King's, the 90th, and the 16th.

The four which I had originally intended for Canada, and which are so stated in my despatch of the 10th August, were the 70th, the 90th, the 98th and the 2nd Batt. of the 93rd.

The change which has taken place in the regiments destined for the service has arisen rather from your having anticipated the arrangements which were in progress or from the desire of His Majesty's Government to place at your disposal such regiments as were most effective.

In addition to this statement, which will, I trust, sufficiently remove the erroneous impression under which you labor with respect to my despatch, No. 41, I have only to assure you that every exertion will be made hereafter, as it has hitherto, to place under your command a respectable force, and that if the reinforcement which you receive shall not always correspond with your wishes it is not because His Majesty's Government undervalue the importance of the Provinces or are indifferent to their defence, but because the demand for reinforcements in other quarters, where interests no less important are to be considered, renders it impossible to detach for your support so considerable a force as under other circumstances would be allotted to you.

(Canadian Archives, C. 682, p 170.)

Extract of a Letter from Kingston, Upper Canada, 7th March, 1814.

We are all quiet here but busily employed in preparing for the next campaign. Some of the brass guns taken at Fort Niagara have arrived, among them: a brass 6-pounder taken from the British at Trenton, New Jersey, the 3rd January, 1777, an eight inch howitzer, taken from Lord Cornwallis at Yorktown in Virginia, also a most beautiful Spanish and two handsome French guns, one of which is named La Trompeuse and the other La Bougissant; on each of them is the motto, "Ultima ratio regum."

(From Poulson's Daily American Advertiser, 15th April, 1814, in the Philadelphia Library.)

Governor Simon Snyder to Colonel James Fenton.

GENERAL ORDERS.

HARRISBURG, March 8, 1814.

The detachment of one thousand men, Pennsylvania Militia, of which you are constituted and appointed colonel commandant, having arrived, or the major part of it, at Erie, the place of general rendezvous, you will, as soon as practicable, organize (and any that may subsequently to a commencement of an organization arrive,) into one regiment, to consist of two battalions, and each battalion to consist of five companies. The officer in command is to be a lieutenant colonel. Each battalion is to be commanded by a major. Each company is to be officered as follows: One captain, one first lieutenant, one second lieutenant, one ensign, four sergeants and four corporals, and each company is to consist of one hundred men, rank and file. The officers to rank and be constituted and appointed according to law. In the performance of which duty it is commanded that the officers of your regiment be to you aiding and assisting and strict, and complete obedience is hereby enjoined on all the officers and men of your regiment to all your lawful commands.

As soon as you shall have organized the regiment as commanded you will report yourself and the number of men under your command to the nearest general officer commanding for the United States, and you are ordered and commanded to yield complete obedience to any orders issued by your superior officer in command at Erie or elsewhere for the United States.

From the alacrity with which very many of your detachment volunteered their services at an inclement season, the Commander-in-Chief anticipates honorable results from citizen soldiers, whose valor is not circumscribed by geographical limits of territory.

SIMON SNYDER,
Governor of the State of Pennsylvania.

(Pennsylvania Archives, Second Series, Vol. XII., pp. 712-3.)

N. B. Boileau to Colonel James Fenton.

Secretary's Office, March 8, 1814.

To Col. James Fenton, Pittsburg:

SIR,—

Agreeably to the authority in him vested by the fourth section of a supplement to the militia law passed 29th March, 1813, (a copy of which, and a copy also of another supplement passed by the present Legislature, is herewith forwarded,) the Governor has by general orders of this day authorized you to organize the fifth detachment of Pennsylvania militia under your command. Blank commissions, forty-two in number, are also forwarded to you to be signed and duly attested. These you will cause to be filled with the names of such officers as shall have been selected before marching from their several brigades, or as may be elected at Erie, agreeably to the first mentioned supplement. You will observe that in all cases of selection it will be necessary to change the word "elected" in the commissions and substitute therefor "designated" or "selected." The number of blank commissions will be sufficient for two majors, ten second and ten third lieutenants and ten ensigns. First lieutenants already commissioned, it is presumed the full number have marched and probably a sufficient number of ensigns, but to guard against deficiency ten blanks are also sent for the last named officers. Not having any return from the several brigade inspectors of the officers marched entitled to command under the militia law, it is probable that those intended for majors and perhaps others may be useless. All such you will return to this office.

By order of the Governor.

N. B. BOILEAU, Aid-de-camp.

From Major General Riall to Lieut. General Drummond.

NIAGARA FRONTIER, March 8, 1814.

SIR,—

I have the honor to enclose you a letter I have received from Mr. Asst. Commy. General Dance, informing me of your order to him to send a sum of money to York. I have called on him in consequence for an account of the money actually in his possession, which I find to be not more than £2874 Halifax curry. It has therefore been impossible for him to comply with your order.

On this subject I feel it my duty to represent it to you that there is an universal complaint throughout the country of the want of punctuality in the payments of the commissariat, so much so that the people absolutely refuse to sell their produce without being paid the money down, having no faith in the promises of that department, by which they say they have been so often deceived, indeed, I believe you yourself have been a witness of this, but which the Commy. says has been unavoidable from the want of funds.

The supplies of timber and materials for the various works ordered will not be procured without prompt payment; so much money is still due for former services of this nature that no person can be found to enter into contracts with the Commissary to furnish them, nor can the labor which will be required be had without regular weekly payments for the same reason.

Although a great deal of money has been paid within a short time to the troops, yet still considerable sums are due, which the specie lately sent up will, I am confident, not be nearly sufficient to pay off, as I this morning received a letter from Colonel Young stating that after having received £1000, £2000 were still due to his Regt. I have directed comm'g officers to send a return of balances due to their Regts. to the 24 Feb'y, which I shall transmit when received.

A large sum will be required to pay the bounties to men whose services are expired and who wish to re-enlist for a further period. Lt. Colonel Gordon mentioned to me that not less than 50 wished to come forward in the Royal Regts.

Exclusive of all these present exigencies the outstanding claims which you have directed me to investigate and order payment of, are a daily and constant draught upon the commissariat for ready money, and I believe you are aware that they are to a very great amount.

For these reasons, therefore, it will be *absolutely necessary* that regular and considerable supplies be furnished to the Commissary for the service of this division of the army.

(Canadian Archives, C. 118, pp. 47-9.)

Major General Riall to Lieut. General Drummond.

NIAGARA FRONTIER, March 10th, 1814.

SIR,—

As the season for active operations is now advancing, and from the preparations and appearance of the enemy it is probable that an attempt may be made on this frontier, it is time that I should give confidential instructions to the officers in command of the different posts for their conduct in case of attack, but in order that my measures may be subordinate to your general intentions, I have thought it advisable previously to make a communication to you on this subject, and to request that you will be pleased to give me such information of your general plan of defence as may be necessary for my guidance in this respect.

As my position is assailable in its front and on both flanks, I have to request that you will favor me with your directions for the line of conduct I should adopt in case of attack upon any of those points, referring more particularly to the right, where there is a possibility the enemy by effecting a landing at Long Point or its vicinity or by advancing along the western road may get into my rear and consequently cut off communication with you.

I feel it my duty to represent to you that it is decidedly my opinion that the very small disposable force on this line is not by any means adequate to its defence in front, and to meet the probable movement of the enemy upon its flanks, and that unless I receive a good and sufficient reinforcement the situation of this division of the army may become extremely critical.

(Canadian Archives, C. 682, pp. 258-9.)

Captain Alex. Stewart to Major General Riall.

DELAWARE, March 6th, 1814.

SIR,—

I have to acquaint you that the enemy retreated precipitately from their position about 8 o'clock on the night of the 4th instant down the river Thames. As the service for which the advance of the troops was intended has been frustrated by the Indians refusing to proceed with the ammunition, and no probability of our being able to come up with the enemy, as they had gained twelve hours' march of us, I have withdrawn the troops to this place where we will remain waiting your further instructions. I enclose Col. Elliott's letter on the subject of the Indians refusing to proceed with the ammunition. Our wounded are to be removed to-morrow morning to Oxford as there is accommodation at that place.

(Canadian Archives, C. 682, p. 191.)

Lieut. Colonel H. Butler to Major General Harrison.

DETROIT, March 7th, 1814.

DEAR SIR,—

By Lieut. Shannon of the U. S. Infantry I have the honor of informing you that a detachment of troops under my command, led by Captain Holmes of the 24th U. S. Infantry, has obtained a signal victory over the enemy. The affair took place on the 4th inst., about a hundred miles from here, on the River La Tranche. Our force consisted of not more than 160 rangers and mounted infantry. The enemy, from their own acknowledgment, had about 240. The fine light company of Scots Greys is totally destroyed; they led the attack most gallantly, and their commander fell within ten paces of our front line. The light company of the 89th has also suffered severely, one officer of the company fell, one is a prisoner, and another said to be badly wounded. In killed, wounded and prisoners the enemy lost about eighty, whilst on our part there was but four killed and four wounded. The great disparity in the loss on each side is to be attributed to the very judicious position occupied by Captain Holmes, who compelled the enemy to attack him at a great disadvantage. This, even more than his gallantry, merits the laurel.

Captain Holmes has just returned and will furnish a detailed account of the expedition, which shall be immediately transmitted to you.

Enemy's forces as stated by prisoners:—
- Royal Scots 101
- 89th Regt................... 45
- Militia 50
- Indians.................... 40 to 60

236

From the Military Secretary to Lieut. General Drummond.

Head Qrs., QUEBEC, 7th March, 1814.

SIR,—

18th Feby, 1814.
19th "   secret.
21st "
21st "

Trowsers.
Shoes.
Felt Caps.
Half Stockings.

Flannel waist coats.

In obedience to the orders of the Comr. of the Forces I am to acknowledge the receipt of your several letters, dated as per margin, and I have His Excellency's commands to acquaint you that directions will be given to the Commisst. to send to Kingston as soon as the navigation opens, for the use of the militia in Upper Canada, 1,500 scarlet jackets with an equal proportion of the articles mentioned in the margin.

The Comr. of the Forces approves of the appointment of Captain Robinson of the King's Regt. to act as an Inspecting Field Officer of militia in Upper Canada, provided the Militia Act contemplated becomes law.

Sir George Prevost has received, with satisfaction, your report of the advance of the Lt.

troops and Indians of Major General Riall's division towards Amherstburg, as it will tend to cramp the resources of the enemy in the direction of Detroit, and will throw open a field for supplying our own troops and the numerous Indians and their families looking to our depots for provisions, but His Excellency regrets exceedingly the disgraceful spirit of desertion which prevails on the Niagara frontier as represented by you.

I avail myself of this opportunity to acknowledge the honor of your three letters of the 19th Feb'y, which, with their enclosures, I have laid before the Comr. of the Forces.

There is no objection to the allowance in lieu of clothing being paid to the recruits of the Royal Scots as proposed by Lt. Colonel Gordon in his letter of 15th Feb'y, and he has the authority of the Comr. of the Forces to do so at the rate established in His Majesty's regulations.

The temporary appointments of Mr. Wilkins, Mr. Jas. McNabb and Mr. Cumming, which you have sanctioned in the Commissariat in Upper Canada, are approved by His Excellency and may continue as long as the service requires their assistance, and the Commander of the Forces consents to your authorizing the issue of 5/ per day pay from the extraordinaries of the army to Lieut. Jomois(?) of the militia, as superintendent of the waggon department, provided you deem such an appointment essential to the service, and that this officer has a claim to this consideration. His pay as lieutenant and an allowance in lieu of forage for a horse will, of course, be drawn from the militia department.

(Canadian Archives, C. 1222, pp. 60-1.)

Lieut. John Le Breton to Captain C. Foster, Military Secretary to Lieut. General Drummond.

DELAWARE, 8th March, 1814.

DEAR SIR,—

As the report of our unfortunate and truly lamentable expedition has reached the General you are no doubt acquainted with the circumstances, I shall therefore forbear making any comments and only send you a sketch of the ground as nearly as I could take it on the spot. The American enclosure is only a brushwood fence with an abattis on the outside to prevent a charge, no defence in front but almost inaccessible except by the road.

I regret very much not being authorized to raise a company. Since I am here I might have got several men. McGregor's company are dissatisfied with him and are about leaving him. Three of them have engaged in Coleman's dragoons and the remainder wish to join Caldwell's Rangers. I have seen several persons from the River Thames and Amherstburg, who all say that the inhabitants are anxiously expecting and a great many ready to join us. The Wyndotts or Huron Indians are also at the back of the lake settlement anxiously expecting us. However, I fear our expedition to westward is now completely frustrated. In consequence of Colonel Elliott being sick and the want of Indian chiefs the Indians who came up latterly are all returned back to the head of Lake Ontario.

I beg you will be pleased to mention to His Honor Lt. General Drummond that I have endeavored to obtain all the information in my power respecting a company of artificers, and am well convinced that a corps (on the) same terms with Sappers and Miners could be raised in a very short time. A man arrived from the River Thames to-day says that 500 Americans had crossed from Detroit to come to the assistance of those engaged on the 4th inst. I have learned that the first party came out with the intention of going to Port Talbot. They have brought with them 3 field pieces, which they were obliged to leave at the Round O.

OXFORD, 10th March, 1814.

Not having had an opportunity of sending the foregoing I have now to acquaint you with our retreat yesterday morning. Intelligence was received that the enemy was advancing and that their vanguard had reached the last settlement on the River Thames. In compliance with General Riall's orders we have retired to this place. In case the enemy should advance I think we may make a good defence here, as we have an excellent position in our front. We have lost 5 or 6 of our wounded men. Some are badly wounded. It is

thought McGregor will lose his arm. Several of his company are
gone off. They are now reduced to about 30 men.

(Canadian Archives, C. 682, p. 233.)

Lieut. General Drummond to Sir George Prevost.

YORK, March 9th, 1814.

SIR,—

I have the honor to transmit to Your Excellency the copy of a
report received by Major General Riall from Captain Stewart of the
Royal Scots light company, relative to an affair which took place in
advance of Delaware town between the detachment under his orders
and a body of the enemy from the westward.

I regret to state that our loss has been considerable in proportion
to the numbers engaged, and that notwithstanding the daring gallantry displayed on the occasion, finding it impracticable to dislodge
the enemy from the security of his breastworks the troops were
reluctantly withdrawn after an action of an hour and a half.

(Canadian Archives, C. 682, p. 186.)

From Lieut. General Drummond to Sir George Prevost.

YORK, March 10th, 1814.

SIR,—

I have the honor to transmit a letter from Major General Riall,
whereby Your Excellency will perceive the absolute necessity there
exists for ample supplies of money being transmitted to the upper
part of this Province in particular, that not only the outstanding
debts of the service may be liquidated but that the Commissariat may
be enabled to procure such resources as the country affords, before the
credit of Government be altogether destroyed.

I beg leave again, therefore, to entreat Your Excellency's serious
consideration of this important service.

(Canadian Archives, C. 118, pp. 45-6.)

From Sir James Yeo to Sir George Prevost (unaddressed).

DEAR SIR,—

An American seaman has this moment arrived from Sackett's
Harbor. He declares that they are building one ship of 162 ft. keel
to carry long 32 prs. on the main deck and 42 pr. carronades on the
spar deck; two of 124 ft. keel to carry long 24 prs. and they have
just laid the keel of a fourth ship the size of the *Pike*.

I am now with Colonel Harvey, who will communicate the particulars to Your Excellency, and I am confident you will see the necessity of engaging every shipwright that can be found in the country for the third ship.

The enemy never will meet us with an equal force, and unless very great exertions are made to finish the third ship we cannot expect to meet them with success.

Thursday, (March 10th,) ½ past 4 p. m.

(Canadian Archives, C. 732, pp. 50-60.)

Captain A. H. Holmes to Lieut. Colonel Butler.

FORT COVINGTON, March 10th, 1814.

SIR,—

I have the honor to submit in writing that the expedition sent under my command against the enemy's posts, by your special orders of the 21st ultimo, had the good fortune on the 4th inst. to meet and subdue a force double its own, fresh from the barracks and led by a distinguished officer. I had been compelled to leave the artillery by the invincible difficulties of the route from Point au Plait to Round O. No wheeled carriage of any kind had ever attempted it before, and none will ever pass it until the brush and fallen timber are cut away and the swamp causewayed or drained. After joining Capt. Gill I began the march for Fort Talbot, but was soon convinced of its being impossible to reach the fort in time to secure any force that might be there or adjacent. This conviction, united with the information that the enemy had a large force at Delaware upon the Thames, that I should be expected at Fort Talbot and consequently that a previous descent upon Delaware might deceive the foe and lead him to expose to me some point in defending others he might think menaced, and coupled with the possibility that hearing of Captain Gill's march to the Round O by McGregor's militia whom he had pursued, a detachment had descended the Thames to intercept him, determined me to exercise the discretion allowed by the order and to strike at once upon the river.

On the 3rd inst., when only fifteen miles from Delaware, we received intelligence that the enemy had left Delaware with the intention of descending the river and that we should probably meet him in one hour; that his force consisted of a light company from the Royal Scots, mustering for duty one hundred and twenty men, a light company from the 89th Regiment of foot, (efficiency not known,) Caldwell's Indians and McGregor's militia, amounting in all to about three hundred. My command had not originally exceeded one hundred and eighty in rank and file. Hunger, cold and fatigue had brought on disease, and though none had died all were exceedingly depressed and sixteen had been ordered home as unable to continue the march. I resolved therefore to avoid a conflict on equal ground and immediately retreated five miles for the sake of a good position on the western bank of Twenty Mile Creek, leaving Gill with twenty rangers to cover the retreat and watch the enemy's motions. We had camped but a few minutes when Capt. Gill joined, after exchanging shots with the enemy's advance in vainly attempting to reconnoitre his force. The Twenty Mile Creek runs from north to south through a deep wide ravine, and of course is flanked east and west by lofty heights. My camp was formed upon the western heights, the enemy's upon the opposite. During the night of the third all was quiet. At sunrise upon the fourth the enemy appeared thinly upon the opposite heights, fired upon us without effect and vanished. After waiting some time for their re-appearance Lieut. Knox of the rangers was sent to reconnoitre. Upon his return he reported that the enemy had retreated with the utmost precipitation, leaving his baggage scattered upon the road, and that his trail and fires made him out not more than seventy men. Mortified at the supposition of having retrograded from this diminutive force, I instantly commenced the pursuit with the intention of attacking Delaware before the opening of another day. We did not, however, proceed beyond five miles when Captain Lee, commanding the advance, discovered the enemy in considerable force arranging himself for battle. The symptoms of fear and flight were now easily traced to the purpose of seducing me from the heights, and so far the plan had succeeded but the enemy failed to improve the advantage. If he had thrown his chief force across the ravine above the road and occupied our camp when relinquished, thus obstructing my communication to the rear, I should have been driven upon Delaware against a superior force, since found to be stationed there, or forced to take the wilderness for Fort Talbot without forage or provisions. Heaven averted this calamity. We soon regained the position at the Twenty Mile Creek, and though the rangers were greatly disheartened by the retreat, and to a man insisted on not fighting the enemy, we decided to exhibit on that spot a scene of death or victory.

I was induced to adopt the order of a hollow square to prevent the necessity of evolution, which I knew all the troops were incompetent to perform in action. The detachment of the 24th and 28th Infantry occupied the brow of the heights. The detachment from the garrison of Detroit formed the north side of the square, the rangers the west, the militia the south. Our horses and baggage stood in the centre. The enemy threw his militia and Indians across the ravine above the road and commenced an action with bugles sounding from the north, west and south. His regulars at the same time charged down the road from the opposite heights, crossed the bridge, charged up the heights we occupied, within twenty steps of the American line and against the most destructive fire. But his front section was shot to pieces. Those who followed were much thinned and wounded. His officers were soon cut down and his antagonists continued to evince a degree of animation that bespoke at once their boldness and security. He therefore abandoned the charge and took cover in the woods at diffused order, between fifteen and twenty paces of our line, and placed all hope upon his ammunition.

Our regulars, being uncovered, were ordered to kneel that the brow of the heights might partly screen them from the enemy's view. The firing increased on both sides with great vivacity; but the crisis was over. I knew the enemy dared not uncover, and of course no second charge would be attempted. On the north, west and south front the fire had been sustained with much coolness and with considerable loss to the foe. Our troops on these fronts being protected by logs hastily thrown together, the enemy not charging, both the rifle and musket were aimed at leisure, perhaps always told. The enemy at last became convinced that Providence had sealed the fortune of the day. His cover on the east front was insufficient, for as he had charged in column of sections, and therefore when dispersing on either side of the road was unable to extend his flanks, and as our regulars presented an extended front from the beginning it is evident a common sized tree could not protect even one man, much less the squads that stood and often breathed their last together, and yet upon his regulars the enemy relied for victory. In concert therefore, and favored by the shades of twilight, he commenced a general retreat after one hour's close and gallant conflict.

I did not pursue for the following reasons:—1. We had triumphed against numbers and discipline and were therefore under no obligation of honor to incur additional hazard. 2. In the requisites, (numbers and discipline,) the enemy were still superior and the night would have insured success to ambuscade. 3. The enemy's bugle sounded close upon the opposite heights. If then we pursued we must have passed over to him as he did to us, because the creek could be passed on horseback at no other point, and the troops, being fatigued and frost bitten, their shoes cut to pieces by frozen ground, it was not possible to pursue on foot. It follows that the attempt to pursue would have given the enemy the same advantage that produced their defeat.

Our loss in killed and wounded amounted to a non-commissioned officer and six privates, but the blood of between eighty and ninety brave Englishmen avenged their fall. The commander, Captain

Basden of the 89th, is supposed to have been killed at an early stage of the contest. The whole American force in action consisted of one hundred and fifty rank and file, of whom seventy were militia, including the rangers. The enemy's regulars were from one hundred and fifty to one hundred and eighty strong, and his militia and Indians fought on three fronts of our square.

I am much indebted to all my regular officers and I trust their names will be mentioned to the army and to the War Department. Without intending a discrimination it must be acknowledged that the exertions of Lieuts. Knox and Henry of the 28th, and Jackson and Potter of the 24th, were most conspicuous, because fortune had opposed them to the main strength of the foe. Captain Lee of the Michigan Dragoons was of great assistance before the action, at the head of the advance and spies, and my warmest thanks are due to Acting Sailing Master Darling of the United States schooner *Somers* who had volunteered to command the artillery. Ensign Heard of the 28th, acting as a volunteer adjutant, merits my acknowledgments, and especially for his zeal in defending my opinion against a final retreat when others permitted their hopes to sink beneath the pressure of the moment.

The enemy's wounded and prisoners were treated with the utmost humanity. Some of our men were marching in their stocking feet, but they were not permitted to take a shoe even from the dead.

Captain Alexander Stewart to Major General Riall.

OXFORD, 11th March, 1814.

SIR,—

I have the honor to acknowledge the receipt of your letter of the 7th inst. at Delaware, and lost no time in retiring to this place with the troops, where we arrived last night, leaving Capt. Caldwell with the Kent Volunteers and Rangers at Putman's, and an advance of an officer and 12 men at McMillan's. I beg leave to state that the Indians joined at Delaware on the 3rd. the day before the light companies marched, and it was my wish they should move next morning. Col. Elliott reported they were much fatigued and would require a day's rest, but that he would find a sufficient number to join Captain Caldwell ; this party of twenty refused to march, which induced me to move forward the light companies on the 4th, not only as a support to Capt. Caldwell but as an incitement to the Indians to follow, and to enable me to carry the service for which an advance was principally intended into effect. I beg further to state that I did not consider the enemy in any force to make a stand, and that the party

Capt. Caldwell fell in with must have been that which went to the Round O at Cranfield's, and I was supported in this opinion by the return of a trusty man of the Kent Volunteers, sent down the River Thames to give information, who reported that none of the enemy were on the river. Little suspecting that an action would take place, I remained behind to fix with Col. Elliott the day on which the Indians would take their departure to the westward with the ammunition, as my future movements must have depended on it, the result of which is already made known to you. I am happy to report that the wounded are doing well.

(Canadian Archives, C. 682, p. 208.)

Lieut. General Drummond to Sir George Prevost.

York, March 11th, 1814.

Sir,—

I have the honor to transmit to Your Excellency the copy of a letter from Capt. Stewart of the Royal Scots Regiment to Maj. Genl. Riall, covering one from Col. Elliott, of the Indian Department, whereby Your Excellency will perceive that the enemy retreated from their position with much precipitancy towards the mouth of the Thames after the affair of the 4th instant.

My desire to furnish such of the Indians as remained to the westward with powder and shot has been frustrated by the refusal of their brethren with us to proceed with the supplies without the advance of our troops at the same time, and through apprehension for the safety of their friends and families, should a knowledge of the circumstances reach the Americans at Detroit.

It is a matter of much gratification to me to learn that Your Excellency has been pleased to order the 103rd Regiment to this Province, but as I have already mentioned to Your Excellency that I propose stationing a strong force near Turkey Point for the defence of the approaches from the westward and the shore of Lake Erie, I consider it my duty to state that from every rational supposition of the direction of the efforts of the enemy in the ensuing campaign, I am apprehensive I shall not have a sufficient disposable force to preserve the western part of the province from insult unless Your Excellency be pleased to reinforce me with another regiment in addition to the 103rd already ordered here, for Your Excellency must be fully aware that it would be highly imprudent to reduce either of the garrisons of Kingston or York by a single man after the Glengarry Light Infantry shall have left the former for the frontier on the opening of navigation, and it would be equally inconsiderate to permit the post and depot at Burlington to remain without the protection and support of a complete battalion.

That the Right Division be supplied as observed upon in Your Excellency's letter of the 28th ultimo, from magazines to be established previous to the opening of the ensuing campaign, I must beg to assure Your Excellency is totally and absolutely impossible. The country is not furnished with the requisite resources. Even already has the scanty supply of salt pork on hand been obliged to be broke in upon, and I must again assure Your Excellency that I conceive that it will be totally impossible for the Right Division to hold its ground on the Niagara Frontier without a very ample supply of provisions from the Lower Province.

(Canadian Archives, C. 682, p. 192.)

Captain Alex. Stewart to Major General Riall.

OXFORD, 12th March, 1814.

SIR,—

I beg leave to report that Lieut. Jackson of my company, the bearer of the flag of truce to Detroit, returned last night with a letter addressed for you, which is herewith enclosed. I also forward a report from Lieut. Jackson to me detailing such circumstances as came within his notice while detained at Detroit. It appears that there are none of the enemy on this side Sandwich. I believe their force in the action of the 4th inst. was not nearly so great as stated in Ensign Mills' report. They came up the lake shore, joined the mounted riflemen at Crawford's at Point aux Pins and were to have moved on to Port Talbot from thence on the new road, which joins the principal one at McMillan's, so as to gain the rear of our division at Delaware. This plan was abandoned in consequence of the bad state of the roads. I omitted to state in my letter of yesterday's date that the place my letter of the 4th was dated from is fourteen miles in advance of Delaware.

I beg leave to state that the family of Capt. Springer, who was carried off by the Americans from Delaware, are reduced to the greatest necessity for want of provisions and clothing, and no means of procuring any. Therefore I beg to recommend them as objects deserving the support of the Government.

(Canadian Archives, C. 682, p 154.)

Lieut. George Jackson, Royal Scots, to Captain Alex. Stewart.

OXFORD, 12 March, 1814.

SIR,—
I beg leave to observe, the reason just assigned for the detaining the flag I carried to Detroit was in consequence of the expedition then on the way from that post to act against the detachment under your command stationed at Delaware. As soon as Col. Butler, the officer commanding at Detroit, received an account of the affair which happened near Delaware, he informed me he would still be under the necessity of detaining me from information he had just received, which stated that a body of British troops, accompanied by a number of Indians, were on their march towards Detroit or the post on the opposite side. On expostulating as to the truth of his intelligence as mentioned, Colonel Butler mentioned that there could be no doubt whatever, as he had it direct and in the most speedy manner from the Council of those we employed, (meaning Indians.) About two hours after I met in Col. Butler's quarters one of the Western Indians employed by the British Government, whose features were to me quite familiar.

In the course of my conversation with Col. Butler he frequently mentioned the excellence of the spies employed by him and other officers of the United States army, and by way of illustration said he was informed of a conversation which happened at night in York some time ago between Lieut. Genl. Drummond and other military men respecting the expedition to the westward, a communication which enabled him to prepare for the defence of Detroit, and, he said, given by a person who sat in the next room, who, from the door being open, was afforded an opportunity of hearing all that had been said distinctly. He mentioned his spies being frequently at Burlington, and everything was known at Sackett's Harbor as soon as resolved on at Kingston.

A party of Indians had arrived from Michilimackinac a few days before my arrival at Detroit. Col. Butler said they were within two hours of taking Mr. Dickson, the Indian Chief, that, however, he was well acquainted with Mr. Dickson's mission, that he thought the fort at that place had been destroyed and the troops retired. Finding it otherwise, he spoke as if something would be attempted against that place. From everything I could learn Lucen, Allen, Norton, Richardson and son, all lately residing on the Thames, are the most useful and daring spies employed by the Americans in this direction. The troops at Detroit are about 400 regulars and 150 militia; at Spring Wells, (where Genl. Brock crossed,) 150 militia; at Malden 250 regulars, and Sandwich 150 regulars.

This is the strength of the enemy's force as near as I could learn. Of the militiamen at Detroit 90 are mounted and use the long country rifle. The Detroit fort has got an abattis on the land side of the north and west faces, which were the only faces I could see. Guns mounted in all the embrasures, and on the parapets two travelling 24-pounders. The redoubt at Sandwich is small, containing a small barracks and defended by an 8 or 10 inch picketing, in the tops of which are large nails.

(Canadian Archives, C. 682, p. 155.)

Captain James L. Basden, 89th Regiment, to Captain A. Stewart.

OXFORD, March 13th, 1814.

SIR,—

I take the earliest opportunity, being a little recovered, to inform you of the circumstances which took place on the 4th inst. for the early information of Major General Com'g the Right Division of the army.

Having on the evening of the 3rd received your orders to march the next morning, I paraded in consequence and received further directions, viz., to move forward, support Capt. Caldwell's detachment and push on as far as Ward's with the whole. I moved on, found Capt. Caldwell with the whole of his party at the 14 Mile Creek. He had seen the enemy that morning in numbers, supposed 150 or 200, drawn up in an irregular column about 5 or 6 miles from his present position, (the 14 Mile Creek.) I here refreshed the men and waited a very long time in expectation of some Indians, (conceiving that a party was following me:) 5 only arrived and it was growing late in the day. I proceeded, leaving Mr. Fraser of the Indian Dept. with orders to hurry on such Indians as might come up. On approaching the place where the enemy had been before seen, it was observed that by the smoke and some noise that they were occupying the same ground. I therefore made my dispositions for an immediate attack, it growing late, they were posted on the opposite side of a ravine on a high bank close to the road, and I thought I colud perceive a slight brushwood fence thrown up, as I presumed to obstruct the road. The Kent Volunteers with the Rangers I directed to file through the woods to my left, and by making an extensive circle they were to post themselves in rear of the enemy, get as near as possible, not to fire a shot but to sound a bugle whenever the position was properly secured and they were prepared to advance. Mr. Fraser now arrived with about 23 Indians. These I stationed to flank my right and advance with the main body. At the sound of the bugle the flank comp(anies) moved on in an open column of sections, (the 89th lt. comp. being weak in sub-divisions,) led by the Royals with an advance from them. The enemy commenced their fire immediately on our appearance, and when the head of the column had proceeded a short distance down the hill the firing from them (the enemy) was so severe as to occasion a check. They, however, instantly cheered and rushed on, making for the road on the opposite side with the intention of carrying this fence. However, this was found impossible, the ascent being so steep and slippery. I now desired the men to follow me and I moved in the ravine to the right for some distance under an uncommon fire. On ascending and gaining the top of the bank I was very much surprised to observe another face of the work. I placed the men in extended order under cover of the trees, and the action was kept up with great vigor till dusk, when that of the enemy became very feeble. I now determined to send to the point on the top of the hill, (from whence the action commenced,) for more men to strengthen the party I then had with me, and on their arrival to storm the enemy's position agreeably to my first intention.

At the instant I received a severe wound in my thigh and was under the necessity of going to the rear. Before I had proceeded far the enemy's fire had ceased. At this period only I received your orders to retire, which order I forwarded to the officer com'g on the field. A few minutes after I met yourself.

(Canadian Archives, C. 682, p. 236.)

General Order.

Headquarters, ALBANY, March 13th, 1814.

The period of service of the militia on the Niagara Frontier will shortly expire. In providing for the future security of the western portion of the State various considerations induce the Commander in Chief, instead of making a further draft on the Seventh Division, which, on account of unfortunate occurrences, has heretofore been greatly harassed, to appeal directly to the citizens of the State at large, and more especially to the acknowledged patriotism of the citizens of the Western District to furnish a select and efficient corps of volunteers.

The organization of the force to be raised by virtue of this order will be as follows: Two regiments of infantry with a colonel, lieutenant colonel, two majors for field officers with the usual regimental staff of militia.

The regiments will consist of ten companies each, and the

respective companies to be composed of one captain, two lieutenants, two ensigns, six sergeants, five corporals, two musicians and ninety privates. One separate battalion comprising four companies, with the like number of officers, non-commissioned officers, musicians and privates as above, will likewise be organized. One company of the battalion to be riflemen, two to be light infantry, and the fourth to consist of mounted riflemen. The field officers may be selected by the captains and subalterns, and the latter by the volunteers of the respective companies. The Commander in Chief earnestly recommends such selection to be made without reference to present rank or any other consideration than those of merit, talents and patriotism. The field and company officers who may be selected, if they should not already hold commissions of the same grade in the militia or in corps of exempts, will be brevetted and commissioned by the Commander in Chief. The regimental staff will be assigned by the Commandant of the regiment and an adjutant for the separate battalion will be appointed by the Commandant thereof.

General Peter B. Porter will command the whole corps. The volunteers will be provided with the same camp equipage, rations, pay and means of transportation as are allowed to the troops of the army of the United States, and the Commander in Chief entertains a confident expectation that an additional monthly allowance on account of clothing will be appropriated by the Legislature of the State. The terms of service of the volunteers will be six months if required. but there is every reason to believe their services may be dispensed with in a shorter time.

Having given the detail of the intended organization and objects of the corps, the Commander in Chief counts with confidence on the immediate completion of the contemplated force. The prompt and patriotic spirit evinced by his fellow citizens on every occasion which has called for their services, will not permit him to doubt the issue of this appeal. The late ravages and barbarities of the enemy on the Niagara Frontier must revive painful recollections and excite the keener sensibilities of all, and will, he hopes, produce a universal zeal to promote the success of the effort to give permanent tranquillity and security to the inhabitants of the Western District.

By order of the Commander in Chief.

SOL. VAN RENSSELAER, Adjt. Gen.

(Tompkins' Papers, New York State Library.)

Third Session of the Sixth Provincial Parliament of Upper Canada.

Met at York on the fifteenth day of February, and prorogued on

the fourteenth day of March following, in the fifty-fourth year of the reign of George the Third.
Gordon Drummond, Esquire, President.
Anno Domini, 1814.

CHAPTER I.

An act to repeal part of the laws now in force for raising and training the militia of this province, and to make further and more effectual provision for the same.

CHAPTER II.

An act to provide for the issuing and circulating of government bills in this province.

CHAPTER VI.

An act to empower His Majesty for a limited time to secure and detain such persons as His Majesty shall suspect of a treasonable adherence to the enemy.

CHAPTER IX.

An act to declare certain persons described therein aliens and to vest their estates in His Majesty.

Passed March 14, 1814.

Whereas, many persons, inhabitants of the United States of America, claiming to be subjects of His Majesty, and renewing their allegiance as such by oath, did solicit and receive grants of land from His Majesty, or became seized of lands by inheritance or otherwise within this province, which persons since the declaration of war by the said United States of America against His Majesty and his subjects of the United Kingdom of Great Britain and Ireland, have voluntarily withdrawn themselves from their said allegiance and the defence of the said province, be it enacted by the King's Most Excellent Majesty, by and with the advice and consent of the Legislative Council and Assembly of the Province of Upper Canada, constituted and assembled by virtue of and under the authority of an act passed in the Parliament of Great Britain, entitled, "An act to repeal certain parts of an act passed in the fourteenth year of His Majesty's reign, entitled an act for making more effectual provision for the government of the Province of Quebec in North America, and to make further provision for the government of the said Province" and by the authority of the same, that all such persons as aforesaid, who, having received grants of land or may have become seized of lands within this province by inheritance or otherwise, as shall have voluntarily withdrawn themselves into the United States of America since the first day of July, one thousand eight hundred and twelve, or who may hereafter during the present war voluntarily withdraw themselves from this Province into the said United States without license granted under authority of the Governor, Lieutenant Governor or person administering the government of this Province, shall be taken and considered to be aliens born and incapable of holding lands within this Province.

II. And be it further enacted by the authority aforesaid, that it shall and may be lawful for the Governor, Lieutenant Governor or person administering the government, by commission under the great seal of this Province to authorize any sheriff, coroner or other person or persons in the several districts of this Province to inquire by the oath of twelve good and lawful men of their respective districts, and by inquisition indented under the hands and seals of the said jurors and of the said commissioner or commissioners to return to His Majesty's Court of King's Bench all such persons as aforesaid who, seized of lands in the respective districts, shall have voluntarily withdrawn into the United States of America since the said first of July and before the conclusion of the existing war with those States without license granted under authority of the Governor, Lieutenant Governor or person administering the government, and from and after the said finding by inquisition His Majesty shall become seized of the lands so found to have been in the seizure of such person on the said first day of July; provided always that nothing in this act contained shall be construed to prevent any persons interested in the said lands from traversing any inquisition or office respecting the same at any time within one year after the finding of such inquisition.

III. Provided always that nothing in this act shall extend or be construed to extend to affect the claim of any *bona fide* creditor or to defeat any just lien or security of or upon any lands, tenements or hereditaments whatsoever.

CHAPTER XI.

An act for the more impartial and effectual trial and punishment of high treason and misprision of high treason and treasonable practices in this Province.

Kingston Gazette, March 22nd, 1814.

MONTREAL, March 1, 1814.

Extract of a letter from York, dated 22d Feb., 1814.

"The House of Assembly of Upper Canada have resolved that the proclamation of Gen. de Rottenburg declaring martial law was an arbitrary and unconstitutional measure, tending to destroy the laws of the Province, and ordered that the said resolution be entered on the Journals of the House."

Proclamation.

PROVINCE OF UPPER CANADA.

Gordon Drummond, Esquire, President administering the Government of Upper Canada, and Lieutenant General commanding His Majesty's forces within the same.

To all to whom these presents shall come:
GREETING,—
Know ye that finding it at present expedient and necessary to prohibit the distillation of spirits, strong waters and low wines from any wheat, corn or other grain, meal or flour within this Province, I do hereby under the authority of several acts of the Parliament of this Province in force for that purpose, and by and with the advice and consent of His Majesty's Executive Council for the affairs of this Province, prohibit the distillation of spirits, strong waters and low wines from any wheat, corn or other grain, meal or flour within this Province from the expiration of five days after the date of this proclamation in the Home District and of ten days in every other district of this Province to the first day of July now next ensuing, under the penalties and forfeitures by the said act imposed.

And I do for that purpose issue this my proclamation declaring the provisions and restrictions of the said acts so far as they relate to the distillation of spirits, strong waters and low wines from wheat, corn or other grain, meal or flour within this Province to be in force from the time and for the period above mentioned.

Given under my hand and seal at arms at York this fourteenth day of March in the year of our Lord one thousand eight hundred and fourteen, and in the fifty-fourth year of His Majesty's reign.

GORDON DRUMMOND, President.

By His Honor's command.

WM. JARVIS, Sec'y.

Thomas Cummings to Captain W. H. Merritt.

CHIPPAWA, 14th March, 1814.

DEAR SIR,—
I have been informed this day that a man named Francis Postel, belonging to your troop, deserted from you last fall at Burlington and came to Lyon's Creek where he sold his horse, regimentals and accoutrements to one of the inhabitants who assisted over the river. Afterwards, as I am informed, the regimentals was seen in the man's chest not long since. I think you ought to prosecute this man and

make an example of him to deter others from being guilty of the same offence. I think sufficient proof can be got to convict this man. If you will have the goodness to let me know the day you intend to come up I will have the parties here ready.

Captain Hamilton Merritt,
    Niagara L. Dragoons,
        St. Davids.

(Merritt MSS.)

Lieut. General Drummond to Sir George Prevost.

YORK, March 14th, 1814.

SIR,—

In reference to Your Excellency's letter of 28th ultimo, I have the honor to acquaint you that I have transmitted to Major General Stovin at Kingston a proclamation which, as Lieutenant General commanding in Upper Canada, I have directed him to issue in the Midland and Newcastle Districts, declaring martial law to be in force as far as relates to provisions and forage for the use of His Majesty's troops in that vicinity.

It is a matter of much regret to me that the House of Assembly would not consent to strengthen the executive in this Province by authorizing the person administering the government to proclaim martial law in special districts only where so violent a measure became indispensable. The question was negatived by a decided majority.

(Canadian Archives, C. 682, pp. 200-1.)

Lieut. General Drummond to Sir George Prevost.

YORK, March 14, 1814.

SIR,—

As the session of the Legislature will close this day I have the honor to acquaint Your Excellency that I propose proceeding to Kingston immediately.

I regret to find by a communication from the Adjutant General that the 103d Regiment, which I was led to understand from Your Excellency's letter of the 28th ultimo would prove to be a very effective corps, is to be broken up by two companies of it being ordered to garrison Fort Wellington.

The flank companies of the 89th Regiment will be ordered to join the regiment. But prior to the march of the light company for that purpose it becomes indispensably necessary that an investigation into the circumstances attending several acts of outrage committed by them at Ancaster should take place. I have already directed Major General Riall to order their return to Burlington from the westward.

On the arrival of the flank companies of the 89th Regiment at Cornwall I trust that Your Excellency will be pleased to direct that the two companies of the 103d may be relieved at Fort Wellington by a detachment of the former from Cornwall, that the 103d Regiment be left fully disposable and that only one regiment be dispersed in detachments.

I have received a communication from Assistant Commissary General Dance in reply to instructions from me on the subject wherein he states that as to laying in a stock of provisions at Fort Niagara it is perfectly out of his power. The quantity of salt provisions for that alone would be more than he has altogether, and could that of flour be spared for one particular object, which at this moment it cannot be, it would be perfectly impossible to bring it from Burlington or Long Point in the present state of the roads, and on this line we have it not.

And in another communication Mr. Dance says, "that if anything can give us a *chance* of getting through with the additional force expected it will be the keeping us literally supplied with money, particularly specie when possible."

(Canadian Archives, C. 682, pp. 196-9.)

From Col. Robert Young to Major General Riall at Headquarters, Roreback's.

FORT NIAGARA, March 14, 1814.

MY DEAR SIR,—

Two steady well behaved grenadiers deserted last night. I am grieved and desponding at the circumstances and absolutely ashamed of the corps. I am, alas, too well persuaded that many more will go. The balances they are receiving will, I fear, have a great influence with them and yet the money has been so long due them that it was impossible, and at any rate highly impolitic, to have withheld it upon any pretext whatever. There is yet a great deal of arrears due the men and when it shall be paid I am confident I shall have more desertions. I am puzzled how to act and what to think of the cursed scheming and general dissatisfaction which prevails in the regiment.

(Canadian Archives, C. 388, p. 46-7.)

From Major General Riall to Lieut. General Drummond.

March 15th, 1814.

My Dear Sir,—

I am very sorry to inform you that desertion from the King's Regiment in that cursed fort not only continues but increases to an alarming degree. I enclose you a letter that I received from Colonel Young yesterday reporting the loss of two grenadiers that morning; two other men deserted on the 12th. The men are sick of the place, tired and disgusted with the labor to which they see no end, and have got sulky and dissatisfied. With the exception of those that are in the large store building, about 150, their quarters are fully as good if not better than either of the other regiments on the line. They receive a ration of spirits, which the others do not, and they receive also the field ration of flour while the Treasury ration only is issued to the Royals and 100th. It is the place and the place only which can be the cause of dissatisfaction, which Colonel Young says prevails amongst them. This is an additional reason to me that the works should be compressed as much as possible so as to make a small garrison only necessary for its defence, and which might be changed every month. I have been obliged to write you an official letter to-day about Mr. Gaugreben. I see now very plainly I shall get nothing done if he is to continue the head of the department here. Col. Drummond is not yet arrived here. I hope he did not venture by the Vincent, which has not yet made her appearance either.

(Canadian Archives, C. 388, pp. 44-5.)

Lieut. General Drummond to Sir George Prevost.

York, March 15th, 1814.

Sir,—

I have the honor to transmit the copy of a letter from Captain Stewart of the Royal Scots light company to Major General Riall, whereby Your Excellency will perceive that much dependence cannot be placed on our Indian allies' co-operation.

Major General Riall has reported to me that the enemy have lately shewn themselves in strong parties along the Niagara line and have been heard at work frequently at night at Lewiston Heights.

The Major General, under the supposition that he would have full employment for all the effectives of the Right Division the ensuing campaign and that his force will become more effective by the acquisition of the greater part of the garrison of Fort Niagara, has suggested the idea of destroying that fort with the exception of the north eastern square tower or stone building and the rampart on the land side, which should be continued to the river and well picketted as a cover to the communication to the tower. The tower to be mounted with a gun of heavy calibre on the top and three smaller within the work, to be surrounded by a strong picketting and a ditch. For its defence a force of about 70 men and 15 artillerymen would be sufficient and the remainder of the present garrison would become disposable.

The weather has been so excessively severe on the Niagara frontier lately that it has been impossible to proceed with any of the works at Queenston and Missassauga Point.

I am sorry to report to Your Excellency that sickness is prevalent in the King's Regiment, principally ague and dysentery, and the senior medical officer of the regiment recommends their immediate removal from Niagara. Major General Riall has directed Staff Surgeon Mabee to inspect the regiment and report upon its state.

From communications which Major Holcroft of the Royal Artillery has had he conceives it probable that he is shortly to be removed from the Right Division. Should such be the case I am convinced that much detriment would accrue to the service, as from Major Holcroft's experience and local information, combined with his abilities and exertions, he is particularly calculated for the command of the artillery on that frontier.

Major General Riall acquaints me that he is constantly urging Mr. Dance, the Assistant Commissary General, to make the greatest exertions to collect the resources of the country for the service of the troops, and he states that the stock of salt provisions is very small, and the fresh meat has nearly failed altogether. I trust therefore that the moment the navigation opens an ample supply will be sent from the Lower Province.

(Canadian Archives, C. 683, pp. 202-7.)

From Colonel Robert Young to Major General Riall.

FORT NIAGARA, March 17th, 1814.

MY DEAR SIR,—

I am heartbroken at the general spirit of defection which has evinced itself in the regiment. I cannot divine the cause. I have indirectly employed agents to discover the source of grievance and complaint, and the full result of my inquiries are that they have incessant fatigues independent of their military duties and no comforts of any kind. In fact the men seem generally dissatisfied, and that spirit once disseminated amongst them not all the exertions and rhetoric of the officers can counterbalance. I feel my personal situation with respect to the regiment more humiliating than I have language to express. The regiment has lost its wonted character, and the more mortifying circumstance to me is that the very best men in the corps have evinced the greatest disposition to desert. I am not myself. I do not know what to say upon the occasion. I am chagrined and desponding and can only most conscientiously aver that I am ashamed and feel disgraced by associating my name with what I formerly and *proudly* designated the King's Regiment. In the name of God remove us as unworthy of retaining the Post of Honour. My confidence in the regiment is now gone, and its villainous conduct will bring my grey hairs with sorrow to the grave. It is hard, nay cruel, that after more than twenty-two years service in the regt. I should live to witness the disgrace which has been brought upon it. In despair I remain,

(Canadian Archives, C. 833, pp. 112-4.)

From Major General Riall to Lieut. General Drummond.

NIAGARA FRONTIER, March 17th, 1814.

SIR,—

I am extremely sorry to have to report to you again the very alarming height to which desertion from the King's Regiment in Fort Niagara has arrived, it having lost nine men in the last five days. From the report made to me by the officer commanding that regiment a spirit of discontent and inclination to desert so plainly appears to have engrafted itself in it that I have determined to withdraw it from that garrison and have accordingly ordered the 100th Regiment to be in readiness to relieve it.

I have already submitted to you my ideas upon the necessity I think there exists, from what I have above mentioned and from other causes, for reducing the works of this fort to a very small compass; but upon more mature consideration I am decidedly of opinion that it will be the most expedient measure to abandon the place altogether and destroy it, for the following reasons:

In the first place, I greatly fear it cannot be maintained if the enemy seriously attempt its recovery and establish mortar batteries against it, from which there is no protection within the fort. Its defence may cost us many men and its fall must greatly inspirit the enemy.

Secondly, the disposition to desert has unfortunately manifested itself in more regiments than one in this army, and it is much to be feared, and indeed to be expected, that from the facility which Fort Niagara affords the contagion may spread much further.

Thirdly, from every report that reaches me of the preparations of the enemy I am naturally to expect that the attack upon this part of the Province will be made in considerable force; it is absolutely necessary, therefore, that I should be provided with sufficient numbers to meet him in the field, and of the small force which I even now have on this frontier, (which should not be weakened by occupying positions which cannot be maintained,) I am deprived of nearly one-third by the occupation of this place.

Fourthly, when the defences of Fort George and the battery on Mississauga Point are completed I conceive the entrance of the river is nearly as well protected as with the occupation of Fort Niagara.

I have abstained from making any remarks upon the expediency of its retention in a political point of view, so far as it regards the power with which it invests the Government of the United States to embody its militia during the invasion or possession of any part of its territory by a foreign power.

(Canadian Archives, C. 833, pp. 115-8.)

New York Evening Post, 30th March, 1814.

AUBURN, N. Y., March 23.

On Saturday last, (March 19,) 1,300 men from French Mills and Sackett's Harbor, of the 11th, under Major McNeil, and 25th Regiment under Colonel Brady, U. S. Infantry, passed through this village on their way to the frontier. On Sunday General Brown went through and on Monday the 3rd Regiment of Artillery, under Colonel Mitchell, amounting to about 600, quartered here. On Tuesday the artillery regiment had orders by express to return immediately and to march 30 miles per day. The 1,300 men of the 11th and 25th Regiments which passed on Saturday last are also repassing through this village to-day. The 9th and 21st, which quartered at Skaneateles, (7 miles below this place,) on Monday, have also returned.

National Advocate, New York, March 31, 1814.

BATAVIA, March 19.

During the above transaction, (the action near Delaware,) a gentleman of the name of Westbrook of Delaware town, whose property was seized on suspicion of disaffection to His Majesty, and placed under a guard of an officer and twelve men, succeeded with a party of mounted men in capturing this guard and collecting his moveable effects together, deposited them in a large barn containing 600 or 700 bushels of grain and caused the whole, together with his dwelling, still and other outhouses, to be set fire to and consumed rather than that they should be enjoyed by his implacable persecutors. He then proceeded with his family to Detroit.

For the above intelligence we are indebted to persons who left Canada by permission the fore part of the present week. Desertions from the enemy at Fort Niagara are frequent. Nine sturdy looking fellows arrived here this morning.

(File in New York Society Library.)

From Sir George Prevost to Lieut. General Drummond.

Head Qrs., QUEBEC, 19th March, 1814.

SIR,—

I have the honor to acknowledge the receipt of your letter of the 4th inst., representing the difficulty experienced by the commissariat in procuring flour at the post of Kingston for the use of the troops.

I have referred this communication to the Commissary General and I enclose the copy of the answer received from Mr. Robinson on this subject, and participate in his regret in your having deemed it expedient suddenly to repeal the proclamation of M. Genl. de Rottenburg imposing a partial existence of martial law by which supplies of provisions were obtained from those inhabitants who now obstinately withhold them to the extent that apprehensions exist in your mind respecting the possibility of victualling the troops and seamen in Upper Canada without a recurrence of that unpopular measure.

In order to lighten the difficulties you have to contend with I have desired every possible exertion to be used to forward supplies from this Province, and the Dy. Commissary General at Kingston will be furnished with a considerable sum in specie and small notes to assist in obtaining provisions on the spot.

Your two letters of the 5th inst. have been duly received—the one enclosing a letter to Colonel Talbot reporting the advance of the enemy up the Thames and of their having destroyed the settlement at Point aux Pins.

I approve of your having directed Captain Rowe of the militia of the United States not taken in arms to be sent back, and of the remonstrance you have made to B. General Cass against the incendiary system he is conducting in the neighborhood of Detroit. You will be so good as to report the reception your representation experienced.

I am concerned to find by your second letter of the same date the inconvenience the public service is likely to suffer by the want of energy and foresight on the part of Asst. Commissary General Dance. A change in that department appears to be necessary, and I have induced Dy. Commissary General Couche, whose health is now restored, to proceed immediately to Kingston to take the superintendence of the commissariat in Upper Canada, and Dy. Commissary General Turquand will repair to Burlington to assume charge with the Right Division; these arrangements, I trust, will remedy the difficulties existing in that branch of the service and lead to measures for satisfying the just demands of individuals upon government for cattle and provisions furnished for the use of troops; at the same time it is necessary before blame attaches to commissariat officers to discriminate whether the demands for which claims remain unsettled were furnished by contract or agreement, or whether at the will of officers commanding detachts. of troops and Indians and without the knowledge of that department; in cases of the latter description the claims of individuals should be investigated by a competent board of officers and the officer in command of the Division on the spot should annex his opinion of the propriety of these claims.

The result of the affair near Long Wood may induce you to consider seriously the disadvantages inseparable from too great an expansion of your force.

It is to be regretted that Captain Stewart was not at his post when the action commenced, as the intrepidity of the handful of troops committed to his charge might have been more judiciously and advantageously directed than I apprehend they were on that occasion.

The Adjutant General has signified to you the extent of the reinforcement in movement for Upper Canada, and I cannot at this moment hold out to you any expectation of my being enabled to make any accessions thereto.

(Canadian Archives, C. 1222, pp. 63-5.)

New York Evening Post, 4th April, 1814.

(From the Northern Luminary, Watertown, N. Y., March 23d, 1814.)

CANADA NEWS.

Since our last we have conversed with several persons of our acquaintance direct from Canada, one of whom, week before last, was several days at Kingston. They informed us that great and spirited exertions have been used the winter past in getting on large supplies of ordnance and military stores to make a bold, firm and vigorous stand. That they had three vessels now upon the stocks, one of which was 150 feet keel, the others 120, but neither of them were in equal forwardness with ours at Sackett's Harbor, that in all probability ours will be ready three or four weeks the soonest. That their Incorporated Militia were sent to York and were fortifying there. That they were building a large number of boats at Lake Simcoe. That their forces were principally gone to the upper parts of the Province, leaving not more than 1,000 regulars at Kingston. That the Legislature in Canada had enacted a law ordering one-third of the militia to be drafted into service, which occasioned such uneasiness that numbers of them were making their escape into the United States. That 100 pieces of ordnance, drawn by 200 yoke of oxen, had been the winter past taken from Montreal to Kingston, and it was well understood the oxen were smuggled into Canada from Vermont and New Hampshire and drove by the men who smuggled them in, having for their pay $400 for each piece of ordnance when delivered at Kingston.

Major Thomas Deane, Royal Scots, to Major General Riall.

OXFORD, 21st March, 1814.

SIR,—

The following information I received this morning from a gentleman of the name of Richardson, who served as a medical officer on board our fleet on Lake Erie and has been a prisoner since that period ; he is on his way to General Drummond.

Mr. Richardson states that he left Sandwich on Tuesday last, that at that time the garrison of Detroit consisted of about 600 men, the garrison of Sandwich of 75 and that of Amherstburg of 120 ; that the post of Amherstburg was to be evacuated in a few days by order, as Mr. R. understood, from General Harrison. The fort of Detroit is made very strong and Sandwich was also strengthened. The garrisons were on half allowance of flour for some time. It did not appear that there was any intention to make a movement this way ; indeed the roads are now almost impassable. Another reason, it was stated by Captain Holmes, the commanding officer at Amherstburg, to a gentleman who gave the information, that all disposable force was collecting and to be collected at Presque Isle for the purpose of making a descent at Long Point and attacking Burlington Heights.

(Canadian Archives, C. 682, p. 283.)

Secret Information.

On Sunday, the 13th inst., about 3,000 troops left Sackett's Harbor for Niagara with an intention of retaking that fort. Their artillery and other supplies had been previously forwarded to Rome.

Before the departure of the above troops for Niagara they had recruited their force to about 5,500. There remains about 2,000 there. They had not yet laid down any new ship at Sackett's Harbor for want of room in the navy yard, but they had the timber prepared and ready in the forest as soon as they launched the one that is nearly ready.

They have at Vergennes on Lake Champlain a brig on the stocks of 20 guns; she is contracted to be finished in 60 days from 1st March. Likewise at same place they have seven galleys on the stocks.

They have at different places on the lake five gunboats.

At Plattsburg not building anything new of any description, that is to say such as fortifications, barracks, &c.

The troops that have left Plattsburg for Chazy were a rifle corps of 250 men, on the 19th inst. two companies of artillery, 100 men with 3 fieldpieces, to join which on Sunday Col. Miller went with 500 infantry.

At Swanton Falls, about 400 rifle corps, under Col. Clark. On Friday, the 18th, Genl. McComb arrived at Swanton with 550 infantry.

At Burlington and Plattsburg the rest of the force remains as before.

General Wilkinson has been directed to move his troops as near the lines as he can. Yesterday an express left him directed to Genl. McComb, Mississquoi Bay.

The inducements held out and the prospect of a speedy peace have made them very successful in enlisting men.

From particular circumstances it was impossible to meet as agreed upon. Deponent will confer with his old friend at the former place. It is desirable it should be as soon as possible. Deponent will observe the movements in their camps as he returns.

March 22nd, 1814.

(Canadian Archives, C. 682, pp. 252-4.)

From Lieut. General Drummond to Sir George Prevost.

KINGSTON, March 21st, 1814.

SIR,—

I have the honor to annex an extract from a letter from Major General Riall of the 15th instant, in consequence of which and of former communications relative to Lieutenant Gaugreben, in the first instance, in consequence of his inability to do duty from severe sore eyes, I have directed Lieutenant Phillpott to proceed without delay from hence to Niagara, and his place to be supplied by Lieutenant Gossett from Prescott. Immediately on Lieutenant Gaugreben being relieved I propose ordering him to Fort Wellington.

(Extract.) " I request that another officer may be placed at the head of the engineer department with the Right Division of the Army in the stead of Lieutenant De Gaugreben, otherwise I very much fear no part of the various works that are to be constructed on this frontier will be completed in sufficent time."

The enclosed letter from Major General Riall, covering one from Colonel Young, marks so strongly the alarming degree to which the desertion from the King's Regiment has risen that I transmit them to Your Excellency as I received them. In a former communication to Major General Riall, I left it discretional with him to relieve the King's with the 100th Regt., should he find it advisable.

Two deserters came in from Sackett's Harbor yesterday evening; they report that Major General Brown proceeded to Niagara with 3,000 men, leaving a force of about 1500 regulars at Sackett's Harbor.

P. S.—I have likewise directed Lieut. Yule of the Royal Engineers to repair to Kingston from Niagara, there to wait further orders.

(Canadian Archives, C. 388, pp. 41-3.)

From Lieut. General Drummond to Sir George Prevost.

KINGSTON, March 22nd, 1814.

SIR,—

I have the honor to state to Your Excellency that I have this instant had a communication with Commodore Sir James Yeo, who asserts he cannot possibly carry on the duty of the Naval Department on the opening of navigation with a less number of Royal Marines than 350; and to fill up vacancies arising from every description of casualty he conceives it absolutely necessary that the entire battalion should be upon the spot at Kingston for that purpose.

I beg therefore to request that Your Excellency will be pleased to permit the remainder of the battalion of marines to proceed to Kingston without delay, whose place at Fort Wellington I take the liberty of suggesting might be supplied by a portion of the Embodied Militia from the Lower Province, or the 89th Regt.

(Canadian Archives, C. 732, pp. 74-5.)

From Lieut. General Drummond to Sir George Prevost.

KINGSTON, March 22nd, 1814.

SIR,—

I have the honor to acknowledge the receipt of your letter of the 9th inst. and to acquaint you for the information of His Excellency, the Commander of the Forces, that I communicated the instructions therein contained relative to the supplies of provisions and stores to be thrown into Fort Niagara without delay to Major General Riall and to Assistant Commissary General Dunce.

The arrangements proposed for forwarding the reinforcements and supplies for the defence of Michilimackinac have been carried into effect with all the energy, I have much pleasure in remarking, and despatch which was practicable.

(Canadian Archives, C. 78, pp. 67-8.)

From Lieut. General Drummond to Sir George Prevost.

KINGSTON, March 22nd, 1814.

SIR,—

In addition to the letter from Major General Riall, covering one from Colonel Young of the King's Regt., which I had the honor to enclose in my letter to Your Excellency of yesterday's date, it is with very great concern that I feel it requisite to transmit another letter and enclosure from Major General Riall, received this day, on the same alarming subject of the desertion and dissatisfaction of the King's Regiment at Fort Niagara.

With regard to the latter part of Major General Riall's letter on the expediency of abandoning and destroying Fort Niagara, I beg leave to observe that I do not altogether coincide in opinion with him, as although a considerable proportion of the Right Division will necessarily be employed for its defence, yet a still much greater force of the enemy must unavoidably be engaged in its investment, which force might otherwise be at liberty to act against us in perhaps a far more vulnerable point.

Two divisions of the 103rd Regiment have marched in here, and as the present state of the roads is so excessively bad I propose detaining them until the opening of the navigation, when Commodore Sir James Yeo will convey them by water, with also whatever stores may then be in readiness. The men of the 103rd Regiment will thus be well refreshed and fit for immediate service on their arrival with the Right Division, and with this same view I would feel particularly gratified if Your Excellency would permit the two companies at Fort Wellington to join their regiment here without delay, to be replaced by two companies of the 89th Regt. from Cornwall, as I, in a former letter, observed upon.

(Canadian Archives, C. 833, pp. 119-121.)

From Sir George Prevost to Lieut. General Drummond.

Head Qrs. QUEBEC, 22nd March, 1814.

SIR,—

I have had the honor to receive your letters of the 10th and 11th inst. In the first I found an urgent requisition for a further supply of money for the Right Division for the purpose of obtaining provisions and liquidating the debt of the Commissariat.

You will have received before this letter reaches you a statement of the several sums in specie and in notes which have been forwarded to Upper Canada since the commencement of the present year, amounting to £231,500, in addition thereto Dy. Commissary Genl. Couche took with him £10,000 in small notes and £5,000 in gold.

As the pecuniary resources of this command partake largely of the limitation of the other means placed at my disposal for the continuance of the present contest it becomes indispensably necessary you should resort to every proper expedient for the removal of the difficulties you occasionally experience, confiding on my earnest desire to afford you on all occasions support and every possible facility in the execution of the arduous duty imposed upon you.

The exigencies of the service have been with me a primary consideration in regulating my conduct, and I trust an anticipation of them will continue to distinguish yours, but still resorting to measures within your own control for the public welfare should not be shrunk from when the benefit resulting from them become evident.

Your second letter was accompanied by Captain Stewart's report of the sequel of the unfortunate affair of the 4th inst. near the Long Wood, with his reason for not pursuing a flying foe.

Without a great deal of management on the part of the officer in the command of a detachment of troops co-operating with Indians, their services are seldom as valuable as they are supposed. I am apprehensive that on this occasion that essential point has not been sufficiently attended to by Captain Stewart, but that the warriors have been treated as a disposable force, which they are not under the most favorable circumstances.

Having understood from the Depy. Adjutant General that Lt. Col. Drummond had been entrusted with the command of the force advanced towards the mouth of the Thames, my expectations respecting the result were considerably raised.

The Acting Comr. is instructed to attend to your requisition for the construction of two fast sailing vessels as soon as it is practicable for men to do so, and until you are in possession of such means for the conveyance of supplies to the Right Division the Commodore will furnish you with accommodation for that purpose from his squadron.

I cannot close this letter without recommending to you, and through you to the general officers in Upper Canada, the most scrupulous attention to the public expenditure in order that an efficient system of economy of the public money may be observed in all the departments of Government, so that by wholesome restrictions a lavish and improvident use of it may be avoided without prejudice to the just expectation of the soldier or the wants of the service.

(Canadian Archives, C. 1222, pp. 67-9.)

Major General Harrison to the Secretary of War.

Headquarters, CINCINNATI, March 22d, 1814.

SIR,—

The tribes of Indians upon this frontier and east of the Mississippi with whom the United States have been connected by treaty are the Wyandots, Delawares, Shawanese, Miamies, Pottawatomies, Ottawas, Chippewas, Piankishaws, Kaskaskias and Sacs. All but the last two were in the confederacy which carried on the former Indian war against the United States that was terminated by the treaty of Greenville. The Kaskaskias were parties to the treaty, but they had not been in the war. The Wyandots are admitted by the others to be the leading tribe. They hold the *grand calumet* which unites them and kindles the council fire. This tribe is nearly equally divided between the *Crane* at Sandusky, who is grand sachem of the nation and Walk-in-the-water at Brownstown near Detroit. They claim the lands bounded by the settlements of this State southwardly and eastwardly, and by Lake Erie, the Miami river and the claim of the Shawanese upon the Au Glaize, a branch of the latter. They also claim the lands they live on at Detroit, but I am ignorant to what extent.

The Wyandots of Sandusky have adhered to us through the war. Their chief, the Crane, is a venerable, intelligent and upright man. Within the tract of land claimed by the Wyandots a number of Senecas are settled. They broke off from their own tribe six or eight years ago, but receive a part of the annuity granted that tribe by the United States by sending a deputation for it to Buffalo. The claim of the Wyandots to the lands they occupy is not disputed that I know of by any other tribe. Their residence on it, however, is not of long standing, and the country was certainly once the property of the Miamies.

Passing westwardly from the Wyandots, we meet with the Shawanese settlement at Stoney Creek, a branch of the Big Miami and at Wapockannata on the Au Glaize. These settlements were made immediately after the treaty of Greenville and with the consent of the Miamies, whom I consider the real owners of those lands.

The chiefs of this band of Shawanese, Blackhoof, Wolf and Lewis, are attached to us from principle as well as interest—they are all honest men.

The Miamies have their principal settlements at the forks of the Wabash, thirty miles from Fort Wayne, and at Mississinneway, thirty miles lower down. A band of them under the name of Weas have resided on the Wabash, sixty miles above Vincennes, and another, under the Turtle, on Eel River; these three bands were passed on General Wayne as distinct tribes and an annuity was granted to each. The Eel Rivers and Weas, however, to this day call themselves Miamies and are recognized as such by the Mississinneway band. The Miamies, Maumees or Tewicktowies are the undoubted proprietors of all that beautiful country which is watered by the Wabash and its branches and there is little doubt that their claim extended at least as far east as the Scioto. They have no tradition of removing from any other quarter of the country, whereas all the neighboring tribes, the Piankishaws excepted, who are a branch of the Miamies, are either intruders upon them or have been permitted to settle in their country. The Wyandots emigrated first from Lake Ontario, and subsequently from Lake Huron; the Delawares from Pennsylvania and Maryland; the Shawanese from Georgia; the Kickapoos and Pottawatomies from the country between Lake Michigan and the Mississippi; and the Ottawas and Chippewas from the peninsula formed by the Lakes Michigan, Huron and St. Clair, and the streight connecting the latter with Erie. The claims of the Miamies were bounded on the north and west by those of the Illinois confederacy, consisting originally of five tribes called the Kaskaskias, Cahokias, Peorias, Michiganians and Illinois speaking the Miami language, and no doubt branches of that nation.

When I was first appointed governor of Indian Territory these once powerful tribes were reduced to about thirty warriors, of whom twenty-five were Kaskaskians, four Peorians and a single Michiganian. There was an individual lately alive at St. Louis who saw the enumeration made of them by the Jesuits in 1745, making the number of their warriors four thousand. A furious war between them and the Sacs and Kickapoos reduced them to that miserable remnant, which had taken refuge among the white people of the towns of Kaskaskia and St. Genevieve. The Kickapoos had fixed their principal village at Peoria upon the south branch of the Illinois river, while the Sacs remained masters of the country to the north.

During the war of our revolution the Miamies had invited the Kickapoos into their country to assist them against the whites, and a considerable village was formed by that tribe on the Vermilllion River near its junction with the Wabash. After the treaty of Greenville the Delawares, with the approbation of the Miamies, removed from the mouth of the Au Glaize to the head waters of the White River, a large branch of the Wabash, and the Pottawatomies, without their consent, had formed two villages upon the latter river, one at Tippecanoe and the other at Chippoy, twenty-five miles below.

The Piankishaws lived in the neighborhood of Vincennes, which was their ancient village, and claimed the lands to the mouth of the Wabash and to the north and west as far as the Kaskaskians claimed. Such was the situation of the tribes when I received the instructions of President Jefferson, shortly after his first election, to make efforts for extinguishing the Indian claims upon the Ohio below the mouth of the Kentucky River, and to such other tracts as were necessary to connect and consolidate our settlements. It was at once determined that the community of interests in the lands amongst the Indian tribes which seemed to be recognized by the treaty of Greenville should be objected to, and that each individual tribe should be protected in every claim that should appear to be founded in reason and justice. But it was also determined that as a measure of policy and liberality such tribes as lived upon any tract of land which it would be desirable to purchase should receive a portion of the compensation, although the title might be exclusively in another tribe. Upon this principle the Delawares, Shawanese, Pottawatomies and Kickapoos were admitted as parties to several of the treaties. Care was taken, however, to place the title to such tracts as it might be desirable to purchase hereafter on such a footing that would facilitate the procuring of them by getting the tribes who had no claims themselves, and who might probably interfere, to recognize the titles of those who were ascertained to possess them.

This was particularly the case with the lands watered by the Wabash, which were declared to be the property of the Miamies with the exception of the tract occupied by the Delawares on White River, which was to be considered the joint property of them and the Miamies. This arrangement was very much disliked by Tecumseh and the banditti he had assembled at Tippecanoe. He complained loudly as well of the sales that had been made as of the principle of considering a particular tribe as the exclusive owners of any part of the country, which he said the Great Spirit had given to all his red children. Besides the disaffected among the neighboring tribes he had brought together a considerable number of Winnebagoes and Folles Avoines from the neighborhood of Green Bay, Sacs from the Mississippi and some Ottawas and Chippewas from Arbre Croche on Lake Michigan. These people were better pleased with the climate and country of the Wabash than with that they had left.

The Miamies resisted the pretensions of Tecumseh and his followers for some time, but a system of terror was adopted and the young men were seduced by eternally placing before them a picture of labor and restrictions as to hunting, to which the system adopted would inevitably lead. The Pottawatomies and other tribes inhabiting the Illinois River and south of Lake Michigan had been for a long time approaching gradually towards the Wabash. Their country, which was never abundantly stocked with game, was latterly almost exhausted of it. The fertile regions of the Wabash still afforded it. It was represented that the progressive settlements of the whites upon that river would soon deprive them of their only resource and indeed would force the Indians of that river upon them, who were already half starved.

It is a fact that for many years the current of emigration as to the tribes east of the Mississippi has been from north to south. This is owing to two causes: The diminution of those animals from which the Indians procure their support and the pressure of the two great tribes, the Chippewas and the Sioux in the north and west. So long ago as the the treaty of Greenville the Pottawatomies gave notice to the Miamies that they intended to settle upon the Wabash. They made no pretensions to the country and their only excuse for the intended aggression was that "they were tired of eating fish and wanted meat." It has already been observed that the Sacs had extended themselves to the Illinois River and that the settlement of the Kickapoos at the Peorias was of modern date. Previously to the commencement of the present war a considerable number had joined their brethren upon the Wabash. The Tawas from the Des Moines River have twice made attempts to get a footing there.

From these facts it will be seen that it will be nearly impossible to get the Indians south of the Wabash to go beyond the Illinois river. The subject of providing an outlet to such of the tribes as it might be desirable to remove has been under consideration for many years. There is but one. It was long since discovered by the Indians themselves, and but for the humane policy which has been pursued by our government the Delawares, Kickapoos and Shawanese would long since have been out of our way. The country claimed by the

Osages abounds with everything that is desirable to a savage. The Indians of the tribes above mentioned have occasionally intruded upon them—a war was the consequence, which would soon have given a sufficient opening for emigration. But our government interfered and obliged the hostile tribes to make peace.

I was afterwards instructed to endeavor to get the Delawares to join that part of their tribe which is settled on the west side of the Mississippi near Cape Girardeau. The attempt was unsuccessful at the time. I have no doubt, however, that they could be prevailed on to move, but it ought not in my opinion to be attempted in a general council of the tribes.

The question of the title to the lands south of the Wabash has been thoroughly examined. Every opportunity was afforded to Tecumseh and his party to exhibit their pretensions and they were found to rest on no other basis than that of their being the common property of all the Indians. The Pottawatomies and Kickapoos have unequivocally acknowledged the Miami and Delaware title. The latter, as I before observed, can I think be induced to move. It may take a year or eighteen months to effect it. The Miamies will not be in our way. They are a poor, miserable drunken set, diminishing every year. Becoming too lazy to work they feel the advantage of their annuity. The fear of the other Indians has alone prevented them from selling their whole claim to the United States, and as soon as there is peace or the British can no longer intrigue, they will sell. I know not what inducements can be held out to the Wyandots to remove. They were not formerly under my superintendence but I am persuaded that a general council would not be the place to attempt it.

(McAfee, History of the late War in the Western Country, pp. 43-7.)

NOTICE.

President's Office, Upper Canada,
Kingston, 24th March, 1814.

His Honor the President has been pleased to appoint by commissions, bearing date this day, the under mentioned gentlemen to be Commissioners for carrying into effect the provisions of an act passed in the late sessions of the Legislature of this Province, entituled, "An act to empower His Majesty for a limited time to secure and detain such persons as His Majesty shall suspect of a treasonable adherence to the enemy," in the several districts of this Province respectively, the Western District excepted, that is to say :—

For the Eastern District—
    Alex. McMillan,
    Samuel Anderson,
    David Sheek,
    William Fraser,
    Thomas Mears,
    Joshua Y. Cozens,
    John Crysler,
    Laurence McKay and
    Albert French, Esquires.

For the District of Johnstown—
    Solomon Jones,
    Joel Stone,
    Daniel Jones,
    William Fraser,
    Thomas Fraser,
    Stephen Burritt,
    William Gilkinson,
    Thomas Smith and
    Thomas Osborne, Esquires.

For the Midland District—
    The Hon. Richard Cartwright,
    Alexander McDonell,
    Alexander Fisher,
    Thomas Dorland,
    Timothy Thompson,
    Thomas Markland,
    Peter Smith,
    John Cumming,
    James McNabb,
    Ebenezer Washburn,
    Robert C. Wilkins,
    James Young and
    William Crawford, Esquires.

For the District of Newcastle—
    Elias Jones,
    Richard Lovekin,
    David McGregor Rogers,
    John Burn,
    Robert C. Wilkins,
    James Young,
    John Peters and
    Richard Hare, Esquires.

For the Home District—
> Thomas Ridout,
> Samuel Smith,
> William Allan,
> Alexander Wood,
> Duncan Cameron,
> Samuel Hatt,
> Richard Beasley,
> Richard Hatt,
> William Applegarth and
> James Fulton, Esquires.

For the District of Niagara—
> Robert Kerr,
> Joseph Edwards,
> Thomas Dickson,
> Samuel Street,
> Robert Nelles,
> Richard Beasley,
> Abraham Nelles,
> Richard Hatt,
> Samuel Hatt,
> Thomas Clark,
> William Claus and
> William Crooks, Esquires.

For the District of London—
> Thomas Talbot,
> Thomas Rolph,
> Robert Nichol,
> John Backhouse,
> Mahlon Burwell,
> George C. Salmon and
> Thomas Bowlby, Esquires.

Lieut. General Drummond to Sir George Prevost.

KINGSTON, March 24th, 1813.

SIR,—

As I had given Major General Stovin, when transmitting to him the proclamation declaring martial law in the Midland and Newcastle Districts, as mentioned in my letter to Your Excellency of the 14th inst., a discretional power to distribute the same should it be found decidedly unavoidable, I was much gratified to find on my arrival here that they had not been issued, in consequence of the reasonable hope which appears to be entertained by the most respectable inhabitants, of the resources which the country is able to afford being brought to market without the infliction of so violent a measure.

I have the honor to acquaint Your Excellency that I propose retaining the proclamation until circumstances of necessity imperiously call for its distribution.

(Canadian Archives, C. 682, pp. 248-9.)

The Deposition of Robert Christie.

March 24th, 1814.

He lives at York. Left it in April, 1812, to see his father and mother, who reside near Philadelphia, where he has been, not having it in his power to return till six weeks ago, when he came to Sackett's Harbor as a ship carpenter. He left Sackett's Harbor the night before last, not having it in his power to make his escape sooner. Says there are two brigs building at Sackett's. He expects they are calculated to carry 24 guns each. They are planked up to the bends but not calked and no part of the deck laid. The large ship building on the point he calculates is to carry 48 guns; says she is planked up to the bends, but, same as the brigs, not calked and no part of the deck laid. He heard Commodore Chauncey say the other night, (last Saturday,) to Captain Crane that they must give the large ship up as they had not sufficient water to launch her. They had tried by making sufficient holes in the ice, and could only find about eleven feet water. They have only got thirteen guns. There are some about eight miles off, cannot say how many. The whole of the rigging has arrived at Sackett's. Eleven hundred and sixty seamen at Sackett's. He saw the troops march from Sackett's on Monday week last, said to be 4,000, under the command of two generals, towards Niagara. Says there are about 1,600 men at Sackett's.

(Canadian Archives, C. 682, pp. 246-7.)

Lieut. General Drummond to Sir George Prevost.

KINGSTON, March 24th, 1813.

SIR,—

I have the honor to transmit for Your Excellency's information the copy of a statement made by a person just arrived from Sackett's Harbor (24th March.)

How far the pleasing intelligence of the impracticability or even difficulty of launching the enemy's largest vessel now building there may be correct I shall endeavor to ascertain by a strict enquiry into the degree of credibility which ought to be given to the informant's assertions.

To this end I have written to York.

(Canadian Archives, C. 683, pp. 244-5.)

Extract of a letter from Colonel Elliott to the Deputy Superintendent General of Indian affairs, dated "Beach, 25th March, 1814."

Two young men of the Potawamy nation arrived here last night from Maipock. They state that the Indians in that quarter are sitting on their warclub waiting to take it up when an opportunity may offer, also that we may as soon as the weather gets warm expect many of the young men to join us and get ammunition, also that the Americans tell them that they intend to attack us by the way of Long Point as soon as the navigation opens, and that the Hurons, Delawares and Shawanese are to accompany them. Should this prove true these nations can send five or six hundred men and leave sufficient with their women and children. I shall send to the other nations to avert if possible this evil. The Heights appear to be their object.

Truly extracted, York, 26th March, 1814.

D. CAMERON,
Asst. Sec'y, I. D.

(Canadian Archives, C. 257, p. 232.)

Lieut. Colonel R. H. Bruyeres to Sir George Prevost.

QUEBEC, 25th March, 1814.

SIR,—

Having attentively considered the proposal made by Major General Riall to Lieut. General Drummond, (whereon Your Excellency had directed me to report,) respecting the eligibility of destroying part of Fort Niagara and reducing the defences of that position to the N. E. square tower, which is to be surrounded by a small work containing three guns, to be secured with a ditch and strong picketting, also to continue the ramparts on the land side towards the river as a cover to the communication to the tower, in order to diminish the number of troops required for the present defences and thereby obtain an increase to the disposable force acting on the west side of the river, I very respectfully beg leave to submit to Your Excellency that I am of opinion that any partial destruction of this fort would render the position totally untenable and could not be maintained with so small a number of men as proposed, particularly when it is considered that the work alone required for the security of this blockhouse is far beyond the means you can have to execute it in the presence of the enemy.

Should it therefore be judged expedient and indispensable to reduce the present strength of that garrison for the purpose of increasing the active force to be employed in the field, I recommend the total and entire demolition of the buildings and the fort and to evacuate that position. At the same time I should be very unwilling to resort to this measure if there is any probability that our naval ascendency on the lake can be so far established at an early season after the opening of navigation that we can by that means ensure the safe communication of troops and stores to that frontier. In this event the advantage to be derived from the acquisition of the river Niagara as a harbor is of such material importance that I would maintain the Niagara fort with a strong garrison as long as possible without diminishing its present defences, but should the ascendency on the lake be doubtful, or even retarded to a late period in the campaign, I am well aware and fully convinced you have not the means to maintain that position if attacked with energy and great superiority of numbers.

In this case I would immediately decide to demolish the American fort and concentrate all our force on the west shore.

(Canadian Archives, C. 682, pp. 255-7.)

Colonel E. Baynes to Sir George Prevost.

DEAR SIR GEORGE,—

I have the honor to return to Your Excellency Bruyeres' report. His reasoning upon the subject seems to me well grounded. The few men that could be spared could not effect the alterations proposed with sufficient expedition or security, and it would be impolitic if not impracticable, to place a greater force on that side. I am not sufficiently acquainted with the nature of Fort Niagara to judge what defence the square tower is capable of making the rest of the work being laid in ruins. It *was not covered* from the fire of Fort George, which, notwithstanding, produced little or no effect upon that building. It is certainly very important to hold it if we have the ascendency on the lake. It is still more so that the fort should be destroyed if we are doomed to experience the reverse. I therefore think the grand expression (?) never ought to be lost sight of under every possible state of things. There is certainly not at present time or means to make the alterations suggested in Lieut. Colonel Bruyeres' report.

(Canadian Archives, C. 682, pp. 250-1.)

Militia General Order.

KINGSTON, March 28th, 1814.

His Honor the President has been pleased to promote Lieut. McGregor of the Kent Volunteers to the rank of captain in the militia for his gallant and meritorious conduct on all occasions since the formation of that corps under his command, with the pay and allowances as such from the 25th inst. inclusive.

Alexander McDonell, Esqr., Dep. Paymr. Genl., having resumed the functions of his office from the 25th inst., the accounts of that department will be handed over to him by Actg. P. Mr. Genl. Street, from that period accordingly. All estimates and other communications appertaining to the duties of that office will be transmitted to him at Hd. Qrs. until further notice.

The proceedings of all regimental courts martial are in future to be transmitted to the Adjt. Genl. of Militia for the information of His Honor the President. They will be returned to the Com'g officers of corps, by whom, however, they are to be approved prior to their being transmitted for His Honor's information.

By His Honor's command,
C. FOSTER,
Adjt. Genl. Mil., U. C.

From the Military Secretary to Lieut. General Drummond.

Head Qrs., QUEBEC, 25th March, 1814.

SIR,—

The Commander of the Forces has directed me to transmit to you the enclosed extract of a letter from Dy. Asst. Comy. Genl. Gilmore to the Commissary General, and I have His Excellency's commands to request that you will call the attention of the Dy. Comy. Genl. in charge of the Commissariat in Upper Canada to the important subject to which it relates, with the view that such arrangements may be adopted as will produce a more economical expenditure of provisions in the issues to the Indians than appears to have existed in supplying the warriors and their families at present attached to the Right Division.

(Canadian Archives, C. 1222, p. 70.)

From Lieut. General Drummond to Earl Bathurst.

No. 2

KINGSTON, UPPER CANADA, 20 March, 1814.

MY LORD,—

I beg to acquaint Your Lordship that the Legislature of this

Province, made at York on the fifteenth of February, and was prorogued on the fourteenth of this month, it being the third session of the sixth Provincial Parliament, during which I have the satisfaction to say that the best understanding subsisted between myself and the other branches.

I do myself the honor of transmitting herewith copies of my speeches on the opening and closing of the session, and of the addresses of the Legislative Council and House of Assembly in answer, with a schedule containing the titles of the acts passed in it, some of which will, I trust, under the present circumstances of the colony, prove eminently beneficial.

Those acts from which such effect may be expected more immediately to result as tending to strengthen the arm of the Executive Government and to suppress or keep in awe that spirit of sedition and disaffection, (promoted, no doubt, by the agents of the enemy,) which, I regret to say, prevails in some parts of the country, are :— That authorizing the suspension of the Habeas Corpus ; that for the more effective trial and punishment of treason and treasonable practices ; and that declaring certain persons therein described aliens and vesting their estates in His Majesty.

That there are many whom it will be found necessary to detain in custody under the provisions of the former, there is too much reason to apprehend, and not a few will experience the effects of the two latter.

Having said this much with respect to the disaffected spirit evinced by some, it is at the same time but justice to say that the greater portion of the inhabitants are well disposed, and many have on various occasions manifested their loyalty and devotion to the service by their actions in the field. Those chiefly who have shewn the opposite disposition, it is satisfactory to know, are such as have from time to time crept into the Province from the neighbouring States and settled on lands which they purchased from individuals. This practice will, I trust, be effectually guarded against in future.

The appropriation of a considerable portion of the provincial revenue for the improvement of the public roads, which are at present in many places impassable for troops, artillery or carriages of any kind, must contribute highly to the promotion and welfare of the service.

The law passed in the session of the last year authorizing the incorporation of battalions of militia volunteers for service during the war not having answered the expectations then formed of it, a small number only having engaged under its provisions, I therefore found it necessary to recommend at the late session some modification of it. Under the present statute a fourteenth of the whole of the population fit to bear arms, who are to be selected by ballot and to serve for a year at least, may be embodied. This proportion, it is supposed, will produce about six hundred men, which with those engaged under the former act will form a battalion of nine hundred men.

I cannot, however, my Lord, but express my regret that our present circumstances should render it necessary to call upon the yeomanry of the country for their services in the field while their farms must consequently be neglected, especially when produce and provisions of every kind have become very scarce and extravagantly dear, and when it is with difficulty the Commissariat are able to procure the necessary supplies for the troops. These considerations would induce me most willingly to dispense with the military for the domestic services of the militia if our regular force here were such as to enable me so to do.

I have given directions for the proper officers to furnish me with authentic copies of all the acts now passed, which I shall have the honor of transmitting to Your Lordship with as little delay as possible.

(Canadian Archives, G. 474.)

Sir George Prevost to Lieut. General Drummond.

QUEBEC, 26th March, 1814.

SIR,—

Since writing to you on the 24th inst. I have received the information, a copy of which is herewith transmitted, and as it comes from a person who has at difft. times furnished me with intelligence which has invariably proved correct, I feel satisfied you may rely and act upon it. On the day the intelligence is dated Colonel Clarke, with his corps, entered the Province and established himself at St. Philipsburg and has since been followed by General McComb with his infantry. These movements, altho' evidently meant as a feint to draw off our attention from the enemy's real views upon Niagara, have induced me to place part of the Left Division, under the command of Colonel Sir Sidney Beckwith with directions to avail himself of the first favorable opportunity to meet the approach of the invaders should they have the temerity to advance further into the Province, and to drive them not only from our territory but from Swanton.

Since my last letter to you of the 24th, I have received yours of the 15th, and having submitted Major General Riall's proposal to the consideration of Lt. Colonel Bruyeres, the commanding engineer, I now enclose to you his report on that subject.

I agree with him in opinion that the question of retaining or destroying Fort Niagara must altogether depend upon the probability of our obtaining the naval superiority on the lake; from the information now transmitted to you, as well as from the means which you possess of obtaining further intelligence on the subject, you will be enabled to judge whether it is likely that the desirable object of our naval ascendency will be obtained. In that event, to which I cannot but look forward with sanguine expectations, beyond all doubts, for the various reasons stated by Lt. Colonel Bruyeres, as well for others equally obvious, Niagara will be invaluable to us and it will be highly important to retain the possession of it as long as possible. You must therefore strongly impress upon Colonel Young and the garrison of that fort that the post of honor is the one they occupy and that it must be maintained to the last extremity. Should you, however, have strong reasons to doubt our acquiring the ascendency on the lake, and that you find that the enemy's preparations are in such forwardness as will enable them to navigate it for any considerable time before our squadron shall be able to meet them, in that case I am decidedly of opinion that Niagara should be completely demolished. I have no doubt from the information I now send to you, connecting it with the communication made to you in my letter of the 24th, that the American Government is determined to make a great effort for the recovery of Niagara before it shall be called upon to decide upon the proposal I might feel disposed to make in consequence of Mr. Monroe's letter to Genl. Winder. It therefore becomes the more important that we should retain possession of that important fortress if practicable, or render it useless to the Americans should we be obliged to abandon it. All these considerations will, I trust, have their due weight with you in leading you promptly to make exertions and to adopt the measures necessary for either event, and I confidently rely upon zealous and vigorous endeavors to prevent the loss of that conquest so gallantly achieved, and to disappoint the enemy in their expectation of these advantages to which, by Mr. Monroe's letter, they seem to look from an armistice, should it take place.

I have already fully written to you on the subject of the Commissariat and respecting your supplies of provisions and money. With regard to Captain Holcroft, there is no intention of removing him from a situation where his services are so much wanted, and in which it now appears his own inclinations lead him to remain. I shall leave Quebec to-morrow for Montreal, where I hope to be on Tuesday or Wednesday next.

(Canadian Archives, C. 1222, pp. 71-3.)

Colonel Wm. Claus to Captain Loring.

YORK, 28th March, 1814.

SIR,—

I received a letter yesterday from Colonel Elliott, of the 25th instant, an extract of which I herewith transmit for the information of His Honor Lieut. General Drummond. I have directed Colonel Elliott to send off runners immediately to Maipock and the Potawatamies.

Colonel Elliott ought to know the strength of the nations that is said to have joined the enemy, but I am at a loss to know where they can have such a force. I know the Hurons are very weak, and most of the Shawanese moved some years ago to the west of the Mississippi. The Delawares, whose place of residence is on the Eel River near the head of the Wabash, are the strongest nation, but the distance is so great that I should very much doubt their coming forward with the enemy. The want of wampum is very great, as no business can be done with the Indians without it. A requisition was sent down more than twelve months ago for that article, but none was received.

I also put under cover a letter from Major Givins of the 23rd instant, addressed to me, on the subject of rations being issued to the families of the officers of the Indian Department. I beg to submit the same to His Honor the President, hoping that the same indulgence may be granted to the Indian Department that this order gives to the staff and the army in the country.

(Canadian Archives, C. 257, p. 223.)

From Lieut. General Drummond to Sir George Prevost.

KINGSTON, March 29th, 1814.

SIR,—

Six of the tumbrils and a similar number of the waggons captured from the enemy at Fort Niagara, having been completely repaired for the service of the ordnance department in the carriage of musket ball cartridges, extra field ordnance ammunition and forage for the light brigade of artillery, whereby the necessity will be superseded of hiring country teams, which are perpetually failing at the moment they are most required, are also an enormous expense, and for want of proper covering are the cause of an immense quantity of ammunition being consequently destroyed, I have deemed it highly beneficial to the service to direct Major General Riall to cause horses to be purchased for them without delay, which, I trust, will meet Your Excellency's approbation.

Harness has been procured from Niagara also.

(Canadian Archives, C. 388, pp. 54-5.)

From Sir James Yeo to Noah Freer.

His Majesty's Ship *Wolfe*,
KINGSTON, 29th March, 1814.

SIR,—

I have had the honor of your letter of the 21st instant, and beg leave to acquaint you, for the information of His Excellency, that the guns of His Majesty's ship *Aeolus* will be required for the upper gun deck of the third ship building at this yard.

(Canadian Archives, C. 733, p. 84.)

Major J. B. Glegg to John Emmott, Living on the Road Between the 10 and 12 Mile Creek.

Headquarters, NIAGARA FRONTIER,
27th March, 1814.

SIR,—

A representation having been made this day by the widow Catherine Sloat that you occupy a house and premises belonging to her late husband, to the prejudice of her interest and contrary to her will, and further that you do this as you allege by the permission and consent of Mr. Merritt, who has in violation of his oath and allegiance deserted his king and country and joined the enemy, you are hereby directed and ordered to immediately retire from and surrender the said house, premises and land to the rightful owner, Catherine Sloat, for her use and benefit, otherwise you must answer all consequences, as the business will be referred to the King's Attorney at York.

(Merritt MSS.)

Major J. B. Glegg to Captain W. H. Merritt at 12 Mile Creek.

NIAGARA FRONTIER, 29th March, 1814.

DEAR MERRITT,—

By direction of Major Genl. Riall I send a person of the name of Robt. Hoyle, who was apprehended under very doubtful circumstances at Chippawa, at which place he appeared anxious to know the way to Long Point and otherwise was rather curious.

He says he has been employed in the Lower Province as a lumber merchant, and has contracted largely with persons at Montreal. He says he sold a small cargo of goods at an advanced price to Mr. Durand, and being required to show his passport he said none had been given him or asked for since he left Montreal. He will be brought to you by a private and sergeant of the 19th Light Dragoons, and Major General Riall desires you will relieve the escort at the Twelve by sending on Cornet McKenney and one private, who must be very careful of their charge and conduct him to Major Maule, where further instructions will be in waiting. You are of course acquainted that Major Maule now commands at Burlington.

(Merritt MSS.)

Chauncey to Secretary Navy.

No. 24.

U. S. Ship *General Pike*,
Sackett's Harbor, 29th Mar., 1814.

Sir,—

I have been duly honored with your letter of the 18th instant, and feel flattered that the alterations made in the large ship has met with your approbation, and that you have allowed me the privilege of naming the vessels now building. I shall endeavor to make such a selection as you will be satisfied with.

I have reduced the quantity of ballast first ordered and shall use stone as far as we can with safety; but the vessels on this lake are so shallow that we find much difficulty in stowing five weeks' provisions even with iron ballast. The large ship could not be ballasted with stone. She will require her ballast to lay low down to counteract the immense weight aloft, which upon her gun deck and above it will be upwards of 200 tons. Be assured, Sir, that I shall use all the economy the nature of the service will admit of. I shall be able to obtain some ballast from Rome and some from Onondaga, and we shall have no difficulty in obtaining a sufficient quantity of shot; those that I contracted for at Onondaga are already coming in. We shall soon receive them from Rome and New York. I am very apprehensive that we shall be detained for our heavy guns, for the winter has been so very open and mild that a large portion of the guns which left New York in the early part of February are still on the road between Albany and New York, and must now come by water by the way of Oswego. I am making every arrangement that there shall be as little delay at Oswego as possible. That post, however, requires a military force at it, as it is now entirely destitute, and I believe not a gun mounted. It would be quite impossible to get either guns or ballast from Lake Erie as long as the enemy has possession of the Niagara frontier.

There are but few guns here belonging to the War Department, and those generally of small calibre. I certainly think that guns might be taken from the works at New York without endangering that post, and I most fervently hope that the Secretary at War will give the order for us to receive those required.

Be assured, Sir, that every exertion shall be used to be prepared to meet the enemy as early as possible.

Lieut. William MacEwen to Mrs. MacEwen at Chippawa.

FORT GEORGE, 81st March, 1814.

I received by the hands of Phillips a ham and a small basket of eggs, which came very opportunely, as there is nothing to be got here for money. The whole place is a ruin, nothing to be seen but brick chimneys standing, what the fire could not destroy, of the once beautiful town of Newark. The whole of the men have been employed in raising batteries and other works for the protection of the place, but I will say nothing as to the issue. We were alarmed last night and were under arms most of the night owing to the enemy firing over the river. As they are within a short distance it was expected they would make a landing on this side; however, they did not make their appearance so we were permitted to go to our quarters, which are beyond any I have occupied in this country, nothing to be had but water, and that would be scarce if the river was not near us.

I am getting into a barrack with Bailey and Vaughan, the only one in the place, and will have it ready in a few days for your reception if you are determined to abide by a stirring and restless life. I am afraid this will be the case throughout the summer, as the Americans are determined to beat us from the place very soon. Give my respects to Captain Muirhead, Margaret and all the family. See if you can get James to give you his Morgan to draw the cart, as my poor Paddy has been lame ever since I left Chippawa and is at present unable to take the journey. Bring some spirits and everything you want, as there is nothing here. At present the roads are very bad and hardly passable for carriage or horse.

(A. Brymner's Excerpts, pp. 12-3.)

Lieut. General Drummond to Sir George Prevost.

KINGSTON, March 31st, 1814.

SIR,—

I am concerned to inform Your Excellency that I have received a report from Major General Riall of the 24th instant stating that no progress had been made in any of the works on the Niagara Frontier in consequence of severity of the weather, there being more snow on the ground in that neighborhood now than there has been during the winter.

I have the honor to enclose for Your Excellency's information the copy of a letter from Major Deane commanding the detachment of the Royal Scots at Oxford. Your Excellency is well aware of the inadequacy of our means in that quarter should it prove to be the intention of the enemy to advance upon Burlington from Long Point and at the same time make an attempt on the Niagara line.

It having been reported to me by Major General Riall and from other sources that Major McKee of the Indian Department has been doing a great deal of mischief among the Indians, upon the beach at the Head of the Lake, not only by getting shamefully drunk himself every day and speaking very improperly to them, but by permitting liquor to be sold to them in great quantities, which renders them outrageous and easy to be worked upon, and having understood that it might prove even dangerous to have him written to or spoken to with anger or displeasure on the subject as he has very considerable influence over them and might lead them astray, I thought it advisable to send for him to Kingston for the purpose of conversing with him on Indian affairs and propose soon after his arrival here to forward him to Montreal where Your Excellency will, I trust, find means to employ or detain him as long as we may find the service of the Indian tribes useful to the cause we are engaged in.

I am happy to inform Your Excellency that no desertions from the King's Regiment have taken place since their relief from Fort Niagara was made known to them, although the same opportunity still existed, which proves, I have satisfaction in observing, a disinclination to the place only and not to His Majesty's service.

(Canadian Archives, C. 682, p. 285.)

From Lieut. General Drummond to Earl Bathurst.

No. 4.   KINGSTON, UPPER CANADA, 31 March, 1814.

MY LORD,—

Since the destruction by the enemy of the Government House and the other public buildings at York, great embarrassment and difficulty in carrying on the public business has been experienced by the officers of the civil departments of this government for the want of proper houses for the records of their respective offices.

In the year 1804 the Legislature of the Province passed an act appropriating annually four hundred pounds with the view of establishing a fund for the purpose of defraying the expense of erecting the necessary buildings for the accommodation of the legislature and for public offices at York, but that act was repealed the last year and the fund which had accumulated under it, with all the surplus revenue of the colony, was liberally granted in aid of the war.

Under these circumstances I beg to solicit Your Lordship's authority to incur the expense necessary for erecting proper buildings for the residence of the person administering the government and for public offices, as soon as the relation of our affairs with the United States may prudently admit of it, the amount of which may be estimated at ten thousand pounds.

His Excellency Sir George Prevost having judged it expedient that I should for the present make this my principal place of residence from its importance in a military point of view, I have therefore been under the necessity of hiring a house at the rate of three hundred pounds a year, which I shall direct the Receiver General of the Province to pay, having no doubt but that it will be approved by Your Lordship.

(Canadian Archives, C. 474.)

From Sir George Prevost to Lieut. General Drummond.

Head Qrs., MONTREAL, 31st March, 1814.

SIR,—

21st March.	I have had the honor to receive your several com-
21st "	munications, dated as per margin, with their respective
24th "	enclosures.
24th "	The papers transmitted from M. Genl. Riall and
24th "	Captain Stewart, with the answer of Colonel Butler of
25th "	the U. States Army, are highly interesting. The sys-

tem of creating distrust employed by Colonel Butler is of French origin. Am I to understand from the reports before me that Colonel Baby did not experience the treatment first represented?

Referring to your second letter of the 21st inst. I rejoice at the fortunate escape from a conflagration of a most alarming nature to which the dockyard at Kingston has been recently exposed.

On a perusal of the further communications you have enclosed to me relative to the affairs on the River Thames, below Delaware town, on the 4th inst., I cannot but lament the injudicious arrangement of Captain Basden in the attack upon the enemy on that day.

I shall be glad to find after inquiry that credit may be given to the deposition of Robert Christie from Sackett's Harbor.

It is with much satisfaction I learn that circumstances have not made it necessary to issue the proclamation declaring martial law in the Midland and Newcastle Districts as mentioned in your letter of the 14th inst., and that reasonable hopes are entertained of being able to obtain a sufficiency of provisions in the Upper Province for the maintenance of the troops without resorting to so violent a measure.

Your letter of the 25th covers an address presented to you by the Commons House of Assembly of Upper Canada during the late session.

I have not failed in giving every consideration to the claims of the militia of Upper Canada, and consider the imputation of a neglect of them as unfounded and unjust. The United States replies reluctantly to any communication on the subject of an exchange of prisoners and always with evasion. This capricious conduct has rendered it almost impossible to carry on any exchange, but you may assure the relatives of those of H. M. brave and faithful subjects of Upper Canada who have unhappily fallen into the hands of the enemy, that it will give me the most cordial satisfaction to effect their exchange as speedily as circumstances will permit, and I am not without hopes that the opportunity will soon be afforded to me, as I am led to believe from a communication I have just received from Mr. Monroe, Secretary of State of the United States, that the tone of the American Government as respects the measure of retaliation and of exchange of prisoners has experienced a favorable change.

(Canadian Archives, C. 1222, pp. 77-9.)

From the Military Secretary to Lieut. General Drummond.

Head Qrs., MONTREAL, 31st March, 1814.

SIR,—

21st March.	The Commander of the Forces has this day handed to me and directed that I should acknowledge the receipt of your several despatches, dated as per margin, which His Excellency is prevented from replying to himself as he had intended by the express, from the
22d "	
22d "	
25th "	
26th "	

circumstances of the advance of the enemy in force by the Odell Town Road, and of information just received of their having commenced an attack on our post at the La Cole. His Excellency proceeds immediately across the river to St. Johns.

The letters remaining unanswered relate to the prevalence of desertion from the King's Regt.; the arrangement you had made for the relief of Lt. Gaugreben from the charge of the Engineer Dept. on the Niagara Frontier.

The requisition of Com. Sir Jas. Yeo for marines. His application for a Fort Adjutant at Fort Wellington, and the confidential instructions you have given to the officer in command of the Right Division.

(Canadian Archives, C. 1222, pp. 79-80.)

District General Order.

KINGSTON, March 31st, 1814.

District General Order.

The Lieut. General Commanding and President having had under his consideration the report of a Board of naval officers assembled for the purpose of ascertaining how far the ration actually issued to the seamen on the lakes according to the scale of naval ration promulgated in the General Order of the 20th January, 1814, is equal to that which is issued to the seamen of His Majesty's Navy serving on other stations, and which board has reported it as their opinion that there exists a material deficiency in the following essential articles, viz.: The allowance of only one pound of soft bread in lieu of one pound of biscuit, and in the substitution of ten ounces and two-thirds of pork per day throughout the week as an equivalent for the usual weekly issues of meat on board His Majesty's fleet and which include four pounds of beef. The Lieut. General having further taken into his consideration the privation the seamen labour under on this station from the impossibility of procuring vegetables, of which they always have an abundant supply on other stations, His Honor moreover, knowing it to be as much the wish of His Excellency the Commander of the Forces and Governor in Chief, as it is his own, to extend to the seamen who have volunteered their services on the lakes, not only every allowance to which they can have any just claim but also every indulgence which our limited means may enable us to afford them, he is pleased to direct, in conformity with the suggestion of Commodore Sir James Yeo, and of the board above mentioned that the following addition shall be made to the naval ration at this station and that the augmentation shall commence from the 25th inst., viz.: One pound and a half of bread or its equivalent in flour, or one pound of biscuit per day. Pork, six pounds per week whenever the usual proportion of fresh beef is not to be procured.

J. HARVEY,
Lt. Col., D. A. G.

(Canadian Archives, C. 733, pp. 88-9.)

From Sir James Yeo to Lieut. Colonel Harvey.

His Majesty's ship *Wolfe*, 1st April, 1814.

SIR,—

I have had the honor to receive your letter of the 31st ultimo., with a copy of a District General Order issued by His Honor Lieut. General Drummond.

I have to request you will express to the Lieut. General the high sense I entertain of his prompt and kind attention to the interest and comfort of the seamen, by whom I am confident his kindness will be sensibly felt.

You will also be pleased to accept my best acknowledgments for the very ready and kind support you at all times give to everything connected with the naval department in this country.

(Canadian Archives, C. 733, p. 87.)

From the Diary of Thomas McCrae.

RALEIGH, Thursday, 31st March, 1814.

A party of 27 Am. horsemen came here by the Round O and proceeded on to Sandwich the same day.

Saturday, 9th April, 1814.

John went down to Jacob's for a barrel of salt bo't of H. Hunt in Detroit for 40 dollars.

Speech of the Sioux Chief Named The Leaf, Indian Name Wabasha.

My Father, when I heard the good news which my father, the Red Head (Robert Dickson) communicated to me I took the same road as my deceased father used to take to come here, (Quebec), and my arrival is a fine day to me for I see the good works of my English father.

You ordered your children to lift the tomahawk, but as for me I have not yet taken it in hand. It is neither from fear nor laziness but because I lack strength. I say because I lack strength. I have neither arms nor ammunition and I live at a great distance; but I should 'ere this have begun it if the want of what I have mentioned had not prevented me.

It is not from to-day that I know you, my father; it is since the old fort was built that you have supported us and we wait for that support this day.

My Father, in speaking to you I say since the old fort was built, as also before, for there it was that my deceased father, "The Leaf," took great pains to support the Sioux nation, but they had the misfortune to lose him too soon and we have suffered much since that time, more especially since the Americans have adopted us for their children, but we have the good fortune to have the Red Head for a friend, who, in spite of the barriers which the Americans made, always found a passage to come and save the Indians from perishing. At present he is our father. He has some difficulty to bring the Indians on the right way but it is requisite he should have a force with him in order to be attended to. I speak not of my nation, for we are his true children.

My Father, I conclude by pressing your hand and begging you to stretch out your arms in support of your children on the Mississippi.

Speech of Little Crow, a Sioux Chief, Indian Name Chatewaconamin.

My Father,—

I present myself this day before you to talk, which gives me much pleasure. I speak of war for I have already begun. I have sent back the Americans from La Prairie du Chien and then I came here to drive them away. Since then I find this island more solid than when they were here. I believe I am now under a clear sky. Last year I undertook to crush an embarrassment that was in the way but I could not do it because I found the Americans, like the beaver, burrowed under ground. My thoughts likewise are often turned to our own side because I fear the Americans who have fine roads to come to us, which causes me to dread for our women and children.

It would be a great charity on your part, my Father, to send some of your big guns and brave warriors to our support. I requested it last year but I have this day to repeat my request.

I have always obeyed your orders, which makes me speak with boldness as I speak according to my works.

My Father, you ordered all your Indian children to be on a good understanding with each other and live in union. Till now I have done so.

To assure you more forcibly, my Father, of my deeds, know that I and my young warriors have devoted our bodies to our father the Red Head.

My Father, we are sorry to learn that we are to have no trader this year. Although you give assistance to all your children yet you have too many to take care of before it can reach us.

We have of late not had much assistance through you, my Father, for one half of our nation have died of hunger with shreds of skin in their mouths for want of other nourishment. I have always thought and do so still that it arises from no other cause but the troubles you have had with the Americans.

Speech of the Manouminie Chief Named Thomas.

My Father,—

It is a long time past that you know us who are called Manouminies and I suppose you are acquainted with our behavior towards the whites, and particularly towards our English Father.

Shall I tell you, my Father, that when I beheld the great fire which shined on this island its light brought to mind times that are passed and I said to myself: "This then is the Fire whose assistance gives life to all the copper colored skins and particularly to our nation, who have so often had the happiness of seeing and approaching it."

My Father, I give you my hand and in so doing it seems to me that I am giving it to our Great Father.

I consider that we are all created in the same likeness and by the same power and it mortifies me to say that there are some of my *sembables* who have many ears and many hearts.

I speak without hesitation, my Father, because I have but one heart and two ears to hear with, and I wish that every chief would be as firm as I am. I call myself happy this day because I have always pressed my English Father's hand and my wish has always been to please you, my Father.

My Father, I embrace the present moment to thank our Great Father for the goods which me and my people have received for a long series of time and likewise to thank the two persons† whom my Father chose for the taking care of us Indians. I say that I thank them, because it is their courage and good hearts which made them proceed in spite of the lateness of the season and its severity and arrive with the goods destined for us, which saved our lives as well as many other nations.

†R. Dickson, Capt. Bullock.

Speech of Lassaminie, Chief of the Winibagoes.

MY FATHER,—

It is true. We are a nation that is known to be brutes and bad people but since we have paid attention to your good advice we have begun to behave better. For some time past a thick cloud hovers near our lands. Every time it approaches we go to meet it and have succeeded so far as to drive it farther from us, but we have lost many of our young warriors. If this had happened to any other nation they perhaps would have asked for goods as a payment for their bodies. As for me, my Father, I speak on behalf of my nation. I only ask for forces to fight the enemy and be persuaded that the tomahawk shall always be lifted up till the period arrives that you will grant peace to the Americans.

My Father, let some of your warriors go with us on our lands. It will be the means of keeping the other nations in respect.

What regards our women and children, my Father, you know their situation and the need they have of your help.

(Canadian Archives, C. 257, p. 268.)

Lieut. General Drummond to Sir George Prevost.

KINGSTON, April 2nd, 1814.

Secret and Confidential.

SIR,—

I have the honor to acknowledge the receipt of Your Excellency's letter of the 24th ultimo, marked private and confidential, enclosing the copy of a letter from Mr. Monroe to Brigadier General Winder of the United States Army on the subject of an armistice, on which Your Excellency desires my sentiments.

I beg leave respectfully to submit as my opinion that the object of Mr. Monroe's letter is two-fold. First, to gain time for organizing their naval and military force. Second, to cause the proposal for the armistice, (the discussion of which is to afford that time,) to originate with Your Excellency.

Unless Your Excellency is in possession of some other pledge than General Winder's assurances of the sincerity of his Government, I should place but little faith in them, as I have ever understood that officer to be one of the most strenuous supporters of the war and withal the most plausible, therefore the most dangerous agent the American Government could employ in this country.

If the American Government be sincerely desirous of a cessation of hostilities, I conceive that it arises from the consideration that the advantages to be derived from the continuation of them are at least doubtful, or more probably that on the opening of the ensuing campaign they will be decidedly on our side.

We should be extremely cautious in doing anything the tendency of which may derogate from the high ground on which His Majesty's Government stands, by affording to the enemy the smallest reason to infer that any diffidence of our ability to defend these Provinces has a secret influence in deciding us to court or even willingly to meet his advances for a cessation of hostilities.

Respecting the motives which should influence Your Excellency to any discussion of a pacific nature, although I admit the communication between Coteau du Lac and Kingston may be liable to occasional interruption, yet I do not consider it so much so as to cause any serious apprehension. That between Kingston and Niagara can only be interrupted in the event of the enemy acquiring the superiority on Lake Ontario, and the accompanying deposition on oath of a person lately from Sackett's Harbor affords strong grounds for hope that the enemy's marine at that place will not soon, if ever, acquire that degree of force alluded to in Your Excellency's letter. The whole of the advantages therefore to be derived from the armistice will be reaped by the enemy.

It is impossible at present to ascertain to which side the naval superiority on the lake will preponderate on the opening of navigation unless full credit can be attached to the enclosed deposition, when, if so, the superiority will be decidedly on our side, and, at all events, we have, in my opinion, as much right to look for its possession as the enemy.

Should an opportunity offer by even a temporary naval superiority for the destruction of the enemy's fleet and arsenal at Sackett's Harbor, a vigorous combined attack by the navy and army would be highly advisable, yet it must be remembered that the squadron will be required to perform another most important service as soon as the season opens, viz., the pushing of troops, (the 103rd Regt. and the Glengarry Light Infantry,) stores, &c., &c., to the relief of Fort Niagara and the Right Division.

The latest information I have received respecting the enemy's squadron has been from the accompanying document. Our two new ships, Sir James Yeo informs me, he is in hopes to launch on the 9th instant if the ice permits, and they will be in readiness with the other vessels immediately after the opening of navigation.

It is highly satisfactory to know that the interests of the Indians will not be forgotten in any arrangement which may take place.

(Canadian Archives, C. 683, p. 1.)

From Lieut. General Drummond to Sir George Prevost.

Kingston, April 2nd, 1814.

Secret and Confidential.

Sir,—

I have the honor to acquaint Your Excellency that on the night of the 30th ultimo, Commodore Sir James Yeo called on me to communicate the very disagreeable intelligence that an alarming spirit of discontent had displayed itself in the sailors of the squadron under his command in consequence of the diminution that had lately taken place in the naval ration, conformably to the General Order of the 20th January last.

The first intimation that the Commodore stated that he had of this appearance of dissatisfaction, he received on the morning of the 27th ultimo, when a deputation composed of a considerable number of the petty officers waited on him for the purpose of respectfully preferring a complaint that the quantity of provisions that had for some time been issued to them was not the same they had always been in the habit of receiving, that neither their allowance of bread (1 lb.) was equal to the same weight of biscuit, nor the proportion of pork substituted in lieu of beef was by any means equivalent to the latter species of meat.

Sir James endeavoured without effect to convince them that their calculation was an erroneous one, as the same quantity of bread was issued to the seamen that the soldiers of the army received, and that it was an invariable custom by the naval regulations to substitute a smaller portion of pork for a greater one of beef. On the day he reported the transaction to me he received private information that the sailors were canvassing the subject in a more unreserved manner, and that they had even gone such lengths as to talk of the appointment of delegates by whom they could more fully give effect to their remonstrances.

It is superfluous for me to observe to Your Excellency how greatly I was distressed on being made acquainted with this intelligence, so dangerous in its consequences, at a time when the greatest unanimity and most strenuous exertions of our fleet on Lake Ontario were so essential for the preservation of the colony. I had it in recollection that every instance of discontent and insubordination in the British Navy had been induced by complaints respecting provisions and I immediately saw the necessity of adopting decisive measures for obviating the evil whilst only in its commencement, as were it suffered to proceed to a more open manifestation, the most fatal effects might result from its being neglected. I therefore requested Sir James Yeo to assemble a board of officers to inquire into and ascertain how far these complaints were founded in reason, the proceedings of which I have the honor to transmit Your Excellency a copy; in consequence of the opinion therein contained I judged it advisable to issue a District General Order respecting the naval ration, a copy of which I also enclose, as well as a comparative schedule of that ration as reduced by the General Order of the 20th January last from those established by the naval instructions, together with copies of letters from Sir James Yeo and Lieut. Colonel Harvey, the latter written by my direction.

(Canadian Archives, C. 732, pp. 90-3.)

From Sir George Prevost to Lieutenant General Drummond.

Hd. Qrs., MONTREAL, 2d April, 1814.

SIR,—

29th March. I have had the honor to receive your letters of the
29th   "   dates stated in the margin, and in reply I beg leave to
29th   "   inform you that in concurring in the sentiments of the
Comg. Genl. with respect to the difficulty experienced by the Commissariat in obtaining provisions for the troops in Upper Canada, I intended particularly to allude to past circumstances, and you will have learnt by my last communication the satisfaction I felt that events had not made it necessary to issue the proclamation declaratory of Martial Law you had prepared, and that you had reasonable hopes of being able to obtain a sufficiency of provisions without resorting to so violent a measure.

I approve of the directions you have given for the purchase of horses for the six tumbrils and waggons in the ordnance department on the Niagara frontier, and I propose sanctioning an attempt being made to recover the boats and craft on the Salmon River alluded to by Colonel Scott, and also of some ordnance which I am informed were buried by the enemy.

(Canadian Archives, C. 1222, pp. 80-1.)

From Sir George Prevost to Lieut. General Drummond.

Hd. Qrs., MONTREAL, 4th Apl., 1814.

I have to acknowledge the receipt of your letters of the 21st, 22d, 26th and 31st ultimo.

The two first relate to changes you have made in the distribution of the officers of engineers in Upper Canada. You are the best judge of the necessity and the advantages of such removals to the future good of the service. They also contain representations of the disgraceful propensity to desertion prevalent in the King's Regiment in Fort Niagara. This circumstance has induced Major General Riall to relieve that corps by the 100th Regt. I feel confident those who so gallantly carried the fort will as gallantly maintain it. In waiting for the movement which is to afford them another opportunity of displaying their valor they will, I trust, give a brighter example of patience and soldier like feelings than were evinced by their predecessors. When an old respectable corps disgraces itself as the King's Regt. has done surely the officers cannot be faultless.

The third was accompanied by a plan of defence suggested by you to General Riall against the attempt it is expected the enemy will make on the Niagara frontier. In the arduous circumstances of that officer's situation in the event of an attack being made upon the positions occupied by the Right Division to the extent you anticipate, I cannot desire any specific instructions sufficient to embrace all the contingencies of the campaign we are about commencing.

Those you have composed appear to be judicious and well calculated to gratify and relieve the Major General, and may prove themselves useful to him in the ulterior arrangements he may be called upon to make.

Your last letter relates to the impossibility of proceeding with the additional works of defence projected at Niagara, in consequence of the severity of the weather. However, that evil is now removed and I trust the facility of execution attends the ability.

As to Major Dean's representations, I confess I feel but little apprehension when I consider the composition and discipline of the force by which the enemy will be opposed.

(Canadian Archives, C. 1222, pp. 83-5.)

From Lieut. General Drummond to Sir George Prevost.

KINGSTON, April 5th, 1814.

SIR,—

Desirous of affording every assistance within my control to Major General Riall in the important command he holds on the Niagara frontier, I have the honor to acquaint Your Excellency that I have directed Lieutenant Colonel Drummond, Acting Deputy Quartermaster General, to repair thither some time since and to remain there until matters should assume an aspect of more promise than they have hitherto done as far as regards the works of defence ordered to be erected on that line. And the whole time of Captain Sabine, Acting Deputy Assistant Quartermaster General here, being occupied in the detail of the duties of the office, there is not an officer of the department disposable upon whom I can call for active service at an emergency. Permit me therefore to request that Your Excellency will be pleased to direct Captain Fowler to join the department here, if he can be spared from the Lower Province, if not, any active and intelligent officer you may think proper.

(Canadian Archives, C. 388, pp. 61-2.)

From Lieut. General Drummond to Earl Bathurst.

No. 6. KINGSTON, Upper Canada, 5th April, 1814.

MY LORD,—

Upon my arrival in this Province, Martial Law, so far as relates to the procuring of provisions and forage for the garrisons of Kingston and Prescott, was in force in the Midland, Johnstown and Eastern Districts, a measure to which Major General de Rottenburg found himself under the necessity of reverting, not only from the very low state to which the supplies in those garrisons was reduced but the evident reluctance on the part of the inhabitants in furnishing those supplies, altho' the most liberal prices had been offered.

Learning, however, upon assuming the command, that the measure had created much discontent, and thinking, as the winter was just commencing when the roads are rendered practicable and which is the season when the produce is generally brought to market, that the necessity for enforcing it would cease to exist, I was induced to revoke it.

The House of Assembly during its late session in March passed a vote of censure on Major General de Rottenburg for having resorted to a measure in their view unconstitutional, notwithstanding which I am sorry to inform Your Lordship I have since been constrained by the most imperious necessity to recur to it, there being at one time lately in this garrison, at which alone a daily issue of nearly five thousand rations takes place, but sixteen barrels of flour in store. It is now in operation throughout the Province, the officer at the head of the Commissariat having strongly urged its absolute necessity, as otherwise the necessary supplies could not on any terms be obtained.

I have taken care to give particular orders that the officers and agents of that department employed in collecting those supplies should observe the greatest moderation and use their best endeavours to conciliate the people, and with a view of acting on the most liberal and just terms between the Government and them have directed the magistrates of each district in full assembly to fix upon a fair price to be paid for every article furnished.

As it is highly probable, however, that a vote of censure similar to that passed on Major General de Rottenburg will in the next session be passed upon me for having resorted to a measure, without which the troops could not possibly have subsisted, and in which I had the full concurrence of His Excellency the Governor in Chief, I have to request Your Lordship will afford me the satisfaction of knowing whether the charge by the House of Assembly of the act being unconstitutional can be substantiated, or if, on the contrary, in continuing to enforce it, should the same necessity exist, I should receive the sanction and support of His Majesty's Ministers.

(Canadian Archives, G. 474)

Lieut. Colonel Mahlon Burwell to Colonel Talbot.

OTTER CREEK, 5th April, 1814.

MY DEAR COLONEL,—

On my way to Port Talbot last evening I met George Coltman at this place, who has informed me that you have gone to Long Point. I intended to have brought my family away immediately, but Wallace tells me that you went away in Hunter's skiff, which I depended on as my only means of getting my family from Port Talbot. Coltman says that Captain Secord has gone to Scram's on the north branch for a box of arms. I shall go to Kettle Creek to-day and get some person to go to Port Talbot to-morrow and see Willson and Patterson, and if Secord gets the arms and I can get word of the enemy I shall call out the militia from the street and meet him at Port Talbot. If there should be no more than 30 dragoons and one company of men, I trust we should have no great difficulty in managing them. I trust you will send back the skiff as soon as possible that I may take my family away, for I can never think of leaving them there alone, which I shall be forced to do if I can't get them away before the enemy's approach. The travelling is so bad I don't believe the Yankees will be there for several days.

(Talbot Papers.)

Seth Grosvenor to ————

WILLIAMSVILLE, 3rd April, 1814.

DEAR SIR,—

I am requested in behalf of the Committee to state the amount of our losses on the western frontier, which are to wit :—

Buffalo—
    69 frame houses, including two brick and stone.

8 log do.
16 stores, including two offices.
35 barns.
15 sheds, or say shops and other outhouses.
Total, 143, amounting to about $190,000.

Black Rock—
16 frame houses.
11 log do.
8 barns.
5 outhouses, say shops, &c., amounting to $19,000.
Total, 183.

From Black Rock to 18 Mile Creek—
20 frame houses.
67 log do.
5 stores.
29 barns.
30 shops, mills and other outhouses.

151 amounting to $141,000.
334 houses, &c., total $350,000.

This does not embrace any further than those who have laid their claims before us. You know Messrs. Porter have not and some at Buffalo have been deficient.

(Poulson's American Daily Advertiser, 27th April, 1814, Philadelphia Library.)

Lieut. General Drummond to Sir George Prevost.

KINGSTON, April 5th, 1814.

SIR,—

The necessity of an additional number of marines for the squadron having been represented by Commodore Sir James Yeo, and in fact the impossibility of its leaving port without them having been so strongly urged by that officer, I have felt myself so imperiously called upon to give every assistance in my power for gaining the naval superiority on the lake that I have considered it indispensably necessary to the safety of the Province to accede to the Commodore's solicitations, and I have in consequence directed two companies of marines to proceed immediately from Fort Wellington to this place and the two companies of the 89th Regiment, under Major Clifford, from Cornwall, to replace them, on whose arrival at Fort Wellington the two remaining companies of marines are to march to Kingston.

I beg leave therefore to suggest to Your Excellency that the

89th Regiment complete be ordered to Fort Wellington, whereby Lieut. Colonel Morrison, being senior to Lieut. Colonel Pearson, the latter will become disposable for service with the Right Division, where an officer of Lieutenant Colonel Pearson's intelligence, zeal and ability is very particularly wanting, and the two companies of the 103rd would become efficient with their corps. The 89th Regiment at Coteau du Lac can be replaced by a regiment of Embodied Militia or such other as Your Excellency may find disposable.

I do not suppose the entire of the marines will be required on board the squadron at the same time, yet I consider it highly necessary that they should be upon the spot to fill up vacancies arising from every description of casualties as they occur.

And I must again take the liberty of pressing on Your Excellency's observation the inadequacy of the force for the security of this all important place as soon as the 103rd Regiment shall be removed from hence and should I find it necessary to detach also the Glengarry Light Infantry.

(Canadian Archives, C. 683, pp. 8-11.)

Sir George Prevost to Lieut. General Drummond.

Head Qrs., MONTREAL, 6th April, 1814.

SIR,—

Earl Bathurst in a communication bearing date the 28th of January, just received, having stated to me the desire of the Lords Commissioners of the Admiralty that the 2nd Battn. of Royal Marines, excepting the Artillery Company, should be placed immediately at the disposal of Commodore Sir James Yeo to enable him to fulfill their Lordship's orders for manning the squadron under his command, I propose to order on to Kingston the detachment of that corps now at Fort Wellington, which will be relieved by five companies of the 89th Regt. under Lieut. Colonel Morrison as soon as the navigation admits of their moving in that direction.

The 89th will therefore be divided between Fort Wellington and Cornwall, and the post at Coteau du Lac will be occupied by a detachment of Embodied Militia.

(Canadian Archives, C. 1222, pp. 85-6.)

From Sir George Prevost to Lieut. General Drummond.

Head Qrs., Montreal, 7th April, 1814.

SIR,—

I was yesterday honored by the receipt of your secret and confidential letter of the 2nd inst., with its several enclosures, on the subject of the dissatisfaction which had shewn itself among the seamen of the squadron at Kingston in consequence of an alteration which has been made in the naval ration. I highly approve of the prompt and effectual measures you adopted to remove the evil, the matter having been communicated to the Commissary General. I enclose herewith Mr. Robinson's letter explanatory of the naval ration.

(Canadian Archives, C. 1222, p. 86.)

Captain Sinclair to Secretary of the Navy.

WMSBURG, VIRGINIA, April 7th, 1814.

SIR,—

Having waited with much anxiety for an answer from you in reply to my letter of the 17th Jan. last, wherein I accepted of your proposition to take the command of the Norfolk Flotilla, and never having recd. one, I am hopeful you have contemplated giving me a frigate in preference; and I have lately observed in one of your official reports that three of the number authorized by Congress to be built will soon require commanders. I hope you will not consider it presumptive in me to solicit you to give me the appointment to one of them, and, as long and constant services will, I am sure, have their due influence with you, I beg leave to suggest that upon that score no officer in service has a superior claim, as my life has been devoted to my country since the commencement of our present naval establishment.

I have the honor to remain, Sir, with high respect,
Your obt. servt.,
(Signed) A. SINCLAIR.

Lieut. General Drummond to Sir George Prevost.

KINGSTON, April 7th, 1814.

SIR,—

I have the honor to report to Your Excellency that Major General Riall's last letter to me states that no regular force has as yet made its appearance on the American side of the Niagara River, and that consequently he supposes no part of the column which left Sackett's Harbor some time since had arrived in that neighborhood, conceiving from the display the enemy used to make formerly, they will not be long in shewing themselves when they do arrive, at the same time expressing his hope and belief that in the hands of the garrison, (the 100th Regiment,) who so gallantly gained possession of it, Fort Niagara is for the present safe.

A Mr. Bell, a respectable man, and two others, lately made their escape from Malden and report that there is not the smallest appearance of any preparation there for a forward movement nor did they hear it spoken of. They were totally unacquainted with the occurrences at Presque Isle. On their way to Port Talbot they discovered the two guns left by the enemy in the woods near Point aux Pins, and hid them so carefully as totally to prevent their being found again except by themselves. Two gun carriages and two ammunition carts with ammunition discovered at the same time and place Colonel Talbot has sent a party to destroy.

I am happy to acquaint Your Excellency that Assistant Commissary General Coffin, in the absence of Mr. Dance, has reported to me that the three months' supply of provisions ordered to be deposited in Fort Niagara will have been laid in there in the course of a week from the 27th ultimo.

(Canadian Archives, C, 683, p. 12.)

Captain Sinclair to Secretary of the Navy.

WMSBURG, Saturday evening,
April the 9th, 1814.

SIR,—

Your express has this moment handed me yours of the 7th inst. No time shall be lost in reaching the department at the earliest moment.

Yours respectfully,
(Signed) A. SINCLAIR.

From Lieut. Colonel Harvey to Sir James Yeo.

KINGSTON, April 9th, 1814.

Most Secret and Confidential.

SIR,—

The season for naval operations being at hand Lt. Genl. Drummond considers it advisable to communicate to you his ideas as to how the squadron under your command may be best employed on the opening of the navigation.

Assuming that your superiority of force will be in the first instance decidedly secured by the accession to your former squadron of the two new vessels, the service that appears to Lt. General Drummond of the greatest importance to the defence of the Province is the reinforcement of the Right Division by the 103rd Regiment, and the conveyance at the same time of a supply of stores and provisions to Fort Niagara and Fort George.

The Lieut. General would therefore wish that you would be pleased to make arrangements for executing this service at the earliest practicable period; the troops to be landed at the head of the lake, the stores and provisions at Fort Niagara and Fort George. On your way up the lake it would be desirable for one of the vessels to look into York to communicate with the officer commanding that post, (Colonel Stewart,) with a view to receiving on board and conveying to Fort Niagara five heavy guns, (3 18s and 2 24s,) destined for that fort, if these have not already been forwarded.

After landing the stores, &c., at Fort Niagara and communicating with M. Genl. Riall it might be desirable, if you find the M. General has no material assistance or co-operation to require from the squadron, that you should proceed down the American shore, looking into the different creeks and particularly reconnoitering Oswego, when, if you find it an object and consider the marines of the squadron sufficient for the service, you might land and bring off or destroy whatever stores, craft or public buildings the enemy might have there.

After which the Lt. General would recommend your proceeding off Sackett's Harbour, endeavour accurately to reconnoitre that place, and if you should consider an attack upon the enemy at that place as offering any rational hope of success, you might in that case despatch a boat or fast sailing vessel to Kingston with the result of your reconnoissance and follow with the squadron, to be ready to receive on board the troops in the event of the Lt. General's determining on the enterprise.

To the foregoing outline Lt. General Drummond has nothing at present to add. New circumstances or fresh intelligence may confirm or render it necessary, wholly or partially, to change the plan of operations, both with regard to the troops and the squadron. In such case the Lt. General will hasten to apprise you of the nature of such change of circumstances, as he will be anxious to communicate and consult with you on the change which it may be advisable to make in the plan of the naval campaign. Considering it essential that you should be apprised of the orders which have been sent to M. General Riall in order that you may be better prepared to appreciate the movements of the troops under his command and more promptly and effectually to co-operate with and assist them, I am directed to transmit, enclosed, such extracts from M. General Riall's instructions as relate to this subject. The instructions to the officer commanding at York are simply to defend that post, which it is considered he has ample means of doing against any force which the

enemy could convey to that point on board their squadron. If forced
or overpowered he is to retire upon Burlington, not *Kingston*.

(Canadian Archives, C. 732, pp. 147-151.)

From Sir George Prevost to Lieut. General Drummond.

Hd. Qrs., MONTREAL, 10th April, 1814.

SIR,—

I am much concerned to observe in your letter of the 5th inst. a want of attention to the purport of my late communications respecting the removal of any portion of the troops employed in the protection of the line of transport from the Coteau du Lac to Kingston without having obtained my previous consent, except under circumstances of a defensive nature. I am induced to dwell on the circumstance from having before me a most extraordinary letter addressed to Lt. Colonel Morrison by the Deputy Adjutant General attached to the Upper Canada District.

The movements of the enemy having made it necessary to suggest to that officer some precautionary measures, he was in the execution of them when your commands arrived, which, dashing and in fact being contradictory to those he was about obeying, Lt. Colonel Morrison very properly resorted to me for an explanation. You will prevent the recurrence of anything of the kind again by proper restraints on the Dy. Adjutant Genl., who will in consequence be more cautious in commanding the execution of a service by troops so near my headquarters and so immediately at my disposal.

You will receive from the Adjutant General of the Forces a General Order expressing the movements I have sanctioned.

When I reflect that the reinforcements of which you now complain as being inadequate are in fact more in number than is consistent with the safety of other parts of my extensive command, I cannot but feel you viewed that subject under the momentary impression of some misrepresentation made to you by an over anxious individual, which, on further consideration, you will be convinced had better have been omitted at a moment when the enemy was pressing on the frontier of this Province.

It has not escaped my observation that you sought my commands on an important subject, (the partial operation of martial law,) on which I could only offer advice, as the power to do so comes from the commission under which you act as a governor; but on various other occasions affecting my responsibilty you have not hesitated to act and afterwards report having done so, tho' nothing pressing attended the case.

(Canadian Archives, C. 1222, pp. 89-91.)

Lieut. Charles Ingersoll to Captain W. H. Merritt.

BURFORD, 11th April, 1814.

DEAR SIR,—
Enclosed you have my weekly report of the dragoons on this station. The horses appear to hold their own very well, better than I have any reason to expect from the badness of the roads. Forage is very scarce. It is with the greatest difficulty that a sufficient quantity can be procured for the horses. I did not mention in my former report that I had taken Dakins from Hopkins and stationed him at Burlington Heights. . . . .

(Merritt MSS.)

Hon James Monroe to Colonel Ninian Pinkney.

Department of State, April 11th, 1814.

SIR,—
You are hereby authorized to discuss and arrange an armistice with such person as Sir George Prevost may appoint, and which when concluded and mutually signed is to be executed as definitely binding on both parties.

(Canadian Archives, C. 683, p. 79.

Commodore Chauncey to Secretary Navy.

U. S. Ship *General Pike*,
SACKETT'S HARBOR, 11th April, 1814.

No. ——

SIR,—The agent that I sent a few days ago to the other side has this moment returned, with information that the enemy has all his fleet ready, (with the exception of the new vessels,) in the stream, he has 12 to 14 gunboats and a number of small craft, and 3,000 troops ready to embark for this place, and it is said they are only waiting for a favorable time to make the attack. My own impression is that they have understood that we are going to York and that they have prepared this force for the purpose of attacking the harbor the moment our fleet leaves it. The enemy, however, may be determined to make the attack at all hazards, as the object to them is of immense importance, and I am sorry to say that our force is but little adapted to the defence of this place. There are not a thousand effective men here besides the sailors and marines. General Gaines arrived here yesterday and assumed the command, and we shall endeavor to defend the place as long as we can with the means we possess.

We launched the other brig yesterday, which I have called the *Jones*, but I am sorry to say that I have neither men or guns for her, and from the present state of the roads but little prospect of getting them soon. I received 21 men a few days since from New York. They were eight days getting from Utica to this place, a distance of about 80 or 90 miles.

From Lieut. General Drummond to Earl Bathurst.

No. 8.　　　　　　　　Kingston, Upper Canada, 12th April, 1814.

My Lord,—

With the circumstance of the printing press belonging to this Province having been destroyed at York in the month of April of the last year, Your Lordship has been made acquainted by my predecessors.

The inconvenience which the public service has since experienced in consequence has been much felt. To obviate this inconvenience in future, I gave directions for the purchase of a press in Lower Canada, but was sorry to find that one could not be procured there.

Learning since that an old one might be obtained at Ogdensburg, a village on the enemy's side of the Saint Lawrence, opposite the port of Prescott, at the low price of eighty-four pounds seven shillings and six pence, I have authorized the purchase of it, which I trust will be approved.

This press being very small and far from complete, the type nearly worn out, can only be expected to be useful until a proper one can be obtained, which I have to request that Your Lordship may be pleased to cause to be sent out as early as possible, addressed to the officer administering this Government to the care of the Commissary General at Quebec.

(Canadian Archives, G. 474.)

Memo. by Captain R. H. Barclay, R. N.

Memo. for His Excellency, as to those Provincial officers who served under my command on Lake Erie, and whose merit deserves his patronage and protection.

Lieut. Rolette in a peculiar manner for his very zealous and able services on all occasions, and his wounds, not only received in the action of the 10th Septr. but before that period. I had promised, (if I had been successful on Lake Erie,) on the arrival of a sufficient number of officers to enable me to dispense with his services to have given a place of the best kind in my power in the dockyard and to recommend him strongly to be confirmed to it.

Mr. Richardson, who served with me as surgeon, is also a most deserving man, he having done everything in his power for the good of H. M. service, although had it not been for that conviction he would have left the Provincial service as interfering with his occupations, particularly as one of the sheriffs of the district.

His health will not admit of his serving afloat, as he is always sick. His absence from his home at the period of the retreat of the army from Amherstburg no doubt militated much against the removal of any of his property, which must be severely felt by him on account of his large family.

Nothing can surpass the merits of Lieut. Irvine. As far as I was able I did justice to him in my official letter. Such a situation as is consistent with his present rank, or that which may be given him as a reward for his meritorious conduct, will be, independent of those claims he may have, conferring a great obligation on myself.

2d Lieuts. Sinclair and Patterson, the former of whom is a prisoner and the other has a place in Kingston dockyard, I mention as very deserving men.

Mr. Campbell, mid., who commanded the Chippaway, deserves every praise and countenance.

I should have begun with Mr. Purvis did I not understand that he has an ensigncy in the 8th Regt.

R. H. BARCLAY,
Apr. 12th, 1814.   Comr. R. N.

(Canadian Archives, C. 732, pp. 124-7.)

From Sir James Yeo to Sir George Prevost.

DEAR SIR,—

I will answer Your Excellency's other despatches by the next express, but it does not require a moment's deliberation to most respectfully coincide with Your Excellency as to the almost impossibility of bringing up the ships in frame. I also agree with Your Excellency as to sending one of the brigs to Isle aux Noix and am of opinion in the meantime Captain Pring ought to strengthen his force by building two or three fine gun boats.

Dockyard, 13th April, 1814.

(Canadian Archives, C. 732, pp. 133-4.)

Captain Richard O'Conor, R. N., to Noah Freer.

Naval Yard, KINGSTON, April 12, 1814.

MY DEAR SIR,—
In reply to your letter of the 7th inst. I have to acquaint you, for the information of His Excellency, that the two ships now *complete*, together with three heavy gun boats, will be launched on the 15th inst. and the exact state of forwardness of the large vessel now in hand is as follows, viz.: Moulds made, keel laid, stem and stern nearly finished, dead wood made, four frames made and timber finished for ten frames.

(Canadian Archives, C. 732, p. 123.)

Major J. B. Glegg to Captain W. H. Merritt.

STAMFORD, 12th April, 1814.

DEAR MERRITT,—
This is the last communication you will receive from me from this station as you must consider the headquarters as established at Fort George to-morrow morning, therefore act accordingly and direct all despatches to be taken to the quarters formerly occupied by Mr. Coffin. I shall order your two dragoons from this place to Fort George, where it will be necessary that you make arrangements for their forage, &c. Perhaps you will meet me there on Thursday or Friday next. My quarters will be near the General's, where Mr. Mc-Donell, paymaster of militia, used to live. I heard from Major Maule that two of the 19th are left by some mistake at Stoney Creek, and these belonging to the Dover troop. You must take immediate measures for their relief by ordering two men there from the 12. I write by this express to this effect to Major Maule. I wish I could find civilians but it is not possible. I enclose a very *fashionable billet doux* which was overlooked this morning.

We have great news from Europe. A tremendous battle was fought about the end of January between the Allies and French quite in the interior of France. Bonaparte commanded in person, and he says had it not been for the *barbarous Cossacks*, (Russian or rather Tartarian Light Horse,) he should *have gained* the victory. . .
This is the French account, therefore from it we expect a very glorious account from the Allies. I have no doubt the victory was most decisive. The Americans have made a fourth desperate attempt to invade the Lower Province (on the 30th ulto.,) under General Wilkinson, and have experienced, as before, defeat and *disgrace*. Genl. *Vincent* is complimented for his able arrangements. Our loss is but trifling, 10 killed and about 40 wounded. Of the latter are two officers.

(Merritt MSS.)

Memorandum by Lieut. Colonel Clegg.

Head Qrs. established at Fort George 13th April; a heavy fall of snow and hard frost on the 14th; 15th, 6 a. m., H. M. schooner *Netley* arrived, having left Kingston on the morning of the 14th. Came in her the 103rd grenadier company and guns for the fort.

(From a field note book in possession of Lieut. Col. Turner, Reading.)

Sir James Lucas Yeo to Sir George Prevost.

KINGSTON, U. CANADA, 13th April, 1814.

SIR,—

I have the honor to acknowledge the receipt of Your Excelleney's letter of the 7th inst. requesting my opinion respecting an overture for an armistice offered by the American Government, together with the information recently obtained from a person from Sackett's Harbor, which Your Excellency is disposed to consider as correct, which you wish me to compare with my former statement to you, (I perceive it corroborates the statement,) and which you wish should assist my judgment in the answer I am about to give.

After the most deliberate consideration I am of opinion that as far as relates to naval operations it is by no means certain that the enemy will have the advantage at the commencement of the campaign, and the reinforcement of seamen and supply of stores which His Majesty's Government mean so frequently to assist us with, will, I have no doubt, enable us to acquire the ascendency on the lake.

The third ship now building is, I believe, of far greater force than any the enemy can launch at Sackett's Harbor, and doubts have arisen as to the practicability of launching the large ship now ready, as will appear by the accompanying deposition of the carpenter of the *Madison*. But even admitting the enemy are able to launch their large ship and have received the whole of their guns and stores, (of which I entertain a doubt,) we never have been so competent to engage them with a reasonable prospect of success as at present. For although the enemy have a greater number of guns of heavy calibre, yet my having two ships of such effective strength as the *Prince Regent* and the *Princess Charlotte* closely to support each other, may give me an advantage in the early part of the action which I feel confident the talents of the officers and the spirits of the men under my command would immediately avail themselves of. I perceive two of the enemy's new vessels are brigs, and however formidable they may be as to *weight* of *metal* should any accident befall their gaff or main boom they become for the time unmanageable. Brigs have never been esteemed so effective as ships in battle. In short, Sir, I am fully persuaded that with the means I now possess with those the Government mean to place at my disposal, I shall be able either to bring Chauncey to a decisive action, or should I find him too superior, (for I cannot rely on his strength until I see his squadron,) manœuvre with him until the third ship is ready, and which vessel I look upon to be of a description to look down all opposition. In the interim of this ship being ready, the reinforcements of seamen can be placed in heavy gunboats that may effectively assist me during the calms at the commencement of the season.

These considerations induce me to be decidedly of opinion that were Your Excellency to accept of the proposed armistice it would neither conduce to the credit of His Majesty's Government or the honor of his arms, while it would enable the enemy to gain time for launching and equipping more ships, augmenting and concentrating his forces and bringing them to bear, (should a rupture of the armistice come, a measure I fear from the known enmity and insincerity of the American Government too likely too occur,) with redoubled force against us.

(Canadian Archives, C. 683, p. 19.)

From a Journal of a Survey of Talbot Road West by Mahlon Burwell.

18th September, 1816.

I passed the place in front of lot No. 177, Tilbury East, where Major Holmes of the United States Army had encamped a day or two when on their intended expedition against Port Talbot in the time of the late war. I find here, as well as upon every other occasion when they remained all night in our woods, they felled large trees flat to the ground all round their encampment to serve as a breastwork in the event of an attack. Two field pieces and ammunition waggons were left here by Major Holmes, which were destroyed by the Loyal Essex Rangers. The carriages were burnt and the guns and ammunition were carried back and deposited in a black ash swamp, where they remained until the treaty of peace.

Proclamation.

By Lieutenant General Gordon Drummond, commanding His Majesty's forces in the Province of Upper Canada, &c., &c., &c.:

A PROCLAMATION.

Whereas it is found necessary for the public safety that the most efficacious means should be used for supplying His Majesty's troops stationed in the Province with provisions and forage, which, though abounding in the Province, are withheld from the Commissariat and their agents, notwithstanding the most liberal prices have been offered for the same, I do therefore hereby declare that so far as relates to the procuring of provisions and forage for the said troops martial law shall be in force throughout the Province, and the same is hereby declared to be in force therein and ordered to be acted upon accordingly.

Given under my hand and seal at Kingston this twelfth day of April, one thousand eight hundred and fourteen.

GORDON DRUMMOND, Lt. General.

(MSS. of G. M. Jarvis, Ottawa.)

Lieut. General Drummond to Sir George Prevost.

KINGSTON, April 13th, 1814.

SIR,—

I have the honor to acknowledge the receipt of Your Excellency's despatches by Captain Tasché of the militia.

I avail myself of this opportunity to acquaint Your Excellency that Major General Riall has taken measures for levelling and destroying the batteries of the enemy which still existed in the neighborhood of Fort Niagara, one of them in particular being a very heavy work, immediately opposite to Fort George, required a considerable degree of labor and time. The quantities of ice which have come down the Niagara River have been so great as to cut off all communication with the opposite shore for some days.

But the Major General hopes in the course of a week to have the Missassaga battery so far advanced as to mount four guns.

He had directed Major Deane to fall back to Burford, having the Rangers in advance at Campfield's house, as the roads from Oxford are at present so excessively bad that should the enemy land at Long Point they could with ease arrive at the Grand River before Major Deane and cut off his passage of that river.

The Major General also states to me that Lieutenant Marsh of the Marine Artillery has been acting as assistant engineer at Fort Niagara from his arrival there, and, Colonel Young reports, with the greatest assiduity, so much so in fact that were it not for him nothing whatever would have been done. I request therefore that Your Excellency will be pleased to confirm the appointment of Lieutenant Marsh from the date of his arrival, with the usual pay and allowances.

And as the Major General, from a representation from the senior engineer to him, has urged the necessity of an assistant engineer being appointed for Fort George and Missassaga batteries, and has submitted the name of Lieutenant Jenoway of the Royal Scots Regiment as fully qualified for the situation, I have the honor to recommend that officer to Your Excellency's consideration accordingly.

I am concerned to report to Your Excellency the desertion of nine men of the 100th Regiment from the working party in destroying the batteries of the enemy before mentioned. One of them has since returned and declares that he had been taken prisoner and made his escape, but his story is not credited.

The Shawanese Indians have elected the Prophet to be their war and Tecumseh's son their village chief. Thirty-five warriors with 90 women and children have arrived at Burlington from the River St. Clair. They report that vast numbers are awaiting our arrival at Detroit.

(Canadian Archives, C. 683, pp. 30-2.)

From John McGill to John Small.

YORK, 13th April, 1814.

SIR,—

I observe that your official note of the 6th instant, stating that His Honor the President in Council was pleased to order that directions should be given to all the public officers residing at York to remove their respective public papers at least one mile out of the said town of York before the 20th of the present month, is only addressed to me as Auditor General. Am I from this to conclude that it is not His Honor's orders that the books and bonds, &c., belonging to the Receiver General's office, nor those belonging to the Inspector General's office should be removed. If they are let me immediately know by a line, as the period for their removal is close at hand.

I have the honor to be, Sir, your most obt. ser.,
JOHN MCGILL,
Act'g Rec. Genl. and Insp. Genl.

John Small, Esq.,
    Clerk Executive Council.

Endorsed, "13 April, 1814, Honble. J. McGill, Act. R. Gl. and Auditor Genl., relative to ye order of 6 Apl. on the subject of ye Public Records."

From Lieut. General Drummond to Sir George Prevost.

KINGSTON, April 13th, 1814.

SIR,—

I have much pleasure in acquainting Your Excellency that Commodore Sir James Yeo proposes launching the two new ships to-morrow.

The harbour is perfectly free from ice and all the cther vessels are completely ready for sea. The *Wolfe*, the *Melville*, the *Sir Sydney* and the *Beresford* are lying in the offing, the remainder are only prevented getting out by contrary winds.

(Canadian Archives, C. 732, p. 132.)

Sir James Lucas Yeo to Hon. John Wilson Croker.

His Majesty's Ship *Prince Regent*,
No. 6.   KINGSTON, in UPPER CANADA, 15th April, 1814.

SIR,—

I have the heartfelt satisfaction to announce to you for the information of the Lords Commissioners of the Admiralty that His Majesty's frigates *Prince Regent* of fifty-eight and the *Princess Charlotte* of thirty-six guns were launched in safety at this yard yesterday evening.

The *Rogal George* has been hove down and repaired ; the *Moira* and *Sir Sidney Smith* cut down to improve their sailing and the whole squadron put in an efficient state, and I hope to have all ready to take the lake by the 25th or 30th inst.

(Canadian Archives, M. 389-6.)

Lieut. General Drummond to Sir George Prevost.

KINGSTON, April 15th, 1814.

SIR,—

I have the honor to acquaint Your Excellency that in compliance with my request Commodore Sir James Yeo directed His Majesty's schooner *Beresford* to receive on board such detachment of troops as she could accommodate for a passage to the Head of the Lake. That vessel in consequence sailed yesterday morning from hence with a leading wind for Niagara with the grenadier company of the 103rd Regiment and a detachment of rocketteers, with a supply of rockets and an 18 pounder.

I have peculiar satisfaction in communicating to Your Excellency that the two new ships, (the *Prince Regent* and *Princess Charlotte*,) were launched yesterday in a very superior style without any accident occurring. The Commodore thinks they will be fit for sea in the course of ten days, but I cannot imagine until about the first of the ensuing month.

(Canadian Archives, C. 683, pp. 25-6.)

The Information of William Tapley.

Home District.   Information of William Tapley, late an artificer
York.   employed in His Majesty's service, now residing in the town of York, taken before me, Thomas Ridout, Esqr., one of His Majesty's Justices assigned to keep the peace in the said District, who, being duly sworn, deposeth and saith that he lodges in the house of Osborne Cox, innkeeper, in the said town, and that yesterday, the 23rd of the present month of April, in the forenoon, a certain Jacob Fraser came to the said house and said he was of the people who had brought up the guns from Smith's Creek and that he was paid a dollar a day. From the language and behavior of the said Jacob Fraser, the deponent was led to expect that he, the said Jacob Fraser, was attached to the Government of the United States, (and) the said deponent pretended to be so too and said that he had been taken up as a spy and to be now under the custody of the constable, Osborne Cox, whereupon the said Jacob Fraser advised deponent to endeavor to escape and then wrote down and gave him the names of several persons residing between York and the Bay of Quinty, at whose homes he might call as friends to the United States, and whose names are on the annexed paper "A" written by the said Jacob Fraser, viz.: Mr. Farrell, Mr. Cornell, James Ash, Mr. John Burk, Jonathan Bedford, J. Tucker, Mr. Stafford, Gershom Tucker.

He, the said Jacob Fraser, further informed the deponent that the above named persons had formed themselves into a club and called themselves the Loyal Club, meaning loyal to the United States, that a boat was building which would take him, the deponent, to the United States, but concerning which the deponent would make further enquiry at the above named Mr. Stafford's. The said Jacob Fraser also informed the deponent that he, the said Jacob Fraser, had been up as far as Newmarket, (in the the township of Whitchurch,) and that he knew the boys who had hoisted the flag of liberty, that there were a thousand of such boys in the country who were armed with rifles, pistols and muskets, secured in different places and were ready to assist the Americans as soon as requisite. Jacob Fraser further informed deponent that he had been at Montreal, came up from there to Kingston and that his business was to see who were loyal or fit members for their club.

(Sgd.) William X Tapley.
His
Mark

Sworn before me at York this twenty-fourth day of April, 1814.
Thos. Ridout, J. P.

(Powell Papers, Toronto Public Library.)

Assistant Commissary James Gordon to Captain W. H. Merritt.

Sunday, Apr. 17th.

. . . I have received 29 steel scabbard swords and 29 marine pistols for you by the *Beresford* schooner, which came in on Friday ev'g; left Kingston the day before; she brought a parcel of 32 and —— pr. rockets with men to use them and signals for this coast—reports that the new ships were launched on Friday last, 3 o'clock. Our fleet to be out in 8 days and Yankee about the same time. One of their vessels mounts 42 pr. long guns and 68 pr. carronades.

(Merritt MSS.)

From A. C. Burke, Late Lieutenant in the 100th Regiment, to Brevet Major Davies.

Beauport, 15th December, 1814.

Dear Sir,—

In answer to your letter requesting me to detail on paper the surprise of the fortress of Niagara under Colonel Murray, I have to state and affirm that I was one of the subalterns of your company at that affair, where you were the third in seniority; that soon after Colonel Murray was wounded and taken off to be dressed, the enemy still keeping up a heavy and galling fire from the southern stone tower, near the magazine, from the six pounder on the top and through two tiers of loopholes below, I heard you suggest to Lt. Colonel Hamilton, the second in command, the absolute necessity of storming it before daylight, lest the enemy should discover where to throw their shots with more effect, &c., and you volunteered your service to do so, which, being assented to, you with your party, (principally men of your own company,) gave the signal to advance, saying, "Follow me, my boys," upon which we rushed forward in despite of the fire to the barricaded entrance door, which was battered in with sledges and large billets of wood. Upon our entering, the enemy who were firing through the loopholes below, (except such as were killed or taken prisoners,) ran to join those above and we pursued. Some of our men, according to your previous instructions to them, carrying large firebrands from which they blew immense sparks and flashes, by the light of which we in some measure found our way to and up the narrow intricate staircase. From your skilful directions and judicious orders, the persevering resolution of the party and the stratagem, threats that nothing but unconditional surrender could save them from instant destruction, the enemy cried for mercy and were made prisoners to the number of sixty-four, more than double the assailants, Lieut. Nowlan and one private only of ours being killed in the tower. Some hundreds of loaded firelocks and a large quantity of cartridges found in this building having been secured; you placed Lieut. Fortune and myself on guard over the prisoners and went to report the circumstances. This took place about an hour before daylight.

(Canadian Archives, C. 1017, p. 72.)

From Colonel John Murray to Colonel Baynes.

MONTREAL, 17th April, 1814.

SIR,—

Brevet Major Davies, 100th Regt., having expressed to me his chagrin at his name not being noticed in the General Order issued on the taking of Fort Niagara, which he attributes to the supposition of his name being left out in my despatch, whereby his services have been passed over while those of inferior officers whose conduct had been less conspicuous were particularly extolled, I considered it my duty to rectify the omission as far as lays in my power by now making known to the Commander of the Forces the services of Brevet Major Davies, which I cannot better perform than by copying an extract from the Major's letter to me, which I have to request you will do me the honor to lay before His Excellency. At the same time I beg leave to accompany it with my testimony and warm commendation of the services of Brevet Major Davies in the affair of the 19th December, and particularly in the spirited assault of his company of one of the blockhouses. I hereby add the latter part of the extract on the supposition that it was the Major's wish that I should do so:

"I consider myself particularly neglected in his, (Lt. Col. Hamilton,) having omitted mentioning to you, (prior to your sending off your despatch of the capture of Fort Niagara,) the circumstance of myself and my company having charged and taken the southern blockhouse, in which were 65 of the enemy, whose incessant tho' random fire killed two and wounded one of my division, and I am persuaded that had not the blockhouse been carried previous to the return of daylight, the enemy would have committed great destruction in our column. The method I took to effect this operation was by advancing with an American prisoner, (threatening him with instant death in default of guiding me to the inner stairs,) and sheltering my men behind the corner of the large store until I judged by what I saw and heard that the enemy were in the act of loading: taking advantage of that moment I gave the signal to run at and force the lower door, which, fortunately we found partly broke open, and in a few minutes we effected an entrance, upon which the enemy, who were firing from the loopholes below, ran to join those above. We pursued them, some of my men, agreeable to my instructions, carrying large firebrands, from which they blew sparks and flashes, by the light of which we in some measure found our way up the intricate stairs, others calling out for ladders to scale the outside. I called out to bayonet the whole, &c., &c., which I suppose so terrified the enemy that they called for mercy and surrendered to the number of 64, only one man being killed. Colonel Hamilton, I must allow, could not have known anything of this except my taking the prisoners along with us by his consent, but I humbly conceive that as commanding officer, after you were wounded, it was his duty to have enquired the particulars and to have made them known to you, especially as it was by his sanction that I, with the 4th Company, attacked the said blockhouse and reported to him the capture of it with the surrender of the 64 prisoners. He could easily have learnt this from two other officers and any of the men of my company present, about thirty-three in number. Fear of being thought an egotist and motives of delicacy hindered me from acquainting you myself the same morning, neither should I at this distant period but for reasons it may be unnecessary for me to explain in this letter, for withal I consider I only did my duty on the occasion, yet I flatter myself that my name should have appeared in your despatch had you in time become informed of the particulars, which I have in part here detailed. Now, Sir, I beg that you will be pleased to take some opportunity of acquainting His Excellency Sir George Prevost personally with the circumstances, that it may operate in favor of my pretensions to promotion in this country, which seniority of rank as a major in the army entitle me to hope for. At present I am the senior and I believe the only major, (one much junior excepted,) who is not provided for by separate command or staff appointments."

I must in justice to Lt. Col. Hamilton add that as soon as he had an opportunity he did report to me the conduct of Brevet Major Davies and his company as one of the most dashing attacks of the morning. From the darkness of the night I could not ascertain who was the particular officer that attacked the blockhouse, and Col. Hamilton's report was too late for me to notice Major Davies in my despatch.

(Canadian Archives, C. 683, pp. 34-9.)

From Lieut. Colonel Hamilton to Brevet Major Davies, 100th Regt.

YORK, 27th November, 1814.

DEAR MAJOR,—

With great pleasure I comply with your desire and bear testimony to your good conduct at the assault of Fort Niagara, when you with great spirit obeyed an order of mine to take possession of the stone tower near the magazine with your company.

I am unacquainted with what difficulties you encountered in performing that service but recollect your reporting to me that you made 64 prisoners in the tower.

(Canadian Archives, C. 1017, p. 71.)

Lieut. General Drummond to Sir George Prevost.

KINGSTON, 19th April, 1814.

SIR,—

I have the honor to acquaint Your Excellency that Major General Riall has reported to me his having been requested to attend a Grand Council of the Indians at the Head of the Lake. The Prophet has been chosen the principal chief of all the Western nations. His having been presented with the sword and pistols from His Royal Highness the Prince Regent gave very general satisfaction. He has promised the most cordial co-operation and says their smallest boys shall be ready to march at a moment's notice.

I am much concerned to communicate to Your Excellency that the Major General states that three of the Six Nations, speaking through their principal chief, have requested the Major General to represent to Your Excellency their dissatisfaction at the appointment of Captain Norton to be their leader. They say they will not acknowledge him as such, will pay him no respect or obedience nor look to him for anything they want; that they know him not except as a disturber of the peace and harmony that ought to exist among them; they have a head man whom the King has appointed and they want no other, (Col. Claus); the representation made to Col. Drummond was the contrivance of a few who had no authority to do so, and it was not the opinion of the Nations. The Major General enquired if such was the general opinion. The chiefs of three, viz.:

The Mohawks, Oneidas and Tuscaroras said it was theirs decidedly; the others, viz.: the Cayugas, Onondagas and Senecas refused to answer.

(Canadian Archives, C. 257, p. 253.)

From Sir J. C. Sherbrooke to Noah Freer.

HALIFAX, 19 April, 1814.

SIR,—

I have the honor to report for the information of His Excellency the Commander of the Forces that Lt. Colonel Robertson with the detachment of the 2nd Battn., 8th (or King's) Regiment, with the women, children and baggage belonging to that corps, arrived here last evening.

The *Lord Somers* transport on which they were embarked separated from the convoy in a fog and was attacked a few leagues off the Halifax lighthouse by an American privateer schooner, which they resisted in a gallant manner and beat off, having sustained, I am sorry to say, a loss of one seaman killed and two wounded, Capt. James Agnew of the 8th slightly, nine privates of that corps severely and three slightly wounded.

Lt. Colonel Robertson having come in the *Manly* sloop of war, Major Phillot of the Royal Artillery was the senior officer on board the transport and he speaks very highly of the steadiness of the detacht. of the 8th on the occasion.

The *Rifleman* sloop of war is gone in pursuit of the privateer and as soon as she returns it is the intention of the Admiral that she shall convoy the vessels now about to sail for Quebec.

I propose sending fifty thousand pounds in specie by her for the service under His Excellency's command.

The guns and equipment required by Commodore Sir James Yeo, a quantity of flour for the Commissary General, the company of Royal Artillery ordered by the Commander of the Forces, the exchanged prisoners of war belonging to the Regts. in Canada and the detachment of the 8th Regt. will sail under convoy of the *Rifleman*, I hope, by the latter end of this or the beginning of the ensuing week.

I have yet rec'd no intelligence of the arrival of the 90th Regiment at Bermuda, but as I wrote to the Admiral immediately on receiving His Excellency's commands to send that corps to Canada, instead of the 98th, requesting him to forward them direct to Quebec, I am willing to hope they have arrived there by the time you have received this.

Had His Excellency, however, continued in his original intention of having the 98th Regt. sent to Quebec, they could not have been sent until the arrival of the other corps at this port, for want of transport, there being at the present scarcely sufficient tonnage of that description in the harbor to convey the troops and stores now going.

(Canadian Archives, C. 834, pp. 5-7.)

From Sir George Prevost to Lieut. General Drummond.

Hd. Qrs., MONTREAL, 20th April, 1814.

SIR,—

I have had the honor to receive your letter of the 12th inst., reporting your having deemed it expedient to issue a proclamation declaratory of martial law as far as relates to the procuring of provisions and forage in Upper Canada, in consequence of the impossibility of obtaining supplies without resorting to that measure.

The circumstances which have compelled you to resort to that measure were a sufficient justification in my estimation, and I can assure you I feel no desire to shrink from any responsibility on the occasion that you may be desirous I should assume, convinced that you were impelled to adopt it for the good of His Majesty's service and the preservation of the Province committed to your charge. However, it is proper that I should state to you that the legal advice I have obtained respecting martial law, for the subject has been frequently discussed, has uniformly been that I could only proclaim its existence by virtue of the King's commission to me as Governor General in the Province in which I might be at the time it became necessary to do so. Major General Sir Isaac Brock, when exactly in your situation, informed me he should be under the absolute necessity of proclaiming martial law. I reported the circumstance to His Majesty's Government and received in reply an unqualified approval of the measure. When I was in Upper Canada I gave authority to the general officers in command at Detroit and Niagara to do so in their respective districts whenever the emergencies of the service should render it an indispensable act for the preservation of their command or the subsistence of the troops, but when I withdrew to the Lower Province I considered my power to have ceased, therefore when M. Genl. de Rottenburg took the command and was under the necessity of declaring martial law he modified its operation, but he did it as administrator of the government, and in that capacity alone during the existence of a civil government do I apprehend it might be done.

(Canadian Archives, C. 1222, pp. 103-5.)

From Sir George Prevost to Lieut. General Drummond.

Hd. Qrs., MONTREAL, 21st April, 1814.

SIR,—

I have had the honor to receive your letter of the 16th inst., and lose not a moment in replying to it.

As I feel satisfied with the explanation you have afforded me, I propose only to advert to some of the observations you have thought proper to annex to it, in order to remove from your mind apprehensions respecting the perfect confidence I repose in your zeal and talent.

I hope the letter which I addressed to you yesterday has convinced you I felt no desire to shrink from necessary and justifiable means, however they might add to my responsibility, and that I consider the present case to come under that denomination is unquestionable.

Your late letters were of a nature to induce me to believe the resorting to martial law was not in your contemplation.

I do not think it expedient to make any change in the limits of the military commands which have been established, as it was to be presumed, that more accurate information existed at headquarters respecting the state of things at the French Mills and in the Salmon River than could be obtained at Kingston, and as General Wilkinson's army was in motion at the time the order was sent to Colonel Morrison, I confess its unconditional tenor struck me as highly improper.

Having replied to your remarks with that candor and frankness which should characterize the correspondence of soldiers, I trust you will again feel possessed of my entire confidence and ready support. I can assure you there is at this moment in Upper Canada a much larger proportion of British soldiers than were ever in it before. It does not appear to be the intention of Government to add to my force beyond the 90th Regt., announced last autumn as ordered from the West Indies to Quebec. The 49th Regt. is completely worn out. The 2nd Battn. of the King's is under 400. The first corps must be sent to Quebec and the latter brought forward in its stead. 24 bateaux with stores and provisions proceeded yesterday from Lachine to Kingston. A Commissariat officer is under orders to proceed to your Head Qrs. with £10,000 for the army in Eagles and Half Eagles.

P. S.—The Bill for the repeal of the embargo laws has passed in the House of Representatives. The majority in its favor was much larger than expected. Great inconvenience is experienced by the American Government in consequence of the scarcity of specie in the United States.

(Canadian Archives, C. 1222, pp. 105-7.)

From Sir James Yeo to Sir George Prevost.

His Majesty's Ship *Prince Regent*,
KINGSTON, 22nd April, 1814.

SIR,—I have the honor to acknowledge the receipt of Your Excellency's letter of the 6th instant, together with the copies and extracts of letters from the Secretary of State, making known the intention of His Majesty's Government to convey immediately to this country the frames of two fir 32 gun frigates and two brigs, each to carry 20 guns, for the service of the lakes. The plans of the vessels proposed, with the schemes of scantling for building them and the lists of timber to be provided in this country, have also come to hand.

I perfectly agree with Your Excellency that the impediments to this scheme are numerous and very difficult to be overcome, if not (under existing circumstances) wholly impracticable. The timber to be provided here can be procured but the time that would elapse 'ere the frames could be transported, considering the immense supplies Your Excellency must also send for the subsistence of the troops and seamen, would be so long that the third ship, equal in force to three or four of such frigates, would be built, equipt and on the lake 'ere the frames of the two fir ships could be sent up. That the enemy would permit such immense convoys to pass unmolested cannot be supposed, and the large escorts which must consequently accompany them would weaken Your Excellency's force in those points where they might be more essentially useful. But what in my opinion should chiefly influence Your Excellency's decision respecting them is that the strength of the third ship, now building, is such as to give us a reasonable hope that their being sent up is unnecessary.

I wish much that one of the brigs could be made serviceable on Lake Champlain, though I fear from their drawing 15 feet of water there is little hope of it. I have directed Captain Pring to ascertain with precision whether a vessel of that draft can navigate there in safety and his report shall be communicated to Your Excellency.

With respect to transporting the frames in the winter season, I see equal objections arise, for should the war continue the additional ordnance and iron work, which we cannot do without, would employ all the sleighs, horses and oxen during the season, and on the whole I am fully of opinion that building here is more beneficial to the public service, not to say a word of the enormous expense that will be saved thereby.

(Canadian Archives, C. 732, pp. 139-42.)

From Lieut. General Drummond to Sir George Prevost.

KINGSTON, April 23rd, 1814.

SIR,—

In reference to a paragraph in Mr. Freer's letter to me of the 19th inst., wherein he states it to be Your Excellency's intention to write fully on the subject of the employment to be made of the two new ships lately launched here, I have the honor to transmit a copy of a communication, marked most secret and confidential, which I directed to be addressed to Commodore Sir James Yeo on the 9th instant, to the end that I may countermand or withdraw the whole or such part thereof as Your Excellency may not consider as sufficiently coinciding with your wishes.

(Canadian Archives, C. 732, pp. 145-6.)

From Sir George Prevost to Lieut. General Drummond.

Hd. Qrs., MONTREAL, 23rd April, 1814.

Confidential.

SIR,—

I have had the honor to receive your letters of the 15th inst. reporting the departure of H. M. schooner *Beresford* for the Head of the Lake with the grenadiers of the 103rd Regt., a proportion of rocketteers and supply of ordnance stores on board, and also that the two new ships were launched on the 11th inst. without any accident occurring. You therein further express an opinion that they would be ready for sea about the 1st May. Presuming that the recent addition to our squadron on Lake Ontario has established the naval ascendency, it becomes expedient you should obtain accurate information of the state of the enemy's fleet at Sackett's Harbor in order to decide whether a combined attack on it offers a reasonable prospect of success. I am induced to urge the serious consideration of this measure because, if the enemy are left undisturbed to prosecute their plans, the vastly superior resources they possess for ship building and in procuring seamen must terminate in their acquiring a superior naval force at no very distant period, and once in possession of that advantage it will not be possible to guard a very extended frontier from insult. The destruction of the American naval force on Lake Ontario would effectually cause all hostile operations in that quarter to cease, while it would afford many facilities to our own.

The enemy's squadron at Sackett's Harbor once destroyed ulterior operations for the support of the Niagara Frontier or recovery of the Western district would be most naturally promoted, and sufficient means would become disposable without the safety of Kingston being risked, which port, from its great importance, must now claim your vigilant attention whilst the enemy possess a naval force at Sackett's Harbor.

A project for a combined attack upon Sackett's Harbor for the destruction of the American fleet is herewith transmitted for your consideration, and I have to request you will favor me with observations upon those points after having consulted with Sir James Yeo, as may apply to them.

It is proper I should inform you that the plan was formed upon correct intelligence obtained of the actual state of things in October last at Sackett's Harbor, assisted by the personal knowledge of the place acquired by the writer. The changes which may have occurred it will be your duty to ascertain.

M. Genl. De Rottenburg informs me he gave over to you a manuscript sketch of Sackett's Harbor and the country in its immediate vicinity. I sent it to him on account of its being as correct a design as the eye unassisted could give, and a reference to it will elucidate the suggestions.

Experience has proved that a surprise is not practicable, therefore a strict blockade should precede your operations.

From the squadron you will require, and I make no doubt receive, the most cordial co-operation in the enterprise, as its fate will depend on the promtitude of its execution, as well as on the energy and judgment displayed in the previous arrangements.

It is difficult to foretell the next offensive measure of the enemy, as their policy has become notoriously miserably shallow since the intelligence of the great and glorious events which have occurred in Europe arrived at Washington, but if a flow of enterprise is rekindled and a descent on Long Point should be combined with an attack on Fort Niagara, it appears to me advisable that Major General Riall should concentrate his force between Chippawa and Fort George in order to crush the enemy marching upon Burlington.

You will decide under what circumstances of danger Niagara (should) be blown to the moon.

Canadian Archives, C. 1222, pp. 107-10.)

Earl Bathurst to Sir George Prevost.

Downing Street, 24th April, 1814.

SIR,—
I take the earliest opportunity of acquainting you that His Majesty's Government have not failed to avail themselves of the present favorable state of affairs in Europe to order reinforcements,

both of infantry and artillery, for the army under your command to proceed to Quebec as soon as they can be collected from the different quarters in which their services have hitherto been required.

(Canadian Archives, C. 683, p. 24.)

Lieut. Charles Ingersoll to Captain W. H. Merritt.

YEIGH'S, BURFORD, 20th April, 1814.

MY DEAR SIR,—

I am sorry to report to you that Henry Young deserted last night from Oxford down the river with his horse and all his appointments. He got so far down before I rec'd intelligence of it that it was impossible for me to overtake him. Westbrook came up the same evening and made Major Tewsley prisoner. He left his compliments for Captain Caldwell, saying that in a short time he would visit Oxford again with a party of Indians. You will only have to return for myself, Doan, Yocum and Lambert, as the remainder of the party I brought with me are furnished by the commissariat. Enclosed you have my weekly report.

(Merritt MSS.)

President's Office, KINGSTON, 20th April, 1814.

His Honor the President has been pleased to appoint the undermentioned gentlemen to be Commissioners for the districts opposite their respective names for carrying into effect the provisions of an act passed in the late session of the Provincial Legislature, entitled an act for granting to His Majesty a certain sum of money out of the funds applicable to the uses of this Province, to defray the expenses of amending and repairing the public highways and roads and building bridges in the several districts thereof, viz.:

The Rev. Alex'r McDonell and Thomas Mears, Esquire, for the Eastern; Joel Stone, Esquire, for the Johnstown; the Honorable Richard Cartwright for the Midland; David McGregor Rogers, Esq., for the Newcastle; Samuel Smith, Esq., for the Home; Samuel Hatt, Esq., for the Niagara; and Thomas Talbot, Esq., for the London District.

Militia General Orders.

Headquarters, KINGSTON, April 24th, 1814.

His Honor the President has much satisfaction in announcing to the militia of Upper Canada that His Excellency the Governor in Chief has been pleased to sanction and confirm, on the 18th instant, articles entered into by Colonel Baynes, Adjutant General of the British forces, and Brigadier General Winder of the United States army, for the mutual release of all prisoners of war or others, with the exception of the 46 American officers held in retaliation as hostages for the 23 British soldiers confined by the United States Government as hostages for the 23 British born subjects taken from the ranks of the enemy and sent to England for legal trial.

And as by the before mentioned convention all officers, non-commissioned officers and soldiers of the militia, and all other persons (with the exception of the hostages already alluded to) who may have been made prisoners of war and are at present on parole are to be released from their obligations on the 15th of the ensuing month, (May,) they are to be considered liable to be called on for militia duties from that date.

Every officer, non-commissioned officer and soldier will therefore report himself without delay to the colonel or commanding officer of the regiment of the county wherein he at present resides, who will transmit a return of the same to the Adjutant General's office, specifying when and where each person was made prisoner, to what regiment or department such person belonged and on what particular service he was employed when so taken.

Such persons as belong to the Incorporated Militia or any public department will equally report themselves, and will also join their respective corps or departments on the 15th of May on pain of being treated as deserters.

By command of His Honor the President.

C. FOSTER,
Adj. Genl. of Militia, U. C.

Brig. General Alex. Macomb to Sir George Prevost.

SIR,—

The Government of the United States has appointed an officer of rank to meet such person as you may appoint on the part of the British Government to discuss and arrange an armistice. The village of Champlain is proposed as the place of conference. Should there be no objection to the spot the officer referred to will meet the person appointed by Your Excellency on the first day of May next.

(Canadian Archives, C. 683, p. 46.)

Proclamation.

PROVINCE OF UPPER CANADA.

Gordon Drummond, Esquire, President, administering the

Government of the Province of Upper Canada and Lieutenant General commanding His Majesty's force within the same.

To all to whom these presents shall come:

GREETING,—

Know ye that finding it at present expedient and necessary to prohibit the exportation of wheat and other corn or grain, meal, flour, beef and pork from this Province, I do hereby, under the authority of the several acts of the Parliament of this Province in force for that purpose, and by and with the advice and consent of His Majesty's Executive Council of this Province, prohibit the exportation of wheat and other corn or grain, meal, flour, beef and pork from this Province from the expiration of five days from the day of the date of this proclamation to the first day of November next ensuing.

And I do for that purpose by and with the advice and consent as aforesaid issue this my proclamation, declaring the provisions and restrictions of the said acts so far as they extend to prevent the exportation of wheat and other corn or grain, meal, flour, beef and pork from this Province to be in force from the time and for the period above mentioned. And I do hereby enjoin all Collectors of Customs, Inspectors, Sheriffs and their deputies to perform their duties strictly and faithfully in obedience to the said acts and this my proclamation.

In witness whereof I have hereunto set my hand and seal at arms at Kingston this twenty-sixth day of April in the year of our Lord one thousand eight hundred and fourteen and in the fifty-fourth year of His Majesty's reign.

WM. JARVIS, Secretary. GORDON DRUMMOND, President.

From Lieut. General Drummond to Sir George Prevost.

KINGSTON, April 26th, 1814.

SIR,—

I have the honor to acquaint Your Excellency that Commodore Sir James Yeo has represented to me that the ring bolts for the guns of the two new ships have never yet been received. Every enquiry has been made in this neighborhood about them but to no effect, and as it is wholly impossible for the squadron to leave harbor without this indispensably requisite part of their equipment, I take the liberty of suggesting to Your Excellency the propriety of the conductor or other person who had charge of these particular stores, being especially called upon to account for them, and that he be sent again upon the road he escorted them in search of them, accompanied at the same time by an officer of intelligence and suitable authority. I conceive the ships would be fit for sea by Sunday next provided the ring bolts were now here. Already three months' provisions have been taken in, yet the *Regent* is by means so deep in the water as necessary from want of proper ballast.

(Canadian Archives, C. 732, pp. 153-4.)

From the Military Secretary to Lieut. General Drummond.

Hd. Qrs., MONTREAL, 26th April, 1814.

(Extract.)

His Excellency regrets that the appointment of Captain Norton to be leader of the Six Nations has not met with approbation. Much dissatisfaction has always been shewn by some to Captain Norton and opposition has been raised against him. He trusts by a steady line of conduct he will be distinguished by his perseverance and usefulness and that he will prove himself worthy of the honor conferred upon him by the Comr. of the Forces, and that the Indians to which he is attached will still be reconciled to him.

With respect to Colonel Elliott, Superintendent of Indian affairs, I am directed to return to you the original papers which accompanied his memorial, and to inform you that His Excellency has recently granted to that officer an increase of £100 to his salary from the 28th June last, in consequence of his long and faithful services and the serious hardships to which he has been exposed.

(Canadian Archives, C. 1222, pp. 110-13.)

Sir George Prevost to Brig. eneral Macomb.

SIR,—

I have had the honor to receive your letter of the 25th inst., acquainting me that the Government of the U. S. has appointed an officer of rank to meet the person I should appoint on the part of the British Government to discuss and arrange an armistice, and that the village of Champlain is proposed as the place of conference. In reply I have the honor to inform you that an officer of rank of the British army will be sent to the place you have mentioned in the course of the first day of May.

(Canadian Archives, C. 683, p. 48.)

Lieut. General Drummond to Sir George Prevost.

KINGSTON, 27th April, 1814.

SIR,—

I have the honor to acknowledge the receipt of Your Excellency's letter of the 23rd instant, enclosing a plan of a combined attack proposed to be made on the enemy's fleet at Sackett's Harbor, to which I have given that serious attention which the great importance of the subject demands.

By my letter to Your Excellency of yesterday's date prior to the arrival of your despatches you will perceive that I have in a great measure anticipated Your Excellency's views with regard to the imperious necessity which exists for an immediate attempt to destroy the enemy's fleet, at the same time that I stated what I now beg leave to repeat, that in my opinion a force of not less than 4,000 effective troops would be essentially necessary to ensure a reasonable hope of success, as from the latest information I have been enabled to collect not only the defences have been much strengthened and multiplied by the erection of blockhouses, but the garrison does not consist of less than 1,800 regular troops with constant reinforcements of recruits, beside which there are between 1,500 and 2,000 seamen.

Previously to the receipt of Your Excellency's commands I had a communication with Sir James Yeo relative to the expediency of a combined attack on the enemy's fleet. I also, in compliance with your wishes, had this morning a conference with him on the same subject, when I submitted to him Your Excellency's letter and its accompanying document.

Sir James entirely coincides with me that the force to be brought against the place ought to be at least what I have before stated.

Enclosed I have the honor to lay before Your Excellency a statement of the force and means that I presume can be collected within my command, by which you will observe it is necessary a reinforcement should be sent from other quarters of the Province to make up the number specified.

In addition to the operation in agitation against Sackett's Harbor, I conceive that a successful attack on their great naval depot at Oswego would nearly, if not altogether, circumscribe the operations of the enemy, because, should we be so fortunate as to destroy the stores, &c., that are now collected there for the use of the fleet, it is very improbable they could show themselves on the lake for some time at least.

I propose giving Sir James Yeo an adequate number of troops to co-operate with him for the accomplishment of this desirable object as soon as the squadron can put to sea, if possible.

(Canadian Archives, C. 683, pp. 57-60.)

Copy of the Proceedings of a Committee of the Executive Council on the 27th of April, 1814, at the House of the Honorable John McGill in the Town of York.

PRESENT.

The Honble. Thomas Scott, Chief Justice, chairman.
The Honble. John McGill.
The Honble. Mr. Justice Powell.

Read the following letter:

President's Office, KINGSTON, 21st April, 1813.

SIR,—

His Honor the President judging it to be expedient and necessary to prohibit the exportation of provisions from this Province until the first day of November next, under the authority of the statute for that purpose, I am therefore directed by His Honor to signify his desire the same for the consideration and advice of the Executive Council.

I have, &c.,
(Signed)   ROBERT R. LORING,
Secretary.

John Small, Esq.,
Clerk of the Executive Council.

The President's Secretary having omitted to communicate the information and facts which may have induced His Honor's judgment on the expediency of the measure proposed, have no data for their consideration and therefore cannot advise it. But having entire confidence that His Honor possesses information and facts justifying the expediency of the measure, on the true ground of scarcity of provisions for the subsistence of the colony should any part be sent to a foreign market, the board cannot hesitate in such case to concur with His Honor in the necessary steps to secure subsistence, as well for the army as for the inhabitants.

(Signed)   THOS. SCOTT, Chairman.

A true copy.

JOHN SMALL,
Clerk of the Executive Council.

(Canadian Archives, C. 688, pp. 25-6.)

Lieut. General Drummond to Sir George Prevost.

KINGSTON, 28th April, 1814.

SIR,—

In addition to the statement I had the honor to address to Your Excellency in my letter of yesterday's date, I now beg leave to transmit some further observations on the subject of the proposed attack on Sackett's Harbor. It is sufficiently obvious that considerable time will be required to collect the troops necessary for the undertaking, that a vessel must be sent to Niagara to carry up the iron 24 prs. and bring down the brass ones, as these guns are indispensable; it is evident also that, taking for granted that 4,000 men is the least number with which the enterprise ought to be attempted, that at least 800 of them must come from the Lower Province: under all these circumstances and with a view to derive every advantage which may be possible from the interval which a reference to Your Excellency for your decision and aid has unavoidably occasioned, I propose that immediately after the squadron is ready to sail, which it is hoped will be in two days, (provided the ringbolts arrive,) Sir James Yeo shall proceed off Sackett's Harbor to reconnoitre the state of forwardness of the enemy's new ship, and from thence along the coast to Oswego, where it is reported there are large depots of provisions and naval stores, and what are of infinitely greater importance, some of the guns and other essential parts of the equipment of the new ship. Should Sir James, in co-operation with the force I intend embarking on board the fleet, be so fortunate as to seize or destroy the guns and stores and thereby retard the progress of this vessel the advantage to be derived from such a measure would be incalculable.

From Oswego Sir James can detach one of the brigs to Fort George and the Head of the Lake to take up the iron and bring down the brass guns, and with the assistance of the *Beresford* and *Vincent* schooners, which are already there, and such craft as can be collected, the detachments of regular and militia troops from York and the Indians from Burlington can be conveyed to Kingston or the point of rendezvous.

Without entering into the numerous reasons in favor of an immediate attack on Sackett's Harbor, it may be sufficient to observe that the exhausted state of this Province in respect to provisions will not admit of protracted operations. I will not say exactly how long our resources may hold out, but I am very apprehensive that at no very remote period difficulties the most serious and alarming in this respect will be felt by the Right Division.

Should the enemy therefore be suffered unmolested to complete his new vessel it is to be feared that he will then be enabled, occasionally at least, to interrupt the communication with Niagara and the Head of the Lake, by which alone the Division can be supported and fed.

(Canadian Archives, C. 683, pp. 61-4.)

Statement of the Force and Means which it is Assumed may be Collected in Upper Canada for the Attack on Sackett's Harbor.

TROOPS.

From the garrison of Kingston—
103rd Regiment, (the whole, grenadier company excepted).. 550
De Watteville's, (200 will remain in Kingston)........... 750
104th, (all fit for active field service)................... 250
Glengarry Light Infantry (do) 250
———1,800

From Prescott and Cornwall—
89th Regiment, (leaving about 100 in Prescott)....... ... 400

From York and Burlington—
41st Regiment (Volunteers)............................ 250
Incorporated Militia (do.) under Captain Robinson of the King's Regiment 150
——— 400

Indians from Burlington (Volunteers) 200
Add 2nd Battalion Royal Marines, (the whole).......... 400

Total regulars....................................... 3,000
Indians 200

NOTE—The militia to be called out at Kingston, Prescott and Cornwall during the absence of the regular troops.

ORDNANCE ON FIELD CARRIAGES.

From Kingston it is proposed to take the two twelve prs., the 5½ and 8 inch howitzers and perhaps one 6 pdr.

None of these pieces, however, except the large howitzer can be of much use against blockhouses. It is therefore proposed to bring down the two brass 24 pdrs. from Fort George, sending the iron guns in their place.

Troops and light artillery alone would be of no use whatever numbers employed. Heavy ordnance is indispensably necessary to the success of an attack on an enemy whose principal defence consists not in a breastwork, as assumed in the memorandum, but in a connected chain of blockhouses armed with guns of heavy calibre.

The two large mortars (or 68 pounder carronades) might be useful both against the blockhouses and shipping.

The rocket detachment under Lieutenant Stevens would also be capable of rendering very great service on shore, but it does not appear advisable to attempt to use the rockets, (Congreve,) from boats or other craft.

(Canadian Archives, C. 683, pp. 65-7.)

Sir George Prevost to Colonel Baynes.

Headquarters, LONGUEUIL, 29th April, 1814.

SIR,—

The Government of the United States appointed an officer of rank to meet such person as I may appoint on the part of the British Government, to discuss and arrange an armistice to the extent of my authority. I have selected you for this important duty in the presumption a suspension of arms is sought by the President of the United States, with a sincere desire of conciliation and in the firm belief the negotiation at Gottenburg will lead to a speedy and amicable adjustment of the differences existing between the two countries, and not merely for the purpose of obtaining a temporary cessation of hostilities. Conceiving myself to be acting in strict conformity to the principles which have marked the conduct of His Majesty's Government, *not the aggressor in the war*, by displaying a readiness to meet that of the United States in every just and honorable measure which has for its immediate object the promotion of immediate difficulties, and viewing the prolongation of hostilities as more calculated to retard than accelerate that object, I have determined on your proceeding to the village of Champlain for the purpose of meeting the officer who has been appointed and ordered to proceed there by the Government of the United States, and you are hereby authorized to discuss and arrange an armistice upon such terms and conditions as are consistent with the liberty of the British nation, and which shall accord with its interest and honor.

(Canadian Archives, C. 683, p. 88.)

Basis for an Armistice.

His Excellency Sir George Prevost, Bart., Commander of His British Majesty's forces in the North American Provinces, on the part of Great Britain, and the Hon. James Monroe, Secretary of State, on the part of the United States, being desirous in consequence of the negotiations pending between their respective nations to prevent the useless effusion of human blood and to put a stop to the future calamities of war, have agreed, His Excellency Sir George Prevost, Bart., by Col. Edward Baynes, Adjt. General of His Britannic Majesty's said forces in North America, who is duly authorized for that purpose, and the said Honorable James Monroe, Secretary of State by   who is duly authorized by the Government of the United States for the like purpose, upon the following terms of an armistice :

First.—That an armistice between the land forces of Great Britain in the Canadas and in the other British Provinces of North America and those of the United States, and between the naval forces of both nations on the lakes will take place from
and shall continue to be in force until an absolute and unequivocal rupture in the negotiations holding at Gottenburg, and further that no act of hostility shall be committed on either side until at least 30 days shall have expired from the hour on which the intended rupture of the intended armistice is received by the party not being the first to revert to hostilities.

2nd.—A cessation of hostilities shall take place on both sides at all distant posts from the moment the arrangement of this armistice shall be announced at each military station, and the same to be promulgated with the least possible delay.

3rd.—All the Indian tribes and their followers and adherents who have borne a part in the war on either side are to be considered as included in the armistice in the most full and liberal manner, and each government respectively pledges itself to exert its utmost influence to endeavor to cause the said armistice to be faithfully observed by all the Indians in habits of intercourse or friendship with either nation.

4th.—The post of Amherstburg and town of Sandwich, if in possession of the troops of the United States when this armistice is notified at Detroit, to be retained by them during the continuance of the armistice, but no armed force is to be sent from either place into the country adjacent, nor are the settlers and inhabitants thereof to be subject to the control or government of the officers commanding at those places.

5th.—The forts of Niagara and Michilimackinac shall also remain in the possession of the troops of Great Britain during said armistice, the officers commanding in those places confining their troops to the limits of their respective posts.

6th.—No armed force or patrols or parties of reconnoissance shall approach within five miles of any frontier military post on either side of Lower Canada.

7th.—No vessels are to be suffered to pass the streights from

Lake Erie to Lake Huron or to visit or hold any communication with any part of the coast or territory of the enemy on any of the lakes.

8th.—Sackett's Harbor and Kingston are to be established points of communication on Lake Ontario; Fort Erie on Lake Erie, and Champlain and Odelltown for the communications of the Lower Province.

9th.—The intercourse of travellers and private individuals between the two nations to be made liable to such restrictions as may be deemed expedient by either party.

Given under my hand at headquarters, Longueuil, the twenty-ninth day of April, one thousand eight hundred and fourteen.

GEORGE PREVOST,
Commander of the Forces in British North America.

By His Excellency's command.

NOAH FREER,
Military Secretary.

(Canadian Archives, C. 683, p. 68.)

Capt. A. Sinclair to the Secretary of the Navy.

ERIE 29th April, 1814.

SIR,—

I merely drop you a line to notify my arrival, as the short time I have been here precludes the possibility of giving you anything like correct information as regards the state of affairs on the station. I can only say the squadron are in no state of forwardness for service. The materials and mechanics are beginning to arrive. Every nerve shall be exerted, as the very life of the expedition depends on the time we may be able to commence it. I have written the Commanding Officer at Detroit apprizing him of the intended expedition, and despatched a vessel with it yesterday morning—from present appearances he will receive it to-morrow morning. I have endeavored to impress upon him the absolute necessity of securing the strongholds which may command our passage to and from the upper lakes, as from every information I can gain there are situations when a very small force could effectually cut off all communication between the two lakes, (Erie and Huron,) a narrow channel bordering close upon the enemy's shore, (within pistol shot,) and a current of $4\frac{1}{2}$ knots setting down, would it not be well to make arrangements with the war office to this effect while it is in our power to secure those important points? It is stated here that Genl. Harrison has ordered all other points to be abandoned except Detroit. Should those passes be secured by the enemy when the squadron are divided on the two lakes, it might be attended with most serious consequences to the country, and the probability is he will not attempt doing so until we are so divided.

There is no bread-stuff as yet on the station, I have, however, made arrangements for an ample supply. There are very few officers here, not one of the least experience from whom I can receive assistance. Commanders for the vessels are immediately and much wanting. Since your last returns from this place there has been many deaths and discharges. Capt. Elliott thinks there are not more than 170 all told, many of whom are unfit for service. I have sent up ordering the prize ships immediately down to this place, and shall use all possible exertion to get them in safety over the bar. There is only 5 feet on the bar; Capt. Elliott thinks it impossible to get them over, as they draw 9½ with swept holds. I shall, however, have some lighters constructed, which I hope will succeed in getting them in.

As soon as returns can be made you shall secure them.

I have the honor to remain with great respect, Sir.

N. B.—Your letter of the 18th instant, respecting the increase of pay of officers, was received yesterday.

From Sir George Prevost to Lieut. General Drummond.

MONTREAL, 30th April, 1814.

Secret and Confidential.

SIR,—

The subject of your letter of the 13th inst. was in a great degree replied to by anticipation, in the communication I made to you on the same day. In your despatch of the 26th, which has this moment been brought to me, I perceive a more decided opinion on the contemplated movement against Sackett's Harbor.

You consider the land forces to be employed on this service should not be less than 4,000 effective rank and file to afford a reasonable hope of success.

In order to render so many men disposable at Kingston, I ought to augment your present force there to at least 5,000 effectives, an increase little calculated to diminish the great difficulties which you are laboring under for provisions and forage to maintain a much smaller force. But the fact is that the force in this country is insufficient to enable me to concentrate at any one point in Upper Canada the number of regulars you require for this important service without stripping Lower Canada of nearly the whole of them that are at present in it, and committing its defence to Provincials and militia.

The views of His Majesty's Government respecting the mode of conducting the war with America, do not justify my exposing too much at one stake. It is by wary measures and occasional daring enterprises, with apparently disproportionate means, that the character of the war has been sustained, and from that policy I am not disposed to depart.

But a presumption that the Government of the United States is animated by a sincere desire of an armistice from a firm belief that the negotiation commenced at Gottenburg will terminate in peace has induced me to accede to the President's proposal to appoint an officer of rank to discuss and arrange to-morrow, on the part of H. M.'s Government, with a similar person on the part of the American Gov't the articles of a suspension of arms, at the village of Champlain.

This circumstance renders it inexpedient that an extensive offensive movement against any of the enemy's positions should be undertaken until you shall again hear from me on the subject.

I do not feel disposed to give credit to the whole of Mr. Constant Bacon's deposition. The circumstances may be true but they are exaggerated, and in one instance I see much improbability in the statement. However, it is satisfactory to know that M. Genl. Riall is fully prepared against any enterprise. The Commiss'y Genl. has the most positive orders to forward provisions to Upper Canada as expeditiously as possible.

You will please to communicate to Commodore Sir James Yeo the subject of this letter, but I do not wish it to restrain him from any operation he may have in view until the armistice is officially announced.

(Canadian Archives, C. 1222, pp. 112-14.)

From Sir George Prevost to Lieutenant General Drummond.

Head Quarters, MONTREAL, 30th April, 1814.

SIR,—

Herewith I have the honor to transmit a copy of a letter addressed to me by Lt. Genl. Sir John C. Sherbrooke and one enclosure.

You will have the goodness to make known the liberality of the Province of Nova Scotia in relief of the distressed inhabitants of Upper Canada to such persons as are concerned in its distribution, and inform me of the most agreeable mode of transferring to your credit the sum voted.

(Canadian Archives, C. 1222, p. 114.)

The Secretary of War to President Madison.

War Department, April 30th, 1814.

SIR,—

So long as we had reason to believe that the enemy intended and was in a condition to re-establish himself on the Thames and open anew his intercourse with the Indian tribes of the west, it was no doubt proper to give our naval means a direction which would best obstruct and defeat such movement and designs. An order was accordingly given by the Navy Department to employ the flotilla in securing the shores of the western lakes, destroying the enemy's trading establishment at St. Joseph's and in recapturing Fort Mackinac. As, however, our last advices show that the enemy has no efficient force westward of Burlington Bay, and that he has suffered the season of easy and rapid transportation to escape him, it is evident that he means to strengthen himself on the peninsula and make Fort Erie, which he is now repairing, the western extremity of his line of operations. Under this new state of things it is respectfully suggested whether another and a better use cannot be made of our flotilla.

In explaining myself it is necessary to promise that, the garrisons of Detroit and Malden included, it will be practicable to assemble on the shores and navigable waters of Lake Erie 5,000 regular troops and 3,000 volunteers and militia, and that measures have been taken to produce this result by the 10th day of June next. Without naval means, however, this force will be necessarily dispersed and inoperative—with their aid, competent to great objects.

Lake Erie, on which our dominion is indisputable, furnishes a way scarcely less convenient for approaching the heart of Upper Canada than Lake Ontario. Eight or even six thousand men landed in the bay between Point Abino and Fort Erie, and operating on the line of the Niagara, or, if a more direct route is to be found, against the British post at the head of Burlington Bay, would induce the enemy so to weaken his more eastern posts as to bring them within our means at Sackett's Harbor and Plattsburg.

In choosing between this object and that to which the flotilla is now destined, there cannot, I think, be much hesitation. Our attack carried to Burlington and York interposes a barrier which completely protects Malden and Detroit, makes doubtful and hazardous the enemy's intercourse with the Western Indians, reduces Mackinac to a possession perfectly useless, renders probable the abandonment of Fort Niagara and takes from the enemy half his motives for continuing the conflict on Lake Ontario. On the other hand take Mackinac and what is gained but Mackinac itself? If this plan is adopted no time should be lost in countermanding the execution of the other.

(McAfee, History of the late War in the Western Country, pp. 421-2.)

Heads of Plan of Campaign within District No. 9.

1st.—That such portions of the Erie fleet and of the garrison of Detroit as the officer commanding may deem necessary for the purpose be despatched without delay to the western lakes, with orders to attack or capture a British fort or post established at Matchedash Bay on Lake Huron, recapture Michilimackinac and break up such other hostile establishments within these inland seas as may be practicable.

2d.—That all surplus vessels belonging to the fleet and left at Detroit be brought down the lake and employed in transporting the division of the left, its arms, ammunition and baggage to such point on the Canada shore as may be indicated, and in such other acts of co-operation with the division as may be proper and necessary.

3rd.—That after landing the troops be marched as expeditiously as possible on the British position at Burlington Bay with orders to seize and fortify that post, and, having thus cut the enemy's line of land communication between York and Fort George, await the arrival and co-operation of the Ontario fleet, which, from statements made by the Secretary of the Navy, will be prepared for action by the middle of June.

4th.—Under these circumstances the commanders of the two arms will have within their choice a speedy investment of Forts George and Niagara; a rapid descent on Sackett's Harbor, a junction with the brigade at that post, and a direct attack on Kingston. In choosing between these objects circumstances must govern. The former will enable us to take a new line of operation from Fort George to Lake Simcoe, shutting out the enemy from all direct communication with the western lakes and thus destroying his means of sustaining his western posts and settlements and of reinstating his influence over Indian wants and policy. The latter, besides comprising all the advantages of the former, will put an end to all farther naval expenditure on Lake Ontario; give us uncontested possession of a great proportion of Upper Canada and enable us to carry our whole concentrated force on Montreal, which, if gained, cannot fail to give to the war a speedy and favorable termination. All which is respectfully submitted.

(Armstrong's Notices of the War of 1812, Vol. II., pp. 218-9, Appendix 17.)

From the Diary of Thomas McCrae.

RALEIGH, Wednesday, 20th April, 1814.

A party of Am. horse came up here to-day under John Walker, Richardson along with them.

Thursday, 21st April.

Westbrook, Doyle and Pelton passed down on the opposite side with Towsley prisoner.

Colonel Baynes to Colonel Pinkney.

CHAMPLAIN TOWN, 1st May, 1814.

SIR,—

I have the honor to furnish you with the enclosed copy of the credentials that I received from Lt. Genl. Sir George Prevost, containing the basis upon which I am authorized to treat for an armistice, and I request to be informed if you are prepared to discuss and arrange an armistice upon the terms proposed or upon what grounds you are empowered to proceed in such an arrangement.

(Canadian Archives, C. 683, p. 93.)

Colonel Baynes to Sir George Prevost.

CHAMPLAIN TOWN, 1st May, 1814.

Confidential.

SIR,—

I have the honor to inform Your Excellency that the officer I have met at this place is the aid de camp of Genl. Dearborn, who brought the intimation of the rejection of the armistice concluded at Albany. The officer proposed by Mr. Monroe was to have been General Winder, and Colonel Pinkney has been substituted as a measure of necessity in his place. He has not been at Washington nor had any communication with Mr. Monroe, nor does he appear to be at all acquainted with the views or designs of his government in the present arrangement. He came prepared with the head of an armistice, which I have not yet learnt, but upon showing him your guide-letter he observed that he had no latitude left at his discretion with respect to pledging his government with respect to the principle upon which the armistice was proposed, or to engage for anything more than ordinary cessation of hostilities to be annulled at the *pleasure* of either party at 20 days' notice, and that he did not feel himself at liberty to pledge himself either for the principle or to the extent of the period stated in Your Excellency's letter. I have assured him that you will not accede to an armistice on any other terms. I have sent him a copy of my credentials with a note requesting him to inform me if he is prepared to negotiate on these grounds, or what others he has to propose. I shall of course await the result and see if any arrangement can be made of a nature that Your Excellency would approve of, but I am not sanguine and think it will end in waiting for General Winder's return, as I suspect Colonel Pinkney will adhere to the mere letter of his instructions, whatever they may be. I return this by Major Coore. If I can be of no further use by waiting I will myself return to-morrow morning.

(Canadian Archives, C. 683, p. 78.)

Colonel Baynes to Colonel Pinkney.

CHAMPLAIN TOWN, May 1st, 1814.

SIR,—

I have the honor to acknowledge your note of this day and to inform you that the proposal entertained in the first paragraph corresponds with the instructions I have received from His Excellency Lt. Genl. Sir Geo. Prevost in as far as they relate to the grounds and conditions upon which he is willing to assent to a cessation of hostilities between the forces under his immediate command including the lakes of Canada, but His Excellency is not empowered to make any stipulation whatever for the naval commander. It is not expected that any assurance can be given that a conciliation shall follow an armistice as a matter of course, but it is required as a pledge of the sincerity of the desire on the part of the United States that the result of the negotiations pending at Gottenburg may terminate in an honorable adjustment of differences subsisting between the two countries shall be the sole ground upon which either party shall be at liberty to dissolve the armistice.

(Canadian Archives, C. 683, p. 87.)

Lieut. General Drummond to Sir George Prevost.

KINGSTON, May 3rd, 1814.

SIR,—

I have the honor to acquaint Your Excellency that I propose embarking on board the squadron, as soon as the wind is fair, the following troops, viz:

Royal Artillery.......................... 24
Rocketteers 6

Sappers	20
Regiment De Watteville	450
Glengarry Light Infantry	50
which, with the Royal Marines	350
will make a disposable force of	900

men for the purpose of destroying, if possible, the enemy's magazines and stores at Oswego, and along the southern coast of Lake Ontario, bringing off, however, such quantities as it may be practicable for the relief of the Right Division.

To satisfy myself that as much is done on this occasion as can be, I propose embarking myself with Commodore Sir James Yeo, but the immediate command of the troops I have entrusted to Lieutenant Colonel Fischer of De Watteville's Regiment.

By the enclosed copy of information from Sackett's Harbor, dated the 28th ultimo, Your Excellency will perceive that a new ship is to be laid down there and finished in six weeks. If such be the case it is impossible for us to keep pace with such exertions. I must again beg leave to repeat my opinion that the only way to completely secure the Upper Province is a vigorous combined attack of army and navy against the enemy's chief means of annoyance, their fleet and stores at Sackett's Harbor.

But on this occasion the most ample measures must be taken to ensure success, and the small force which the Upper Province can afford must be assisted by a regular force from Your Excellency of certainly not less than 800 effective men from the Lower Province. In all these opinions I am joined by the naval commander, Sir James Yeo.

Major General Riall has reported that the enemy are encamped at Buffalo with about 800 men, with three field pieces.

(Canadian Archives, C. 683, pp. 93-6.)

Capt. A. Sinclair to the Secretary of the Navy.

ERIE, 2nd May, 1814.

SIR,—

Yours of the 27th ultimo has this moment come to hand. I had anticipated that part of its contents which required the curtailing the indents made on the navy agent at Pittsburg. I have, however, difficulties to contend with in order to inform myself of the state of the station which you can form no idea of. It appears that since Mr. Hambleton left this, there has been no responsible person whose duty it is to keep copies of requisitions, receipts, returns of expenditures, etc. I am using every possible exertion in my power to enable me to give you a correct and circumstantial account of what has been done, what requires doing, what is on hand and what required to complete the outfits of the intended expedition. You will readily see the difficulties existing when I tell you that there is no account of the articles on hand of any description, and that they are scattered over a space of several miles. Shot are to be raked from below high water mark, covered in sand, materials of every kind unstored. Private store houses, which have been rented and used for storing, have been so repeatedly broken into that they are now nearly useless, therefore inventories of every article must be taken before I can inform you with any degree of accuracy. From the view I have taken of things I am very confident that, system once established, there will be a saving of 25 % to the public.

I shall endeavor in the course of this week to give you a general view of the station, and suggest such alterations as may appear necessary for the public good. The mechanics are arriving here daily—no provision had been made for their reception, and such are the difficulties for provision in this country that I have been compelled, tho' against my inclination, to advance some from our stock in order to get them boarded at all. There are no boats on the station, not a boat a piece for each vessel of any description.

The small vessels are in some state of readiness, the *Niagara* is over the bar, but wants considerable repairs, caulking entirely. The *Lawrence* shall pass the bar the first good weather, in the meantime her repairs are going on. The *Lady Prevost*, a vessel only 72 feet on deck and 18 feet beam, was altering into a brig, the lower masts only are repaired. I have stopt the alteration, not only on account of expense, but utility also. She will not answer for the Upper Lake, her draft is two feet more than our brigs. The *Hunter* is sunk with a quantity of powder and stores in her, much of which is damaged. The *Amelia* is in the same situation. I am now getting them on float and saving what can be saved from them. The report is that they are rotten and unfit for service—a survey shall be held and a report made accordingly.

The prize ships arrived last night. I have not yet visited them—their safety, etc., shall be immediately attended to. They have considerable quantity of powder and ordnance stores on board, full sufficient, I fancy, with what we have on hand, to answer all our purposes.

I am much pleased at the prospect of some officers of experience being on their way here—none, however, have arrived yet. I would suggest that an old and experienced purser be ordered to the station. *One* of that description would answer all purposes, Mr. Harris, Mr.

Hambleton or one of their standing. A master commandant also of considerable experience, and who has system about him, will be absolutely necessary during my absence. I trust, Sir, that in doing my duty I shall not make unfavorable impressions as regards Capt. Elliott. He is very young as a commander, has had but little experience, surely none to justify the difficulties he has had to contend with here—they have been many and of magnitude.

I have not yet heard from Detroit; but as the same vessel which carried my orders for bringing the ships down took my despatches for that place, I shall expect her the first wind.

The vessels which were on shore, (except the *Ariel*,) were burnt. She, I am told, is a fine vessel and lays four miles this side of Buffalo uninjured. There is a considerable quantity of ice yet between this and her. I shall, however, send down immediately and request Genl. Scott, who is in her neighborhood, to have her protected until I can make the necessary arrangements for getting her on float, which shall be in the shortest possible time.

Colonel Baynes to Sir George Prevost.

Headquarters, MONTREAL, 3rd May, 1814.

SIR,—

I have the honor to report to Your Excellency that in obedience to your command I proceeded on the first instant to Champlain Town and was received at Judge Moore's house by Colonel Pinkney, Inspector General of the army of the United States, who communicated to me a letter from the American Secretary of State, appointing him to discuss and arrange an armistice with such person as Your Excellency might appoint for that purpose, with full power to conclude and ratify the same.

I also communicated to Colonel Pinkney the credentials I had received from Your Excellency and requested to be informed if he was prepared to proceed in the discussion of the proposed arrangements on the basis therein suggested, or on what terms he would propose to ground the negotiations for a cessation of hostilities. Colonel Pinkney shortly after enclosed a note, which I have the honor to enclose with a copy of my answer, and I further learnt verbally from that officer that it was the intention of the Secretary of State to have employed Brigr. Genl. Winder as a negotiator on this occasion, but that officer having proceeded on his journey to Washington had missed a packet addressed to him to the care of the general officer commanding on the frontier, who had in conformity with instructions from his government substituted Colonel Pinkney's name and transmitted for his guidance and information an instruction containing the principal heads of a convention for a proposed armistice: that he possessed no other documents nor had he any other knowledge of the views and intentions of his government. That the express had brought a sealed packet for Brig. Genl. Winder, but that the commanding officer not considering himself at liberty to inspect its contents had returned it to the Secretary of State; that he had no doubt that the packet contained private and confidential instructions for Genl. Winder, who had besides recently held personal interviews with the minister, but that as he had no clue for his guidance he felt himself under the necessity of adhering to the strict letter of the only instructions he possessed, viz., to conclude an armistice that should include the whole Atlantic coast of America, and that for an indefinite period to terminate at pleasure at the expiration of twenty days' notice. He, however, earnestly requested that his objection to the terms proposed by Your Excellency should not be considered as breaking off the negotiations, as he felt confident that Brig. Genl. Winder would still be sent furnished with information of the views of his government, which he did not think himself at liberty to hazard on conjecture. Under these circumstances I thought it would be unavailing to press the subject any further, and Col. P. having stated to me his intention of immediately transmitting to his government the result of our conference, I considered nothing more could be done for the present and returned to headquarters.

While at Champlain I availed myself of the opportunity of learning from Judge Moore the grounds upon which Mr. Monroe had founded his present overtures for an armistice to have originated in a conversation in which I was represented to have expressed myself to that effect. The judge assured me that no communication from him could have sanctioned such an assertion; that he had mentioned in a letter the conciliating spirit with which an exchange had been proposed by Your Excellency of prisoners of war, hostages as well as others, and added that from the liberal sentiments which appeared to influence your conduct and the general tenor of my conversation he had no doubt you would feel inclined to renew the armistice, which had been so wantonly and imprudently rejected by the President, but that it could not be expected that any overtures of that nature would again originate with Your Excellency. I learned from Judge Moore that the war party was reduced to the lowest ebb and daily becoming more unpopular, so that it was not believed that any offensive measure of any magnitude or for the purpose of invasion would be again attempted. That all eyes were anxiously directed to the council of Gottenburg as the only hope of emancipation.

(Canadian Archives, C. 683, p 83.)

Lieut. General Drummond to Sir George Prevost.

KINGSTON, May 3, 1814.

SIR,—

I am extremely concerned to acquaint Your Excellency that I have received information from the Head of the Lake that Colonel Elliott, Superintendent for Indian affairs, has been given over by his physicians for three successive days.

His very great mental anxiety relative to the Western Indians under his charge, and his bodily exertions beyond what his strength at his advanced age could support, so completely exhausted nature that I am apprehensive long 'ere this His Majesty has lost one of his most faithful and zealous servants, and before he could have received intelligence of your gracious intentions towards him, (with respect to the increase of his salary,) to soothe him in his hours of pain.

Should this melancholy event have taken place, I am extremely apprehensive that serious evils will arise if Major McKee, next in seniority to Colonel Elliott, should succeed to the charge and superintendence of the Western Indians, and I know of no other remedy than by appointing Col. Caldwell, who is well known to and by these nations, to the situation of Dy. Supt. General of these Indians or in any other manner whereby he would become senior to Capt. McKee.

Major General Riall has directed Col. Claus to proceed to Burlington to assume the general superintendence of the Indians at the Head of the Lake.

(Canadian Archives, C. 257, p. 250.)

From the Diary of Thomas McCrae.

RALEIGH, Thursday, 3rd May, 1814.

A party of American horsemen, about 25, went up the river to-day, some on this side and some on the other. Nine more passed here just at dark on foot, armed.

Wednesday, 4th May, 1814.

The Am. party returned this evening. They have just taken John Truxter and Billy Ward.

Major General Stovin to Sir George Prevost.

KINGSTON, 5th May, 1814.

SIR,—

I have the honor to inform Your Excellency that a detachment from this garrison embarked on Tuesday evening, the 3rd, on board the fleet, consisting of :—

Twenty-four artillery non-com. and privates with one brass field piece, 12 pdr. and one 5½ inch howitzer, under Captain Cruttenden.

Twenty sappers and miners, under Lieut. Gosset.

The rocketteers, under Lieut. Stevens.

Six companies of De Watteville's, 75 r. and f. per Co. with off. and non-com. do., and one Co. Gleng. Light Inf., 50 r. and f.

The whole under Lieut. Col. Fischer, De Watteville's.

Lieut. General Drummond embarked at five o'clock on Wednesday morning and the whole fleet were under weigh about ¼ before six o'clock. The appearance of the *Prince Regent* and *Princess Charlotte* on so small a piece of water was truly magnificent. They appear to sail remarkably well. They were not out of sight at 5 o'clock p. m.

This day about ¼ before four o'clock p. m. a heavy firing was heard by many people in the town, and a party that were on a fishing excursion on Long Island on the bateaux passage very distinctly heard a heavy firing about the same time. It appeared to be in the direction of Oswego.

The moment any despatch arrives it shall be instantly forwarded, or should I obtain any intelligence it shall be immediately communicated to Your Excellency.

As the express goes early to-morrow morning I thought it proper to communicate what I have written.

(Canadian Archives, C. 683, pp. 97-9.)

Capt. A. Sinclair to the Secretary of the Navy.

ERIE, 6th May, 1814.

SIR,—

I herewith enclose you a return of officers and men on the station and an inventory of such articles as I have been able to come at, and I shall endeavour to give you a view of the station generally.

There has not been a responsible officer at the head of any one department, whose duty it was to keep an account of the expenditure of stores. There is a Col. Forster of this place, (who appears to be a respectable man,) and who Capt. Perry or Elliott appointed as receiver of provisions and other stores, (with the pay of a master,) and to superintend the transportation from Waterford to this place. He is the only person who could give me any insight or information of what had been received, but as most articles, except provision, was either taken over to the peninsula or on board the fleet without order or requisition, it was out of his power to say more than that they had been received. Timber, which has been contracted for, not only for the use of the fleet but for a public store house which Capt. Elliott has framed and is finishing by contract on the peninsula, has been exposed to pilfer and at the mercy of the waves, and I am told there are great quantities of 32 pd. shot which have been brought from the ships, and where the boats grounded, thrown overboard and are covered with sand. I am in hopes, however, to recover them, and from that source have a sufficient quantity for the use of the station. Great quantities of timber and plank are contracted for, at very large prices, and the transportation to this place from the mills, which are only two miles distant, amounts to more than half the cost of the articles; but as the work has been done under written contract, I shall be bound to pass the bills, but I absolutely feel mortified to place my signature to them as a sanction of their correctness. The store house building for the public is much wanting for the security of provisions and stores, and also that part of it which is intended for a hospital; but its situation is illy chosen, so much so that I am yet doubtful whether I ought to have it finished, notwithstanding it is all ready for covering in, the materials nearly all delivered and the finishing it contracted for. I will enclose you a rough sketch of it with my opinion of the advantages and disadvantages attending its situation, and shall be glad to receive your instructions on the subject as early as possible, that the necessary arrangements may be made with the contractors previous to my leaving the place.

The temporary manner in which the brigs have been repaired has added nothing to their strength—they have merely had graving pieces put in without regarding the injury done their timbers, and they have not been caulked in the upper works, as appears from their state to be absolutely necessary, both for their preservation, safety and the comfort of those on board. I have yet to get their spars from the forest. The *Hunter* is from 12 to 16 years old and much decayed. They have put powder and other articles in her, then suffered her to ground with her decks full of shot and other heavy articles, where she has fell over, filled to water mark, and damaged half her contents. I have had her pumped out and have secured what remained unspoiled. The *Amelia* is also sunk and reported to be rotten in her bottom—she shall be attended to as soon as possible. The *Ohio*, the *Porcupine*, the *Somers*, the *Scorpion* and *Tigress* are all over the bar. I keep two of them cruising between this and Long Point—two others anchored for the protection of those vessels over the bar which have not yet got their guns on board, for such is the scarcity of boats, and so heavy has the wind been since the *Niagara* passed the bar that I have not been able to get off all her ballast and guns, nor has the *Lawrence* been able to move towards the bar in consequence of the sea on it. I was anxious to stop the purchase of articles, which might not be wanted, and which had been ordered by Captain Elliott when he contemplated fitting out the two ships, but was at a great loss how to proceed, as he had only a copy of a part of his requisitions. I was therefore obliged to make a rough and hurried estimate of what they would have required and send it on as articles not wanting, but I very much fear most of the heavy articles have been contracted for by the agent at Pittsburg. I would have curtailed the indents when passing through that place, but it was impossible for me to know what Capt. Elliott's views were, or what the station absolutely required. I am of opinion that the article of shot, the transportation of which is so very heavy, might have been dispensed with, as there is on the station a very ample supply for any service we have in view. The arrangement as regards provision is bad, the flour is brought here to be baked, and with the utmost exertion which can be made here no more than 10 barrels can be baked per day. I have urged the agent at Pittsburg to forward on bread with the least possible delay, and by paying extra to the bakers here I get soft bread baked sufficient of a night to serve the crews the following day, by which means we do not encroach upon our stock intended for the supply of the expedition, the beef and pork contracted for to be delivered at this place, Capt. Elliott has directed the contractor to deposit at different points on the lake from 70 to 150 miles distant from here, which not only subjects us to the inconvenience of sending for it, but it is entirely unprotected from any expedition which might be formed against it by the enemy, and altho' not at our risque the want of it might prove of serious inconvenience, I have therefore, as there are no private craft on the lake, employed one or two of the public vessels to transport it here immediately—they have arrived with a part of it and have gone for a second load.

The small part of the ration such as beans, peas, rice, molasses, butter, suet and even vinegar, the men have been very long destitute of, and it is, as may be expected, a source of great discontent. I have written in the most pressing manner to the agent at Pittsburg to endeavour to supply them immediately. They had been some days without spirits when I came, and but a very few barrels has yet arrived. I am doing everything in my power to reconcile them to the service here, as their times are daily expiring, but with all the inducements held out I fear I shall lose a large portion of them, and as for getting volunteers among the people of this country it is out of the question, when the common laborer gets his dollar per day— you will perceive there are only 31 marines fit for service. That description of men might be procured, as there are a number of substitutes among the militia here who have evinced a disposition to enlist were it not for their officers preventing it; they have gone so far as to confine their men to camp and prohibit our recruiting parties from passing their line; you will perceive by the enclosed list of men how little was known of the state of the station when I informed you, by authority from Capt. Elliott, that all told there was not more than 170 attached to it. A muster had not been had for a very considerable time.

The mechanics have nearly all arrived, but their tools are yet behind. I have mustered for their use all I can procure on the station, have got the spars under way and am preparing to build a couple of launches fit for anchor boats, etc., which are indispensably necessary, as we are going into strange, narrow and shallow waters. I shall not be detained for any other class of boats, but endeavour to substitute such as Col. Croghan mentions in his letter, (in answer to mine on the subject of our expedition,) can be furnished at Detroit, a copy of which letter I herewith enclose you.

So great is the scarcity of provision in this quarter that in order to get board upon any terms for the mechanics I have been compelled to advance provisions to each house keeper who would take 10 men at $4 per week. Better arrangements might perhaps have been made had it been thought of before they arrived, but it appears their arrival had not been anticipated in *any respect*.

The gun carriages disabled in the action are yet to be made. I have been thus particular in giving you a correct state of things, that you may know the means with which I am furnished and calculate accordingly. Whatever industry and the exertion of all the means in my power can perform, shall be done to hasten my departure and the equipment of that part of the force intended for this lake, but you will readily perceive that too much depends upon contingencies for me to speak with anything like certainty of the time I shall have it in my power to leave this, my situation is peculiarly mortifying, as I feel that the very soul of the enterprise depends upon the time I shall be able to commence it.

I do not think that Mr. Magrath, (the only purser we have on the station,) is entirely himself at all times, he is certainly occasionally deranged. I suggested to you in my last letter the necessity of ordering an old and experienced purser on the station. I think the good of the service requires it, and if he, instead of the commanding officer, could be made the agent and responsible person, through whom all money expended here should pass, it would take great trouble and responsibility from the commander.

Mr. Magrath has been advancing some of the men three months' pay, said to be voted by Congress, on account of their services here

Is it correct and shall it be allowed to all? My having no instructions to that effect, I have stopt it until I hear from you.

What shall I do with the invalids who have been disabled on the station? Shall a certain allowance be made them to carry them home, and what shall that allowance be?

Is there any allowance to seamen who have served their times out and discharged here, and if there is what shall it be?

Am I to continue the acting appointments made by Captains Perry and Elliott where I find them deserving?

Shall I draw on the agent at Pittsburg or on the navy department for the requisite funds to meet the expenses of the station? I have been able to trace most of the difficulties existing among the officers to their proper source, and am in hopes to adjust them without court martial. None of the officers mentioned in your letter of the 27th have yet arrived—their services are very much wanting, as you know they are all very young here. A gang of blockmakers, which I knew nothing of being ordered, have just arrived. A very industrious young man has been employed here all the season, and has an ample supply for all our purposes already on hand, they were therefore by no means wanting. I shall, however, as they are here and already incurred the greatest expense of getting themselves tools and materials on the spot, let them make a stock sufficient to meet contingencies and then discharge them. I have written the agent at Philadelphia to send no more mechanics, as it seems they are not all yet underway that were required. I have sent an officer on to Pittsburg to forward the articles wanting, provisions especially.

N. B.—The next mail will bring on a regular muster roll to the accountant of the navy.

(Enclosure.)
Lieut Col. Croghan to Capt. A. Sinclair.

DETROIT, 1st May, 1814.

SIR.—

I have this moment received your confidential communication of the 28th ult., and am happy in assuring you that every assistance which my diminutive force can afford will be freely offered you. Knowing that an expedition would be fitted out against the posts on the upper lakes, I was enabled to anticipate your enquiries relative to the situation strength, &c., of those several places, and have taken such steps as are most likely to secure me correct information on the subject. I have not been able to ascertain *directly* the strength of the several garrisons of Michilimackinac, St. Marys and St. Josephs, but from the latest Indian accounts they are stated to be weak, that of Mackinac cannot exceed 40 regulars and Canadians. The Indians from the neighborhood of the River Sable generally agree in saying that the enemy have built at Matchitash, (Gloucester Bay,) 25 boats, each carrying two guns, but as for the correctness of this tale I cannot vouch, I am rather disposed to disbelieve it. I think it highly probable that boats are building on Lake Simcoe, but as there is a portage of some miles between Lake Simcoe and the waters of Gloucester Bay, over which those boats must be hauled, I am induced to believe that they are not larger than ordinary bateaux, and that they are intended more for the purpose of keeping up the communication with, and of provisioning those posts above mentioned than for acting offensively. I am well aware of the annoyance that your fleet would meet with in passing up the strait should the enemy by batteries, gunboats or otherwise command or block up the entrance into Lake Huron and shall therefore make immediate preparations for establishing a strong post at the point on which Fort St. Clair formerly stood. I fear, Sir, that in the present reduced state of my force, I shall not be able to afford you any valuable assistance, indeed I cannot, (unless previously reinforced,) pledge myself to co-operate with you in any way which would be likely to draw my troops from the *immediate* defense of this place and its dependencies. With regard to provisions I cannot speak confidently; our supply at present is but scanty, nor am I aware of the arrangements made by Genl. Harrison for increasing the stock. I find on enquiry that a sufficient number of boats can be furnished you at this place; the two masters return reports 40, each capable of landing from 50 to 80 men.

P. S.—About 10 days since I sent up some active spies in the direction of Lake Simcoe and Gloucester Bay, for the purpose of ascertaining the exact situation of the enemy in that quarter—within 10 or 15 days their return is expected.

Lieut. General Drummond to Sir George Prevost.

H. M. S. *Prince Regent*, Lake Ontario,
off OSWEGO, May 7, 1814.

SIR,—

I am happy to have to announce to Your Excellency the complete success of the expedition against Oswego. The troops mentioned in my despatch of the 3rd instant, viz., six companies of De Watteville's Regiment under Lieutenant Colonel Fischer, the light company of the Glengarry Light Infantry under Captain McMillan, and the whole of the second battalion of the Royal Marines under Lieutenant Colonel Malcolm having been embarked with a detachment of the

Royal Artillery under Captain Cruttenden with two field pieces, a detachment of the rocket company under Lieutenant Stevens, and a detachment of Sappers and Miners under Lieutenant Gosset of the Royal Engineers, on the evening of the 3rd instant, I proceeded on board the *Prince Regent* at daylight on the 4th and the squadron immediately sailed. The wind being variable we did not arrive off Oswego until noon the following day. The ships lay to within long gun shot of the battery, and the gunboats under Captain Collier were sent close in for the purpose of inducing the enemy to show his fire, and particularly the number and position of his guns. This service was performed in the most gallant manner, the boats taking a position within point blank shot of the fort, which returned fire from four guns, one of them heavy. The enemy did not appear to have any guns mounted on the town side of the river.

Having sufficiently reconnoitered the place arrangements were made for its attack, which it was designed should take place at eight o'clock that evening, but at sunset a very heavy squall, blowing directly on the shore, obliged the squadron to get under weigh and prevented our return until next morning, when the following disposition was made of the troops and squadron by Commodore Sir James Yeo and myself. The *Princess Charlotte*, *Wolfe* (1) and *Royal George* (2), to engage the batteries as close as the depth of water would admit of their approaching the shore, the *Sir Sydney Smith* schooner (3) to scour the town and keep in check a large body of militia who might attempt to pass over into the fort; the *Moira* (4) and *Melville* (5) brigs to tow the boats with the troops and then cover their landing by scouring the woods on the low point towards the foot of the hill by which it was intended to advance to the assault of the fort.

Captain O'Conor had the direction of the boats and gunboats destined to land the troops, which consisted of the flank companies of De Watteville's Regiment, the company of the Glengarry Light Infantry and the second battalion of the Royal Marines being all that could be landed at one embarkation. The four battalion companies of the regiment of De Watteville and the detachment of artillery remaining in reserve on board the *Princess Charlotte* and *Sir Sidney Smith* schooner.

As soon as everything was ready the ships opened their fire and the boats pushed for the point of disembarkation in the most regular order. The landing was effected under a heavy fire from the fort as well as from a considerable body of the enemy drawn up on the brow of the hill and in the wood. The immediate command of the troops

---

(1) Montreal, (2) Niagara, (3) Magnet, (4) Charwell, (5) Star.

was entrusted to Lieutenant Colonel Fischer of the Regiment of De Watteville, of whose gallant, cool and judicious conduct, as well as of the distinguished bravery, steadiness and discipline of every officer and soldier composing this small force, I was a witness, having, with Commodore Sir James Yeo, the Deputy Adjutant General and the officers of my staff, landed with the troops.

I refer Your Excellency to Lieutenant Colonel Fischer's letter enclosed for an account of the operations. The place was gained in ten minutes after the troops advanced. The fort being everywhere almost open, the whole of the garrison, consisting of the third battalion of artillery about 400 strong, and some hundred militia, effected their escape, with the exception of about 60 men, half of them severely wounded.

I enclose a return of our loss, amongst which I have to regret that of Captain Holtaway of the Royal marines. Your Excellency will lament to observe in the list the name of that gallant, judicious and excellent officer, Captain Mulcaster of the Royal Navy, who landed at the head of 200 volunteer seamen from the fleet and received a severe and dangerous wound when within a few yards of the guns which he was advancing to storm, which, I fear, will deprive the squadron of his valuable services for some time at least.

In noticing the co-operation of the naval branch of the service, I have the highest satisfaction in assuring Your Excellency that I have throughout this as well as on every other occasion, experienced the most zealous, cordial and able support from Sir James Yeo. It will be for him to do justice to the merits of those under his command, but I may nevertheless be permitted to observe that nothing could exceed the coolness and gallantry in action or the unwearied exertions on shore of the captains, officers and crews of the whole squadron.

I enclose a memorandum of the captured articles which have been brought away, in which Your Excellency will perceive with satisfaction seven heavy guns that were intended for the enemy's new ship. Three 32-pounders were sunk by the enemy in the river, as well as a large quantity of cordage and other naval stores. The loss to them therefore has been very great and I am sanguine in believing that by this blow they have been deprived of the means of completing the armament and particularly the equipment of the large man of war, an object of the greatest importance.

Every object of the expedition having been effected and the captured stores embarked, the troops returned in the most perfect order on board their respective ships at four o'clock this morning, when the squadron immediately sailed, the barracks in the town as well as those in the fort having been previously burnt, together with the platforms, bridges, &c., and the works in every other respect dismantled and destroyed as far as was practicable.

I cannot close this despatch without offering to Your Excellency's notice the admirable and judicious manner in which Lieutenant Colonel Fischer formed the troops and led them to the attack; the cool and gallant conduct of Lieutenant Colonel Malcolm at the head of the second battalion Royal Marines; the intrepidity of Captain De Bersey of the Regiment De Watteville, who commanded the advance; the zeal and energy of Lieutenant Colonel Pearson, inspecting field officer, who, with Major Smelt of the 103rd Regiment, had obtained a passage in the squadron to Niagara and volunteered their services on the occasion; the gallantry of Captain McMillan of the Glengarry Light Infantry, who covered the left flank of the troops in the advance, and the activity and judgment of Captain Cruttenden, Royal Artillery, Brevet Major De Cousten of the Regiment De Watteville, Lieutenant Stevens of the Rocket company, Lieutenant Gosset, Royal Engineers, each in their respective situations.

Lieutenant Colonel Malcolm has reported in high terms of Lieutenant Laurie of the Royal Marines, who was at the head of the first men who entered the fort, and I had an opportunity of witnessing the bravery of Lieutenant Hewett of that corps, who climbed the flag staff and pulled down the American ensign, which was nailed to it. To Lieutenant Colonel Harvey, Deputy Adjutant General, my warmest approbation is most justly due for his unremitting zeal and useful assistance. The services of this intelligent and experienced officer have been so frequently brought under Your Excellency's observation before that it would be superflous my making any comment on the high estimation in which I hold his valuable exertions.

Captain Jervois, my aid de camp, and Lieutenant Colonel Hagerman, my provincial aid de camp, the only officers of my personal staff who accompanied me, rendered me every assistance.

Captain Jervois, who will deliver to Your Excellency with this despatch the American flag taken at Oswego, is fully able to afford every further information you may require, and I avail myself of the present opportunity strongly to recommend this officer to the favorable consideration of His Royal Highness the Commander in Chief.

(Canadian Archives, C. 683.)

Lieut. Colonel Fischer to Lieut. Colonel Harvey.

H. M. S. *Prince Regent*, off Oswego,
Lake Ontario, May 7, 1814.

Sir,—

It is with heartfelt satisfaction that I have the honor to report to you, for the information of Lieutenant General Drummond commanding, that the troops placed under my orders for storming the fort at Oswego have completely succeeded in this service.

It will be superfluous for me to enter into any details of the operations, as the Lieutenant General has personally witnessed the conduct of the whole party, and the grateful task only remains to point out for his approbation the distinguished bravery and discipline of the troops.

The second battalion of Royal Marines formed their column in the most regular manner, and by their steady and rapid advance carried the fort in a very short time. In fact, nothing could surpass the gallantry of that battalion, commanded by Lieutenant-Colonel Malcolm, to whose cool and deliberate conduct our success is greatly to be attributed.

The Lieutenant-Colonel reported to me in high terms the conduct of Lieutenant James Laurie, who was at the head of the first men who entered the fort. The two flank companies of De Watteville's, under Captain De Bersey, behaved with spirit, though laboring with more difficulties during their formation, on account of the badness of the landing place and the more direct opposition of the enemy. The company of Glengarry Light Infantry, under Captain McMillan, behaved in an equally distinguished manner by clearing the wood and driving the enemy into the fort. I beg to make my personal acknowledgements to Staff Adjutant Greig and Adjutant Mermet of De Watteville's for their zeal and attention to me during the day's service. Nor can I forbear to mention the regular behavior of the whole of the troops during their stay on shore, and the most perfect order in which the re-embarkation of the troops has been executed and every service performed.

I enclose herewith the return of the killed and wounded as sent to me by the different corps.

(Canadian Archives, C. 683.)

Return of killed and wounded of the troops in action with the enemy at Oswego, on the 6th of May, 1814 :—

Second Battalion Royal Marines—One captain, two sergeants, four rank and file killed.

De Watteville's Regiment—One drummer, eleven rank and file killed.

Second Battalion Royal Marines—One sergeant, 32 rank and file wounded.

De Watteville's Regiment—One captain, one subaltern, one sergeant, 17 rank and file wounded.

Glengarry Fencibles—Nine rank and file wounded.

Total—One captain, two sergeants, one drummer, 15 rank and

file killed; one captain, one subaltern, two sergeants, 58 rank and file wounded.

OFFICER KILLED.

Second Battalion Royal Marines—Captain William Holtaway.

OFFICERS WOUNDED.

De Watteville's Regiment—Captain Ledergrew, severely; Lieutenant Victor May, dangerously (since dead.)

J. HARVEY,
Lieut.-Col. D.A.G.

His Majesty's Brig "Magnet," (late Sir Sidney Smith) Off Oswego.

May 7, 1814.

Return of ordnance and ordnance stores taken and destroyed at Oswego, Lake Ontario, the 6th May, 1814, by His Majesty's troops under the command of Lieut.-Gen. Drummond:—

Taken—Three 32-pounder iron guns, four 24-pounder iron guns, one 12-pounder iron gun, one 6-pounder iron gun. Total—9.

Destroyed—One heavy 12-pounder, one heavy 6-pounder. Total, 2.

Shot—81 42-pounder, round; 32 32-pounder, round; 36 42-pounder, canister; 42 32-pounder, canister; 30 24-pounder, canister; 12 42-pounder, grape; 48 32-pounder, grape; 18 24-pounder, grape.

Eight barrels of gunpowder and all the shot of small calibre in the fort and stores thrown into the river.

EDWARD CRUTTENDEN,
Captain Commanding Royal Artillery.

Memorandum of provisions, stores, &c., captured at Oswego:—

One thousand and forty-five barrels of flour, pork, potatoes, salt, tallow, &c., &c.; 70 coils of rope and cordage, tar, blocks (large and small,) two small schooners, with several boats and other smaller craft.

NOAH FREER,
Mil. Sec.

Sir James Lucas Yeo to Hon. John Wilson Croker.

His Majesty's Ship *Prince Regent*,
9th May, 1814.

SIR,—

My letter of the 15th April last will have informed their Lordships that His Majesty's ships *Prince Regent* and *Princess Charlotte* were launched on the preceding day. I now have the satisfaction to acquaint you for their Lordships' information that the squadron, by the unremitting exertions of the officers and men under my command, were ready on the 3rd inst., when it was determined by Lieutenant-General Drummond and myself that an immediate attack should be made on the fort and town of Oswego, which in point of position is the most formidable I have seen in Upper Canada, and where the enemy had by river navigation collected from the interior several heavy guns and naval stores for the ships and large depots of provisions for their army.

At noon on the 5th we got off the port and were on the point of landing, when a heavy gale from the N. West obliged me to gain an offing. On the morning of the 6th, everything being ready, one hundred and fifty troops, two hundred seamen armed with pikes, under Captain Mulcaster, and four hundred marines, were put into the boats. The *Montreal* and *Niagara* took their stations abreast, and within a quarter of a mile of the fort, the *Magnet* opposite the town, and the *Star* and *Charwell* to cover the landing, which was effected under a heavy fire of round, grape and musketry, kept up with great spirit. Our men, having to ascend a very steep and long hill, were consequently exposed to a destructive fire. Their gallantry overcoming every difficulty, they soon gained the summit of the hill, and, throwing themselves into the fosse, mounted the ramparts, vieing with each other who should be foremost. Lieut. Laurie, my secretary, was the first who gained the ramparts, and Lieut. Hewett of the same corps climbed the flagstaff under a heavy fire, and in the most gallant style struck the American colors, which were nailed to the mast.

My gallant and much esteemed friend, Captain Mulcaster, led the seamen to the assault with his accustomed bravery, but I lament to say that he received a dangerous wound in the act of entering the fort, which, I apprehend, will, for a considerable time, deprive me of his services (the benefit of which I have many years experienced,) and the country of a brave and experienced officer. Mr. Scott, my first lieutenant, who was next in command, nobly led them on, and soon gained the ramparts.

Captain O'Conor, of the *Prince Regent*, to whom I entrusted the landing of the troops, displayed great ability and cool judgment, the boats being under a heavy fire from all points.

Captain Popham, in the *Montreal*, anchored his ship in a most gallant style, sustaining the whole fire until we gained the shore. She was set on fire three times by red hot shot, and much cut up in her hull, masts and rigging. Captain Popham received a severe wound in his right hand, and speaks in high terms of Mr. Richardson, the master, who, from a severe wound in the left arm, was obliged to undergo amputation at the shoulder.

Captain Spilsbury of the *Niagara*, Captain Dobbs of the *Charwell*, Captain Anthony of the *Star*, and Captain Collier of the *Magnet* behaved very much to my satisfaction.

The 2nd Battalion Royal Marines excited the admiration of all. They were led by the gallant Colonel Malcolm, and suffered severely. Captain Holtaway, doing duty in the *Princess Charlotte*, gallantly fell at the head of his company.

Having landed with the seamen and marines, I had great pleasure in witnessing not only the zeal and prompt attention of the officers to my orders but also the intrepid bravery of the men, whose good and temperate conduct under circumstances of great temptation (being a whole night in the town, employed in loading the captured vessels with ordnance, naval stores and provisions,) most justly claim my high approbation and acknowledgements, and I here beg leave to recommend to their Lordships' notice my first lieutenant, Mr. Scott, and aide-de-camp, Acting Lieutenant Yeo, to whom I beg leave to refer their Lordships for information; nor should the meritorious exertions of Acting Lieutenant Griffin, severely wounded in the arm, or Mr. Brown, both of whom were attached to the storming party, be omitted.

It is a great satisfaction to me to acquaint their Lordships that I have on this, as well as all other occasions, received from Lieutenant-General Drummond that support and attention which never fail in securing perfect cordiality between the two services.

I herewith transmit a list of the killed and wounded, and of the ordnance, naval stores and provisions captured and destroyed by the combined attack on the 6th inst.

(Canadian Archives, M. 389-6, pp. 116-120.)

A list of officers, seamen and marines of His Majesty's fleet on Lake Ontario, killed and wounded at Oswego, on the 6th of May, 1814:

PRINCE REGENT—
    Abel John, seaman, killed.
    G. A. Griffin, acting lieut., wounded.
    Thomas Harrington, seaman, severely wounded.
    James Heagsham,   do   do   do

PRINCESS CHARLOTTE—
    John McKenzie, seaman, killed.
    W. H. Mulcaster, captain, wounded (severely.)

MONTREAL—
    Thomas Gorman, seaman, killed.

Wounded.

Stephen Popham, captain.
James Richardson, master, severely, lost an arm.
John Baxter, seaman.
Thomas Gillingham, seaman.
Joseph Padds, do
John Oscar, do

ROYAL MARINES—*Killed.*

William Holtaway, captain.
Sergt. Green.
Joseph Brown, private.
Corp. Battle.
Sergt. Kain.
Thos. Hooper, private.

Wounded.

John Hewett, lieut.
William Mcredith, private.
James Lee, do
J. Callahan, do
Thos. Greenlove, do
Samuel Wright, do
John Newburg, do
Thos. Russell, do
Peter Keener, do
John Bax, corpl.
John Blundell, sergt.
John Tacked, corpl.
John Caveny, private.
Edward Fell, do
William Wench, do
Thos. Making, do
John Webber, do
John Gillingham, do
William Trout, do
Isaac Taylor, do
John Baxter, do
John Jackson, do
Francis Marlow, do
Matthew Hoosey, do
Philip Ridout, do
Thos. Beckford, do
John Smith, do

(Canadian Archives, M. 389-6, pp. 113-4.)

A statement of ordnance and naval stores and provisions brought off and destroyed in a combined attack of the sea and land forces on the town and fort of Oswego, on the 6th of May, 1814:—

BROUGHT OFF.

Ordnance Stores—
Guns—3 long 32-pounders, 4 long 24-pounders. A quantity of various kinds of ordnance stores, naval stores and provisions.
3 schooners.
800 barrels of flour.
500 barrels of pork.
600 barrels of salt.
500 barrels of bread.
A quantity of large rope.

DESTROYED.

Guns sunk—3 long 24-pounders, 1 long 12 pounder, 2 long 6-pounders.
One schooner and all barracks and other public buildings.

JAMES LUCAS YEO,
Commodore.

(Canadian Archives, M. 389-6, p. 115.)

Commodore Chauncey to the Secretary of the Navy.

U. S. Ship *Pike*, SACKETT'S HARBOR,
May 7, 1814, 5 o'clock P. M.

SIR,—

The enemy's fleet passed in sight about an hour since at a great distance and standing for Kingston. We have some vague reports that the enemy landed from 1,500 to 3,000 men, and that they carried the fort at Oswego by storm and put the garrison to the sword. Others that the garrison, with Captain Woolsey and the seamen, surrendered, and that the enemy were marching to the falls. All these reports are unquestionably much exaggerated, and if it should turn out that Oswego has been taken, it will be found that the troops and seamen did their duty, and that the enemy paid dearly for the place.

"New York Evening Post," 19th May, 1814.

Extract of a letter from a United States officer to his friend in Boston :—

OSWEGO FALLS, May 7, 1814.

I arrived at this place about sunset last evening, in company with about 200 troops. We escaped from the fort about 3 p. m., after a very severe contest. Our force was in all about 300 men. The enemy's fleet made its appearance on the morning of the 5th, about six o'clock, and consisted of four ships and three brigs. We had no doubt of their object, and fired alarm guns to collect the militia. About 3 p. m. the fleet formed a line and commenced embarking their troops in boats. We had only four pieces of ordnance to oppose their landing. The cannonade began on our side about 4, and was immediately returned by them. It continued until 6, at which time we saw them take their men on board and cut four of their boats adrift, there being every appearance of a squall. The fleet left us and came to anchor about ten miles from the fort down the lake.

On the morning of the 6th the fleet again made sail for the fort. The wind being nearly ahead, it could not form its line until 11. The militia had assembled to the number of 200. The enemy placed their troops in boats, and the cannonading began on our side immediately. Our battery prevented their landing until about half-past one, when they effected their purpose under cover of a continued stream of grape and canister shot. The militia at this time thought best to leave us. I do not think they fired a gun. The enemy was met by two companies of our troops at the landing, but his advantage was so great that it became impossible to prevent his progress, and our soldiers retreated to the breastwork. We now formed our line of defence and stood our ground for about 30 minutes, when the retreat was ordered by Lieut.-Colonel Mitchell, a brave and active officer. We retired in good order, tho' exposed to the brisk fire of the enemy. Our loss in killed and wounded we have not yet ascertained. Only one officer, however, was killed—Lieut. Blaney of our corps. He fought in the most gallant manner until about the commencement of the retreat, when he was shot dead. Lieut. Robb of the light artillery was wounded, but very slightly.

General Orders.

Adjutant General's Office, Headquarters,
MONTREAL, May 12, 1814.

His Excellency the Governor-in-Chief and Commander of the Forces has the highest satisfaction in announcing to the troops that he has received a despatch from Lieutenant-General Drummond reporting the result of a most spirited and successful attack on the enemy's fort and position of Oswego, which was carried by assault at noon on the 6th inst.

The Lieutenant-General reports that, having caused six companies of the Regiment De Watteville and one company of the Glengarry Light Infantry to embark on board the squadron, in addition to the 2nd Battalion of Royal Marines, he accompanied Sir James Yeo in the *Prince Regent*, and on the evening of the 5th instant anchored off Oswego, but a violent gale of wind driving the squadron off shore the position was not recovered until noon on the following day, when the disposition for landing was instantly carried into execution in the following order: The frigates taking a position from whence they could cannonade the fort and the brigs, schooners and gunboats in proportion to their respective draft of water covered by their fire the several points of debarkation of the troops, which was attended with considerable difficulty, owing to the shoalness of water the boats grounding, the troops were in many instances obliged to leap out and wade through the water to their middles to gain the landing, and the enemy having strongly occupied the favorable positions near the shore and the woods with which it is surrounded, the disembarkation was attended with some loss but effected with the utmost promptitude, under the direction of Lieut. Colonel Fischer, led by two new formed companies of De Watteville's Regiment under Capt. De Berzy, the remaining four companies and detachment of artillery being held in reserve. The 2nd Battalion of Marines, under Lieutenant Colonel Malcolm, supported by a detachment of 200 seamen under Captain Mulcaster, Royal Navy, formed a second column to the right. Captain McMillan's company of the Glengarry Light Infantry gained the skirt of the woods to the left and covered the advance of the columns to the fort, which was gained and carried in ten minutes from the advance of the troops after landing. The enemy's garrison consisted of Macomb's 3rd Regiment of artillery 400 strong, and a numerous body of militia, saving themselves by a precipitate flight.

Lieutenant General Drummond speaks in the strongest terms of the cordial, judicious and able co-operation of Commodore Sir James Yeo and the officers and seamen of his squadron, and laments the temporary loss the service has sustained in Captain Mulcaster of the Royal Navy, who is severely wounded. The eminent services of that officer and of Captains O'Connor, Popham and Collier are particularly noticed.

The Lieutenant General bestows the highest praise on the cool and judicious conduct of Lieutenant Colonel Fischer of De Watteville's and Lieutenant Colonel Malcolm of the Royal Marines, on the intrepid gallantry displayed by Captain Berzy, who led the flank companies of the Watteville's, and by Captain McMillan in the judicious execution of the duties assigned to his light company in covering the advance; to Lieut. Colonel Pearson, inspecting field officer and Major Smelt, 103rd Regiment, who, being passengers in the fleet, volunteered their services; Captain Cruttenden, Royal Artillery, Brevet Major De Cousten of De Watteville's; Lieutenant Stevens, Rocket Company; Lieutenant Gosset, Royal Engineers; Lieutenant Laurie of the Marines, who led the first party that entered the fort, and Lieutenant Hewitt of the same corps, who climbed the flagstaff and pulled down the American colors which were nailed to it, are respectively noticed by the Lieutenant General, who represents in the strongest terms the zealous and able assistance he has experienced on this and every other occasion from Deputy Assistant Adjutant General Lieutenant Colonel Harvey and from his aid de camp, Captain Jervois.

It is particularly gratifying to His Excellency to have to notice that to the high honor of both branches of the service that there was not a single soldier or sailor missing, nor a single instance of intoxication, although surrounded by temptation.

The service has lost a brave and meritorious officer in Captain Holtaway of the Royal Marines.

Every object of the expedition being accomplished, the barracks burnt and the fort dismantled, and all public stores which were not brought away destroyed, the troops re-embarked at 4 o'clock the following morning and the squadron sailed for Kingston.

The enemy's loss amounts to at least 100 killed and sixty prisoners, the greater part wounded.

EDWARD BAYNES, A. G. N. A.

General Order.

Headquarters, SACKETT'S HARBOR,
May 12, 1814.

Major General Brown has the satisfaction to announce to the forces under his command that the detachment stationed at Oswego, under the immediate orders of Lieutenant Mitchell of the Third Artillery, by their gallant and highly military conduct in sustaining the fire of the whole British fleet on the lake for nearly two days, and contending with the vastly superior numbers of the enemy on the land as long as the interests of their country or the honor of their profession required, and then effecting their retreat in good order in the face of this superior force of the enterprising and accomplished foe to the depot of naval stores, which it became their duty to defend, have established for themselves a name in arms worthy of the gallant nation in whose cause they fight and highly honorable to the army. Lieutenant Colonel Mitchell had in all less than 300 men, and the force of the enemy by land and water exceeded 3,000.

R. JONES, Assist. Adj. Gen.

Commodore Chauncey to the Secretary of the Navy.

U. S. Ship Superior, SACKETT'S HARBOR,
May 12, 1814.

I have not heard from Oswego since I wrote last. The enemy's fleet left Kingston again yesterday. The *Lady of the Lake* dogged them until evening and was several times chased by one of their brigs. The enemy had with him a number of small vessels and gunboats and at sundown were standing about S. W., evidently bound again to Oswego or the Genesee river on some marauding expedition.

New York Evening Post, 25th May, 1814.

(From the Ontario Repository.)

On Friday last, May 13, a British force of seven sail appeared off the mouth of the Genesee river, where we have a small force under General Peter B. Porter. They sent in a flag to demand a surrender of all public stores, which was refused. The flag returned and then they sent some gunboats, between which and our men some shots were exchanged. Another flag was afterwards sent renewing the demand with some threats. They also sent to General Porter a paper purporting to be the terms on which the people at Oswego gave up the public property at that place and offered the same terms to the people at the river, viz., not to molest private property.

On Saturday, (May 14,) the enemy appeared off the village of Pultneyville and sent a barge ashore, which took off as prisoners a Mr. Fuller and two other persons.

Biographical Note.

Colonel John Hewett entered the Royal Navy in 1803 as rated midshipman of H. M. S. *Windsor Castle*, 98 guns, and besides serving in several minor actions took part in the general engagement fought on 22nd July, 1805, between the British fleet, (15 ships of the line and 3 frigates,) and the combined French and Spanish fleets, (20 ships of the line, 7 frigates and 2 brigs,) and subsequently saw active service in W. Indies at Cadiz and Corunna, (under Sir John Moore,) and the Baltic, in Spain and Portugal, on the staff and attached to the 33rd Regt. under Sir Arthur Wellesley, in the United States and in Canada, at the storming of Hampton, Ocracoke, taking of Kent Island and Queenstown and capture of Oswego.

On one occasion the *Windsor Castle* being in immediate danger from a white squall the topmen hesitated to go aloft till Midshipman Hewett sprang forward and showed them an example, which was immediately followed. For this act of daring he was publicly thanked by the captain. He was severely wounded in the head in the action of the 22nd July, 1805. Four commissions in the Royal Marines were offered to those midshipmen who had most distinguished themselves, the first of which was offered to and accepted by Mr. Hewett.

L'Impeteuse, (French 74,) having been driven on shore at Cape Hatteras, Lieut. Crook, R. N., and Lieut Hewett with 18 marines were sent to take possession. On their approaching L'Impeteuse it was found that she had not struck her colors and the enemy attempted to tip one of the main deck guns into the English boat, but after considerable difficulty the party reached the quarter deck. Being hard pressed Lieut. Hewett placed his small party of marines between two quarter deck guns and then joined Lieut. Crook in endeavoring to persuade the French commander to surrender. This he refused to do, stating that his captain had gone to the British Admiral to claim American neutrality, and he insisted that the British party should become prisoners, to enforce which he attempted to draw his sword. Lieut. Hewett immediately seized the French officer's sword arm and prevented this, at the same time giving his marines the order to charge. This was done with such effect that the French were taken by surprise and the deck was so crowded that in the struggle 80 of them jumped overboard and were mostly drowned in attempting to swim ashore, and the remainder were driven off the quarter deck. Lieut. Hewett had the honor of hauling down the French flag. The French crew, many of whom were intoxicated, then lost all discipline and became beyond control. In the awful position in which they were placed the gallant Lieut. Crook kept possession of the quarter deck until reinforcements arrived, while Lieut. Hewett with one marine and a noble French officer went below and secured the magazine and spirit room. To this French officer Lieut. Hewett attributed the safety of the ship's crew and the British party.

Lieut. Crook's report states that "in a moment those gallant marines were at the side of their officer, and Lieut. Hewett and his party after a severe struggle cleared the deck and drove the entire French crew under hatches and subsequently secured the magazine and spirit room, (a service of extreme peril,) where the enemy were in possession, intoxicated, with unguarded candles and several hundred loose gun cartridges under their feet, thereby preserving the lives of upwards of 800 men."

At Craney Island Lieut. Hewett was thanked by Lt. General Sir Charles Napier and General Sidney Beckwith for volunteering to lead the way over a bridge which the enemy had mined.

At the storming of Fort Oswego Lieut. Hewett had the honor of being selected with his company to cover the retreat should the attack fail, but at his earnest request was permitted to lead the forlorn hope. The Americans had nailed their ensign to the flagstaff, which had been cleated for the purpose of ascending it. On his party entering the fort Lieut. Hewett with his color sergeant cut their way to the flagstaff, which the former climbed under a heavy fire and tore the colors from the masthead. In executing this he was wounded in several places, and just as he regained the ground and leaned for a moment, faint from loss of blood, against the mast, a wounded American lying on the ground within a couple of paces raised his musket and was about to fire at him when the color sergeant bayonnetted him. Lieut. Hewett was thanked for "the manner in which he with his company covered the landing of the assaulting column under a heavy fire from the fort and from American infantry and riflemen in the adjacent woods, and for the gallant manner in which he led the assault, entering where the opposition was greatest and then charging on the flagstaff." Lieut. General Sir Gordon Drummond and Commodore Yeo were eye witnesses and on Lieut. Hewett presenting the captured colors the former said: "No one so worthy of them as yourself;" the Commodore adding "Taken in a manner unparallelled in history."

While Col. Hewett remained in the army and even for some time afterwards his men used to present to him a wreath of laurel annually on the anniversary of the capture of Oswego.

On another occasion the British and Americans were marching through a dense wood unknown to one another when the enemy being suddenly observed the British received the order to "front form." So close were the opposing forces that the Americans mistook the command for that of their own officers and performed a similar movement thus bringing the leading companies of the opposing forces face to face within a few yards of one another. Taking instant advantage of the momentary hesitation and surprise Lieut. Hewett ordered his company to fire a volley low from the hip, and to charge, with the result of killing a large number of the enemy and dispersing the rest.

When in charge of outposts watching the American forces on the south side of the St. Laurence Lieut. Hewett sought for, discovered, and at night tested, by personally wading, a ford close above some rapids, which was hitherto entirely unknown, and which from the roughness and velocity of the water was always deemed to be utterly impassable. This discovery subsequently proved of great advantage.

Lieut. Hewett on promotion received a brevet majority for services. He was officially thanked "for the example he had always shown as an officer at headquarters for always volunteering for service, and for the honor he had done to his corps while on service." He received by command of William IV, through Sir Herbert Taylor, His Majesty's approbation of his merit and gallant services.

Col. Hewett died in 1876 at the age of 84 at Llantwit in Glamorganshire.

(MS. Pedigree of the family of Hewett, in possession of Major E. V. O. Hewett.)

From Sir George Prevost to Lieut. General Drummond.

Secret and Confidential.

HEAD QRS., MONTREAL,
7th May, 1814.

Sir,—I have this day had the honor to receive your communication of the 3rd inst., stating the forces you proposed embarking on board the squadron for the purpose of acting against the enemy's magazines and stores at Oswego and along the southern coast of Lake Ontario. My letter to you of the same date will have anticipated your wishes by conveying my approval of that measure.

I cannot at this moment supply you from this Province with the 800 effective men you deem necessary to enable you to attempt, by a combined operation, the destruction of the enemy's fleet and stores at Sackett's Harbor, and it will depend upon the force which His Majesty's Government may place at my disposal from England during the next month whether the seat of war may be transferred to the enemy's possessions contiguous to Upper Canada, or whether, as at present the case, I shall be obliged to retain the whole of the troops I have in Lower Canada for its defence.

In acknowledging the honor of your second letter of the 3rd inst. and its enclosure, relative to the serious indisposition of Colonel

Elliott of the Indian Dept., of whose recovery but little hope was entertained, I perfectly agree with you that Colonel Caldwell, from his acquaintance with the Western Indians, is best calculated to succeed to the situation and as soon as the account of Colonel Elliott's death may reach me, Colonel Caldwell shall be ordered to proceed forthwith to the head of the lake and he will receive such an appointment as will place him senior to Major McKee.

(Canadian Archives, c. 1222, pp. 117-8.)

From Sir J. C. Sherbrooke to Sir George Prevost.

HALIFAX, 9 May, 1814.

Sir,—I have the honor herewith to transmit for Your Excellency's information a copy of a letter which I have received from Vice Admiral Sir Alexander Cochrane. I am much disappointed at the information it contains, as I had hoped the 90th Regt. would by this time have reached Canada. Sir Alexander Cochrane's letter reached me fortunately on the evening before the packet sailed for England, and I immediately reported its contents to Lord Bathurst.

I trust, however, that the Vice Admiral's representation on the subject will have induced Rear Admiral Durham to forward the 90th Regt. without delay to Quebec.

(Canadian Archives, c. 1006, pp. 3-4.)

From Vice Admiral Cochrane to Sir J. C. Sherbrooke.

Asia, BERMUDA, 20th April, 1814.

Sir,—I have the honor to acknowledge the receipt of Your Excellency's letter of the 26th ultimo respecting the 90th Regt., which shall be forwarded on to Halifax the moment it arrives here, but, as I understand, Rear Admiral Francis Laforey or his successor have received no orders to send on this regiment to Bermuda, which has been waiting with the transports sent out for its conveyance at the Leeward Islands since October last. I am apprehensive some mistake has arisen at home. A convoy sails for the Leeward Islands in a few days, when I will acquaint Rear Admiral Durham of your expecting this regiment and recommend his sending it on to Quebec without a moment's delay.

(Canadian Archives, c. 1005, pp. 5-6.)

INDEX.

A.

Abell, M. W. ... 125
Achinson, Lieut.-Colonel ... 93
Adams, Captain G. ... 39, 51, 105
Adams, Major ... 93, 94, 136, 142, 143, 186
Aeolus, ship of war ... 171, 174, 199, 264
Agnew, Captain James ... 301
Albany, N. Y. ... 47, 52, 99, 138, 139, 203, 211, 212, 231, 265, 322
Albany Argus, newspaper ... 55
Albany Gazette, newspaper ... 40
Allan, William ... 255
Allen, ——— ... 229
Allen, Major ... 42, 48
Allen, Holden ... 88
Allen, Joel ... 88
Alvord, Dr. ... 55, 78
Amelia, schooner ... 325, 330
American State Papers ... 18, 40, 46, 109, 129, 146, 156
Amherstburg ... 47, 52, 99, 138, 139, 141, 154, 155, 158, 172, 220, 221, 244, 289, 316
Ancaster ... 154, 237
Anderson, Lieut. ... 75, 80
Anderson, Mr. ... 126, 203
Anderson, Samuel ... 254
Anthony, Captain Charles ... 341
Applegarth, William ... 255
Arbre, Croche ... 252
Ariel, schooner ... 35, 83, 84, 109, 143, 326
Armsden, John ... 88
Armstrong, Captain R. S. ... 75
Armstrong's Notices of the War of 1812 ... 69, 202, 321
Arnold's Mill ... 109
Ash, James ... 296
Asia, ship of war ... 351
Askin, Charles ... 26
Atkins, Captain ... 145
Atkin's house ... 82
Atkinson, Captain ... 163
Auburn, N. Y. ... 52, 241
Au Glaize river ... 249, 250, 251
Avon, N. Y. ... 79, 88

B.

Baby, Lieut.-Colonel Francis ... 75, 144, 179, 193, 206, 207, 210, 212, 268
Backhouse, John ... 255
Bailey, Captain ... 12, 14, 266
Baker, Asa ... 27
Baldoon ... 176
Baldwin, John ... 100, 112
Ball, ——— ... 198
Ball, Lieut. ... 12, 15

Ball, Miss Amy ... 161
Ball's Mills ... 26, 27
Bar Point ... 139
Barbadoes ... 214
Barclay, Captain R. H. ... 8, 27, 47, 140, 288, 289
Barker, Captain Oliver ... 105
Barnard, Lieut. ... 66
Barnett, George ... 29, 30
Barnes, Major Isaac ... 8
Barrett, ———— ... 21
Barrett, Benjamin ... 88
Barton, Benjamin ... 40, 55
Basden, Captain James L. ... 72, 194, 204, 205, 226, 230, 269
Batavia, N. Y. ... 32, 40, 45, 48, 54, 61, 77, 80, 82, 83, 88, 92, 93, 97, 98, 100, 101, 106, 107, 111, 117, 118, 122, 123, 124, 125, 130, 133, 135, 136, 137, 141, 144, 173, 187, 189, 202, 241
Bathurst, Earl ... 30, 41, 58, 59, 98, 110, 191, 212, 213, 254, 267, 279, 282, 288, 306, 351
Battle, Corporal ... 342
Bax, Corporal John ... 342
Baxter, John ... 342
Baynes, Colonel Edward ... 32, 57, 92, 104, 105, 177, 258, 298, 308, 315, 316, 322, 323, 326, 346
Beasley, Richard ... 255
Beasley's house ... 117
Beauport ... 297
Beaver Dams ... 27, 121
Beck, Lieut. ... 39
Beckford, Thos. ... 342
Beckwith, Sir Sidney ... 105, 174, 197, 199, 261, 349
Bedford, Jonathan ... 296
Bell, Mr. ... 140
Bell, Mr. ... 284
Bennett, Major ... 39, 50
Benninger, Michael ... 160
Beresford, schooner ... 295, 297, 305, 313
Bermuda ... 301, 351
Bersey, Captain de ... 337, 338, 345, 346
Bessey's house ... 27
Big Miami river ... 250
Blackhoof, Indian chief ... 250
Black River ... 126
Black Rock ... 8, 46, 48, 50, 51, 55, 61, 62, 63, 64, 66, 67, 68, 70, 71, 72, 73, 74, 77, 78, 79, 80, 81, 82, 83, 84, 85, 86, 87, 88, 91, 93, 94, 96, 97, 99, 100, 103, 104, 109, 110, 111, 112, 114, 117, 120, 125, 126, 133, 135, 156, 157, 159, 172, 178, 281
Blakeslee, Lieut.-Colonel ... 79, 91, 93, 94, 95, 96
Blaney, Lieut. ... 244
Blodget, P. ... 194, 207
Blodgett, Sylvester ... 88
Bloom, Lieut.-Colonel Henry ... 49, 68
Bloomfield, N. Y. ... 88, 97, 100, 135, 178
Blundell, Sergt. John ... 342
Bodwell, Lieut. ... 105
Boileau, N. B. ... 193, 216
Bomford, Major ... 42, 47

Boston, Mass. ...211
Bostwick, Lieut.-Colonel Henry ...43
Boughton, Levi ...88
Boughton, Lieut.-Colonel Seymour ... 79, 83, 88, 91, 93, 94, 96
Bowlby, Thomas ...255
Boynton, Ensign ... 105
Brady, Lieut.-Colonel Hugh ... 241
Brampton, Staff Adjutant ... 12
Brenton, E. B. ...90, 116
Brewster, Captain ... 72
Bridge, Captain ... 71, 74, 75, 86
Brigham, Captain Brewster ... 144, 179, 193, 196, 206, 207, 210
Bristol, Anson ... 88
Brock, Major General ...203, 209, 229, 302
Brooks, Colonel ...97
Brown, Major General Jacob ... 29, 136, 201, 241, 246, 346
Brown, Major ... 101
Brown, Joseph ...342
Brown, Dr. ...97
Brown, Mr. ... 341
Brownell, Wanton ... 88
Brownstown ...249
Bruyeres, Lieut.-Colonel R. H. ... 105, 140, 150, 151, 257, 258, 261, 262
Brymner's Excerpts ... 266
Buel, Willis ... 88
Buffalo ...5, 6, 7, 8, 9, 24, 25, 26, 31, 36, 38, 39, 40, 46, 48, 50, 51, 52, 53
   54, 55, 56, 61, 62, 63, 64, 65, 66, 67, 68, 70, 71, 72, 73, 77, 78,
   79, 80, 81, 82, 83, 84, 85, 86, 87, 88, 90, 93, 94, 96, 97, 100, 101
   103, 104, 108, 109, 110, 111, 112, 117, 120, 121, 122, 123, 124,
   125, 126, 132, 133, 135, 143, 144, 157, 178, 180, 183, 197, 213,
   249, 280, 281, 324, 326
Buffalo Creek ...62
Buffalo Gazette ... 9, 45, 155
Bullock, Captain ... 273
Bullock, Lieut. ...12, 14
Bullus, Dr. ... 6
Burford, (U. C.) ... 287, 290, 307
Burgess, ——— ... 136
Burgess, Samuel ...88
Burk, John ...296
Burke, Lieut. A. C. ...297
Burlington, (U. C.)... 7, 18, 20, 21, 26, 45, 51, 53, 56, 57, 85, 105, 154, 157,
   170, 209, 228, 229, 235, 237, 243, 265, 267, 286, 306, 313,
   314, 326, 328
Burlington, (Vt.) ... 101, 103, 136, 245
Burlington Bay ... 55, 320, 321
Burlington Beach ... 257
Burlington Heights ...9, 18, 31, 49, 56, 66, 117, 133, 194,
   197, 244, 257, 287, 294
Burn, John ... 254
Burnett, Brig.-General ... 143, 177, 178
Burritt, Stephen ...254
Burton, Captain ... 273
Burwell, Lieut.-Colonel Mahlon ... 255, 280, 292
Butler, Lieut.-Colonel Anthony. (H.)... 129, 206, 218, 223, 229, 268
Butler's Rangers ... 97

C.

Cahokia Indians ... 250
Callahan, J. ... 342
Caldwell, Captain ... 158, 204, 205, 221, 223, 226, 227, 230, 307
Caldwell, Colonel ... 328, 351
Caldwell, Mr. ... 28
Caledonia, schooner ... 8, 31
Caledonia, N. Y. ... 79, 88
Camden, (U. C.) ... 106, 109
Cameron, Captain ... 75
Cameron, Duncan ... 255, 257
Cameron, Phoebe ... 161
Cameron, William ... 161
Camp, Captain ... 93, 96, 157
Campbell, Lieut. John ... 88
Campbell, Midshipman ... 289
Campfield's house ... 289
Canadian Archives. 3, 4, 8, 11, 13, 14, 23, 24, 25, 30, 31, 33, 38, 39, 41, 43, 45,
    52, 58, 59, 60, 63, 65, 67, 72, 73, 74, 76, 85, 86, 99, 100, 105,
    106, 110, 111, 130, 132, 140, 141, 143, 146, 147, 149, 150, 152,
    153, 155, 156, 158, 159, 162, 164, 166, 167, 169, 170, 171, 172,
    173, 175, 179, 180, 185, 188, 189, 190, 192, 194, 195, 197, 198,
    199, 201, 203, 204, 208, 209, 210, 212, 213, 214, 217, 218, 220,
    222, 223, 227, 228, 230, 231, 236, 237, 238, 239, 240, 241, 243,
    244, 245, 246, 247, 248, 249, 256, 257, 259, 261, 262, 263, 264,
    267, 268, 269, 270, 271, 274, 275, 277, 278, 279, 280, 282, 283,
    284, 286, 287, 288, 289, 290, 292, 294, 295, 296, 298, 300, 301,
    302, 303, 304, 305, 306, 307, 308, 310, 311, 312, 314, 315, 317,
    319, 322, 324, 327, 328, 329, 337, 338, 341, 342, 343, 351
Canadian Courant, newspaper ... 16
Canandaigua, N. Y. ... 40, 43, 47, 52, 77, 78, 80, 82, 84, 88, 92,
    101, 106, 121, 187
Canute, ——— ... 117
Cape Girardeau ... 253
Cartwright, Hon. Richard ... 254, 307
Caryl, Benjamin ... 123
Cass, General Lewis ... 80, 108, 129, 145, 146, 194, 210, 242
Catfish Creek ... 167
Cattaraugus, N. Y. ... 87, 143
Caveny, John ... 342
Cayuga, N. Y. ... 52
Cayuga Indians ... 301
Chamberling, John ... 144
Chambers, ——— ... 143
Champlain, N. Y. ... 310, 315, 317, 319, 322, 323, 326, 327
Champlain Lake ... 126, 155, 197, 199, 245, 304
Champlin, Lieut. ... 127
Champlin, Ludowick ... 88
Chapin, Lieut.-Colonel Cyrenius ... 26, 35, 45, 52, 67, 77, 79, 81, 88, 90, 93,
    94, 104, 121, 122, 123, 125
Chapin, Lieut. James ... 186
Chapin, Seth ... 88
Chateauguay ... 101, 102, 126, 127, 168, 169
Chatewacomin, Indian chief ... 272
Charleton, Lieut. ... 12, 15, 75

v.

Charwell, Brig. ...325, 340, 341
Chatham, (U. C.) ...175, 194
Chauncey, Commodore Isaac ... 4, 6, 49, 116, 196, 201, 203, 256, 265, 287, 292, 343, 347
Chautauqua County, N. Y. ... 8, 40, 89, 93, 133
Chazy ... 245
Chesapeake Bay ... 153
Chillicothe ... 212
Chippawa ...35, 36, 51, 57, 58, 60, 61, 63, 64, 74, 89, 105, 133, 137, 150, 156, 235, 265, 266,306
Chippawa Creek ... 74
Chippewa Indians ... 185, 249, 250, 252
Chippewa, schooner ... 35, 77, 83, 84, 87, 143, 289
Chippoy ... 251
Chisholm, Mr. ... 173
Christie, Robert ... 256, 269
Church, Lazarus ... 88
Churchill, Lieut.-Colonel ... 35, 91, 93, 94, 178
Cincinnati ... 249
Cincinnati Gazette ... 77
Clarence, N. Y. ...89, 123, 124, 125
Clark, Colonel Isaac ... 245, 261
Clark, Memoirs of Lieut.-Colonel John... 20
Clark, Lieut.-Colonel Thomas ... 91, 255
Clark, Judge ... 35
Clark, Samuel ... 88
Clark, ——— ... 198
Clark's house ... 27
Claus, Colonel William ... 133, 167, 255, 263, 300, 328
Clifford, Major Miller ... 281
Cochrane, Admiral Sir Alexander ... 162, 351
Cochrane, Captain... 99, 117, 212
Cold Springs, N. Y. ...35, 84, 122
Coffin, Assistant Commissary General... 284, 290
Coffin, Lieut.-Colonel N. ... 27, 130
Coit, Daniel S. ... 89
Coleman, Captain Thomas ... 43, 138, 162, 173, 186, 195, 221
Collier Captain ... 335, 341, 345
Collins, Mr. ... 78
Colrain, Mass. ... 88
Colt, Lieut.-Colonel ... 178
Coltman, George ... 280
Commissariat Department ... 61
Conant, John ... 88
Conjunckaty, (Conjockity, Conguichity,) Creek ... 62, 70, 78, 79, 94, 95, 178
Coore, Major ... 323
Corbett, ——— ... 198, 210
Cork ... 214
Cornell, Mr. ... 296
Cornwall, (U. C.) ...58, 100, 102, 103, 150, 166, 176, 177, 179, 189, 204, 237, 248, 281, 282, 314
Cornwallis, Lord ... 214
Coteau du Lac ... 29, 100, 165, 171, 174, 175, 197, 204, 275, 282, 286
Couche, Deputy Commissary General Edward ... 243, 248
Cousten, Brevet Major de ... 337, 346
Covington, Fort ... 223

Cox, Osborne ...296
Cozens, Joshua Y. ...254
Crane, Captain ...196, 256
Crane, Indian chief ...249
Cranfield's house ...227
Crandall, John ...144
Crawford, John ...198
Crawford, William ...254
Crawford's house ...228
Creighton, Captain ...199
Croker, Hon. J. W. ...162, 295, 339
Crooks, Lieut. ...348, 349
Crooks, Major ...145
Crooks, John ...100, 112
Crooks, William ...255
Crookshank (Cruikshank,) Asst. Commissary General George. 141, 151, 165
Cross Roads ...48, 159, 160, 161
Cruttenden, Captain ...329, 335, 337, 339, 346
Crysler ...254
Cull, John ...198
Culver's house ...208
Cumming, John ...254
Cumming, Mr. ...220
Cummings, Thos. ...235
Curtis, Captain ...105
Curtiss, Mr. ...122

D.

Dakins, ——— ...287
Dallaba, Major ...201
Dance, Assistant Commissary General ...148, 209, 216, 237, 239, 243, 247, 284
Darling, Sailing Master ...226
Davies, Brevet Major ...297, 298, 299, 300
Davis, Lieut.-Colonel ...35, 97, 178, 187
Davis, Lieut. ...75
Davis, Lieut. ...80
Dawson, Lieut. Irwin ...12, 15, 19, 20, 22, 30
Dawson, Mrs. ...30
Davy, John ...144
Deacon, ——— ...117
Deane, Major Thomas ...244, 267, 278, 293
Dearborn, Major General Henry ...51, 112, 322
Defields, ——— ...198
Delaware, (U. C.)..109, 144, 170, 179, 193, 195, 204, 205, 206, 208, 210, 212,
218, 221, 222, 223, 224, 226, 228, 229, 241, 250, 268
Delaware Indians ...185, 202, 249, 252, 253, 257, 263
Dennis, John ...144
De Puysay's house ...27
Derby, Vt. ...105
Des Moines river ...252
Detroit ...6, 36, 37, 77, 106, 109, 110, 113, 129, 137, 138, 139, 140, 143,
145, 146, 152, 154, 155, 158, 161, 172, 178, 180, 192, 194, 206,
207, 209, 210, 218, 220, 221, 224, 227, 229, 230, 242, 244,
249, 270, 294, 302, 316, 317, 320, 321, 332, 333.
Detroit river ...139
Detroit, ship of war ...158

Dickson, Robert ... 229, 270, 272, 273
Dickson, Lieut.-Colonel Thomas ... 91, 255
Dickson, William ... 100, 112
Dickson's house ... 27, 85

Dingman, David ... 144
Dingman, William ... 144
Doan, ——— ... 307
Dobbins, Lieut.-Colonel ... 68
Dobbs, Captain Alexander ... 341
Dolsen, widow ... 21
Dolson, John ... 144
Dolson's house ... 109
Dorland, Thomas ... 254
Dorsey, ——— ... 21
Douglas, Sergt. ... 44
Dover, (U. C.) ... 43, 173, 208, 290
Dover Mills ... 43
Downing, Henry ... 88
Doyle, ——— ... 322
Drake, Roderick ... 44
Driscoll, Lieut. ... 18
Drummond, Lieut.-General Sir Gordon..3, 6, 11, 14, 15, 21, 23, 33, 35, 38, 40,
51, 57, 60, 61. 62, 63, 64, 65, 66, 67, 70, 74, 76, 78, 85, 86, 91,
95, 98, 99, 100, 103, 104, 106, 107, 108, 109, 110, 111, 119, 120,
129, 130, 131. 132, 133, 137, 140, 141, 143, 146, 147, 148, 150,
151, 153. 155. 158, 159, 162, 163, 165, 166, 167, 169, 170, 171,
172, 173, 175, 176, 179, 185, 188, 189, 191, 192, 193, 194, 196,
197, 200, 202, 203, 206, 207, 208, 210, 213, 216, 217, 219, 221,
222, 227, 229, 233, 235, 236, 238, 240, 242, 244, 245, 246, 247,
248, 255, 256, 257, 259, 261, 263, 267, 268, 269, 270, 274, 276,
277, 278, 279, 281, 282, 283, 284, 285, 286, 288, 292, 293, 295,
300, 302, 303, 305, 308, 309, 310, 311, 312, 313, 318, 319, 323,
328, 329, 334, 337, 339, 340, 341, 345, 349, 350
Drummond, Lieut.-Colonel William ... 3, 228, 248, 278, 306
Duff, Mr. ... 52
Dundas Militia ... 177
Durand, Mr. ... 265
Durham, Rear Admiral ... 351

E.

Eagle, sloop ... 31
East Bloomfield, N. Y. ... 79
Eastern District ... 147, 254, 279, 307
Eastman, Dr. ... 128
Eckford, Mr. ... 116, 196
Edgecombe, Mr. ... 171
Edwards, Joseph ... 100, 112, 255
Edy, Squire ... 107
Eel River Indians ... 250
Eighteen Mile Creek ... 78, 281
Eleven Mile Creek ... 51, 53, 62, 66, 67, 77, 80, 81, 96, 97, 101,
104, 110, 126, 142, 177
Elgor, John ... 88
Eliot, Captain G. A. ... 7, 12, 15, 21, 22, 28, 52, 63, 75
Ellicott, N. Y. ... 88

Elliott, Captain Jesse D. 5, 6, 129, 130, 131, 133, 318, 326, 329, 330, 331, 332, 333
Elliott, Colonel Matthew ..3, 7, 23, 24, 27, 32, 36, 41, 72, 133, 157, 173, 189, 204, 205, 218, 221, 226, 227, 257, 263, 310, 328, 351
Elliott, Captain William 185
Emmott, Joseph 264
Emmott's house 27
Erie, Pa. 31, 80, 81, 87, 109, 130, 133, 137, 143, 161, 164, 168, 178, 193, 216, 312, 324, 329
Erie, Fort 5, 27, 36, 46, 51, 70, 74, 105, 110, 133, 137, 150, 317, 320
Erie, Lake 6, 24, 31, 47, 71, 77, 103, 137, 143, 153, 154, 163, 172, 180, 192, 196, 200, 201, 208, 210, 213, 227, 244, 249, 250, 266, 288, 317, 320, 321

F.

Fairbanks, Mr. 55
Farnum, Lieut. 95, 96
Farnum, Levi 88
Farrell, Mr. ... .296
Fawcett, Captain ... .12, 15, 22, 28, 67, 72, 73, 104, 111
Fell, Edward 342
Fenton, Colonel James ... .193, 215, 216
Fifteen Mile Creek ... .27
Fischer, Lieut.-Colonel ... .324, 329, 334, 336, 337, 345
Fisher, Alexander 254
Fisk, Lieut. ... .80
Five Mile Meadows 27, 39, 78
Five Nations Indians 202
Fleming, Lieut.-Colonel 68
Folles Avoines Indians 252
Fordham, Apollo 88
Forster, Colonel 329
Forsyth, Major 116
Forsyth's house 93, 98
Fort, Jacob L. 123, 124
Fort Findley 152
Fort George 5, 8, 9, 24, 27, 31, 32, 36, 41, 42, 48, 49, 54, 55, 56, 57, 58, 61, 68, 98, 99, 104, 105, 112, 114, 115, 126, 153, 159, 160, 161, 241, 258, 266, 285, 290, 291, 293, 294, 306, 313, 314, 321
Fort Wayne ... .250
Fort Wellington ... .236, 237, 246, 248, 270, 281, 282
Fortune, Lieut. 298
Forty Mile Creek ... .26, 122, 149
Foster, Captain and Lieut.-Colonel C.L. L....23, 52, 191, 193, 221, 259, 308
Four Mile Creek, (U. C.) 7, 33, 48, 120, 159, 161, 188
Four Mile Creek, (N. Y.) 84
Fourteen Mile Creek ... .204, 205, 230
Fowler, Captain 279
Fowler, S. ... .88
Fox Indians ... .185
Franklinton, Ohio 153
Fraser, Lieut. Donald ... .10, 34, 38, 97, 124
Fraser, Jacob 296
Fraser, Lieut.-Colonel Thomas 149, 254

Fraser, William 254
Fraser, Mr. 230
Frazer, Volunteer John 65
Freer, Noah 167, 179, 185, 198, 202, 203, 219, 259, 264, 269, 290,
              301, 305, 310, 317, 339
French, Albert 254
French Mills 54, 101, 102, 116, 126, 127, 134, 147, 168, 169,
              171, 174, 195, 202, 241, 303
Frenchtown 138
Frend, Major 15, 63, 70, 72
Frey, Captain, Bernard 159
Frey, Mrs. Hannah 159
Frink, Dudley 123, 124
Frisbie, Major 61
Frost, Dennis 88
Fuller, Mr. 347
Fulton, James 255

G.

Gaines, Brig.-General E. P. 287
Gananoqui 150
Gano, Brig.-General 128, 145, 152
Ganson, Major James 100
Garden, Lieut. James 47
Gardner, Captain 129
Gardner, Lieut.-Colonel Peregrine 79, 88, 178
Gardner, William 55, 78
Gaugreben, Lieut. 12, 36, 104, 238, 246, 270
General Pike, ship of war 4, 100, 170, 174, 208, 211, 222, 265, 287, 343
Genesee County, N. Y. 8, 24, 35, 40, 92, 93, 124, 136
Genesee River 52, 69, 88, 347
Geneseo, N. Y. 97
Geneva Gazette 78
Georgia 54
Georgetown, D. C. 68
Gerrard, Youmans & Co. 119
Gilkinson, William 254
Gill, Captain 190, 223, 224
Gillette, Mr. 78
Gillies, Elias 193
Gillingham, John 342
Gillingham, Thomas 342
Gilmore, Deputy Assistant Commissary General 259
Givins, Major 263
Glanford Township 263
Glegg, Major J. B. 66, 117, 133, 157, 192, 264, 290, 291
Glengarry Regiment 7, 38, 227, 275, 282, 314, 324, 329,
              334, 336, 337, 338, 345, 346
Gloucester Bay 334
Gordon, Assistant Commissary James 237
Gordon, Lieut.-Colonel John 15, 63, 71, 72, 95, 217, 220
Gorman, Thomas 341
Gossett, Lieut. 246, 329, 335, 337, 346
Gottenburg 315, 316, 319, 323, 327
Gould, Daniel G. 89
Graeme, Lieut. P. 205

Grand Island	74, 79, 178
Grand River	148, 202, 208, 293
Grand River Indians	202
Granger, Lieut.-Colonel Erastus	34, 35, 46, 61, 84, 93, 95, 123
Granger, MSS. of Lieut.-Colonel J. N.	35
Granger's Mills	181
Grant, Thomas	88
Grass, George	160
Grass, Mary	160
Grass River	176
Gray, John, Indian chief	185
Green, Sergt.	342
Greenbush, N. Y.	147
Greenlove, Thomas	342
Greenville	249, 250, 251, 252
Greig, Staff Adjutant	338
Grier, John	51
Grieves, Colonel	25, 50, 53, 100
Griffith, Admiral	199
Griffin, Acting Lieut. G. A.	341
Grosvenor, Seth	280
Growler, sloop	31
Guernsey	214

H.

Haddock, Mr.	157
Hagerman, Lieut.-Colonel	337
Halifax, N. S.	99, 197, 213, 214, 301, 351
Hall, Major General Amos	42, 43, 46, 47, 54, 61, 63, 64, 65, 66, 68, 77, 78, 79, 80, 82, 88, 91, 92, 97, 98, 100, 107, 111, 118, 130, 133, 134, 135, 136, 137, 144, 161, 166, 173, 177, 178, 185, 189
Hall, Enoch A.	177, 178
Hall, Captain J.	195
Hambleton, Mr.	324, 326
Hamilton, N. Y.	114, 149, 176, 177
Hamilton, A.	27
Hamilton, Lieut.-Colonel Christopher	11, 12, 14, 15, 17, 19, 22, 32, 36, 41, 133, 297, 298, 299, 300
Hamilton, Lieut.	12, 15
Hampton, Captain Frank	109, 123, 124
Hampton, Major General Wade	58, 59, 102
Hardscrabble, N. Y.	141, 177
Hare, Richard	254
Harrington, Thomas	341
Harris, Lieut.-Colonel John	141, 142, 144, 178
Harris, Lieut.	79
Harris, John	89
Harrisburg, Pa.	143, 164, 167, 193, 215
Harrison, J.	18
Harrison, Major General W. H.	48, 49, 56, 102, 116, 128, 145, 149, 150, 206, 207, 212, 218, 244, 249, 317, 334
Harvey, Lieut.-Colonel John	3, 4, 13, 15, 23, 38, 52, 61, 66, 75, 76, 85, 86, 91, 104, 171, 223, 271, 277, 284, 337, 339, 346
Harvey, Midshipman John	29, 30

Hathaway, Wm. G.	88
Hatt, Richard	255
Hatt, Samuel	255, 307
Hatt's house	66
Haun's house	137
Hawkesworth, Midshipman	29, 30
Havre de Grace, Md.	38
Heacock, Reuben	124
Head of the Lake	169, 170
Heagsham, John	341
Heard, Ensign	226
Hearn, Andrew	147
Hemmingford	102
Henry, Lieut.	226
Henry's house	117
Heron, Andrew	51
Heward, Mrs.	159
Hewitt, Lieut. John	337, 340, 342, 346, 347, 348, 349, 350
Hibbard, Ensign Harris	185
Hickox, Mr.	88
Hill, Captain	129
Hill's house	27
Himrod, Brig.-General	177
Hitchcock family	294
Hitchcock's house	171
Hitson, Oliver	89
Hodge, W.	84
Holcroft, Major William	15, 150, 139, 262
Holland, Captain, J. H.	63, 72, 75, 111
Holmes, Captain A. H.	14, 129, 218, 219, 223, 244, 292
Holmes, B.	173
Holtaway, Captain	336, 339, 341, 342, 346
Home District	108, 255, 307
Honeoye, N. Y.	79, 88
Hooper, Thos.	342
Hoosey, Matthew	342
Hopkins, Colonel Caleb	80, 106, 107, 111, 122, 135
Hopkins, Brig.-General Timothy	24, 25, 51, 54, 61, 88, 93, 94, 117, 118, 135
Hopkins, ——	287
Hosmer, Captain George	66, 97, 100, 106, 117, 118
House, Joseph	144
Howel, Captain	145
Hoyle, Robert	264
Hull, Captain William	73, 80
Hull, Brig.-General William	113, 120
Hunt, H.	271
Hunter, Lieut.-General	10
Hunter, Jeffrey	280
Huron Indians	221, 257, 263
Huron, Lake	132, 140, 151, 165, 174, 250, 317, 321, 324
Hutchinson, Wm.	88

I.

Illinois Confederacy	250
Illinois River	251, 252

Indians 6, 7, 8, 10, 11, 16, 23, 24, 25, 26, 27, 28, 31, 33, 34, 35, 36, 37, 38, 39, 40, 42, 49, 51, 52, 53, 55, 56, 61, 62, 63, 64, 68, 70, 72, 74, 78, 79, 80, 81, 82, 84, 87, 90, 93, 95, 97, 109, 110, 120, 133, 146, 155, 157, 161, 169, 170, 172, 185, 189, 194, 201, 202, 204, 205, 209, 213, 218, 219, 220, 221, 224, 226, 227, 229, 230, 238, 244, 249, 250, 251, 252, 253, 257, 263, 267, 272, 273, 274, 294, 300, 307, 310, 313, 314, 316, 320, 321, 328, 333, 334, 351

Indians, Cahokia 251
    Chippewa 185, 249, 250, 252
    Cocknawaga 22
    Delaware 158, 185, 202, 249, 250, 251, 252, 253, 263
    Eel River 250
    Five Nations 202
    Folles Avoines 253
    Fox 158, 185
    Huron 221, 257, 263
    Illinois 250
    Kaskaskia 249, 250
    Kickapoo 185, 250, 251, 252, 253
    Manouminie 273
    Miami 249, 250, 251, 252, 253
    Michiganian 250
    Moravian 202
    Munsey 158, 185, 202
    Osage 253
    Ottawa 185, 249, 250, 251
    Peoria 250
    Piankishaw 249, 251
    Pottawatomie 249, 250, 251, 252, 253, 263
    Saakie 158, 185
    Sac 249, 251, 252
    Shawanese 185, 249, 250, 251, 252, 263, 294
    Sioux 252, 271, 272
    Six Nations 22, 34, 133, 138, 148, 163, 185, 300, 301, 310
    Tawa 252
    Tewicktowie 250
    Tuscarora 34, 56, 301
    Wea 250
    Western 3, 11, 16, 23, 32, 37, 41, 99, 137, 138, 158, 163, 167, 172, 300, 320, 328, 351
        Winnibiegoe 185, 252, 284
        Wyandot 221, 249, 250
Ingersoll, Lieut. 117, 287, 307
Irvine, Robert 289
Isle aux Noix 102, 171, 259
Ithaca, N. Y. 52

J.

Jackson, Lieut. Royal Scots 206, 228, 229
Jackson, Lieut. 24th U.S.I. 226
Jackson, Jacob 88
Jackson, John 342
Jacobs, Mr. 110
Jacobs, ———— 270
James, Lieut.-Colonel R. 106, 109

xiii.

Jarvis, MSS. of G. M. ... 293
Jarvis, William ... 108, 119, 235, 309
Jefferson, President ... 251
Jenoway, Lieut. ... 294
Jervois, Captain ... 72, 76, 111, 337, 346
John, Abel ... 341
Johns, Tom ... 143
Johnson, Friend ... 89
Johnson, J. ... 80
Johnston, Captain D. ... 205
Johnstown District ... 147, 254, 279, 307
Jomois, Lieut. ... 220
Jones, Captain Horatio ... 34, 37
Jones, Assistant Adjutant General R. ... 347
Jones, Daniel ... 254
Jones, Elias ... 254
Jones, Solomon ... 254
Jones's house ... 168
Jones, brig ... 288

K.

Kain, Sergt. ... 342
Kaskaskia ... 251
Kaskaskia Indians ... 249, 250
Keener, Peter ... 342
Kenailounak, Indian chief ... 185
Kentucky ... 53, 54
Kentucky river ... 251
Kerby, Captain James ... 12, 15, 28
Kerr, Captain ... 176
Kerr, Dr. Robert ... 66, 255
Kerr, ——— ... 177
Ketchum's History of Buffalo ... 82, 83, 120, 126, 136
Kettle Creek ... 280
Key's tavern ... 124
Kickapoo Indians ... 185, 250, 251, 252, 253
Kilute, ——— ... 117
Kingston, (U. C.) ...5, 7, 18, 30, 37, 38, 51, 53, 58, 90, 100, 104
106, 109, 116, 119, 127, 128, 129, 130, 131, 132, 137,
140, 141, 143, 146, 147, 148, 149, 150, 151, 152, 158,
159, 162, 163, 165, 166, 167, 169, 170, 171, 173, 174,
178, 185, 189, 190, 198, 199, 200, 201, 202, 204, 208,
210, 214, 219, 227, 229, 236, 242, 243, 244, 245, 246,
247, 253, 255, 256, 259, 263, 267, 268, 270, 274, 275,
276, 279, 281, 282, 283, 284, 285, 286, 288, 289, 290,
291, 293, 295, 297, 300, 303, 304, 305, 307, 309, 311,
312, 313, 314, 317, 318, 321, 323, 328, 343, 346, 347
Kingston Gazette ... 10, 47, 77, 116, 234
Kiskiwabik, Indian chief ... 185
Kitray, Abner ... 88
Kitson, Lieut. ... 141
Knox, Lieut. ... 224, 226

L.

L'Acadie ... 102
La Cole ... 270

Lady of the Lake, schooner 210, 211, 347
Lady Prevost, brig 325
Laforey, Rear Admiral Francis 351
Lamb, Colonel Anthony 118, 135
Lambert, ——— 307
Lamberton, James 193
Landon, Mr. 82
Langham, Major 21
Larwill, Lieut. 80
Lassaminie, Indian chief 274
La Tortue 102
La Tranche river, (Thames) 80, 218
Laurie, Lieut. James 337, 338, 340, 346
Lawe, Eliza 159
Lawe, George 159
Lawrence, Captain George 159
Lawrence, Sarah 159
Lawrence, Lieut.-Colonel 92
Lawrence, brig 325
Leaf, The, Indian Chief 272
Le Breton, Lieut. J. 221
Ledergrew, Captain 339
Lee, Captain 224, 226
Lee, James 342
Lee, Robert 16, 18
Leeward Islands 351
Leonard, Captain 11, 17, 28, 39, 42, 45, 50, 68, 109, 195
Lerche's Ferry 185
Leroy, N. Y. 88
Lewis, Indian chief 250
Lewiston, N. Y. 8, 11, 14, 15, 16, 18, 23, 24, 25, 26, 28, 31, 33, 38, 39, 40, 50, 51, 52, 54, 55, 64, 78, 92, 93, 97, 98, 99, 101, 112, 133, 134, 141, 161, 173, 178, 189, 213, 238
Lewiston Heights 15, 26, 39, 40
Lima, N. Y. 8
Lisle, Major 71, 132
Little Belt, sloop 35, 83, 84, 87, 143
Little Crow, Indian chief 272
Livonia, N. Y. 88
London District 43, 60, 204, 205, 255, 307
London Gazette 31
Long Island 329
Long Point 60, 146, 148, 162, 200, 208, 209, 218, 237, 244, 257, 265, 267, 280, 293, 306, 330
Longueuil 315, 317
Longwoods 204, 205, 243, 248
Loomis, Lieut. 42
Loomis, Jacob L. 88
Lord Somers, transport 301
Loring, Capt. R. R. 191, 263, 312
Lovejoy, Joshua 80
Lovejoy, Mrs. 80, 135
Lovekin, Richard 254
Low, John M. 55, 88

Lowe, Lieut. ...140
Loyal Club ...296
Lucen, ——— ...229
Lundy's Lane ...86
Lusk, Lieut. John ...79, 88
Lyon, James ...88
Lyon, William ...88
Lyons, Captain William ...39, 51, 105
Lyons' Creek ...235
Lyons' Mills ...27

M.

Mabee, Staff Surgeon ...239
Machedash Bay ...132, 321, 334
Madison, President ...320, 337
Madison, ship of war ...6, 100, 170, 174, 211, 291
Madrid, N. Y. ...176
Magnet, schooner ...335, 339, 340, 341
Magrath, Mr. ...332
Maitland, Sir Peregrine ...85
Maipock, Indian chief ...257, 263
Making, Thomas ...342
Malcolm, Lieut.-Colonel ...334, 337, 338, 341, 345, 346
Malcomb, Major ...133
Malden, (U. C.) ...6, 106, 129, 145, 179, 229, 254, 320
Mallory, Major Benajah ...25, 30, 46, 50, 93, 95, 97, 118
Malone, N. Y. ...101
Manchester, N. Y. ...39, 93, 141
Manlius Times, newspaper ...82
Manly, sloop of war ...301
Manouminie Indians ...273
Markland, Thomas ...254
Marlow, Francis ...342
Marsh, Lieut. ...293
Martin, Captain ...12, 14, 22, 28
Martin, Asahel ...88
Martin, William ...88
Marvin, Captain N. ...93, 136
Maule, Major ...265, 290
May, Lieut. Victor ...339
Mead, Major General David ...130, 133, 137, 161, 163, 164
Meadville, Pa. ...133
Mears, Thomas ...254, 307
Medcalf, Lieut. Henry ...43, 60, 66, 76, 92, 146
Meek, Major ...129
Meigs, Fort ...129, 145, 146, 154
Melville, schooner ...295, 335
Meredith, William ...342
Mermet, Adjutant ...338
Merritt, Captain W. H. ...26, 117, 131, 173, 185, 192, 235, 236, 264, 287, 290, 297, 307
Merritt, William ...264
Merritt MSS..117, 173, 174, 185, 193, 196, 236, 264, 265, 287, 290, 297, 307
Merry, Anson ...88
Messa, Lieut. ...105
Miami Indians ...249, 250, 251, 252, 253

Miami River	249,	250
Michigan Lake	250,	251
Michigan Pioneer and Historical Society		29
Michigan Territory	13,	207
Michiganian Indians		250
Michilimackinac, (Mackinac) ...36, 37, 51, 113, 132, 140, 141, 143, 151, 156, 176, 229, 247, 316, 320, 321, 333, 334		
Midland District ...236, 254, 255, 269, 279,		307
Middlesex Militia		44
Millard, Almon H.		88
Miller, Colonel		245
Miller, Major	25,	82
Miller Frederick	125,	126
Miller, William		88
Miller, William T.		126
Miller Road		178
Miller's Tavern ...35, 82, 83, 84, 117, 123,		124
Mills, Ensign F. ...204, 205,		228
Mississauga Point ...104, 239, 241, 293,		294
Mississinneway		250
Mississippi River ...249, 250, 252, 253, 263,		272
Mississquoi Bay		245
Mitass, Indian chief		185
Mitchell, Colonel ...241, 344, 346,		347
Mockler, Captain		47
Mohawk Indians		301
Mohawk River	126,	303
Moira, ship of war	295,	335
Monroe, Hon. James ...262, 269, 274, 287, 315, 316, 322, 326,		327
Montgomery, General		128
Montreal ...5, 7, 16, 105, 119, 153, 155, 156, 167, 175, 178, 185, 195, 198, 201, 202, 234, 244, 262, 265, 267, 268, 269, 277, 288, 296, 298, 302, 303, 305, 310, 318, 319, 321, 326, 344, 350		
Montreal, ship of war ...335, 340,		341
Moore, Judge	326,	327
Moravian Indians		202
Morrison, Lieut. Colonel J. W. ...58, 176, 177, 179, 196, 204, 282, 286,		303
Muirhead, Captain		266
Mulcaster, Capt. W. H. ...29, 30, 176, 336, 340, 341,		345
Mullineux, Mr.		56
Munsey Indians ...158, 185,		202
Murray, Colonel John...3, 7, 11, 13, 14, 16, 17, 21, 22, 23, 26, 27, 32, 41, 57, 58, 65, 78, 85, 99, 133, 195, 297		
Murray, Lieut.		20

Mc.

McAfee's History of the War in the Western Country	253,	321
McBean, Lieut.-Colonel		150
McCarthy, Lieut.		36
McClellan, Captain Martin		160
McClellan, Elizabeth		160
McClure, Brig.-General George ...8, 9, 10, 23, 24, 31, 34, 35, 38, 39, 42, 45, 46, 47, 48, 50, 51, 52, 53, 54, 56, 57, 61, 63, 66, 68, 90, 92, 93, 97, 105, 120, 121, 122, 123, 124, 125, 153, 177		

Macomb, General George 245, 261, 308, 310, 345
McCrae, diary of Thomas 21, 110, 143, 175, 190, 212, 271, 322, 328
McCrae's house 44, 92
Macdonald, Lieut. A. 205
McDonell, Rev'd Alexander 307
McDonell, Alexander 254, 259, 290
McDouall, Lieut.-Colonel Robert 155, 156, 167, 171
McDougall, Mr. 28
McEwen, Lieut. William 266
McEwen, Mrs. 266
McFarland, Lieut. 129, 145
McFarlane, ———— 51
McGill, Hon. John 294, 312
McGregor, Lieut. James 44, 66, 176, 194, 209, 210, 221, 223, 259
McGregor, Billy 144
McGregor, James 144
McKay, Lawrence 254
McKay, Captain R. 79
McKay, Robert 88
McKee, Major Thomas 267, 328, 351
McKenney, Cornet Amos 173, 265
McKenzie, John 341
McLean, Allan 185
McMahon, Edward 119
McMahon, Lieut.-Colonel John 87, 91, 93, 94, 95, 143
McMillan, Alexander 254
McMillan, Captain 334, 337, 338, 345, 346
McMillan's house 226, 228
McNab, Volunteer Allan 65
McNabb, James 220, 254
McNeil, Major 241

N.

Naiwash, Indian chief 185
Narramon, Chester 88
National Advocate, newspaper 40, 42, 241
National Intelligencer, newspaper 55, 56, 87, 88
Navy Yard 82
Nelles, Captain Abraham 39, 51, 105, 255
Nelles, Robert 255
Nelson, gunboat 29
Netley, schooner 291
Newark 10, 15, 24, 31, 38, 40, 41, 42, 50, 54, 56, 57, 87,
        99, 112, 115, 121, 122, 123, 153, 195, 266
Newburg, John 342
Newcastle District 236, 254, 255, 269, 307
New Hampshire 244
Newmarket, (U. C.) 296
New York 5, 6, 47, 55, 167, 211, 235, 266, 288
New York Evening Post, newspaper 16, 31, 77, 78, 80, 84,
                            143, 192, 212, 241, 243, 347
New York Society Library 40
New York State Library 25, 26
Niagara County, N. Y. 8, 10, 16, 40, 89, 123, 124, 125, 126, 178
Niagara District 11, 41, 119, 159, 255
Niagara Falls 180

Niagara Fort ...3, 7, 9, 11, 13, 14, 15, 16, 18, 21, 23, 24, 25, 26, 28, 30, 31, 33, 36, 38, 39, 40, 42, 45, 48, 50, 51, 52, 54, 55, 56, 57, 61, 64, 65, 68, 71, 76, 77, 78, 82, 83, 85, 86, 92, 99, 102, 104, 105, 109, 112, 117, 121, 130, 133, 135, 140, 149, 150, 156, 159, 173, 186, 187, 188, 197, 200, 202, 214, 237, 239, 240, 241, 242, 245, 246, 247, 257, 258, 261, 262, 263, 264, 266, 267, 278, 284, 285, 293, 295, 297, 298, 300, 306, 316, 320, 321
Niagara Frontier...5, 9, 32, 38, 41, 42, 47, 52, 65, 68, 70, 74, 76, 85, 90, 91, 92, 100, 112, 114, 117, 119, 120, 122, 129, 133, 134, 137, 154, 185, 189, 192, 196, 201, 208, 212, 216, 217, 220, 231, 232, 238, 239, 240, 246, 264, 266, 267, 273, 275, 277, 278, 305, 320
Niagara Town 23, 27, 32, 41, 54, 75, 148, 149, 159, 160, 161, 180, 183, 313, 314, 337
Niagara River 31, 41, 42, 54, 70, 77, 86, 97, 120, 133, 137, 172, 180, 202, 238, 258, 278, 283, 293
Niagara, American brig ... .325, 330
Niagara, British ship of war 335, 340, 341
Nichol, Lieut.-Colonel Robert 137, 154, 255
Niles' Weekly Register, newspaper 43, 48
Norfolk flotilla 283
North River 203
Northern Centinel, newspaper ... .87
Northern Luminary, newspaper ... .243
Norton, Captain Heman ... .64, 78, 97
Norton, Captain John 7, 22, 202, 203, 213, 300, 310
Norton, ———— 143, 175, 229
Nottawasaga Bay 151, 165
Nova Scotia 319
Nowlan, Lieut. 11, 13, 14, 20, 22, 28, 298

O.

O'Connor, Captain R. 119, 290, 335, 340, 345
Odelltown 169, 317
Odelltown Road 269
Ogden, Judge 176
Ogdensburg, N. Y. 113, 114, 288
Ogilvie, Assistant Surgeon 13
Ogilvie, Lieut.-Colonel 63, 67, 70, 72, 73, 104, 111
Ohio 138
Ohio River 251
Ohio, schooner 330
Oliver, 'Mr. 145
Oneida, brig 211
Oneida Indians ... .301
Onondaga 265
Onondaga Indians 301
Ontario County, N. Y. 79, 88, 94, 135
Ontario Dragoons 83
Ontario Lake ... ...175, 180, 197, 199, 200, 209, 221, 250, 275, 276, 305, 317, ...320, 321, 324, 334, 337, 339, 341, 350
Ontario Repository, newspaper ... .78, 347
Osage Indians 253
Osborne, Deputy Assistant Commissary General Thomas 149, 254
Oscar, John 342

Oswego, N. Y....126, 167, 170, 174, 203, 265, 311, 314, 324, 329, 334, 335, 337, 338, 339, 340, 341, 343, 345, 346, 347, 348, 349, 350
Oswego Falls ...344
Ottawa Indians ...249, 250, 252
Otter Creek ...280
Ounagechtai, Indian chief ...185
Oxford, (U. C.) ...138, 169, 180, 208, 218, 221, 226, 228, 229, 230, 244, 267, 293, 307

P.

Packet, Lieut. ...129
Padds, Joseph ...342
Palmer, David ...88
Palmer's House ...63
Pamamai, Indian chief ...185
Parish, Captain ...40
Parmalee, Hezekiah ...88
Patterson, Captain Leslie ...198, 280
Patterson, Mr. ...289
Payne, Captain ...152
Peacock, sloop of war ...196
Pearson, Lieut.-Colonel Thomas ...282, 337, 346
Pelton, ——— ...322
Penetanguishene ...132, 140, 143, 151, 165
Pennsylvania Archives ...164, 168, 193, 215
Pennsylvania Militia ...168, 216
Peoria ...251, 252
Peoria Indians ...250
Perrish, Larkin ...160
Perry, Daniel ...88
Perry, Captain O. H. ...6, 77, 329, 333
Peters, Isaac, Indian chief ...185
Peters, John ...254
Porter's house ...27, 117
Phelps, N. Y. ...88
Philadelphia ...253, 333
Philadelphia Library ...16, 280
Phillips, ——— ...266
Phillot, Major ...301
Phillpot, Lieut. ...246
Piankishaw Indians ...249, 250, 251
Pierce, Reuben ...88
Pigot, Volunteer Thomas ...65
Pike, Brig.-General Z. M. ...202
Pilkington, Quartermaster ...12
Pinkney, Colonel Ninian ...287, 322, 323, 326, 327
Platt, George ...195
Plattsburg, N. Y. ...54, 102, 103, 114, 126, 127, 136, 153, 168, 169, 188, 195, 245, 320
Point Abino ...320
Point au Plait ...223
Point aux Pins ...138, 210, 228, 242, 284
Point Pelee ...138, 163, 223
Pomfret, N. Y. ...89
Popham, Captain Stephen ...340, 342, 345
Porcupine, schooner ...330

Port Talbot	44, 163, 179, 198, 209, 210, 221, 223, 224, 228, 280, 284, 292
Portage, Ohio	128, 129, 145, 146, 152
Porter, General Peter B.	53, 81, 83, 232, 347
Porter, Messrs.	281
Porter's house	94, 95
Porter's Mills	33, 40, 99
Porter's tavern	124, 125
Postel, Francis	235
Pottawatomie Indians	249, 250, 251, 252, 253, 257, 263
Potter, Lieut.	226
Poughkeepsie, N. Y.	203
Poulson's Daily American Advertiser, newspaper	215, 281
Powell, Justice William Dummer	312
Powell, Sergt.	110
Powell Papers	297
Poyntz, Lieut. N.	171
Prairie du Chien	272
Prescott, (U. C.)	7, 38, 51, 127, 149, 150, 167, 169, 176, 178, 196, 246, 279, 288, 314
Presqu' Isle	8, 87, 158, 178, 179, 144, 284
Prevost, Sir George	6, 7, 16, 21, 23, 32, 33, 35, 40, 41, 51, 58, 59, 60, 63, 67, 74, 76, 86, 89, 90, 98, 103, 104, 105, 106, 109, 110, 112, 113, 114, 115, 116, 120, 129, 130, 131, 132, 137, 140, 143, 146, 147, 148, 149, 150, 151, 153, 155, 156, 159, 162, 163, 166, 167, 169, 170, 171, 172, 173, 175, 176, 177, 179, 188, 189, 192, 194, 196, 197, 199, 200, 201, 202, 203, 208, 210, 212, 213, 219, 222, 227, 236, 238, 242, 245, 246, 247, 248, 255, 256, 257, 258, 259, 261, 263, 267, 268, 269, 274, 276, 277, 278, 281, 282, 283, 286, 289, 291, 293, 295, 299, 300, 302, 303, 304, 305, 306, 308, 309, 310, 311, 313, 315, 316, 317, 318, 319, 322, 323, 324, 326, 327, 328, 334, 336, 344, 350, 351
Price, Captain	26
Price's house	117
Prince Regent, ship of war	199, 291, 295, 296, 304, 310, 329, 334, 335, 337, 339, 340, 341, 345
Princess Charlotte, ship of war	291, 295, 296, 329, 335, 339, 341
Pring, Captain Daniel	171, 289, 304
Procter, Major General Henry	7, 59, 99, 195, 212
Prophet, the, Indian chief	294, 300
Pultneyville, N. Y.	347
Purvis, Lieut.	289
Put-in-Bay	6, 77, 128, 129, 138, 145, 146, 152, 154, 179, 192
Putman's house	226
Putnam, Lieut.	75
Putnam, John	88

Q.

Quebec	5, 10, 32, 40, 41, 67, 98, 103, 104, 105, 110, 116, 157, 165, 171, 172, 175, 185, 188, 196, 200, 203, 213, 214, 219, 233, 242, 248, 257, 259, 261, 262, 271, 278, 301, 302, 303, 351
Quebec Mercury, newspaper	10

Queenston, (U. C.) ...7, 8, 16, 17, 23, 27, 29, 35, 38, 85, 105, 126, 133, 172, 193, 197, 239
Queenston Heights ...105, 133
Quinte, Bay of ...140

R.

Ransom, Captain ...93
Ransom, Asa ...123
Rapid Plat ...204
Raymond, Edmund ...124, 125
Rea, Brig.-General ...177
Read, Captain ...68
Riall, Major General Phineas ...7, 11, 14, 15, 16, 22, 23, 28, 33, 60, 61, 63, 64, 67, 70, 74, 75, 79, 85, 87, 95, 98, 99, 104, 110, 111, 120, 130, 131, 133, 148, 149, 150, 155, 158, 168, 169, 172, 173, 186, 193, 194, 204, 206, 210, 213, 216, 217, 218, 220, 221, 222, 226, 228, 237, 238, 239, 240, 244, 245, 246, 247, 257, 261, 263, 264, 265, 267, 268, 278, 285, 293, 300, 301, 306, 307, 319, 328
Rice, Lieut. Moses ...44
Richards, Mr. ...176, 177
Richardson, Sailing Master James ...340, 342
Richardson, John ...88
Richardson, Robert ...244
Richardson, Mr. ...289
Richardson, ———— ...229, 322
Richardson's house ...143, 144
Richmond, (U. C.) ...20
Riddle, Major ...34, 45, 92, 117, 126, 133, 134, 135
Ridge Road ...48, 77, 80, 93, 98, 134, 135
Ridgeway, Captain ...187
Ridout, Philip ...342
Ridout, Thomas ...255, 296, 297
Rifleman, sloop of war ...301
River Raisin ...208
Robb, Lieut. ...344
Robertson, Lieut.-Colonel ...301
Robinson, Commissary General W. H. ...105, 242, 283
Robinson, Captain and Lieut.-Colonel William 71, 72, 75, 11, 190, 219, 314
Rodgers, Captain John A. ...10, 49, 109, 124, 125
Rolette, Lieut. Frederick ...288
Rolph, Thomas ...255
Rome, N. Y. ...245, 265
Rondeau, (U. C.) ...44, 176, 221, 223, 227, 271
Roreback's house ...237
Ross, William ...100, 112
Rottenburg, Major General Francis, Baron de ...100, 114, 147, 185, 200, 234, 242, 279, 280, 302, 306
Rowe, Captain ...194, 210, 242
Rowley, Captain J. ...79, 88
Royal George, ship of war ...295, 335
Ruland, Lieut. ...176
Runchey's house ...27
Russell, Benjamin ...89
Russell, Thomas ...342

Ryan, Isaac 147
Ryerson's house 208

Regiments and Corps.

Royal Artillery 3, 4, 11, 12, 13, 15, 21, 32, 41, 51, 75, 163, 167, 239, 301, 323, 329, 335, 346
Royal Engineers 41, 246, 335, 337, 346
Royal Marines 59, 162, 176, 246, 282, 314, 324, 348
Royal Marines, 2nd Battalion 38, 112, 177, 204, 246, 282, 314, 334, 336, 337, 338, 339, 345, 346
Royal Marine Artillery 138, 162, 163, 201, 204, 282, 293
Royal Sappers and Miners 221, 324, 335
Royal Navy 167, 336, 345, 347
19th Light Dragoons 71, 100, 132, 189, 208, 265
1st Foot or Royal Scots...3, 4, 11, 12, 14, 15, 16, 18, 21, 23, 28, 33, 43, 60, 63, 67, 70, 71, 72, 73, 74, 84, 95, 104, 105, 138, 163, 169, 195, 197, 205, 206, 208, 209, 217, 219, 220, 222, 223, 227, 231, 238, 294
8th Foot or King's...33, 51, 63, 67, 70, 71, 72, 73, 84, 104, 105, 111, 133, 163, 190, 197, 214, 217, 238, 240, 246, 247, 267, 270, 278, 289, 301, 303
13th Foot 37
16th Foot 214
41st Foot 3, 4, 11, 12, 13, 14, 15, 16, 18, 21, 23, 28, 33, 63, 67, 70, 71, 72, 73, 84, 104, 105, 138, 163, 167, 314
49th Foot 33, 303
70th Foot 59, 213, 214
89th Foot ... .38, 63, 65, 67, 70, 71, 72, 73, 84, 104, 105, 138, 169, 194, 204, 205, 208, 209, 219, 223, 226, 231, 236, 237, 246, 282, 314
90th Foot 214, 303, 351
93rd Foot 214
98th Foot 214, 302
99th Foot 30
100th Foot 3, 4, 11, 12, 14, 15, 16, 18, 20, 21, 22, 27, 28, 30, 31, 32, 36, 41, 63, 65, 67, 70, 71, 72, 73, 84, 104, 105, 138, 163, 208, 238, 246, 278, 284, 294
103rd Foot 22, 204, 227, 236, 237, 247, 275, 282, 284, 291, 295, 305, 314
104th Foot 314, 337, 346
Royal Newfoundland Regiment 47, 167, 169
10th Royal Veteran Battalion 36
3rd Garrison Battalion 30
De Watteville's Regiment 163, 314, 324, 329, 334, 335, 336, 337, 338, 339, 345, 346
Canadian Fencible Regiment 179
Frontier Light Infantry 105
Glengarry Light Infantry ... ...7, 38, 227, 275, 282, 314, 324, ..329, 334, 335, 337, 338, 345, 346
Western Rangers 204, 205, 221, 223, 226, 227, 230, 292, 293
Provincial Light Dragoons 44, 131, 132, 138, 162, 163, 173, 195, 221, 236
Embodied Militia 59, 73, 246, 282
Incorporated Militia 63, 73, 75, 85, 95, 178, 190, 244, 308, 314
Militia Artillery 75, 160
Township Battalions of Militia 105

Kent Volunteers 169, 176, 194, 205, 209, 210, 221, 223, 226, 227, 230
2nd Gore Militia 85
1st Kent Militia 76
1st Lincoln Militia 159, 160
2nd Lincoln Militia 91
1st Middlesex Militia 70, 198
1st Norfolk Militia 69
2nd Norfolk Militia 69
2nd York Militia 85
1st Regiment United States Artillery 42, 68
3rd Regiment United States Artillery 345, 346
9th United States Infantry 168
11th United States Infantry 241
15th United States Infantry 45
21st United States Infantry 95
24th United States Infantry ... 28, 39, 49, 123, 124, 218, 224, 226
25th United States Infantry 168, 241
26th United States Infantry 43, 92
28th United States Infantry 224, 226
Canadian Volunteers 25, 40, 50, 56, 93, 95, 97

S.

Saakie Indians 158, 185, 249
Sabine, Captain Edward 278
Sac Indians 249, 251, 252
Sackett's Harbor...4, 7, 37, 48, 49, 54, 100, 102, 116, 119, 128, 132,
136, 147, 149, 150, 166, 168, 169, 174, 178, 179, 195,
196, 203, 210, 211, 222, 229, 244, 245, 246, 250, 265,
269, 275, 283, 287, 291, 305, 306, 311, 313, 314, 317,
320, 321, 324, 343, 346, 347, 350
Sailors' Battery 79
Salaberry, Lieut.-Colonel Charles de 59
Salmon, George C. 255
Salmon River 29, 136, 147, 169, 277
Sandusky 249
Sandusky, Lower 128, 145, 152
Sandusky, Upper 152
Sandwich, (U. C.) 113, 129, 138, 145, 154, 172,
228, 229, 230, 244, 271, 316
Schlosser 8, 24, 25, 31, 33, 40, 50,
55, 88, 114, 125, 141
Schram, Benjamin 144
Schram, William 144
Scioto River 250
Scorpion, schooner 330
Scott, Colonel Hercules 277
Scott, Chief Justice Thomas 312
Scott, Colonel and Brig.-General Winfield ...43, 60, 66, 91, 194, 204, 205,
209, 218, 222, 227, 228, 229, 230,
238, 243, 248, 268, 285
Scott, Captain 118
Scott, Lieut. 340, 341
Scram's house 280
Secord, Captain David 280
Secretary of the Navy for the United States...4, 196, 203, 283, 284, 287,
317, 321, 324, 329, 343, 347

Secretary of War for the United States...42, 43, 45, 48, 49, 50, 101, 103, 126, 131, 136, 201, 212, 320
Seeley, Captain ... 91, 93, 95, 96
Seeley, Nehemiah 124
Seneca, Ohio ... 128, 129, 152
Seneca County, N. Y. ...177
Seneca Indians ... 249, 301
Servos, Captain ...73
Servos, Lieut. ...12, 15
Sharmon, Lieut. ...218
Shattuck, Eli ...88
Shaver, Lieut. ...177
Shaw, Major General Aeneas ... 70, 130, 196
Shawanese Indians ... 185, 249, 250, 251, 252, 294
Sheek, David ...254
Shelby, Governor Isaac ...53
Sheldon, N. Y. ...88
Sherbrooke, Sir J. C. ...213, 301, 319, 351
Sherwood, Captain Reuben ...171, 174, 176, 177
Shineck, Frederick ...144
Sill, Joseph ...81
Sill, Nathaniel ...82
Simcoe, Lake ...51, 132, 146, 156, 165, 244, 321, 344
Simons, Major Titus G. ... 63, 75, 85, 86
Sinclair, Captain A. ... 283, 284, 317, 324, 329, 333
Sinclair, Lieut. ...289
Sioux Indians ...252, 271, 272
Sir Sidney Smith, schooner ... 295, 335, 339
Six Nations Indians ...22, 34, 133, 138, 148, 163, 185, 300, 301, 310
Skaneateles, N. Y. ...241
Skinner, H. ...51
Slingerland, Gerritt ...160
Sloat, Catharine ...264
Small, John ... 294, 312
Smelt, Lieut.-Colonel William ...337, 346
Smiley, Major ... 110, 129
Smith, Colonel ...166
Smith, Jabez ...88
Smith, John ...342
Smith, Peter ...254
Smith, Samuel ...255, 307
Smith, Thomas ...254
Smyth, Brig.-General Alexander ...120
Somers, schooner ... 226, 230
Spearman, Sergt. Andrew ... 19, 20
Spencer, John C. ...52, 121
Sporbeck, Polly ...161
Spring Wells ...229
Springer, Captain Daniel ...144, 179, 193, 196, 206, 207, 210, 212, 228
Squaw Island ... 62, 79
Snyder, Governor Samuel ...164, 168, 215
Stafford, Mr. ...296
Stamford, (U. C.) ...290
Star, brig ...335, 340, 341
Stephenson, G. B. ...39
Steuben County, N. Y. ...122

Stevens, Lieut. ... 315, 329, 337, 346
Stewart, Captain and Lieut.-Colonel Alexander...43, 60, 66, 91, 194, 204, 205, 209, 218, 222, 227, 228, 229, 230, 238, 243, 248, 268, 285
Stewart, Ensign Ebenezer ... 88
Stiles, Samuel ... 144
Stiver, ——— ... 173
Stone, Colonel Joel ... 254, 307
Stoney Creek ... 26, 250
Stovin, Major General ... 7, 106, 109, 169, 185, 236, 255, 328
Stow, George ... 88
Street, Samuel ... 255, 259
Stroback, Frederick ... 144
Sugar Loaf ... 137
Superior, ship of war ... 347
Swanton, Vt. ... 245, 261
Swanton Falls ... 245
Swartwout, General ... 127
Swift, General John ... 111, 134, 144
Swift, Lieut.-Colonel ... 107, 141
Swift, Socrates ... 88
Sylph, ship of war ... 5, 211

St.

St. Clair, Fort ... 334
St. Clair, Lake ... 139, 250
St. Clair, River ... 192, 209, 210, 294
St. Davids ... 3, 6, 21, 23, 27, 33, 35, 51, 60, 76, 91, 189, 236
St. Francis, Lake ... 155, 171
St. Genevieve ... 251
St. John ... 102, 270
St. John, Ezra ... 55
St. John, widow ... 83, 84
St. Josephs ... 233
St. Lawrence River ... 102, 114, 195, 288, 350
St. Louis ... 250
St. Mary's ... 333
St. Pierre ... 102
St. Philip ... 102
St. Philipsburg ... 261
St. Thomas ... 20

T.

Tacked, Corporal John ... 342
Talbot, Colonel Thomas ...66, 155, 163, 198, 209, 210, 242, 255, 281, 284, 307
Talbot Papers ... 66, 70, 144, 280
Talbot Road ... 138, 210, 292
Tapley, William ... 296, 297
Taplin, Captain ... 105
Tasche, Captain ... 293
Tawas Indians ... 252
Techcumtha, young ... 158, 185, 189
Tecumseth, Indian chief ... 167, 251, 252, 253, 294
Tecumseth's sister ... 185
Ten Mile Creek ... 27, 261

Tennessee ... 54
Tewicktowie Indians ... 250
Tewsley, Major Sykes ... 307, 322
Thames River ... 43, 44, 45, 66, 113, 129, 139, 145, 170, 179, 180, 192, 196, 202, 204, 207, 209, 210, 218, 221, 223, 227, 242, 268, 320
Thomas, Indian chief ... 273
Thompson, Amos ... 88
Thompson, Lieut.-Colonel Timothy ... 254
Thorne, Mr. ... 101
Tigress, schooner ... 330
Tilbury township ... 194, 292
Tillotson, Brig.-General ... 177
Tippecanoe ... 251
Tompkins, Governor D. D. ... 24, 25, 42, 46, 47, 48, 52, 54, 55, 64, 68, 92, 93, 97, 100, 101, 102, 111, 118, 128, 133, 161, 186
Tompkins Papers ... 25, 26, 54, 97, 98, 101, 112, 134, 232
Tonewanda Creek ... 40, 99
Totman, Joshua B. ... 88
Trenton ... 214
Trippe, sloop ... 35, 83, 84, 87, 143
Trout, William ... 342
Truxter, John ... 328
Tucker, Gershom ... 296
Tupper, Samuel ... 123
Turkey Point ... 106, 208, 227
Turquand, Deputy Commissary General Peter ... 243
Turtle, the, Indian chief ... 250
Tuscarora Indians ... 34, 56, 301
Twalwa, Indian chief ... 185
Twelve Mile Creek ... 27, 49, 56, 264, 265
Twenty Mile Creek ... 27, 49, 224
Two Mile Run ... 7

U.

United States Gazette ... 16
Utica, N. Y. ... 101, 288

V.

Vance, Major ... 129
Van Rensselaer, Colonel Solomon ... 232
Vaughan, Lieut. ... 266
Vergennes, Vt. ... 245
Victor, N. Y. ... 79, 88
Vincennes, Ind. ... 250, 251
Vincent, Major General John ... 7, 15, 22, 43, 63, 66, 162, 195, 290
Vincent, schooner ... 238, 313
Virginia ... 54

W.

Wabachkweela, Indian chief ... 185
Wabash River ... 250, 251, 253, 263
Wabasha, Sioux chief ... 271
Wadsworth, James ... 92, 97, 177
Waikitchai, Indian chief ... 185
Walisseka, Indian chief ... 185

Walker, an American interpreter 110, 190, 322
Walk-in-the-Water, Indian chief 249
Wallace, Colonel J. C. 87, 143
Wallace, Major 109
Wallace's house 280
Wapockanata 250
Ward, Billy 328
Ward's house 212
Warren, Admiral Sir John B. 133, 210
Warren, Lieut.-Colonel 91, 93, 94, 96
Warren, Jesse 88
Warren, Pa. 80
Washburn, Ebenezer 254
Washington, D. C. 8, 87, 116, 306
Wassaskum, Indian chief 185
Waterford, N. Y. 126
Waterford, Pa. 329
Watertown, N. Y. 170, 174, 243
Watson, Lieut. 110
Wayne, General 250
Wea Indians 250
Webber, John 342
Wench, William 342
West Bloomfield, N. Y. 79
Westbrook, Andrew 175, 179, 193, 206, 210, 241, 307, 322
Western District 47, 146
Wheldon, Jared 88
Whitchurch township 296
White Horse, Indian chief 185
Wilcox, (Willcocks), Colonel Joseph................. 8, 25, 56, 88, 121
Wilcox, Hiram 88
Wilkins, Robert C. 254
Wilkinson, Major General James 48, 58, 68, 90, 98, 101, 103, 126,
                                            133, 136, 150, 153, 168, 188, 194,
                                            195, 202, 245, 290
Wilkinson's Memoirs 128, 136
Willett, ———— 21
Williams, Lieut.-Colonel 162
Williamsburg, Va. 283, 284
Williamsville, N. Y..48, 82, 83, 107, 108, 117, 123, 134, 135, 137, 143,
            .155, 161, 177, 178, 186, 280
Willson, Captain 280
Wilmot, Major S. S. 151
Wilson, Brigade Major, John 10
Wilson, Captain 52
Wilson, Ensign 44
Winchester, Fort 145, 152
Winder, Brig.-General W. H. 262, 274, 308, 322, 323, 326, 327
Windsor Castle, ship 347, 348
Winibiegoe Indians 185, 252, 274
Wood, Alexander 255
Wood, Major E. D. 201
Woodford, Asa 88
Woodhouse, Commissioner 199
Wolf, Indian chief 250
Wolfe, ship of war 30, 170, 174, 198, 210, 264, 271

Wright, Charles ...160
Wright, Eliza ...160
Wright, Levi ...88
Wright, Samuel ...342
Wyandot Indians ...221, 149, 250

Y.

Yeigh's house ...307
Yeo, Sir James Lucas...29, 30, 31, 51, 137, 140, 153, 154, 162, 165, 170, 174, 197, 198, 199, 210, 222, 246, 247, 249, 264, 270, 271, 275, 276, 277, 281, 282, 289, 291, 295, 296, 301, 304, 305, 309, 311, 313, 319, 335, 336, 339, 343, 345, 349
Yeo, Acting Lieut. ...341
Yocum, ——— ...307
Yonge Street ...51, 173
York, (U. C.) ...38, 40, 51, 53, 86, 104, 108, 114, 119, 120, 132, 140, 151, 162, 169, 170, 179, 180, 185, 189, 191, 192, 194, 207, 208, 210, 216, 229, 232, 236, 257, 260, 263, 267, 268, 285, 287, 288, 296, 306, 312, 313
Yorktown, Va. ...214
Young, Colonel Robert ... ...,133, 217, 237, 238, 239, 246, 247, 293
Young, Lieut. B. ...73
Young, Henry ...307
Young, James ...254
Youngstown, N. Y. ...18, 19, 28, 29, 39, 78
Yule, Lieut. ...246

www.ingramcontent.com/pod-product-compliance
Lightning Source LLC
Chambersburg PA
CBHW030402230426
43664CB00007BB/716